A HISTORY OF MURDER

A HISTORY OF MURDER

Personal Violence in Europe from the Middle Ages to the Present

Pieter Spierenburg

Polity

First published in 2008 by Polity Press
Reprinted 2009, 2010 (three times), 2011, 2012 (twice)

Polity Press
65 Bridge Street
Cambridge CB2 1UR, UK

Polity Press
350 Main Street
Malden, MA 02148, USA

ISBN-13: 978-0-7456-4377-9
ISBN-13: 978-0-7456-4378-6(pb)

A catalogue record for this book is available from the British Library.

Typeset in 10 on 12 pt Sabon
by Servis Filmsetting Ltd, Stockport, Cheshire
Printed and bound in Great Britain by the MPG Books Group

For further information on Polity, visit our website: www.politybooks.com

Contents

Acknowledgments   vi

   Introduction   1
1 Romeo's Kindred: The Fragility of Life in Medieval Europe   12
2 Sealed with a Kiss: From Acquiescence to Criminalization   43
3 Swords, Knives, and Sticks: The Social Differentiation of
   Male Fighting   65
4 Patriarchy and its Discontents: Women and the Domestic
   Sphere   114
5 Marks of Innocence: Babies and the Insane   143
6 M for Less: The Marginalization of Murder, 1800–1970   165
7 The Tables Turned: 1970 to the Present   206
   Conclusion   223

Notes   227
References   247
Index   270

Acknowledgments

A work of synthesis like this is indebted to all authors upon whose publications I rely, whether I agree with them or not. In addition, the book draws on Amsterdam archival sources; the material was collected during the 1990s with help from several people who were then students: Désirée Herber, Stephanie Reesink, Jeroen Blaak, Janita van Nes, and Aries van Meeteren. Their assistance was financed by the History Department of Erasmus University. I am grateful to the Netherlands Organization for Scientific Research (NWO) for providing me with a grant that set me free from teaching in order to finish the book during the academic year 2006–7. Michel Porret kindly supplied the material for the opening story of chapter 4. Jan van Herwaarden and John Najemy alerted me to publications on medieval themes. René Lévy and Laurent Mucchielli made available French books not available in Dutch libraries; in addition, René secured photographs from the Paris archives. Omri Manoach prepared the graphs. Several colleagues and friends took the time amidst their own activities to read and comment on one or more draft chapters: Clive Emsley, Willem de Haan, Tomás Mantecón, Ed Muir, Dorothea Nolde, Paul Schulten, Jim Sharpe, Marty Wiener, and Damián Zaitch. Roger Lane and an anonymous reader commented on the manuscript for Polity. At Polity, my thanks go to Emma Longstaff and Jonathan Skerrett for their assistance, and the copy-editor Sarah Dancy.

The usual caveat that I am solely responsible for the final result applies.

Introduction

Murder is as old as the marks of external violence found on the skulls of prehistoric skeletons. It is with us today and likely to continue to be part of the human experience. More than 100 years ago Frederic William Maitland remarked that, if a fairy were to offer him the opportunity of personally witnessing the same type of scene across societies, he would choose a murder trial, because it reveals so many matters of the first importance.[1] This book examines homicides on record without a trial as well, but Maitland's remark serves for the coming chapters. Killing always affects the fundamental values of those who participate in and witness the act, thus providing valuable information about culture, social hierarchy, and gender relations. In turn, a consideration of broad social change over the long term increases our understanding of the history of killing. Hence, the subject lies at the crossroads of historical scholarship and criminology.

The word "murder" has the advantage of belonging to everyday language. Most people have a clear idea of what it means. We rarely use it to refer to a soldier shooting an enemy or a traffic accident, whatever our personal views of such events. For that reason, scholars often employ the term murder as shorthand for all forms of private and non-accidental killing. That is the case, for example, in Roger Lane's (1997) overview of the subject in American history. This book conforms to that usage, interchanging murder with the formal concept of homicide just for variation. In the few instances where the reader should understand the former word in a strictly legal sense, this will become clear. Killing is, of course, the most extreme form of personal violence. The scripts of many homicidal incidents are akin to those of violent encounters that do not result in a person's death. Such incidents will be included in our examination, but the focus on murder structures the book. It pays little attention to minor assaults or threats. On the other hand, it excludes subjects that fall outside the realm of "private" violence: revolutions and other forms of large-scale collective action, military activities, or physical punishment (except where this involves the legal punishment meted out to killers). By violence, I mean any intentional encroachment upon the physical integrity of the body.[2] Readers who favor a wider definition of this term may simply insert the word "physical" each time. Finally, neither violence nor murder should be equated with crime. Their gradual criminalization, in fact, constitutes one of the major themes discussed.

It is only in relatively modern societies that we can apply the category of crime or distinguish between interpersonal violence and state violence. From a world-historical perspective, Johan Goudsblom (1998) distinguishes three sequences of monopolization. First, adult males monopolized violence, excluding women and children from its organized use. The beginning of this hypothetical process coincided with the differentiation between hunting as a male activity and gathering vegetables as a female one. Next, in military-agrarian societies, an elite of warriors monopolized violence, excluding other social groups, mainly peasants and priests. Whereas the earlier situation was rooted in psychological persuasion, the second was reinforced by a related monopoly, that of bearing arms. During the third stage, relatively autonomous warrior elites increasingly had to yield to larger organizations. Violence became monopolized within the framework of the institutions that we now call states. All specialists in organized violence were either incorporated into the state or eliminated. This process gained momentum from the sixteenth century onward, and independently from each other, in North-West Europe and Japan. The subsequent uses of state monopolies include war against other states and, internally, physical punishment, torture, and the forceful restraint of lawbreakers. As in earlier phases, the monopoly remained relative: all assaults and murders, as well as riots and occasional civil war, implied a breach of it, while some states lost their exclusive control on violence

Covering seven centuries, this book takes up the history of murder in Europe when it begins to be possible to distinguish private killing from state violence. The later Middle Ages witnessed the transition from the second to the third phase of monopolization. The oldest reliable evidence about the number of murders, moreover, dates from around 1300. Such evidence forms a crucial basis, but this book goes beyond a study of the frequency of killing. Nor does it jump from one narrative to the other. Instead, it adopts a social scientific perspective, examining patterns in the character, incidence, social meaning, and cultural context of murder. Sub-themes such as the representation of violence get attention in passing, but the main focus is on events that actually happened.

The Long-term Decline of Murder

Our starting-point, nevertheless, is a quantitative time series. For several decades, numerous historians, in painstaking empirical studies, have been collecting data that reveal the incidence of murder in individual towns and regions over several centuries. Although researchers already had access to the more easily accessible national statistics of recent periods, this new archival work has greatly enhanced our knowledge of the extent of killing. Several scholars, beginning with Ted Robert Gurr (1981), have used these studies to compile long-term graphs of the incidence of murder. Currently, Manuel Eisner's database represents the most comprehensive effort at systematizing the quantitative work done so far.

Figure 0.1 shows the so-called homicide rate. This is the term always used, although "ratio" would be more accurate. As in all studies of crimes, the homicide rate refers to the number of murders relative to the total population of the area in which they occurred. It is always measured per year. For earlier centuries, this often means the annual average over a longer period, because, if we only have a single-year count, we cannot tell whether it is normal or exceptional for its century. The number of inhabitants taken as a measure is usually 100,000. We could just as well compute the rate per 10,000 inhabitants or per million, but the measure per 100,000 is so extremely common that it is often implicitly assumed. Throughout this book, when the homicide rate is rendered by just one number, this means the annual average per 100,000 population.

The relative scarcity of medieval data has led me to combine them all in one count.[3] The downward trend since then is clearly visible. Whereas homicide rates of several dozen were common in medieval towns, the figure hovered around one in mid-twentieth-century Europe. Of course, such a highly aggregated graph obscures geographic differences and temporary fluctuations. The coming chapters will discuss the principal middle-term trends, along with the qualitative changes in the character of murder that accompanied them. Since about 1970, the long-term trend of decline appears to have been reversed, although the recent rise – hardly visible in figure 0.1 – remains modest when compared to the starting level. The final chapter deals with this contemporary development.

Some readers may wonder how we can be so sure of the data. Isn't there a "dark number" in play? The dark number, or figure, a basic concept in criminology, refers to the difference between recorded criminality and all crimes actually committed. It constitutes a methodological problem in the quantitative study of the incidence of crime. If someone steals my bike and I choose not to report this to the police, I am contributing to the dark number. If, on the other hand, I report it to a researcher who calls me at the

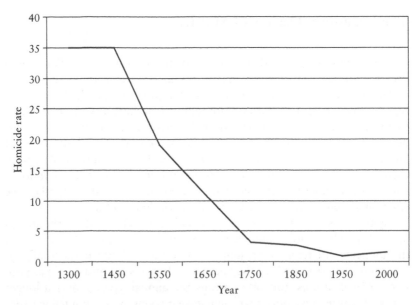

Figure 0.1: The long-term decline of homicide in Europe per 100,000
population annually: average estimates per century
Sources: Eisner 2001 and 2003; Monkkonen 2006

end of the year because I am in his sample, my stolen bike becomes part of
an estimate. Nowadays, victimization surveys constitute the primary means
of getting around the dark number. For obvious reasons this does not apply
to murder, but there are alternatives. Except in a few special cases, a homicide is usually noticed and recent police registrations are reliable.
Moreover, medical statistics of the causes of death, including violent death,
date back, on average, 100 years. As it happens, such data also exist for the
past, often even for as far back as the Middle Ages. The authorities ordered
the investigation of all suspect corpses for signs of a violent death, whether
or not they had information about a perpetrator. These body inspection
reports, called "coroner's records" in England, constitute the basis for our
long-term graphs of homicide. The only remaining dark figure is that of
corpses that have been successfully hidden, but scholars assume that their
number is negligible. Advances in the medical skill of treating wounds,
moreover, hardly affected homicide rates before the twentieth century.[4]

The quantitative record, supplemented by judicial evidence, yields
information beyond the mere incidence of murder. Gender is a crucial
factor. High homicide rates almost always result from a prevalence of
male-on-male fighting. Several chapters discuss this in detail, with examples such as the vendetta and the duel. In the wake of the decline in

homicide, on the other hand, we observe an increasing proportion of intimate victims among the remaining murders. The incidence of the killing of newborn babies is related primarily to the intensity of concern over extramarital sex. Most scholars reserve separate graphs for this phenomenon. After gender, the categories of age and social class are important for an understanding of murder in its wider context. Not only were fighters usually male; they were also relatively young. That is a surprisingly constant factor, regardless of the long-term decrease. The pattern of social stratification matters because of the pacification of the elites.[5] Whereas the medieval upper classes exceeded their social inferiors in propensity for violence, the adoption of a peaceful life style by their descendants marked the decline in homicide. The question of race looms large in the history of murder in America, but less so in Europe. Apart from tensions between Jews and Christians, racial and ethnic differences scarcely affected the character of European murder until the later twentieth century. The United States, moreover, witnessed less of a long-term decline in homicide, always retaining higher levels than those of Europe.[6]

In order to explain the long-term decline of homicide, most scholars prefer Norbert Elias's theory of civilizing processes.[7] Its exposition here, for readers not already familiar with it, is geared toward its application to our subject. It should be emphasized nevertheless that the theory deals with the overall development of societies. In the title of his initial publication of 1939 Elias used the word "civilization" in a polemical sense on purpose. Whereas a lot of his contemporaries worried about a crisis of civilized values, he asked himself: "What, then, does this civilization consist of?" To answer that question, Elias turned to books on etiquette written in various periods from the Middle Ages onward. He found that they dealt with such surprising problems as how to act when a person needed to urinate or felt the urge to spit. Such books were especially elaborate about dining. Whereas medieval table companions ate with their hands from a common dish and drank from the same cup, forks and individual plates only came into use from the sixteenth century on. Gradually, the rules for dining expanded and people became increasingly sensitive to the movement of each other's mouths and hands at the table. That applied equally to other functions of the human body. Elias supplemented the evidence from etiquette books with that from other sources, providing information, notably, on standards of behavior with respect to sex and physical aggression.

A major conclusion that Elias drew from these data was that civilization is never static; it involves complex processes of change. Over some six centuries, standards of behavior became ever stricter, requiring greater self-control from individuals. Although Europeans in, say, 1900 were proud of being civilized, the fact that they cherished certain standards of conduct was merely the result of having been born in the nineteenth century. In many ways, the Victorian period was the heyday of internal psychic repression, but since then, as many scholars have argued, individual behavioral controls have become more stable, balanced, and spread across time. Hence, the average level of self-control is higher still in the modern world. The regulation of urges and emotions is loosely connected across most areas of life, including eating, sex, and conflict. A telling example is the prohibition, repeated in many seventeenth-century manner books, on putting one's knife into one's mouth. Ostensibly, this is a rule of dining etiquette, reflecting the unease that table companions experience at seeing someone display such an offensive habit. But the rule also reflects the awareness of contemporaries that the knife is a dangerous weapon and that a polite person should both act with dignity at the dinner table and also take care not to engage in frequent quarrels and fights.

Finally, these socio-psychological processes are connected to changes in society as a whole, in particular to the development of the modern state. At the most general level, the theory of civilization posits that changes in the way of handling natural resources, in inter-human organization, and in the nature of individual people's emotions and behavioral style are all interrelated. In particular, this applies to the level of control in each of these three fields. If controls decrease or increase in one field, they will tend to do so in the other two as well. The amount and stability of self-control went up on average over the last six centuries of European history, along with heightened social integration and differentiation of functions. Among these changes in behavioral controls, the transformation of aggressive urges and emotions occupied a prominent place. Individuals' propensity for physical assault diminished, as pacification and monopolization by state organizations, as well as economic differentiation and urbanization, progressed. The potential lethality of inter-state conflict, on the other hand, increased significantly. Differences in power between social groups constitute an important element in the theory of civilization. For the established, the adoption of behavioral controls and the pride in being "civilized" are sources of power that are lacked by outsiders.

Not every scholar agrees with this theory. Some historians simply doubt the validity of all theoretical explanations. A few sociologists turn to Durkheim instead, in particular his theory of individualism and the decreasing force of collective bonds, which is well-suited to explain such sub-processes as the disappearance of feuding, in which the decline of extended family ties was a crucial factor. The Eliasian and Durkheimian perspectives, it appears, can easily be integrated.

A theory that applies to the quantitative decline of murder must take its changing faces into account. Homicides and assaults can be characterized according to their position on two related but distinct axes.[8] One axis extends from the extreme of impulsive violence to that of planned violence. It has to do primarily with the mental *habitus* of the perpetrator, inquiring into the degree of spontaneity or control in the act. The second axis, extending from ritual to instrumental violence, refers to the social and cultural meaning of an aggressive confrontation. The more that violence has a ritual character, the more it is done for its own sake. Violence with a highly instrumental nature is employed not for its own sake, but in order to attain something else. Robbery is the classic example, but, historically, bandits also performed rituals. Thus, human behavior always falls between the extremes of both axes, but not necessarily in the middle. In principle, every violent incident can be situated at some point on each of the axes. These can be represented as crossing each other, which leads to four distinct boxes. This way of representing alerts us, for example, to the possibility of violence that is both instrumental and impulsive. The axes can also be represented as parallels. In that case, they imply the hypothesis that, over time, violence on average moves away from the ritual pole in the direction of the instrumental pole, and away from the impulsive pole in the direction of the planned pole. In a formal sense, a high number of planned murders, reflecting self-control, would be compatible with a civilized mentality, but any murderer today acts against the civilized standards cherished by the large majority of the population.

Rituals, it should be emphasized, concern real behavior. Authors studying contemporary phenomena sometimes speak of ritual violence when they mean that playful acting rather than serious fighting is involved. Mimetic aggression and play, however, should be called symbolic violence. For example, when the inhabitants of a village decapitate Lord Carnival at the end of Mardi Gras (Shrove Tuesday), this is a symbolic killing because a puppet cannot actually die. While symbolic behavior often is also ritual, not every ritual is symbolic. Ritual extends into the sphere of reality. Knife-fighters, for example, often aim at their opponent's face because of its ritual significance. Rituals can be cruel and degrading and, although not all historians agree on this, ritual and impulsive violence are wholly commensurable.

The Crucial Role of Honor

In an examination of the character of violence over the long term, the most important element is that of honor. It was involved in the overwhelming majority of murders in Europe – and not only there. Honor is highly gendered. What counts as honorable for a man is often dishonorable for a woman. It is only in the modern world, where power differentials between women and men have diminished, that female and male honor begin to converge. By contrast, in many societies, past and present, the two were highly divergent, paralleling a similar divergence in social roles. In the cultural complex that concerns us here, female honor was based, first, on chastity and, second, on passivity and silence. The passive role accorded to women meant that they had only limited possibilities for maintaining their honor themselves. In patriarchal societies, an important component of men's honor was to uphold the honor of women, which they did in particular by attacking and taking revenge on other men whose actions had compromised a woman's honor. The woman in question was usually her defender's wife, daughter, mother, or dependent. But a man also reacted with violence when another man encroached upon his honor directly. Thus, for men, honor and its defense were practically the same. Male honor depended on physical courage, bravery, and a propensity for violence. Being insulted either verbally or physically equally amounted to an attack on a man's honor, which could be repaired only by counter-attack. Any conflict, about an entitlement to land use for example, had repercussions for male honor. Many murders, therefore, resulted from such conflicts.

This honor complex first received systematic attention from anthropologists such as Julian Pitt-Rivers and Pierre Bourdieu. They discovered it, still very much alive in the 1950s and '60s, among nations on both sides of the Mediterranean. Bourdieu incorporated his findings into his theory about the various forms of capital. According to him, honor did not conform to the logic of economic profits and losses; instead, it constituted a symbolic capital that people valued highly.[9] For his part, the historical anthropologist Anton Blok emphasizes the association of traditional male honor with the body. All body parts had distinct symbolic meanings. In many languages, a man's face stands for his honor, while his testicles make him a real man. This association extends to animal bodies, in particular to the contrasting behavior of rams and billy goats. As country people know from direct experience, a he-goat will allow other males to mate with the females, whereas rams continually fight each other over such an intrusion. All horns that figure as negative markers in folklore – those of a cuckold and the devil, among others – refer originally to goats' horns. An honorable man acts like a ram: he fights other men and controls his female dependents.[10] This attitude is reflected in the popular ballads of early modern England, telling us that only men who rule their wives are capable of eating roast ram. Weak men refuse it from fear of displeasing their sweethearts and cuckolds cannot swallow it at all.[11] Human body symbolism is reflected in the image of blood in the vendetta. A man's blood, rather than his life, constituted the proper revenge for bloodshed and, therefore, vengeance could be taken on the killer's blood relative.[12]

Indeed, the body-related concept of honor was widespread in medieval and early modern Europe and numerous historians have found a close tie between male honor and male violence.

Theories about honor vary. Whereas Daly and Wilson (1988) argue that traditional male honor and the concomitant propensity for violence are so widespread across societies because they have evolved as traits bringing reproductive success, most other authors prefer cultural explanations. According to Frank Henderson Stewart (1994), honor should be conceptualized as a right to respect. He adds another important element by distinguishing between its vertical and its horizontal dimensions. Studies of past violence usually observe the latter. For example, two artisans are drinking in a tavern and one calls the other a dirty dog. The man so degraded makes a threatening gesture with his knife, which wipes out the insult. If a man had the reputation of always reacting violently in such situations, and few others dared to challenge him, he counted as very honorable. Thus, horizontal honor derives from a man's peers. It is a zero-sum game, in which one person's gains are another's losses. Vertical honor, on the other hand, stems from a person's office or rank. People of inferior social status simply cannot attain it. This type of honor is also closely related to violence. It was improper, for example, to issue a challenge to a formal duel across class boundaries. Elite duelists considered their violence to be legitimate, denying that honor could be involved in fights involving craftsmen or peasants.

Like the theory about violence, a convincing theory about honor should include a time perspective. If many murders were honor-related and the murder rate declined over time, did the sense of honor decline too? In fact, honor was subject to change rather than decline. Blok notes this with reference to the work of George Fenwick Jones. Examining German literature, Jones speaks of a shift from external to internal honor, beginning in the mid-eighteenth century and leading to a universally accepted ideal by the end of the nineteenth. Whereas honor first denoted respect, deference, prestige, rank, or superiority, it came to denote admirable conduct, personal integrity, or inner sense of right and wrong. A similar development, he maintains, took place in other European countries.[13] Instead of opposing two types of honor, however, or even calling only the traditional type honor and the newer one virtue or dignity, it makes more sense to emphasize the process of gradual change. Over several centuries, the basis of honor, the male variant in particular, drifted away from its close association with the body. Honor gradually became associated with inner virtue. Consequently, the need to employ violence in order to save one's face when insulted or challenged greatly diminished. Finally, a man could be non-aggressive and honorable at the same time. We call this process "the spiritualization of honor."[14]

Rather than belonging to a particular period of history, the spiritual-ization process depends on the type of society in which it occurs. We observe it in Antiquity, for example. In Roman society, the word "honor" primarily connoted vertical honor, as exemplified by the fact that Romans referred to offices as *honores*. The process of spiritualization revolved around the word *virtus*, originally meaning masculinity. In the early Republic, *virtus* indeed implied traditional male honor, linked to the body and won especially by military courage. In the later Republic and the Empire, on the other hand, it came to connote temperance, sobriety, and chastity, thus meaning "virtue" in the modern sense.[15] Conversely, later European history witnessed counter-movements to the process of spiritu-alization, such as the revival of dueling among the nineteenth-century bourgeoisie. More recently, traditional, body-related male honor resur-faced in urban neighborhoods – a subject for the final chapter.

The body-related concept of honor, it appears, is strongest in societies that lack a stable state system and a differentiated economy, while most, but not all, of the counter-movements to the spiritualization process occurred during temporary lapses in the pacification brought about by state institutions. This brings us back to Elias's theory. Elias dealt at length with the notion of shame, but hardly at all with the theme of honor. Nevertheless, the honor perspective can easily be integrated into the theory of civilization. As a working hypothesis, we expect the murder rate to be highest, and traditional male honor to be most intense, when the monopolization of violence by state institutions and economic differenti-ation are at their lowest point. That situation prevailed in the European Middle Ages. Most men had to rely on their own resources in order to defend themselves, their dependents, and their property, and they took pride in this. As state and economic institutions developed, the spiritual-ization of honor set in and the incidence of personal violence decreased. The details and specific mechanisms of this development, along with related processes such as transformations of the family and campaigns to change popular culture, will receive attention in connection with the empirical evidence in subsequent chapters.[16]

Outline of the Book

The coming chapters mix a chronological with a thematic structure. The book's geographic scope extends roughly to the countries that lay west of the "Iron Curtain" during the Cold War. Within that vast region, the United Kingdom, France, Germany, the Low Countries, and Italy consti-tute the core area, but the principal trends in murder were Europe-wide.

A work of synthesis always depends to a large extent on the efforts of other scholars. Additionally, I rely on my own research in the rich Amsterdam archive, in particular when it provides more detailed evidence and answers to questions not raised in the historical literature. The subject of the popular duel, for example, is crucial to our understanding of the evolution of violence and honor, but it has been neglected in historiography so far. Thus, a balance is sought each time between the scope of the geographic and that of the thematic coverage.

Each chapter has its principal focus. Chapter 1 deals with medieval murder, focusing especially on the feud. Everything related to the judicial handling of homicide is left for chapter 2, which treats its gradual criminalization. That process connected the later Middle Ages with the beginning of the early modern period. Chapter 3 deals with male fighting in early modern Europe, with its social differentiation, marked by the coexistence of the formal and the popular duel, as the principal theme. The fourth chapter examines murder of and by women and intimates. It takes up this subject in the Middle Ages and discusses its increasing visibility from the seventeenth century to the mid-nineteenth. The growing willingness to consider some types of murder as symptoms of madness is the theme of chapter 5. This applied in particular to infanticide, first harshly repressed and then treated as a consequence of unfortunate circumstances, until its incidence became insignificant in the twentieth century. The marginalization of murder after 1800 constitutes the theme of chapter 6, which further deals with the revival of dueling as well as new phenomena such as the *crime passionnel*, serial killing, and the emergence of the underworld. Chapter 7's main focus is on the modern rise in homicide, which reverses the centuries-long trend. Is this temporary or is it with us to stay?

These chapters contain a certain number of violent incidents. Most of the time, the principal function of the protagonists' names is to enable an easy "who's who." This function is best served by first names, especially when men as well as women are involved. In any case, most lower-class people of the early modern period lacked a family name other than a patronym. Historians dealing with the nineteenth century, in particular, are accustomed, after giving the full name, to further designate the protagonists by their last names only. I find this tedious to read. I have chosen to refer to people mostly, but not systematically, by their first names. This is to improve readability, and not because I want to make them look nicer. It has the additional advantage of being more in line with the historical actors' own experiences.

I

Romeo's Kindred: The Fragility of Life in Medieval Europe

Juliet Capulet and Romeo Montague promise to be true to each other for better or for worse, in secret, with only a friendly friar present. A little later, the young bridegroom and some of his kinsmen, on a walk through town, encounter a party of their enemies. One of them, Tybalt, hurls an insult at Romeo. The power of love stops him from immediate retaliation, but his companion Mercutio draws his sword. Exclaiming that the Prince of Verona wants peace in the city, Romeo intervenes in the fight to stop it, but too late. Mercutio is seriously injured. Then Romeo deplores his own cowardliness:

> . . . O sweet Juliet
> Thy beauty hath made me effeminate
> And in my temper soften'd valour's steel.[1]

A little later Romeo learns that Mercutio has died. When Tybalt returns, Romeo has recovered his manliness and challenges the killer: one of them has to die too. This time, Tybalt does not survive the fight. Romeo runs away to a hiding place, but he leaves it during the night to spend a few happy hours with his lovely bride before his fleeing for good. He bids farewell to Juliet as the lark announces the morning: "I must be gone and live, or stay and die."

Ignorant of the clandestine union, the Capulet family arranges for their daughter's wedding to the young nobleman, Paris. Juliet turns to the friar for help. Not daring to admit that he has already married her to Romeo and afraid that he will have to preside over a bigamous ceremony, the friar makes a plan. He has a mysterious potion, which will make Juliet appear dead for two days. She is indeed buried in the family vault, not in a coffin but dressed in her finest clothes. Then fate strikes. The messenger whom the friar has sent to Mantova to inform Romeo of the ruse, so that he can snatch away the sleeping Juliet, is held up because of a plague rumor. From another acquaintance, Romeo hears that his loved one has suddenly died. With poison procured in Mantova, he rides back to Verona; he breaks open the vault and through the dim light sees Juliet's body:

> . . . O my love! my wife!
> Death, that hath suck'd the honey of thy breath,
> Hath had no power yet upon thy beauty . . .

Then he swallows the poison:

> Here's to my love! O true apothecary!
> Thy drugs are quick. – Thus with a kiss I die.

Immediately after this, Juliet wakes up from her long sleep and notices her dead husband:

> What's here? a cup, clos'd in my true love's hand?
> Poison, I see, hath been his timeless end: –
> O churl! drink all, and left no friendly drop
> To help me after? – I will kiss thy lips;
> Haply some poison yet doth hang on them,

But there is not enough poison left on Romeo's lips and when Juliet hears watchmen approaching, she quickly grabs his dagger and stabs herself. Soon all the principal characters assemble around the two lifeless bodies. United in sorrow, Capulet and Montague make peace. The Prince concludes: "For never was a story of more woe / Than this of Juliet and her Romeo."

These events, purported to have happened in the northern Italian town of Verona at the beginning of the fourteenth century, are rendered here as retold by the English playwright William Shakespeare (1564–1616). Obviously, they are not plain history. The admiration of posterity, not the judgment of modern scholars, ought to be invoked to plead the case for Romeo and Juliet. The young couple has fascinated audiences since the sixteenth century, through the Romantic age, until today. Actors, directors, and writers of new versions have interpreted the motif, which has changed with every generation that considered it afresh. *West Side Story*, the popular musical and film of some 50 years ago, is the best-known modern interpretation. Romeo and Juliet, then, are characters who constantly appear to us in a new guise. It would be utterly superfluous to issue the stern caveat of a professional historian, warning that this play does not accurately depict fourteenth-century Verona, or, indeed, late medieval Italy. This chapter reintroduces the legendary couple because of the family enmities that tragically thwarted their brief romance. That part of the story, whatever its fictional content, alerts us to events and situations which really took place, in Italy and elsewhere.[2]

That the story migrated from one society to another is actually an advantage. A consideration of Shakespeare's sources makes that clear. He wrote the play in the early 1590s, when English versions of the legend were already available. The English, along with French and Spanish writers, had adapted the tale from a novel by Luigi da Porto (1485–1529).[3] This nobleman from Vicenza had situated the tragic love of Giulietta and Romeo in the city of Verona at the time of Bartolomeo della Scala's rule (1301–4). Based on an ambiguous stanza in Dante's *Divina Commedia*, da Porto had assumed that the Montecchi and Cappelletti were Veronese families enmeshed in a feud.[4] This author, however, although he significantly reworked the theme, had not invented it. The original source, until literary historians discover a still earlier version, is Masuccio Salernitano's *Il Novellino*, written in the 1450s. Masuccio (1410–75), whose real name was Tommaso Guardati, worked at the court of the Aragonese kings of Naples. His *Novellino* is a collection of short stories, one of which tells about the secret love of Mariotto and Ganozza. According to Masuccio, this affair took place "not long ago" and, more important, in Siena. Mariotto Mignanelli is "a youth of a good family" and Ganozza, whose surname is not mentioned, the daughter of an esteemed citizen. The motifs of clandestine wedding, exile because of homicide, the sleeping potion, and the lovers' deaths are all there, although Mariotto does not commit suicide but is decapitated at the court's order.[5] Surprisingly, however, the Sienese story by Masuccio has no rival families. Mariotto simply gets into an argument with "another honorable citizen," and this escalates into a fight; the citizen is hit on the head with a stick and dies. This was a homicide for honor, no doubt, but without, apparently, a family feud.

The Sienese and Neapolitan origins of the story of Romeo and Juliet serve as a warning. Not every medieval homicide can be traced back to a vendetta. Spontaneous street brawls, spousal conflicts, and violent robberies also occurred, as they would in subsequent periods of European history. And yet, a consideration of later periods makes the vendetta a crucial phenomenon. Every other type of serious violence which can be observed in the Middle Ages was equally characteristic of the early modern era, or even beyond. If we wonder what really was specific about the violence of the period that ended around the middle of the sixteenth century, it is precisely the omnipresence of feuds – feuds between rival families, competing factions, neighboring lords and their retainers, members of opposed camps in a military conflict, or between two groups that had close internal bonds for still other reasons. In the words of a distinguished French historian: "The vendetta made its imprint on every aspect of medieval life, in particular in the towns and that until the fifteenth century at least."[6]

Thus, despite the absence of rival families from Masuccio's tale, Siena had its share of bloody feuds. By the mid-fourteenth century, the Tolomei and Salimbeni families were enemies, as were the Malavolti and Piccolomini families. As a prominent historian of Siena explained four decades ago: "To expand upon the numerous episodes involving members of powerful noble families would belabor the obvious. Published chronicles alone are replete with tales of their murders, assaults and minor battles."[7] Middle Ages, in this chapter, stands for the period from about 1300 to the mid-sixteenth century, when it is more or less possible to distinguish between interpersonal and state violence, although state institutions were only just nascent. They nevertheless ensured a measure of regulation of violence, but this was no more than rudimentary and was easily circumvented.

Murder and the Medieval City

The prevalence of feuding was a major factor contributing to the elevated homicide rates found in the Middle Ages. They leave us in no doubt that violence was endemic in Europe. Surprisingly, however, the oldest reliable figures, for thirteenth-century England, are relatively modest – though not really low – compared to those available for the fourteenth and fifteenth centuries. James Given compiled the thirteenth-century rates from eyre rolls (accounts of visitations by justice officials) supplemented with coroner's records – sources which include cases with unknown offenders. The averages, over periods of three or four years, for the counties of Bedford, Kent, Norfolk, Oxford, and Warwick lay between 9 and 25 per 100,000 inhabitants, depending on the population estimate. For the cities of London and Bristol it was, respectively, 12 and as low as 4, but these urban figures refer to just two years in each case. Note, moreover, that the counties and towns studied are concentrated in the relatively small core area of southern England. Given does concede that Wales and Scotland were notorious feuding areas, but it is possible that the rest of England, too, was more violent than the region he investigated.[8] In any case, higher figures have been calculated for fourteenth-century England. In London, between 1300 and 1340, the average was 42 per 100,000 inhabitants.[9] In about the same period, it was lower in Surrey (12) but at a similar level as that of the capital in Herefordshire (40).[10] The homicide rate for the town of Oxford in the 1340s, just before the Black Death, stood at a record high of 110.[11] No English rates are available between the mid-fourteenth century and the mid-sixteenth.

Continental homicide rates are overwhelmingly urban. The Oxford record was matched by the city of Florence, which, in the second half of the fourteenth century, also boasted 110 per 100,000 inhabitants.[12] Apart from these extreme figures, rates around 50 were not uncommon – in Dutch and German towns among others. Utrecht's homicide rate averaged 53 in the first half of the fifteenth century and in Amsterdam it was 47 by the middle of that century. In Freiburg im Breisgau in the second half of the fourteenth century, the rate fluctuated between 60 and 90.[13] From various local publications, Martin Schüssler collected homicide rates for a number of towns in present-day Germany, Poland, and the Czech Republic in the fourteenth century: Speyer (30), Nürnberg (42), Augsburg (60), Regensburg (20), Olmütz/Olomouc (77), Liegnitz/Legnica (70), Breslau/Wroclaw (27), and Kracow (64).[14] Available Swedish rates are for Stockholm (38 in the 1470s and 1480s) and the small town of Arboga (23 between 1452 and 1543).[15] In a few cases, inflicted wounds appear to have been registered more or less systematically, but there was probably still some "dark number" remaining. The annual physical injury rates per 100,000 inhabitants are 234 for Regensburg (1324–50) and 175 for Kracow (1361–1405).[16] Another Regensburg source, complete for the years 1410–59, lists oaths taken by people who left the city after a term in jail; 647 of them, about 108 per 100,000 annually, had committed assault.[17]

The unavailability, outside England, of reliable quantitative data about rural homicide is unfortunate. Partly to compensate for this, I have calculated minimum estimates referring to the end of the period dealt with in this chapter. They are based on data, provided by Marjan Vrolijk, concerning petitions either for a safe conduct or for a pardon after a murder in the Dutch provinces of Holland and Zeeland, both still largely rural at the time. The rates of homicide for which a petition was drawn up average 15 in the years 1531–5, 18 in 1546–50, and 16 in 1561–5.[18] These are minimum rates, because they exclude an unknown number of murders which resulted in no petition at all. But even if the majority of killers had written a request to the Court of Holland, the numbers suggest the untenability of a "peaceful countryside versus violent towns" hypothesis.

Admittedly, the historical literature, including Schüssler's article, contains lower figures as well. However, these are derived, without exception, from criminal prosecutions or similar types of court proceedings; i.e., they refer only to killers who were arrested and tried. The higher rates just mentioned refer to cases with known killers, usually including fugitives who might be banished by default or offenders who escaped trial through reconciliation. Although a few historians argue that we should simply consider all homicide figures together, from whatever source they derive, this argument cannot be accepted. Obviously, in every case in which an unknown number of killers escaped trial, the real number of murderers – those tried plus the dark figure – cannot have been lower than the number of prosecuted homicides; it must have been higher. Even most of the elevated homicide rates just mentioned exclude cases whose killers remained entirely unidentified and who could therefore not even be banished from the city. Clearly, the higher figures are closer to the mark. The more reliable source of body inspections, available in parts of Continental Europe from the mid-sixteenth century onward, never yields rates above 20 per 100,000 – and usually much lower, except in a few marginal regions. To conclude, the quantitative figures unequivocally point out that interpersonal violence was a relatively common element in medieval life compared to later periods in European history.

Not only homicide rates, but also most of the qualitative evidence about medieval violence derives from urban settings. This state of affairs necessitates a closer look at urban life. Who inhabited and who ruled the towns of the fourteenth and fifteenth centuries and what kinds of activity went on in them besides fighting?[19] Although these towns differed from each other in some respects, the resemblances, ultimately, were more important. The differences primarily concerned their size and economic function. As far as we can tell from the available evidence, economic or demographic conjunctures do not seem to have had a significant influence on the amount of interpersonal violence or the ferocity of vendettas. Homicide rates continued to be high and feuds flared up time and again throughout the period 1300–1550. The Black Death, too, although the occasion for collective violence against Jews and lepers, made little difference over a longer term.[20]

The oldest towns had been built around a pre-existing structure, often a castle or an abbey. Newer markers were the cathedrals that the citizens themselves had built, and the various market squares. The palaces which great families erected in Italian cities and the public buildings of Northern Europe were made of solid stone, but by the fifteenth century timber still predominated among the great majority of ordinary dwellings. The danger of fire always lurked around the corner and the inhabitants probably feared it more than the violence associated with feuding. Volunteers manned the fire brigades, organized by district or street. Bathhouses, bakeries, and breweries were obliged to open their wells if necessary. The narrowness of the streets contributed to the hazard of fire. In Paris, for example, the main streets were five to eight meters across and the alleys two to three meters. Everywhere, they were paved, if at all, with cobblestones. Streets were important for social life, too. A craftsman fabricated his wares in the house, but would trade them, preferably, in front of his door. Next to buying and selling, there was talking and fighting in the streets. Today, a person witnessing a row would quickly shut his door, but medieval people, more familiar with violence than we are, often saw it as just another part of their social lives.

Because the available drinking water was notoriously suspect, all inhabitants, even prisoners, drank beer to quench their thirst. The beer was light; anyone who became involved in a fight as a result of alcohol consumption would have been drinking either a stronger beer or wine. Perhaps the killing of animals led to violence being seen as a normal event. Butchers drove live cows and pigs through the streets to the meat hall, slaughtered them there, and immediately offered the beef or pork for sale. Customers watching this spectacle were probably reassured that they were clearly buying fresh meat. Butchers often threw the offal, including blood, into a nearby canal, but in due course some towns began to insist that they used flowing streams or rivers instead. Latrines, few in number, were often no more than a dead-end street near the market square. These facilities served residents as well as a host of travelers. It wasn't only pilgrims and vagrants who were on the move, but also merchants and their agents – i.e., mostly men. Plenty of lodging houses and inns accommodated travelers, who, as a rule, had to share beds. The more adventurous among them would visit the prostitution quarter or stay in the "women's house," as it was called in Germany.

All towns were highly stratified and dominated by an elite whose origins varied. Its members sometimes descended from landed nobles, at other times from ordinary tradesmen. Even the latter claimed a venerable ancestry, and everywhere the dominant group cherished its armories and took part in tournaments. The elites monopolized urban government, although the feudal lord on whose territory the city had come into being often had some say in it. At the same time, many towns acquired a degree of control over the surrounding countryside. This form of control was most elaborate in Italy, many of whose towns had completely subjugated their *contado*. The principle of elite domination was shaken, but not undermined, by the popular movements and uprisings of the later Middle Ages. For one thing, "the people" never meant the really poor. In the towns of northern and central Italy, the old elite, which included the magnates, was challenged in the late thirteenth century, but the new leaders also were wealthy merchants. Guildsmen of Northern European towns acquired rights to seats on city councils and other offices during the fourteenth century, often after bloody uprisings, which continued into the early fifteenth century. But even where their demands for a share in the urban government were granted, the spoils usually fell to guilds of relatively prosperous merchants such as wine traders. Successful guild or *popolo* families formed a new closed group, aligning itself with the older elite and, whether governments were "popular" or not, a strong family competition for offices remained the rule. In Italian towns, a single family often managed to gain pre-eminence, with its leading member acting as the *signore*, and these urban lords were of *popolano* as well as magnate origin.

This portrait of medieval cities is biased in favor of the upper classes, but that bias is easily justified. The social elites of the Middle Ages were just as heavily and sometimes disproportionately involved in assault and murder as was the rest of the population. It is fair to say that the history of interpersonal violence in Europe begins with the upper classes. Before the rise of towns, men of the secular elite were warriors whose only neighbors were unarmed peasants and peace-loving clerics. Manorial lords levied fines on serfs who fought each other, but their mutual fights were usually trivial. For the elites, violence was part of their lifestyle. When towns emerged, their leading patricians merged or allied themselves with the aristocracy and, more often than not, soon adopted their lifestyle. Medieval patricians and aristocrats alike considered violence to be their special prerogative.

Elite Violence

Quantitative judicial data provide only partial confirmation of an excessive upper-class aggressiveness. Records of chattels confiscated from murderers in thirteenth-century England, for example, indicate that the overwhelming majority were of rather humble means.[21] The offenders' occupations in the Regensburg injury book form a cross-section of the town's population, save for an overrepresentation of tailors.[22] Figures from other places come closer to implicating the elites. In fourteenth-century Venice, nobles were about averagely represented as offenders in murder cases but overrepresented in cases of assault, rape, and insult.[23] In Konstanz, in the mid-fifteenth century, the group of highest tax-payers was considerably overrepresented among the citizens punished for crimes involving the use of arms. Within 30 years, the council fined 19 of its own members and a number of its servants and messengers for assault.[24] Still another pattern prevailed in Florence in around 1400. Both the magnates and the very poor were overrepresented among citizens convicted for assault. However, because it was harder for poor people to escape judicial prosecution, the overrepresentation of magnates was, in reality, greater.[25]

The Florence pattern probably prevailed in other places as well.[26] If a large proportion of elite violence remained unrecorded, the extant statistics have only a limited value.

Aggression from nobles and patricians had the greatest chance of remaining unpunished when the victims came from the humble poor. Although vendettas characterized the Middle Ages, most common people experienced violence as being aimed principally at themselves, and mostly without justification. The prerogative of the elites included the right, self-evident to them, to harass any social inferior who happened to displease them. A lot of top-down casual violence ensued, most of which remained unreported; even if it did become a case, the attacker usually got away with it. A nobleman taking a ride finds a peasant in his way: he might take his sword and cut the peasant's arm. An artisan knocks over the beer can of a wealthy merchant in a tavern: he might himself be knocked down by the merchant. Alternatively, a servant might beat up an impertinent inferior. Aristocrats regularly got angry when an innkeeper or some other service provider asked them to pay the bill. Any hindrance from or self-conscious behavior of a commoner was interpreted by the great as an act of impertinence. The fact that this interpretation was self-evident to them is a constitutive part of the huge inequality of power prevailing in the Middle Ages. As late as the early sixteenth century, the Flemish legal writer Filips Wielant wrote that a gentleman was allowed to ward off with his sword a commoner who attempted to give him a slap on the cheek. If he killed his assailant, it counted as self-defense because he "ought not to tolerate such a shaming act" from a "villain."[27]

This kind of routine aggression is attested widely in England, Germany, and Italy, among others.[28] Italian youths from magnate families would ride out to the *contado* and commit "recreational" violence against peasants. Almost everywhere, such activities only reached the judicial record when an aristocrat was guilty of a long series of particularly callous acts. Noblemen usually had sufficient connections among office-holders to ward off any judicial proceedings. English Justices of the Peace and sheriffs, for example, were all attached, through clientship, family ties, or otherwise, to a great lord, which made them hesitant to undertake action not only against the lords, but also against any of their dependents. In addition, these office-holders used the control they had over the judicial system to resolve personal disputes.[29] Throughout Europe there were cases of disorderly judges, who drank, gambled, fought, and intimidated people, or who promised to release a prisoner on condition of having sex with his young wife.[30] Wealthy merchants found it easy to bribe judges. Only rarely did a higher authority stop such abusers of office. Italian nobles often indignantly and impulsively attacked a city guard or a court messenger who approached them in performance of their duty; nobles did stand trial for such acts, but they were merely fined, whereas a commoner would receive a heavier punishment.[31]

The casual violence of elites against commoners fits perfectly into Elias's model of established versus outsider relations.[32] This unequal relationship between two groups can be observed in practically every society, regardless of its overall level of "civilized" behavior. Members of a group with a large surplus of power over another group often consider themselves as intrinsically "better" than their social inferiors. Established groups view themselves as first-rate human beings and deny the outsiders their full humanity. In relatively pacified societies, the established take pride in their civilized manners and stigmatize outsiders as dirty, sexually immoral, or aggressive. Outsiders are socially excluded, through contact avoidance and similar measures. In societies that value honor and bravery, outsiders can literally be pushed aside. The established, proud of their valor and arms, do not feel stained by physical contact with an inferior, at least not by one-sided violent contact. If an outsider gets in the way of an elite person or in any way spoils his pleasure, he is beaten and injured, and he will bear the mark of his inferiority.

When the power of an established elite is challenged, the balance may turn. The rise of "people's governments" in the Italian communes constitutes an ambiguous example. Medievalists disagree about the effectiveness of their attempts to curb the aggression of aristocrats. As just mentioned, the leaders of the *popolo* constituted a new elite, interested primarily in restricting the magnates' arbitrary behavior against themselves. The new elite's attitudes toward feuding were no different from those of their predecessors. In Florence, in the thirteenth and fourteenth centuries, Andrea Zorzi identified 66 feuds involving patrician families. Of these, 28 conflicts involved *popolo* houses and in 11 cases, both parties belonged to "the people." One vendetta pitted the Mannelli clan, of the old magnate class, against the Velluti clan, rich merchants who had started as wool traders. Although the Velluti participated in drafting the 1295 anti-magnate statutes, Lippo Mannelli was killed just a few days before these statutes were promulgated.[33]

This murder is a famous case in historiography. Ostensibly, it was done in retaliation for a loss the Velluti had suffered no fewer than 28 years earlier. Their descendant, Donato, writing in the 1360s, recalled the case. He explained that his father, a few cousins, and some clients from their neighborhood took revenge in 1295 for the death of Ghino, killed by Mannello Mannelli in 1267. When Donato wrote his *ricordanze*, he had held various offices in the city, among them that of judge. Nevertheless, he praised this act of retaliation by his ancestors, done for the love of lineage and neighborhood. Donato's account has led to different interpretations of feuding and family obligations. According to John Larner, the long time that might elapse between a murder and its reprisal, as well as the feud's recollection by later generations, perpetuated the need for relatives to rely on each other. Families that slayed together stayed together, he concludes.[34] Trevor Dean, on the other hand, believes that Donato may have interpreted the 1295 murder as an act of revenge in a feud, while, in fact, it was not. Moreover, Donato's cousins blamed his branch of the family for taking a leading role in the vendetta.[35]

Thus, the feuding group could be smaller or larger than the family group. Donato was on bad terms with some of his cousins, but he attributed Lippo's murder to the love of lineage *and* neighborhood. As in *Romeo and Juliet*, feuds involved servants and clients too. This broad range of potential avengers was matched by an equally broad range of potential victims. Following a murder, an act of revenge could as easily be perpetrated on a relative or dependent as on the culprit himself. Demographic realities, on the other hand, limited the group likely to take an active part in the vendetta. In all societies, violence is the special preserve of adolescents and young adults. A murder victim's father, if still alive, often was too old to take revenge. Legitimate sons almost always were too young, especially among the Italian elites, where men married in their mid-30s. That is why many accounts of vendettas refer to brothers who take revenge.[36] When a married murder victim had no living brothers, and cousins or nephews declined to act, this might cause retaliation to be postponed until a son had grown up. Indeed, lacking other opportunities, he often used it as a coming of age ritual that gained him recognition as a family leader.

The ambiguity of the composition of the feuding group is no problem for writing about the history of murder. Vendetta circles varied in structure, depending on region and period. Sometimes, although all the avengers might have been related to the victim, they were not necessarily related to each other. At other times their relationship was not of blood at all. Moreover, because feuding belonged to the realm of social custom rather than formal law, there were no definite rules for participation. Questions about the exact applicability of terms like clan or lineage can be left to family historians. For the history of violence, the crucial observation is that internal solidarity often included the sense of revenge. As strong as this solidarity could be, it never was automatically given. Every group with close mutual bonds, actively or potentially engaged in defense or feud against outsiders, had to take care that there was no internal conflict. Among groups not related by blood, statutes forbidding internal quarrels, and subjecting them to arbitration when they nevertheless occurred, are well known in medieval and early modern history. Guilds, brotherhoods, and commercial companies, including merchant associations such as the hanse, had such statutes. In Italy they have been discovered for family clans. A group of united families was called a *consorteria* or *albergo*. Italian *consorterie*, as well as family groups in Germany, France and the Iberian peninsula, routinely erected towers or fort-like strongholds within their towns, as bastions against their enemies and visible signs of their power.[37]

A considerable share of the evidence about Italian vendettas comes from Florence, but this state of affairs may simply reflect the disproportionate attention this city has received from historians. Other towns and regions experienced similar incidents. A Milan feud, for example, shook the city as late as the 1490s. It opposed the Caimi to the Castiglioni clans, both high-ranking families with connections to the Sforza court. According to a contemporary document, both sides suffered serious physical injury and several homicides were committed. The prince (an appropriate term for Milan at this time) had to exercise extreme caution in trying to establish peace between the two parties.[38]

Venice, on the other hand, seems to have been largely free from feuding since the early fourteenth century. In 1320, its ruling class, although of bourgeois descent, was formally defined as an aristocracy. As elsewhere, these nobles were violent, but the commune managed with considerable success to prevent them from taking revenge on each other. The only vendettas appearing in the judicial record were petty ones, mostly among lower-class groups, such as between two neighbors. Interestingly, one of the earliest reported instances of the modern type of contract murder took place in the world of Venetian aristocrats. In 1355, the noble banker Zanino Soranzo hired a shipwright he knew to eliminate his business rival Semelino da Mosto. The assassin was unable to profit from the fee of 100 ducats and living expenses while hiding in Treviso, because he was caught there. It led to Soranzo's flight from Venice.[39] The city witnessed a few similar cases around 1400. It would be too easy, however, to postulate a relationship between contract murders and absence of feuding. In 1396 a murder by a hired assassin took place in vendetta-prone Florence.[40]

From the Italian city-states to the town of Marseilles is no big step. The Mediterranean area from Venice to Catalonia formed a cultural and economic unit. Politically, Marseilles belonged to the kingdom of France, but the French presence amounted to no more than a *viguier* (magistrate), his deputy, and a few assistants. Real authority was wielded at the family and neighborhood level. In the mid-fourteenth century, the entire city was divided into two rival factions, headed by the Vivaut and Martin families on the one hand and the De Jerusalem family on the other. Members of these three families sat on the city council and held other important offices. Their antagonism structured a large part of all urban violence, because families of lesser status and other solidarity groups were allied with one or other of the two factions. In 1356, a murderer from the Vivaut faction had himself arrested, for his own safety, by the *viguier* and his assistants. When some of the De Jerusalems tried to wrestle the arrestee from the men of law, the *subviguier*, Peire Guibert, drew his sword saying "You'll have him only over my dead body." His courage probably derived less from his office than from the fact that he was associated with the Vivaut faction; later, he was accused of killing a De Jerusalem. Thus, at times, even the royal officials took part in local feuding. Unafraid of the French king, attackers committed their acts in full daylight, often near markets, so that everyone would see that a just revenge had been taken. One day in 1403, when Johan Areat returned home from the market, his enemy and two companions ambushed him in Caysarie street, a crowded thoroughfare, and killed him on the spot while numerous people watched.[41]

In France, north of the Languedoc, feuding was equally common, but from the mid-fourteenth century an act of vengeance rarely led to successive acts of counter-vengeance. Gauvard attributes this to the development of a social code which ensured that most feuds ended relatively quickly. This code accorded great importance to the peace-making activities of female relatives from both sides, who exhorted the men toward reconciliation and organized meals or drinking ceremonies where it was sealed. The increasing influence of the French state played a part as well, since most avengers fled their locality in order to escape from justice. Protracted vendettas that nevertheless arose usually lasted no longer than one or two generations.[42]

The evidence from the Low Countries, like that for Marseilles, reveals a concern for making revenge public. In Holland and Zeeland, it was often taken at the church door on Sunday with the whole community watching. Sacrament's Day, with its long procession of clergymen, magistrates, and ordinary laity, was an especially favorite occasion. In Vossemeer, on Sacrament's Day 1495, three men broke into the procession and stabbed to death the village's bailiff for murdering their relative.[43] The evidence further confirms that, when it came to feuds, fairness in numbers was no virtue. Revenge and vendetta always counted as honorable, even when four or five men together killed one opponent. In 1449, for example, a party of relatives from Utrecht crossed the Holland border in order to exact vengeance upon a man who had wounded the bastard son of one of them. When they spotted the aggressor's brother working in his farm field, they immediately attacked him. Another such incident took place in a Zeeland village in 1498. Two brothers and two of their cousins pursued one Hallinck Cornelis, but he managed to kill one of his assailants with a pike and escaped. Thereupon, the other three went to the home of Hallinck's aged father, forced open the door, dragged the old man from his bed, stabbed him 17 times, and finished him off by smashing his head with a club.[44] Even women were not safe. In 1533, three brothers from the village of Rijnsburg in Holland rushed to the home of a man who had killed the son of one of them. When they found that the killer had fled, they broke through the windows and beat up his mother.[45]

England again was relatively free from vendettas, but to a lesser extent than Venice. A milder variant of Continental feuding persisted across the Channel.[46] English nobles differed from French aristocrats or Italian magnates because they tended to leave the actual fighting to their servants and retainers. This was already so in the thirteenth century.[47] Whether it concerned conflicts over land, entertainment, or preference, the servants of a gentleman patron were his watchdogs. On the rare occasions that a gentleman personally participated in a feud, he attacked not the enemy himself, but his retainer. In a feud between two London factions, however, several young patricians from each side actively participated. It occasioned at least two murders: the first in 1228 and the subsequent revenge in 1243. The victim of the second murder was himself the faction leader.[48] Other cases of upper-class violence were reported in England well into the fifteenth century. In 1446, a gentleman landowner made an unusual will by dividing his estates among his bastard children, instead of leaving his property to his widowed sister. After the landowner's death, a conflict ensued between his illegitimate children and their gentry protectors, on the one hand, and the family of the sister's late husband on the other. In the course of this conflict, four men of the latter party killed one of the former.[49] Nine years later, a feud between two Devonshire factions, each led by a gentry family, caused the death of a barrister identified with one of these factions. The barrister's murderers had forced him to provide them with food, stripped his house of all valuables, and then butchered him with their swords and daggers.[50] In both these fifteenth-century cases, retainers of the feuding magnates had performed the actual violence.

Vendetta stories about ambushes and uneven fights represent only a part of the total incidence of violence, which included all kinds of trivial clashes. Quantitative data concerning multiple perpetrators and victimization testify to that. In fourteenth-century Olomouc, for example, out of 246 homicides, 195 had been committed by one person, 25 by two people, and 26 by three or more. Among 67 reported injuries, 49 had been caused by a single person. Victimization was even less of a collective affair in Olomouc: 223 single corpses versus 10 groups of corpses, and 51 single injury victims versus 6 groups of injury victims.[51] Six of the 42 Amsterdam murder victims in the period 1431–62 had been killed by two men and two of the victims had been killed by three.[52] In late fifteenth-century Paris, three-quarters of all fights were one-on-one, but these were usually simple fist fights.[53] Interestingly, we find the largest share of group involvement in the near-complete murder records of thirteenth-century

England. About 60 percent of the killers had acted with one or more co-killers, not just passive accomplices, and in 35 percent of all incidents more than one person was killed.[54]

Not only did feuds with unequal attacks represent just a modest share of all violence, revenge per se, also by an individual assailant, was never an automatic response. Florentine patricians, for example, at times chose to continue a feud by peaceful means, such as economic competition or canvassing for offices.[55] Everywhere, feuds could end or be nipped in the bud through reconciliation. After a single homicide or a feud, reconciliation gradually became systematic (see chapter 2). Trevor Dean emphasizes that three conditions had to be met before vengeance became a reality: escalation of the conflict; incitement by a relative or a reproachful third party; and overcoming the forces aimed at pacification.[56] He considers the third factor as especially strong, warning that researchers should look for cases of vendetta avoidance as well.

In a notorious case in 1405, the question whether to continue a feud or to reconcile was the subject of a bitter father–son conflict.[57] When the young Remigio Lanfredini, scion of a distinguished Florentine family, returned from a trip to Ferrara, he happened to meet Giacomo Pascilocha, an enemy of the Lanfredini family. To the young man's surprise, Giacomo offered him his hand, which prompted Remigio to threaten him with his sword. The presumed enemy then explained that Lanfredino Lanfredini, the father, had made peace with him. They had even sealed it by drinking together in the presence of witnesses, but Lanfredino had negotiated ten days of silence in order to convince his family. The chance meeting had subverted this arrangement. Remigio was furious and his mother, too, took his side with the comforting statement that God would provide for a just vendetta after all. The son remained angry, calling Lanfredino a shameful traitor who had jeopardized the family honor. The conflict ended only with Remigio's emigration to Venice, where he changed his surname to Bellini. We don't know what had caused the hostility between the two families in the first place, but it is suggested that Giacomo had offended Remigio personally.

There are different angles from which to comment on this case. It shows that a son might challenge his father's authority, in particular to decide in matters that concerned the family as a whole, as sons did in many societies. It suggests, moreover, that such disputes had a greater likelihood of erupting when the father's authority was weak, as evidenced by the ten-day silence he thought necessary. With respect to the history of murder, the case is rather ambivalent. If we focus our attention on Lanfredino, we can consider it, with Dean, as an example of vendetta avoidance. Turning to Remigio, now Bellini, and his mother, we realize that for many men and women, honor dictated that a feud should be pursued, and not reconciled lightly. A combination of both views suggests that internal conflict within a solidarity group led to uncertainty about the course of future events. Peace had the greatest chance of being maintained, and a vendetta the greatest chance of being continued, when all members of both parties involved were of one mind. The adage about families slaying and staying together has to be revised to include families surviving by reconciling. Yet, the first happened frequently enough to make the Middle Ages a period in which feuds were common and homicide rates higher than in later centuries.

The urban bias of the evidence about vendettas is partly a result of our starting point around 1300. By then, the heyday of noble feuding had passed, except in the Holy Roman Empire. In the fourteenth and fifteenth centuries, large parts of the Empire lacked even a rudimentary central authority and the most extensive documentation about rural feuding is from these areas. However, contemporary Germans used the word feud (*Fehde*) in a broad sense. Many of these feuds were actually petty wars between two neighboring independent nobles.[58] Such wars hit back on the urban world when feudal knights, scarcely different from robber barons, were said to have a feud against a city. Cologne even kept a register of the persons feuding against it, distinguishing between leaders, their relatives, and their helpers. Between 1384 and 1400, the register identified 177 leaders who had a total of 232 feuds with the city. Cologne routinely bought off the vendetta with "reconciliation money," with which the other party usually was content. By contrast, Frankfurt am Main actively declared feuds against knights who robbed merchants on the way to its fairs: 229 between 1381 and 1425.[59] Such vendettas involved few murders, but assault and injury were common. Messengers who had to declare an urban feud were especially vulnerable and one from Göttingen felt lucky merely to return without his pants.[60]

Clearly, the word feud was "abused" in the Empire. The case of Friuli, analyzed by Edward Muir, offers a better example of classical feuding in a rural setting. In this relatively backward area, the vendetta was rampant throughout the fifteenth century, with conflict culminating in a blood bath in 1511 and even then not fully resolved until the Venetians managed to impose a pacification settlement in 1568. These struggles pitted against each other factions whose membership was highly transitory, but their nucleus consisted of a few aristocratic families who owned castles in the region. Conflicts over mundane issues such as water supply or collective rights to pastures often formed the basis. As in urban feuds, fairness was no virtue. Enemies from rival clans were butchered, as if prey in a hunting party. Clients and servants called themselves their lord's faithful dogs and many a fight did indeed start over injury done to a person's dog. According to contemporary views, these animals, like men, were not wild by nature, but could sometimes go mad. In human feuding, ambushes were common. When Antonio Savorgnan, the expelled leader of a once powerful faction, was killed in Villach in 1512, 10 men jumped on him from their hiding place, drove him to a corner, and offered his archenemy the opportunity to deal the final blow. It was rumored that they fed his brains to a big dog.[61] Ambushes continued to be employed until the 1560s.

Feuding and Urban Governance

Feuding and governance would appear to be irreconcilable. This is suggested on the famous frescoes by Ambrogio Lorenzetti which, to this day, adorn the meeting room of the Government of the Nine in Siena's Palazzo Comunale. Good government means that workers build houses, merchants sell their wares, and ladies dance in the streets; the *contado*, dominated by the city, is safe for travelers. The damaged fresco of bad government depicts, among other things, a robbed merchant, murder, rape, and justice in chains.[62] Does the murder refer to a vendetta? Whether it does or not, the vendetta was such a self-evident reaction to an offense, that the territorial and urban governments on whose authority vendettas in theory encroached could not imagine a world without them. Even for scholars who believe that Donato Velluti was mistaken in considering the murder that his ancestor had committed to be an act of revenge, one conclusion remains the same: this judge condoned feuding for his own family. Councils, judges, and burgomasters showed considerable understanding toward people who killed for honor, because they themselves were active participants in the game.

Official toleration of feuding everywhere was bound to certain conditions. These were written down throughout the Low Countries, in Ghent for example. The blood feud was lawful there when it was officially declared in writing to the other party and each murder committed in the course of it had to be followed by a reconciliation procedure.[63] Murderers in the Low Countries additionally performed rituals such as leaving the weapon and a few coins on the victim's body, which signified that the act had been a lawful revenge. Swiss towns, on the other hand, allowed blood revenge in practice, without issuing official rules, although the Zurich council determined in 1448 that avengers could only be the closest relatives.[64] Such rules were also common across the Alps. The statutes of the *podestà* (chief magistrate) of Florence of 1325, repeated in 1356 and 1415, forbade judges and executors of justice to proceed against men involved in a lawful vendetta. The vendetta was lawful when the following conditions applied: the original offense was manifest; vengeance was appropriate; it was enacted against the offender's children only when the offender was dead; it was carried out by the offended man's family within the fourth degree of cousinship. The Florentine notary Filippo Ceffi considered preparation for a vendetta to be a civic duty and even defined a magistrate's actions following a legal complaint as making a vendetta against the offender.[65] Although Trevor Dean argues that no Italian town was as permissive as Florence, in practice tolerance prevailed everywhere.[66] Communes laid value on limiting the number and duration of feuds, but did not prohibit them in principle.[67] Towns in the Romagna region, for example, forbade exacting vengeance on anyone but the original offender.[68] William Bowsky concludes: "The vendetta could be limited and regulated but not eliminated."[69] This applied to monarchies as well. A Catalonian royal decree of 1360 laid down the following rules: the prospective avengers had to register their claim in a letter to their target's house, then wait for 10 days and take revenge only on the killer or assailant himself.[70] French statutes, from the late thirteenth century onward, limited the size of the group of relatives entitled to revenge, but such statutes expressed the wish of royal and urban governments rather than actual practice.[71]

One of the best illustrations of the intertwining of feuding and governance is a protracted vendetta which divided the entire ruling class of Ghent. Bloodshed was concentrated in the years 1294–6, but the matter was not definitively settled until 1306. A single murder for honor in 1282 intensified the animosities that were always around. The victim, whose name, Arnulf Papenzoon, strongly suggests that he was the bastard son of a priest, had managed successively to charm two patrician young ladies. He was first engaged to Elisabeth Borluut, but left her for the pretty Annekin de Brune. Thereupon, Elisabeth's two brothers, assisted by eight other well-bred young men, killed Arnulf, even though he had taken refuge in a churchyard. A formal peace among all leading families, instigated by Gerelm Borluut, chief magistrate and grandfather of the two avengers, prevented further violence. As part of the settlement, Annekin's brother Jan had to acknowledge that his sister had done wrong in committing herself to a man who was already engaged. At Gerelm's death four years later, however, the balance of power was shaken. As his successor, the majority of the council preferred, instead of his son, a scion of a rival family, whose home base lay in the district across the Scheldt river. Moreover, the new chief magistrate was Jan de Brune's cousin. Again eight years later, a confrontation between Jan de Brune and one of the two avengers, Jan Borluut, escalated the existing tensions.

It was a sunny afternoon in August, the eve of the Feast of the Assumption. Borluut had some business in the cloth hall and afterwards he chatted with a few weavers. Then De Brune came by, accompanied by his wife. Seeing an opportunity to provoke his enemy, he asked with a smile on his face: "Is it because your father failed to become a magistrate that you are obliged to converse with simple craftsmen?" Borluut: "You De Brunes are pathetic upstarts who pretend to be magnates, whereas my family is among the oldest in this town." De Brune: "You come to the cloth hall merely to show your face, since your affairs have been slackening for years." Because this statement contained some truth, Borluut got even more infuriated: "Mind your words; the honor of the Borluuts will have no mockery." This was precisely what De Brune continued to do: "You were forced to hide your sister in a convent, because after even a priest's son had scorned her, no one wanted her any more." These words enraged Borluut so much that, while seated on his horse, he gave his adversary a slap in the face. De Brune intended to fight back, but his wife intervened and, moreover, his adversary had four male servants with him. The slap had multiple meanings. It humiliated De Brune yet, when viewed as purely physical violence, it was insignificant; but this violence was enough to brand Borluut as the one who had broken the peace of 1282. Therefore, De Brune's wife persuaded her husband to withdraw and await judicial satisfaction. His withdrawal caused the many artisans, who had watched the confrontation, to deride him as a coward. At the square they celebrated Borluut's victory all night, praising him as a friend of the people. For more than two months nothing happened, but on October 18 the Ghent court, presided over by De Brune's cousin, condemned Borluut not only to pay the regular £100 fine but also, without any legal base, to ten years' banishment. The following night, a large party, led by Borluut, crossed the Scheldt and besieged the chief magistrate's residence. They failed to lay hands on him, but they killed his nephew, the district's bailiff. This murder set the feud in motion. It pitted two sizeable groups of families against each other. They all took their own grudges to the struggle, while party alliances involving the town's position vis-à-vis the count of Flanders and the French king played their part as well. By January 1296, there were 13 victims altogether: five patricians and two servants dead and six men seriously injured. The family alliances persisted into the political struggles that opened the fourteenth century, and plans by one party to revive the feud in 1306 could only just be thwarted through a grand scheme of arbitration.[72]

More examples of private feuds with political or judicial office-holders as leading actors come from the region North of Flanders. Well into the fifteenth century, urban magistrates were involved in cases of revenge, vendetta, or private justice, as perpetrators as well as victims. Between 1365 and 1404, the Haarlem *schout* (prosecutor) and his relatives were enmeshed in a bloody feud with a few other leading families. This conflict led to a second one, which involved courtiers of the Count of Holland. The murder of a courtier and a lady in The Hague in 1392 then led to a vendetta between two noble factions that lasted until 1414.[73] A particularly brief feud in Heusden, on the border of Holland and Brabant, set the town's *schout* up against a former magistrate, each supported by their relatives. The conflict went through a cycle of first quarrels, then arbitration, broken peace, and lethal confrontation, all on one Sunday in December 1463. Kinsmen from both sides were severely injured and late that night the former magistrate stabbed the *schout* to death.[74]

Among this evidence, the importance of the Ghent vendetta lies in its ample documentation. Blockmans stresses the case's "modern" context, such as the setbacks that the Borluut family had suffered in their cloth business over several decades, due to economic competition between Flanders and England. The interweaving of personal quarrels and the position of people in the town's political hierarchy is also clear, as well as the structural conflict between patricians and artisans. Such pre-existing tensions played a part in feuds everywhere. We may call political and social conflict and economic competition "modern," but that does not diminish the fact that attitudes toward violence were decidedly different from what they were to become in, say, the nineteenth century. The open consent to murder formed part of medieval culture and this is a key element differentiating this culture from later ones. We see it most tellingly in the tacit agreement among the large majority of the urban patriciate that a man could be killed for breaking his marriage vow, which is not a criminal act at all. And we see it in the private and murderous resistance to a judicial judgment and to a bailiff's attempt to uphold it. These murders all took place among patricians, but it is clear, from the celebration at the cloth hall square, that common people understood this value system and shared it. It would even be wrong to say that economic and political conflict had primacy of which violence was the result. One has the impression that Borluut's confrontation with De Brune, primarily about personal animosity and family honor, drew the former into the people's camp.

Factional antagonism played an important role indeed in the great urban revolts of the period 1360–1440, particularly in Flanders, Italy, and the Seine basin. They had a more clearly lower-class signature than the earlier *popolo* movements in Italian communes, but nevertheless, in almost every case, the rebels did not include the very poor. Their leaders, moreover, were distinguished citizens, such as Etienne Marcel in Paris, the Artevelde of Ghent, and Salvestro de Medici in Florence's Ciompi uprising. The Ciompi "revolution" arose to a considerable extent from the desire of the party excluded until then from the city government to continue its vendettas and take revenge for the exile of its members. A similar situation prevailed as far north as Stralsund, Germany in the 1390s.[75] In Leuven in the 1370s, two families were at first enmeshed in a feud and then became leaders of the patrician and popular factions respectively.[76] An interrelationship of family rivalry and political contest can be observed in many German and Swiss towns, as well as in the factional struggles between Hoeken and Kabeljauwen that divided the cities and gentry of Holland after the mid-fourteenth century.[77]

Ghent is exemplary once more. The lives and careers of father and son Van Artevelde, the famous popular leaders, revolved around all the great social antagonisms of their time, but a strong sense of family, underlined by violence, was the connecting thread.[78] Jacob and his son Philip both nursed grudges for years, waiting for the right time to strike. After his election as captain at the beginning of 1338, Jacob kept some 60 to 80 bodyguards, who were ordered to kill any suspected opponent when he signaled them to do so. He had set the example himself by murdering his rival, Fulk uten Rosen, a partisan of the Flemish count, in the presence of the count in August 1338. In March 1345, Jacob's adversaries deposed him and deprived him of this team of guards, which resulted in his assassination in July. The act owed much to personal grudges. Although his assassins were political enemies, they avenged family honor, washing away perceived insults and condescending behavior toward them and their relatives. In their turn, Jacob's sons killed several of their father's and their family's rivals in feuds that sometimes had no recognizable political aspect at all. In January 1382, amidst a severe economic and political crisis, Philip van Artevelde was unexpectedly elected captain, which prompted various prominent citizens, whose families had been opponents of Jacob, to flee Ghent. Those who stayed behind were murdered at Philip's instigation. Philip died, the last male of his line, in November of that year in a battle with the French. In 1384, when the duke of Burgundy succeeded as count of Flanders, the tide for vendetta began to turn.

Ritual, Masculinity and Impulse

The two principal themes of vendetta and elite violence should not be conflated. First, feuding had a broad social base, as in fifteenth-century Holland. Revenge victims there included skippers who returned without one or more of their crew, for whose drowning the community held them responsible.[79] Second, the great as well as commoners also committed violence without a revenge motive. Whereas nobles and patricians might do this for fun, conflicts among common people often arose out of day-to-day affairs like work. Homicides in the villages of fourteenth-century

England, for example, were more common at planting and harvest time.[80] Third, almost all violence was highly ritualized. Ritual has been discussed in connection with the vendetta, but it was an element in ordinary violence too.

The role of ritual in physical aggression is emphasized in every study of the period. In Zurich, for example, in ordinary fights with stones, fists, or knives, the head and especially the face were the most frequent targets of attack. In symbolic language, the face stood for the whole person and his reputation. Insults were a common cause of fights: for men, primarily, for being called a "liar" or "perjurer" and, secondarily, "thief" or "malefactor;" for women, invariably, being dubbed a "whore." These words of abuse were employed against Christian as well as Jewish inhabitants of Zurich.[81] Comparable insults were frequent causes of violence in the Low Countries and France. Women were called whores with various negative adjectives, or "priest's concubine." Names against men included "thief," "traitor," "cuckold," and "bastard," or they were belittled by a diminutive following their name. "Cuckold" and "bastard" implied sexual faults, but not primarily of the insulted man himself. "Son of a whore" was the prime insult, because this word encroached upon the honor of two people and it questioned the authenticity of descent. Illegitimate sons of noblemen, however, enjoyed a relatively high status, so it did not hurt them to be called bastards. A particular insult was to take away or strike at a man's headgear. This often caused a fight. Gauvard attaches great significance to the fact that medieval men usually wore pointed hats, which symbolically stood for their male member. To maltreat a man's headgear thus meant to ridicule his masculinity. This also explains why men were obliged to take off their hats in church, whereas women, whose caps meant chastity, had to keep them on.[82] The face and the whole head were favorite objects of ritual attack throughout Europe and well beyond the Middle Ages. There is a much larger body of evidence about the repertoire of insult and ritual violence in the early modern period, discussed in chapter 3.

Ritual and honor were intimately related, because the message that ritual conveyed almost always touched on a person's honor. The reputation of the assailant or the victim might be at stake and the message could pertain to personal as well as group honor. In order to obtain satisfaction for an attack on a person's honor, however, the assailant did not have to use violence. Almost everywhere, in town and countryside, the judicial authorities routinely fined people for insults and verbal abuse. Hence, the offended party could opt to go to court for a redress of honor. In connection with this, Schuster distinguishes between "honor" and "sense of honor." Medieval magistrates, he argues, protected the first by punishing insults, but they refused to recognize the second and therefore they also punished violent reactions to breaches of honor. The more aggressive a man was, the greater his care for his good reputation: "The sense of honor as well as the tendency to act upon it increased with the decrease of restraint on aggression."[83] However, the relatively light punishments for honorific violence and the tolerance of feuding show that the magistrates' non-recognition of people's sense of honor had definite limits.

The practice of violence took place in a male world. That was evident from the vendetta stories and it is true for many times and places, though less so for victimization. For the Middle Ages, a few quantitative figures suffice. In the coroner's and eyre rolls of thirteenth-century England, just over 90 percent of the killers and 80 percent of the victims were male.[84] In fourteenth-century coroner's rolls, where there is information on the victims only, 94 percent were male in Northamptonshire, 96.5 percent in Oxford, and 90 percent in London.[85] In Florence, in three sample periods (1344–5, 1374–5, 1455–66) the percentage of men prosecuted for assault was 93, 88, and 97.5, respectively.[86] The male preponderance is overwhelming in Gauvard's large dataset of French pardon letters of the fourteenth and fifteenth centuries: 99 percent of the killers and 97 percent of the homicide victims.[87] In a study of pardon letters from Picardy in the first half of the sixteenth century, this is 99.4 percent and 96.5 percent respectively.[88]

Offended masculinity occasioned a murder within the Augsburg patriciate in September 1535, indicating that elite violence was still common toward the end of the period covered by this chapter. Because the killer's brother had broken off a trading partnership with the victim's father six years earlier, it is likely that family conflict lay behind the incident. It began in the Herrenstube, the tavern reserved for male patricians. The company was merry that night. Upon entry, Jeremias Ehem tuned into the merry atmosphere, saying that his wife had chased him from the house. Perhaps in order to counterbalance this joke, he then contested the masculinity of one of the others present, Joachim Herwart. Afterwards, the witnesses had contradictory recollections about what object Ehem held up to Herwart, but they all agreed that it was phallic-shaped. Ehem: "Yours is of no use any more since you cannot get it up." The suggestion of impotence was rebuffed in a classic manner: "Let me ride your sweetheart and I am sure she will enjoy it." Since Ehem's wife was a mere butcher's daughter, the remark implied that she was a cheap whore whom he had married only for her beauty. After another exchange of words, Herwart requested his teaser to go find someone else to make a fool of, whereupon Ehem left the tavern. Sensing that he had not gone home, the company tried to make Herwart stay, but he left as well. Outside both men drew their swords and Ehem fatally stabbed Herwart. The killer fled Augsburg, but he was able to return soon afterwards when a few council members negotiated a settlement between him and the victim's widow by which he was to pay her 500 guilders.[89]

Whereas the link between violence and masculinity was to remain relatively unchanged in later periods, the choice of weapons reflected medieval life and technology. In thirteenth-century England, 30 percent of murder victims died of knife wounds and the rest had been hit with sticks, stones, or agricultural implements. In the next century, knives accounted for 42 percent of murder victims and all stabbing instruments for 73 percent (the remainder had been killed with a blunt object).[90] In fights between men in late fourteenth-century Zurich, the weapon was usually a knife, but axes, hammers, halbards, swords, and lances were also used.[91] Sharp instruments were particularly preponderant in the homicides and non-lethal injuries registered in Krakow's suburb Kazimierz: 458 with a knife, 122 with a sword, and a mere 11 for other categories.[92] These figures are all influenced by a variety of registration and prosecution policies, but it is clear that many men carried sharp weapons, especially knives, and that they were prepared to use them in a fight. Knives, of course, were also used for cutting food. Military weapons often remained in people's hands when they were disbanded as soldiers. At night, Paris was full of men carrying swords of various kinds, as well as daggers, pikes, and lances, even though this was unlawful.[93] In the fifteenth century, Italian cities regularly issued prohibitions on bearing arms, but these included so many exceptions that their effect was negligible.[94] Towns in the Low Countries held official measurements to determine whether knives were too thin or too long. Glaudemans's list of weapons prohibited at one occasion or another consists of all objects that could conceivably kill.[95]

Taverns were a common location for violence, as they would be in later centuries. Even small towns had many of them. Gambling houses, outlawed in some places, were an official source of municipal income in others.[96] Where the judicial records are silent about fights in such establishments, narrative sources supplement them. This was the case in England, where local courts dealt with taverns because of late opening hours, serving to priests or apprentices or being an unofficial brothel, but only rarely for fights.[97] A well-documented incident in a Norwich inn in 1519, however, began with a conflict between five artisans over who had won a game of dice. Stabbed with a dagger, the victim exclaimed: "By the mass, I am slain" – before falling down.[98] Parisian courts regularly dealt with tavern violence, but from French pardon letters, it can be seen that streets and crossroads were more frequent scenes of homicide.[99] Pardon letters from Holland in the first half of the sixteenth century show that taverns there too were important sites of violent conflict.[100]

Scholars who pioneered in the modern history of crime had few reservations in considering the majority of medieval violence as arising on the spot out of impulse or "uncontrollable rage."[101] A synthesis from the 1990s concludes, in a similar vein, that, apart from upper-class vendettas, most medieval violence was spontaneous and occurred during chance encounters.[102] When statements like these are made in absolute terms, they should be rejected. Impulse is always a matter of degree. Human behavior, in any society, depends on prior learning. To get angry and aggressive, you first need a reason, however suddenly found. You have to differentiate between situations with a friendly atmosphere and situations of hostility. A potentially hostile situation arises, for example, whenever a member of a rival faction enters the room. The real issue is whether the behavior of medieval men and women was characterized by a higher degree of impulsiveness than that of modern people. Although they cannot dismiss the higher incidence of violence, some historians deny that the evidence points at a greater element of spontaneity. Their principal argument is based on the alleged incompatibility of ritual and impulse. Because most medieval violence had a ritual character, they claim, it was controlled violence. However, ritual implies a fixed pattern that people know in advance, which does not necessarily point at self-control or calculation. Ritual and impulse are compatible.[103] In Daniel Smail's eloquent formulation, "loves and hatreds, according to vernacular classification, were like clothes: rich in significance, worn on the outside of the body for all to see, and easily changed."[104]

Ritual conveys a message – all kinds of messages, which sometimes entail the victim's humiliation. Considerations of ritual and honor had a softening or aggravating effect according to the occasion, as among the Venetian nobility. When a noble attacked a lower-class person, the confrontation was almost always non-lethal, but when he directed his aggression at a fellow noble, the victim usually lost his life. As Ruggiero explains, members of the nobility considered themselves so much better than the rest that it would be "honoring" a lower-class man too much to kill him. "A slap expressed disdain, a murder suggested equality."[105] Thus, the honor/ritual complex had an aggravating effect on behavior toward fellow nobles and a mitigating effect on the treatment of other people. According to the axes presented in the introduction to this book, impulsiveness is not ruled out by ritual, but by planning. Murder by way of ambush necessarily involved some measure of planning, and the degree of impulsiveness cannot have been high in cases where vengeance was postponed for a long time. In Italian towns, no less than in Marseilles, the avenger often acted on the anniversary of the original murder, preferably in or near the spot where it had occurred.[106] He could only realize this preference if the prospective victim was also there on that day, which he might be in order to show his provocative defiance.

The degree of planning was again low when it came to voluntary pastimes. As some people committed recreational violence, there was violence in recreation. For many, tournament and the Middle Ages belong together, but the history of this game extends beyond the confines of this chapter. Over time, three principal variants can be distinguished, the first of which, called by the Latin name of *hastiludium*, was reported from the eleventh century on. It pitted two teams of knights against each other, both of them riding fast toward the opponent and trying to unseat him from his horse with a lance. Sometimes the teams consisted of real enemies who played during a time-out from a dull siege, or they were simply regional rivals. Many players lost their lives. It was an exercise for real battle, and when they realized that the game also prepared men for a crusade, even clerical writers dropped their misgivings. During the thirteenth century, the second variant, called by the French name of *joute*, hence joust, took over in most of Europe. The principal difference from its predecessor was that two individual players now fought each other. Riding elegantly, moreover, and impressing the noble ladies among the audience, became important goals. There were fewer casualties than before, partly because the use of blunted arms became more common. Tournaments did not remain an exclusively noble pastime. They were organized in north German and Flemish cities for example.[107]

At the end of the medieval period, tournaments became even less wild and turned into theatrical pageants. Even then, participants occasionally lost their lives, as happened to Henry II of France in 1559.[108] At royal and ducal courts of the sixteenth and seventeenth centuries, the third variant, radically different from its two predecessors, prevailed. Players no longer aimed their lances at a human opponent. Still on horseback, their task was to pierce a small ring or to stab a wooden image representing a Moor or Turk. Thus, the physical attack was merely representational. Although the agility which this game required was still good military practice, its non-violent character, compared with medieval tournaments, stands out. Between 1680 and 1730, ring-piercing was played even by ladies, usually from a carriage.[109] The taming of the tournament had few direct links with the criminalization of homicide (discussed in chapter 2), but both changes were part of the overall development of civilizing and state formation processes.

Whereas the tournament remained a game for the elite, folk football was a popular pastime. This game, too, resulted in injuries and occasionally in deaths.[110] Both the English and French governments frowned upon football because it kept people from archery, which was a better exercise for defending the country. Fourteenth-century Siena witnessed the games of *pugna* and *boccata*, played by groups of youths. It began as a fist fight or as a mock battle with wooden weapons, but it often escalated. Then the participants threw stones at each other and exchanged their wooden sticks for staves, knives, and spears. A pitched battle ensued, with the youths loosely divided along the lines of traditional rivalries between the three districts that made up the city. These battle games were often played at the Campo beneath the windows of the Palazzo Comunale. The magistrates only feared them if, on occasion, the opponents united and, aggrieved by the regime, turned the mock battle into an attack on the palazzo.[111] Thus, violent games could give rise to new conflicts. In 3.5 percent of the homicides in French pardon letters, a playground formed the location of the crime.[112]

Outcasts

Medieval attitudes toward violence were based on a simple principle: decent people may fight, but they don't steal. Theft was dishonorable and, consequently, violence performed to enrich oneself at the expense of a fellow person was dishonorable too. There were exceptions even here, as when a magnate organized a raid on another's property in the course of a feud or conflict. But at the local level, whenever a man used violence to appropriate his neighbor's goods, he ceased to be a respectable member of the community. Furthermore, to attack someone secretly, from behind or in the night, was disdainful, because its motive, if not robbery, was akin to that of robbers. Hence the medieval legal distinction between murder and manslaughter, which defined the first not primarily by the criterion of premeditation, but by that of sneakiness. A case could be prosecuted as murder and lead to execution when the act had been particularly heinous, because it had been committed at night, without a warning, because the body had been hidden afterwards, or simply because the victim was a pregnant woman.[113] According to contemporary belief, the corpse's wounds would start to bleed again and reveal the identity of the sneaky murderer, when he dared to come back and look at it. This belief is visually illustrated in the 1513 Luzern chronicle of Diebold Schilling.[114]

Murder, in the legal sense, was infamous, whereas open and public fighting, even when a casualty ensued, was honorific. Many German and Swiss towns officially called the second "honorable or common homicide." When a Zurich butcher had stabbed to death a colleague in the meat hall in 1377, the victim's brother tried to sue the killer for murder, but the magistrates established that it had been an honorific fight, started because the victim had called the killer's family a bunch of rogues.[115] Deceit was obviously involved in 1375, when a Lincolnshire knight was found dead in a field, finely dressed and wearing spurs and belt as if robbers had attacked him. It turned out, however, that men of his own household had killed him and dragged the corpse away, with the complicity of his wife and a possible gentleman lover. Even in this case, and in a Nottinghamshire love drama of 1464, the murderers were pardoned or got away with a light penalty.[116]

Suicide was clearly outside the domain of honor. The family of a person who killed him- or herself often tried to obscure the true cause of death. Partly this served to avoid confiscation of the inheritance, and investigating officials were instructed to be vigilant against such concealment. But the family's reaction also originated from a deep sense of shame, at the act itself and the degrading treatment of the body that usually followed. Punishment by exposure of the corpse or the ignominious burial of persons who had killed themselves continued well into the early modern period. Clerical writers concentrated on the profoundly unchristian character of suicide. Invariably, it was the devil who tempted people to commit the ultimate sin, from which it was, by its very nature, impossible to repent. Indeed, doubts about one's salvation, along with more mundane misfortunes, were among the commonly acknowledged reasons for suicide. Insanity, adduced in a minority of cases, was the only reason that kept the family honor more or less intact.[117] It would require changes in the concept of honor much later in European history for people to save their reputation acceptably by taking their own lives. Reliable suicide rates for the Middle Ages are much scarcer than homicide rates, but a recent careful estimate for England and France shows that the high incidence of violence toward others was accompanied by a much lower incidence of violence against oneself. Homicide/suicide ratios of twenty or more to one were common.[118]

Next to these suicide rates, some quantitative data about instrumental violence against others are available for England. For the thirteenth century, Given calculated a separate homicide-by-bandit rate, which was 2 per 100,000 in the counties but insignificant in London and Bristol. About 10 percent of all homicide victims were explicitly said to have been killed by bandits or thieves.[119] In two rural areas in fourteenth-century England no fewer than 25 and 30 percent of homicides were connected to robbery or burglary, whereas this was 5 percent in London.[120] Bandits often employed extreme violence, torturing their victims into revealing where they had hidden their treasures and hacking them to death with all kinds of weapon.[121] In fifteenth-century East Anglia, however, their weapons were usually cheap knives and farm implements.[122] Narrative evidence refers not to Robin Hood, but to the notorious Coterel and Folville bands. They were troublesome enough to be bought off with pardon and enlistment into military campaigns and even with local offices.[123] Throughout Europe, robbery accompanied by serious violence was mostly a rural phenomenon. Although the citations of fugitive murderers in the Swiss town of Fribourg include a large share of robbers, they probably had their base in the surrounding countryside.[124]

Although not real outcasts, students and young academics often lived a boisterous and sometimes violent life in the margins of society. The famous poet François Villon is one such. As a young scholar, he killed a priest in a street brawl and participated in the robbery of the Collège de Navarre in Paris. He was condemned and pardoned more than once and forced to roam around France for years.[125] Villon's colleagues were less notorious, but large-scale fights between students and citizens or students and sergeants were a common occurrence in Paris and elsewhere. Students were mentioned as eager participants in a factional conflict that erupted in the Castilian town of Salamanca in 1462.[126] Next to students, marginal populations of substantial size existed in London and Paris. Beggars' propensity for violence, along with laziness and sexual lust, probably owed as much to contemporary stereotypes as to their actual behavior.[127] Paris consciously channeled disorder, whether dishonorable violence or just nuisance, away from the center toward the walls. This area, although within the city's jurisdiction, constituted a symbolic frontier: "Students took their mistresses there; drunks sang at the top of their lungs; neighbors fought; and would-be rapists dragged their victims to the ramparts."[128]

The vulnerability of prostitutes to violence is a universal phenomenon. In fifteenth-century Paris, they complained about beatings, threats, kidnapping, and rape. Sometimes, two or more men together would attack a prostitute, and one sergeant was arrested for assaulting a whore; sometimes, men would break into a woman's lodgings at night. But men also attacked other men in brothels, aided and abetted by the prostitutes, while many prostitutes were themselves violent against each other. Part of the explanation for the late-medieval transition from female to male brothel-keepers, attested for in Germany, France, and Spain, lies in the need to contain violence. Despite obligations to hand over one's weapons upon entry, clients repeatedly maltreated whores or fought each other. Regulations in German towns allowed the "women's host" to carry a knife to defend himself and his trustees, but he was not expected to use it against a client without good reason.[129]

Thus, whereas certain categories of violent people were outcasts, social marginalization made becoming a victim of violence more probable. This is especially clear in the repeated attacks on such minority groups as lepers and Jews. On the Iberian peninsula, after the Reconquista, these minorities included Muslims. In many ways, violence against minorities was the opposite of the honorific fighting of the vendetta. Feuds were fought among equals; not necessarily between parties equal in strength of manpower, but between families or factions of roughly the same social status. Minority groups were, by definition, lower in status; although they were often not economically marginal, the majority denied them an entitlement to honor. In the Crown of Aragon, Muslims and Jews were officially denied the right to engage in a vendetta. Whereas, in feuding, being part of a larger or a smaller group could alternate between the parties, members of minority groups were always in that position. Much of the violence against them was collective. Even when one Christian had a fight with one or more Jews or Muslims, the social context put the latter in a position of symbolic inferiority. The danger of retaliation was always felt. Food was a frequent source of conflict. Each of the three religions had different rules about what to consume and how; they refused to eat each other's meat and they had separate meat markets and butchers. Mixed sexual unions were another possible cause of violence. Although prohibitions of inter-faith sex applied to everyone, the stereotypical images of filth connected to it came down especially on non-Christians. On the other hand, they could usually invoke the special protection they enjoyed from kings, ter-ritorial lords or city rulers.[130]

Annually recurrent were the ritual attacks on Jews by Christians on the Thursday before Easter, a custom practiced on the Iberian peninsula, in Italy, and in the south of France. In the Rhineland and other regions, Jews had been slaughtered on occasion since the First Crusade, but anti-minority violence on the Iberian peninsula was rarely lethal before the Black Death. Violence against Jews continued after the plague epidemic, often incited by the sermons of wandering zealots. In 1411, for example, the preacher Vincent Ferrier led mobs in Toledo, Salamanca, and Perpignan who chased the Jews from their synagogues and turned these into churches.[131]

Social Change?

Several historians see the vendetta, or elite violence generally, declining well before the close of the Middle Ages. According to a specialist of Florence, the aggression committed by members of the leading Medici and Strozzi families was less frequent and lethal in the fifteenth century than it had been in the fourteenth.[132] A more recent study credits the Florentine authorities with actively combating violence after the Black Death.[133] In France, private vengeance is said to have been on the decline in the fif-teenth century, due to the extending grip of the courts and an increasing importance of the notion of peace in public opinion.[134] Daniel Smail adds a crucial element to the analysis. The growth of state power, limited as it was, came about in part, paradoxically, by the continued wish for vengeance. State formation processes did not simply involve top-down change. Monarchs, councils, and tribunals wished to extend their influ-ence, but the demand-side from below was an important factor. This demand-side included people and groups who, for tactical reasons, thought they could better strike at their enemies through denunciation and litigation. Hostile emotions continued to play an important role, but vengeance was channeled into judicial action. In this way, structured conflicts from below influenced the modest increase in the strength of state institutions.[135]

Moreover, we should take changes in the strength and scope of family bonds into consideration. Although feuding and revenge involved social groups of various kinds, the ties of blood remained of paramount importance. The gradual emergence of a more individualistic attitude reduced the circle of relatives that a person felt attached to. We may listen once more to Shakespeare, who put a radical dose of individualism into the mouth of Juliet:

> JULIET   O Romeo, Romeo! wherefore art thou Romeo?
>   Deny thy father and refuse thy name;
>   Or, if thou wilt not, be but sworn my love,
>   And I'll no longer be a Capulet.
> ROMEO   [*Aside.*] Shall I hear more, or shall I speak at this?
> JULIET   'Tis but thy name that is my enemy; –
>   Thou art thyself, though not a Montague.
>   What's Montague? It is nor hand, nor foot,
>   Nor arm, nor face, nor any other part
>   Belonging to a man. O, be some other name!
>   What's in a name? that which we call a rose
>   By any other name would smell as sweet.

Such a radical rejection of kinship identity was impossible for nearly all those who lived through the age to which the play referred. The nuclear family started to receive greater emphasis from the second half of the sixteenth century onward, along with the Reformation and Counter-Reformation and the rise, in several parts of Europe, of stronger and more stable state institutions. Any change in attitudes toward or in the practice of violence observed before the mid-sixteenth century remained very modest. The available homicide rates suggest that the average level of internal control over aggression was not raised much during the fourteenth and fifteenth centuries. The same applied to behavioral control generally, for which Erasmus's 1530 manner book represents a new spurt. Popular attitudes toward lethal but honest fights were even slower to change. Only one transformation had its first vestiges visible well before the mid-sixteenth century: the criminalization of homicide.

2

Sealed With a Kiss: From Acquiescence to Criminalization

After killing Lippo Mannelli on June 24, 1295, the Velluti avengers promptly left Florence. They realized that a banishment would follow, but they also knew that they could soon buy their way back into town. But this time, the magistrates wanted more. They started negotiations in the hope of reaching an agreement between the two prominent families. A first attempt failed. Then the killers paid their fines and returned to Florence, and the stage was set for reconciliation. On July 17, members of the Mannelli and Velluti clans, including the avengers themselves, came together in the church of San Pietro Scheragio, kissed each other on the mouth and promised to refrain from further feuding. Although concluded under pressure from the urban government, the maintenance of this private peace pact depended on the goodwill of the participants. The peace held, even though the Mannelli continued to consider themselves superior and to treat the Velluti with disdain.[1]

The kiss is a ritual gesture of venerable antiquity. Among the Hebrews, Greeks, and Romans, it primarily signified the affection and peace inherent to kinship ties and it possibly had a similar meaning for the ancient Germanic peoples. The early Christians exchanged kisses in order to demonstrate that they were all brothers and sisters. In the later Roman Empire, the application of the kissing ritual extended to the sphere of patronage ceremonies, which paved the way toward its subsequent use in feudal rites of vassalage. The homage of joining hands and the kiss on the mouth signified that the vassal owed his lord loyalty, but also that the lord would protect and respect his vassal. It is not entirely clear at what moment in time the kiss came to imply reconciliation as well, but this meaning received increased emphasis along with the consolidation of

Christianity. The Church fathers promoted the kiss of peace, which became a prominent element in Catholic liturgy.[2] When the priest kissed all parishioners after confession, this implied that they had been reconciled with one another. It is no surprise, then, to find the kiss as an element in reconciliation ceremonies following homicide. To the modern speaker of Dutch, this would even be self-evident, because the old word for reconciliation (*zoen*) has become an equivalent to the word for a kiss.

The Reconciliation Ceremony

The story of the criminalization of homicide begins with the reconciliation ceremony. The entire process from acquiescence to criminalization, which stretched from the late fourteenth century to the mid-seventeenth, has as yet occasioned few systematic descriptions or analyses. Nevertheless, this process forms a crucial part of the overall history of homicide and interpersonal violence.

Although the kiss provided this chapter with its title, we cannot simply equate kiss and *zoen*. Ritual kissing extended beyond the sphere of peacemaking, while the reconciliation ceremony involved more ritual elements than just the pledging of lips. The kiss, moreover, disappeared from this ceremony in many places toward the end of the Middle Ages. This happened in Holland as well, despite the association of the two words.[3] As the content of the ceremony was subject to change, it would be pointless to look for the origins of particular elements. It is more fruitful to imagine a chain of ritual repertoires that has no beginning and no end. As private reconciliation was an important tool of social control in many, if not all, societies without elaborate state structures, individual enactments of reconciliation drama always drew on even older traditions. Likewise, individual reconciliation ceremonies could be influenced by ritual from other spheres of social life or even from foreign cultures. In the context of medieval Europe, it is not surprising that Catholicism and feudalism were important sources.

A similar argument pertains to the very existence of reconciliation for homicide. Whether we trace it back to the *Treuga Dei* (the clerical movement to stop the petty wars of knights) or to Germanic wergild procedures, such exercises are no explanation. Explaining a ritual, custom, or law means placing it in the context of the society in which it is found. In the case of reconciliation, the essential element is its private character, undiminished by arbitration or pressure from the authorities. Basically, there were two types of voluntary settlement: one to prevent revenge – and with it the possible start of a vendetta – after a single murder and one to end feuding after at least one member of each party has been killed by the adversary party. As the extent of feuding gradually decreased, the first type became numerically dominant. The vendetta and the private settlement are two sides of a coin. The coin as a whole says: relative absence of state authority and a system of justice. Any society without a stable state structure witnesses feuds *and* private settlements. Two sides of a coin, moreover, means no negative correlation between the incidence of revenge and that of reconciliation. Some authors believe that stateless societies witness frequent palavers and informal settlements, hence few murders. Such societies, however, have been the exception rather than the rule.[4] Likewise, in the European Middle Ages, despite the prevalence of reconciliation, homicide rates were higher than in later periods.

A few early examples suffice to show that reconciliation for homicide predated the period covered by this book and that it was geographically more widespread than the uneven treatment in the literature would suggest. In March 1134, one of the murderers of the sub-dean of Orleans was prepared to repent. He assembled his accomplices, his vassals, and the best of his kin, 240 people altogether, and performed the homage of mouth and hands to the victim's relatives.[5] A similar ceremony took place in Galicia in 1162. In an aristocratic feud, the son of Juan Arias had killed three members of the Ovequo clan. The monks of the Sobrado Abbey, with whom both the Arias and Ovequo had dealings, offered to mediate. Reconciliation was scheduled for the Feast of the Assumption of the Blessed Virgin Mary in the abbey's chapter. The feuding parties came together, shook hands, and exchanged the kiss of peace and security. Reconciliation was common in Italian towns and also throughout the Holy Roman Empire. The archive of Florence contains a series of private peace pacts, concluded after homicides, fights of honor, or other conflicts, which covers a period from the late twelfth century to the late fourteenth.[6] German customs traditionally included the *Urfehde*, also *Unfehde* (literally: "un-feud"), an oath by which both parties solemnly swore to refrain from further hostilities.

One of the problems with the evidence about reconciliation concerns the intervention of political and judicial authorities. Although peace settlements following a single homicide or a feud depended on private goodwill, lords and magistrates usually were pleased with them and actively encouraged their conclusion. The more intensively the authorities meddled with the ceremony, the greater the likelihood that it was recorded. Thus, although it concerned voluntary agreements, our information is most scarce on the conclusion of settlements that were altogether private. The authorities increasingly intervened toward the end of the Middle Ages, so most of our evidence dates from that period and beyond. Moreover, the available evidence appears to be richest for the

Low Countries. Our information regarding the reconciliation ritual and the ceremony's role in the eventual criminalization of homicide is concentrated within an area that comprises the present countries of the Netherlands and Belgium and some adjacent regions in northern France and western Germany. The cursory treatment given to the subject in Edward Muir's *Ritual in Early Modern Europe* is indicative of the state of the evidence.[7] Let us first look at the Low Countries, then, and take what we see as an example of how the reconciliation and peace processes that were practiced elsewhere in Europe too could be acted out.

In its most elaborate form, the reconciliation ceremony lasted for three days. Any grouping of the details is a little arbitrary, but it might be useful to break the ceremony down into four basic components: payment of financial compensation, rituals focusing on the killer's regret, rituals focusing on peace between the parties, and religious provisions.[8] Obviously, two of these elements look more appropriate after a single murder than they would at the end of a longer-lasting feud. When both sides claim about an equal number of victims, the financial compensation would even out and there would be no clear distinction between the guilty party asking for forgiveness and the offended party granting it. It would be rash, however, to conclude that this type of reconciliation ceremony could not be applied to the feud. Note that the Ghent statutes required that, for a vendetta to be lawful, each murder committed in the course of it had to be followed by reconciliation. Pervading all components of the ceremony, finally, was its most important characteristic: it was a family event. Reconciliation never took place between individuals; it was always a collective affair.

At first sight, financial compensation might seem to be mundane, but its transfer constituted an integral part of the ceremony. There were three distinct transfers. The pre-reconciliation money was for the arbiters or any other third party who had made an effort to bring the adversaries together. On the main day of the ceremony, the killer handed over the principal sum to the victim's nearest relative, who had to share his gift with the dead man's other heirs, if any. On the third day, the other participating relatives received the remainder or kin money, their share diminishing with the distance in relationship. Numerous exact amounts in various currencies are mentioned in the literature, but it is rare to see this translated into the cost of concrete economic goods. In a Finnish case in 1550, however, the "blood money" was equivalent to six cows.[9] We can be sure that contributing to financial compensation often was a great burden on the killer and his relatives. Sometimes, if the victim had not died immediately or if the reconciliation was for assault only, the money included the reimbursement of medical costs. Of course many victims had offered resistance. In Ghent it was customary that, if the killer or one of his party had suffered injuries, his medical costs were subtracted from the compensation due by that party.[10] The entire ritual of handing over the various sums reminds us of the importance attached to the gift in many societies studied by anthropologists. Although the money was compensation, hence a kind of debt, its ceremonious transfer symbolized the creation of a new tie of mutual respect between the two families.

The non-monetary rituals concentrated on the ceremony's main day, when the largest groups of participants gathered. They often chose an ecclesiastical feast day. The guilty party had to ask forgiveness from the victim's kin. The essential scene had the killer and his relatives, with folded hands, kneeling down before the other party, one, two, or three times. For the rest, local variants existed. In some places, the penitent group entered the church first, while the forgivers waited until they had received their money, handed over by the mediators. In other places, the penitents came later, because they had ceremoniously taken off their outer garments. The entire penitent group was always clad simply, with bare heads and feet and wearing just a woollen or linen vest, grey, white, or black. The central part of the prostration might be followed by an act of paying homage. The killer and a few of his relatives laid their hands in those of the victim's nearest relatives. As a corollary to the guilty group's submission, the other group promised to refrain from revenge. This promise could take the form of the oath of *Uhrfehde* or just consist of a sign of pardon. Every single ritual was often performed in a sequence, first by the principal representatives of the two parties, then by the others.

The rituals of peace originally focused on the kiss. The kiss on the mouth in particular is a gesture implying complete mutual equality. There is perfect bodily symmetry and it is impossible to distinguish the kisser from the kissed person. As late as 1568, the peace negotiated by the Venetians between the warring clans of Friuli was sealed in this way.[11] In Holland the kiss was usually exchanged between the killer and the victim's nearest relative, the official chief of his party. Hence this chief was called the *mondzoener* ("mouth-reconciliator") and the day of the kiss and the transfer of the principal sum was known as the *mondzoen*. In time, however, the word "mouth" was understood as referring equally to the nearest relative's role as spokesman for the whole kin group. By the fifteenth century, "mouth-reconciliator" had become a traditional term for the victim's representative regardless of the ritual's content. If no close kin were available, a distant relative might take up the task, as in a Ghent agreement of 1459. It stipulated that Jan Merckaert, the son of Michiel, should produce proof, within a month, that he was authorized to act as mouth-reconciliator for the murdered Joris Merckaert.[12]

By this time, the kiss had largely disappeared from reconciliation ritual as practiced in the Low Countries. Possibly, it was associated with ceremonies of a more equal nature. In that case, its decline exemplified the growing prevalence of unequal ceremonies, in which one group unequivocally acted as the guilty party. Significantly, an unequal variant of the kiss was recorded in Aalst, near Brussels, in 1437 after the murder of Willem Scinkel by Marten Joris. At the reconciliation ceremony in a convent, presided over by several authorities, Marten, his father, and his brother each kissed Willem's brother on the cheek.[13] But perhaps we should not make too much of the disappearance of the kiss from the reconciliation ceremony. Other gestures of peace, such as the handshake, remained or served as a replacement. These gestures also implied equality. A meal or just a drink after the ceremony, in which the two parties joined together, became increasingly common toward the end of the Middle Ages, and it remained an element of reconciliation until the end.

The religious provisions of the peace settlement reflected the social hierarchy. The number of masses for the victim's soul, for example, often depended on his status in the world of the living. Five hundred was not uncommon but a few reconciliation agreements mentioned one thousand or more. The souls of important victims were placated with the foundation of a chapel, sometimes with its own priest. More common, and open to everyone, was the victim's posthumous admission into a monastery. The murderer paid a sum to the monks, for which they inscribed the murdered man's name on their list of deceased brothers and prayed for his soul on the anniversary of his death. Many ceremonies were sealed with charitable gifts, to the poor or to mendicant friars. Furthermore, reconciliation agreements throughout the Low Countries obliged the offender to undertake a pilgrimage – an obligation that could also be imposed by a court as punishment for various crimes. Finally, the religious atmosphere was enhanced by the location of the ceremony, very often a church or a monastery. Between 1389 and 1472 in Holland, 25 reconciliation ceremonies were reported to have been held in churches all over the county.[14]

One might think that contemporaries perceived reconciliation as such as a religious duty, diametrically opposed to the secular custom of the feud. That view is too simple. Because everyone believed in an afterlife, the masses and pilgrimages were useful donations to the victim, complementary to the financial compensation for his kin. The forgiving relatives considered this part of the transfer as a concrete contribution that benefited the deceased's soul. The purpose of helping salvation is implicit in the frequent obligation to erect a commemoration sign at the site of the murder or on the victim's grave. The two killers of Joris Merckaert, for example, had to ensure that a painting representing a crucifix, Our Lady, and St John was made on the wall opposite the house where the murder had taken place. A reconciliation ceremony in Antwerp in 1475 was held not only 20 years after the murder but in the absence of the killer, who was reputed to have died in Lombardy. Both kin groups found that the deceased man's soul nevertheless deserved it. The agreement concentrated on religious provisions and, should the killer unexpectedly come back from Lombardy alive, he was to redirect his steps immediately in order to go on a pilgrimage to Rome.

The collective character of the reconciliation ceremony is paramount. Without exception, the nucleus of each party consisted of a family, while most of the others were servants and clients. The reconciliation group was the same as the feuding group. Occasionally, the former, too, included circles of solidarity other than the family, as after the murder of a Solingen trader at the Antwerp fair in 1429. One of the provisions of the settlement obliged the killer's father to pay for a window-glass in a church in honor of the ordinary merchant of Germany and the Hanse.[15] Most reconciliations involved families though. From the killer's side, all relatives had an interest in participating, because they were all targets for revenge if no peace were made. And participation in the ceremony included a contribution to the reconciliation money. There are fewer examples of kin who refused to contribute than there are of killers who abused the system by asking more than their due share from their relatives. As the killer's kin would all be targets, they wanted all potential avengers to be present and to commit themselves. Hence it was not uncommon to see a group of several hundred men prostrating themselves before a party of equal size. Reconciliation created a special bond between the two families, akin to that of vassalage. The sacredness of that bond was to ensure that no new hostilities would erupt. The family was central to the entire social and cultural context of reconciliation, in which one person's actions always had repercussions for the entire kin group to which he belonged.

Documents pertaining to private reconciliation have been preserved in Italian, Iberian, and southern French cities from the fourteenth century until the first half of the seventeenth. The parties usually registered their agreement with a notary. These notarial documents differ from Northern European reconciliation protocols, because they refer not only to homicide but also include numerous settlements for assault and all kinds of conflict among neighbors. This may explain why peacemaking sometimes seemed to be a sober affair involving only a few relatives or mediators. When it concerned homicide or protracted conflict, however, larger kin groups were present, who sealed their reconciliation in a church, monastery, or hospital in the presence of priests as witnesses. The rituals included forgiveness by the offended party, a handshake, embrace, or kiss, and a shared meal.[16] The business-like character of a notarial document did not preclude the expression of emotions. In Siena, where peace settlements registered by a notary were extremely common, a mid-fourteenth-century artist, known as Barna da Siena, painted *The Mystic Marriage of St Catherine*. Commissioned in commemoration of the ending of a feud, the bottom of the painting represents a reconciliation scene, with the former enemies induced by saints to throw down their weapons and embrace each other.[17]

At first sight, England seems exceptional, because private reconciliation was outlawed at an early date. Were attitudes to violence there subject to advanced modernization? The previous chapter showed that this was not really the case. Although English elites were less violent than their Continental counterparts, they kept vendettas alive by having their servants and retainers do the fighting. Homicide rates, somewhat low for the region around London in the thirteenth century, were again comparable to Continental ones in the fourteenth. A similar caveat is in order with respect to reconciliation. The Anglo-Saxons practiced the feud, or bought off vengeance, by paying the victim's wergild, but in the twelfth century the Crown managed to take control of the handling of homicide. Private settlements, which included the payment of wergild, were no longer allowed. However, there is evidence that such settlements continued to be made informally and Thomas Green believes that this practice persisted throughout the Middle Ages.[18] There is hardly any information, though, about the amounts paid and the rituals performed at these informal settlements.

We can conclude that the reconciliation ceremony was complementary to revenge to a large extent. It was equally private, at least in origin. Reconciliation can even be considered as the more voluntary of the two, because it needs the agreement of both parties. Although the continuation of a feud in principle requires the will of both parties, just one of them can decide on an individual act of revenge. With respect to the participants in the vendetta and the reconciliation ceremony, a perfect symmetry obtains. Both customs revolved around solidarity groups, usually families, which might include servants, retainers, and neighbors. Because the Church and upcoming state institutions often served as counter-forces to families and clans, it is no surprise to find them combating the feud and meddling with peacemaking. Some scholars draw even more of a parallel between the vendetta and reconciliation. They consider feuding to be just another system of exercising social control. After all, vengeance is performed as a reaction to a wrongful act and the fear of vengeance may deter people from committing offenses. The problem with this argument is that, in feuding, the offense and the reaction to it are practically indistinguishable. As a rule, they both consist of manslaughter. Even more important, revenge always depends on a one-sided appreciation of events. In the course of a feud, what is an intolerable outrage to one party is an honorific act of vengeance for the other. It is more appropriate, therefore, to consider this the principal difference between the vendetta and reconciliation: the second, but not the first, was a tool of social control.

We can take them together once more when we consider social attitudes to violence. Readiness for vengeance, as well as the idea that a murderer's guilt could be washed away by reconciliation, were expressions of a widespread acquiescence in interpersonal violence. Contemporaries accepted honorific bloodshed as a fact of life. Communities often tolerated revenge, and homicide in an honest fight never led to social ostracism. After reconciliation or the payment of a fine, a killer lived among his neighbors as if nothing had happened. In due course, murderers from amongst the elite might become magistrates or they simply continued in their offices.[19] Some German studies tackle the problem of social attitudes to violence systematically. They show that, although homicide rates were highest in the Middle Ages, town-dwellers had little fear of this endemic violence. First and foremost, they feared punishment from God. They were afraid to travel outside their town, because dangerous robbers awaited them there, and they worried when a neighbor died a seemingly natural but incomprehensibly sudden death. Conflicts among citizens, even when lethal, failed to prevent them from sleeping at night. A discourse about security did not emerge in Germany until after 1500.[20] Frenchmen, too, thought the highways and forests unsafe because of robbers. Their concern extended to crimes connected to or in the wake of military activities. A crime literature emerged in France in the second half of the fifteenth century, but it mainly dealt with cases of adultery, abduction, rape, and political machination – and hardly at all with murder.[21] The absence of a security discourse in medieval Europe is in line with Elias's theory. To a larger extent than in modern times, people lived from day to day instead of basing their activities on a longer-term perspective.

Reconciliation, Prosecution and Pardon

City councils and princes did not just sit back and do nothing. An obvious tool of pacification was to tilt the balance between the two types of private reaction to suffering wrongs. Throughout Europe, nascent state institutions and their courts attempted to combat revenge by encouraging reconciliation and peacemaking. At the beginning, their principal instrument was to renounce the third possibility: that of criminal prosecution. A murderer who made amends avoided not only revenge on himself or his relatives, but also a summons to court. In Siena, for example, the magistrates promised impunity to every killer who was prepared to make it up with his enemies instead of starting or continuing a feud. In particular, they preferred the notarial agreement, which the Sienese called an "instrument of peace." A killer should negotiate it with his victim's family, or an aggressor with the victim himself. Even if a defendant produced such a document while already on trial, the court dropped all criminal proceedings immediately. The instrument of peace also served as a prerequisite for having a ban lifted or getting amnesty on the occasion of a religious festival.[22]

By the fourteenth century, the third type of reaction to homicide – that of criminal prosecution – was a possibility almost everywhere. Perpetrators who had killed by stealth or violent highway robbers, when caught, faced execution. Such infamous murderers often had no strong family connections to begin with. When courts prosecuted honorific perpetrators, on the other hand, who had committed a homicide in a fair fight or in order to take revenge, the judges usually imposed light punishments. Throughout Europe, the authorities and the public agreed that, if it came to judicial prosecution, a fine was the normal penalty for manslaughter. Sometimes courts imposed banishment instead, usually followed by a quick return after the payment of monetary compensation.[23]

As an intermediate measure, the authorities might proclaim a formal peace between the parties. In the Low Countries, the proclamation of peace was institutionalized in the fourteenth century. Urban governments determined that an automatic peace period of six weeks should follow every act of serious violence. Any revenge taken within those six weeks was notoriously unlawful. Such enforced truces were accompanied, in their turn, by various forms of ritual. The town bell was tolled, for example, or the court sent a messenger to offer the peace, which the victim's family was to accept with a handshake. Unwilling kinsmen refused the messenger entry or fled to the churchyard, presumably thinking that this then gave them the right of revenge. On the contrary, throughout the fifteenth century people who refused or broke the peace were routinely fined and sometimes even banished. In provinces that came under the Burgundian dynasty, the prince tended to reinforce such measures. In 1446, Philip the Good made the six weeks truce after a homicide or assault obligatory for the whole of Holland.[24]

The role of the judiciary was largest, from an early date, in England, but once again we should not be deceived by this apparently early sign of modernization. When jurisdiction over all homicides fell to the king in the twelfth century, the culpable ones were easily distinguished from those that were either pardonable or justified. Very strict rules for self-defense came to apply. All culpable homicides were capital offenses, including those committed in the heat of a fight. The law did not even mention the word honor. On the face of it, this looks like a modern system. The nominally great step toward judicial centralization, however, could only be made by a compensatory concession to local communities. Local men were to determine the guilt of each defendant and, after the ecclesiastical ban on ordeals in 1215, this task fell to lay jurors. The jury system ensured that the treatment of killing in England differed less from that on the Continent than the king's laws would have it. In each community, jurors made the same distinction between devious murders by stealth and simple homicides committed in a fair fight that was common on the Continent. Men accused of simple homicide were routinely acquitted or recommended for pardon. Jurors found that the defendant had acted in self-defense, establishing on shaky grounds that he had retreated all the way according to the requirement of the law. In reality, such defendants had often struck back immediately when they felt that their lives were in danger. In the fourteenth century, jurors accorded self-defense to men who had stabbed to death an unarmed opponent for insulting them or grabbing them by the beard. Royal officials knew of such practices but had to acquiesce in them.[25]

The jury system failed to raise any enthusiasm on the Continent. One way of making its inhabitants accustomed to the judicial prosecution of homicide was to tune in to vendetta lore. In this way courts showed their respect for feuding customs as well as their desire to bend them in the direction of criminal action. Rituals that served to encourage revenge were known in various parts of Europe. In Florence, for example, it was said that those who laid out the corpse of a man killed by a sword should refrain from washing his wounds, so that the blood-stained body would cry out for vengeance from the grave.[26] A custom reported for Holland, the Rhineland, and northern Germany in the fourteenth and fifteenth centuries links such lore to judicial prosecution. Courts encouraged the relatives of a homicide victim to file a judicial complaint and to take the dead person's hand with them at the start of the accusatory trial. Ideally, the relatives were to amputate the victim's hand directly after he had died. If they were unwilling or unable to do so, a judge or bailiff took care of it. The hand was cleansed or laid in salt water for a few hours and then preserved in wax. Often, the court printed its seal in the wax. After this ceremony, the hand was either kept in the court building or entrusted to the relatives to take it to trial. When the trial was over, another ritual followed, that of reuniting the hand with the corpse in the grave. The custom of the dead hand was abolished in the early sixteenth century. A Leiden ordinance of 1509 called it "a way of acting that is unnatural, immoral and sorrowful for the dead person's relatives."[27]

The growing frequency of judicial prosecution did not diminish the importance of reconciliation in the Low Countries. To the contrary, urban and territorial rulers tended to make the reconciliation settlement obligatory. Princely intervention had started as a form of mediation between more or less autonomous parties, who accepted it on account of the prince's social status and prestige, rather than as an act of government.

From the late fourteenth century, mediation began to give way to active intervention. Town councils and courts increasingly tried to force a reconciliation between the families of slayer and victim.[28] Voluntary reconciliation persisted in German towns, but it was no longer a guarantee against criminal prosecution. The Nuremberg council legislated in 1482 that, henceforth, everyone who committed manslaughter would receive a penalty, regardless of whether he had concluded an agreement with the other party.[29] At about the same time, the Swiss town of Zurich began to distinguish between honorable manslaughter and infamous or unreasonable manslaughter, the latter carrying a double fine or, increasingly, decapitation.[30] Powerful princes reinforced the urban tendency toward the criminal prosecution of homicide. Throughout their domains, the Burgundian dynasty actively tried to combat feuding. By the late fifteenth century, revenge murders were usually prosecuted, whether or not the ritual signs of revenge had been placed on the dead man's body. Many avengers continued to consider the act as a sacred duty, despite the risk of severe punishment that accompanied it now.[31] The Habsburgs continued the policy of their predecessors and carried it into Spain. Reworking the old constitutional law of the Siete Partidas in 1555, the legal scholar Gregorio López wrote that, although peacemaking involved a private contract that would fail to hold without the parties' total commitment, it was nevertheless enforced and monitored by the state.[32]

While criminal prosecution increased in frequency and severity and feuding met with active resistance, the reconciliation ceremony grew more sober. Again, the evidence is most detailed for the Low Countries, where the number of participating relatives from both sides declined. Whereas, formerly, the offender's as well as the victim's group had included men from the fourth degree of kinship, by around 1500 this was restricted to the third degree. In addition, the authorities guaranteed that relatives who had no complicity in the murder were exempt from contributing to the reconciliation money. The number of prostrations, prayers, and commissioned masses declined correspondingly, and pilgrimages were restricted to nearby shrines. The reconciliation money, originally meant to buy off revenge, was increasingly seen as being compensation for the widow and children for their loss of the victim's income. By the early seventeenth century, when reconciliation ceremonies were still held, they involved only a handful of relatives from both sides, and the ritual consisted of handing over a relatively modest sum and a simple demanding and granting of forgiveness.[33]

When a killer faced judicial action, the two principal means of escaping punishment were sanctuary and pardon. The first was the oldest and it usually served to avoid being tried at all. Throughout Europe, all holy places – churches, churchyards, and monasteries – counted as sanctuaries.

Until the mid-sixteenth century the Church did not automatically acknowledge the ephemeral monopolies of violence of secular rulers. Next to
holy places, some lay territories, often in border regions, traditionally had
the privilege of granting sanctuary. In theory, it was restricted to fugitives
who had killed in an honorific manner, but that clause was not always
observed. If the authorities, bent on prosecution, tried to make a fugitive
surrender, the usual way was to lay a cordon around the sanctuary and
starve him. Occasionally they ignored the religious taboo and arrested him
nevertheless. Local people often had a reason, too, to harass and grab the
offenders. Instead of quietly obeying the place's rules, some of them used
their hideout as a base from which to rob neighbors and travelers. For
many killers, on the other hand, the sanctuary served as a safe haven from
which to start negotiations and initiate reconciliation. In the sixteenth
century, all powerful monarchs of Europe, Protestant and Catholic, issued
decrees abolishing or severely limiting the right of asylum, but a number
of sanctuaries, religious and lay, continued to exist until the end of the
ancien régime.[34]

Pardon served either as an escape from punishment or as a way of stopping the trial altogether. Princes exercised an unquestioned right to let
their personal mercy overrule the decisions, past or future, of their courts.
Unlike sanctuary, which attracted debtors as well, pardon was reserved
for those who had committed a crime, often homicide but also treason.
Many lords and local rulers were accustomed to remit sentences. By the
fifteenth century, however, pardon had become a systematic practice by
three powerful princes in particular: the kings of England and France and
the duke of Burgundy.

The centralized legal system with fixed penalties that prevailed in
England meant that pardon constituted the principal method of getting
away with murder. Early pardons for homicide remind us of the reconciliation practiced on the Continent. They were granted on condition that
the perpetrator had made peace with the victim's kin and they sometimes
included a clause stating that he should enter a monastery or go to the
Holy Land.[35] The offender always had to pay a sum to the royal treasury,
which meant, in practice, that a fine replaced the death penalty. The king
was often motivated by the extra income, extending his clemency to burglars and highwaymen who had murdered their victims. From the mid-
fourteenth century, parliamentary statutes limited the king's authority to
pardon such infamous killers.[36] Under the Tudors, the pardon procedure
had become an alternative to the non-existent possibility of appeal. Royal
officials examined the case anew, which for homicide meant an assessment of the perpetrator's culpability. Relatively broad notions of self-
defense still prevailed and, consequently, many honorific homicides were
excused. The Tudor monarchs used pardon as a tool of royal power, by

showing the king's benevolence and ensuring that no lesser lord had the prerogative to grant it. "Mercy became a tool of state formation." But in England this applied to cases of rebellion even more than to cases of homicide.[37]

Pardons in France and the Burgundian territories were granted almost exclusively for homicide. By 1400, the French king, too, had largely superseded lay and ecclesiastical lords as the sole source of remission. Only the duke of Burgundy refused to comply. Together, the Burgundian possessions, many of which belonged to the Holy Roman Empire, increasingly constituted a kind of rival kingdom. Acting as sovereign, consecutive princes granted pardons to their subjects and, when the Habsburgs succeeded in these dominions in 1482, they continued the Burgundian policy. Essentially, pardon was a corollary to the gradually increasing judicial grip on homicide. "You must be tried by my courts," was the princely message, "but you can ask for a revision of the sentence." The promise of a correction of abuses made judicial prosecution of homicide more palatable. Most offenders distrusted the local court to such an extent that they did not await their trial. They fled and petitioned for pardon as a first recourse. If the local court acted on the case in the meantime, this resulted in banishment by default.

Because of the usual unavailability of trial papers, Continental pardons were based on the petitioners' own elaborate stories of what had happened. The criteria for mercy were the same as in England and similar notions of excusable homicide prevailed. A sane petitioner, whose deed had not been totally accidental, would explain that he had been utterly provoked and had not meant to kill his opponent. The stereotypical content of these documents has led Natalie Davis to the conclusion that they contain "fiction in the archives" and must be analyzed primarily as specimens of storytelling. She noted, nevertheless, that French royal letters of remission could be dismissed by a court and that some of these dismissals did, after all, result in execution.[38] In fact, throughout France as well as in the Burgundian lands, letters of remission always had to be ratified by the local or provincial court. In Picardy in the first half of the sixteenth century the various *bailliages* and *sénéchaussées* took care of ratification, or *interinement* as it was called.[39] In Holland this was a task for the provincial court.[40] The ratification procedure was just like another trial, in which the prosecutor might demand a dismissal and the victim's relatives got the opportunity to dispute the killer's portrayal of the events. Frequently, the offender had no more cards to play than the fact that the prince had believed him. It might reassure him that the victim's party was often bent more on financial compensation than on his execution. In such cases the ratification procedure resulted in a kind of renewal of reconciliation, or a first reconciliation if it had not been made, with prostrations and the handing over of a sack or glove with money. Marjan Vrolijk, who compared tales in pardon petitions and their review in ratification procedures in Flanders and Holland, concludes that there is no reason to distrust the offenders' stories systematically.[41]

On the Continent too, the prerogative of pardon served to bolster the power of the sovereign. As in England, its heyday came just after the Middle Ages. For the province of Artois, Robert Muchembled drew up a graph of the frequency of pardons between 1470 and 1660, using five-year averages. There were two peaks, a huge one between 1520 and 1540 and a more modest one from the late 1590s to the early 1630s.[42] Such long-term graphs are lacking for other regions of Europe. The part played by remission in the overall process of the criminalization of homicide is more difficult to assess than its role in processes of state formation. Perhaps it is wisest to think of two phases. During the first, remission served as an antidote, perceived as a necessary correction, to the increasing frequency of criminal prosecution. For judicial intervention to become acceptable, there had to be a safety valve. The second phase set in after prosecution had become the norm and was largely accepted by the public. Then pardon no longer served as a safety valve for all, but primarily as a form of extraordinary mercy in exceptional circumstances. In the modern world, pardon usually means being spared the most severe sanction, not punishment as such; hence, it does not diminish the criminalization of the offense in question.

Criminalization: The Final Phase

The culmination of the criminalization process is the phase most patchily documented. In the core area of Continental Europe it began during the 1530s, and full criminalization of homicide was reached probably by the mid-seventeenth century. Full criminalization must be inferred largely by way of the "argument from silence," in particular the disappearance of references to private reconciliation and the appearance of strict criteria for self-defense. Decrees establishing primacy for the inquisitorial trial procedure stood at the beginning of the last phase. In the absence of a plaintiff, the inquisitorial procedure entailed the possibility of trying an offender who was suspected of a serious crime, and of subjecting this suspect to torture. This possibility extended to cases of manslaughter. A French royal decree of 1539 established primacy of the inquisitorial procedure in that country, without referring to reconciliation for homicide.

For the Holy Roman Empire, the 1532 criminal law, known as the Carolina, constituted a landmark. The Carolina, too, fails to make mention of reconciliation, but a preference for criminal prosecution is implied in article 137, which says that every killer who cannot establish a lawful exculpation has forfeited his life. Self-defense was the most common form of exculpation. Charles V's law tuned into the broad conception of self-defense that still prevailed. Article 140 says, in John Langbein's translation: "When someone challenges, attacks or strikes another with a deadly weapon or arm and the imperiled person cannot reasonably escape without danger or injury to his body, life, honor and good repute, he may save his body and life through appropriate counter-force without any criminal penalty."[43] The formulation is a bit ambiguous, but it ostensibly treats a threat to the defender's life and to honor as one and the same thing. Given that it is dishonorable to retreat, the Carolina does not make it obligatory to do so. Contemporary legal writers confirmed this interpretation.[44] The influence of this imperial law should not be overestimated. Outside the Habsburg domains, princes and cities were largely autonomous and criminal courts enjoyed considerable discretion. In the course of the early modern period, however, the influence of academic lawyers on criminal matters in the Holy Roman Empire increased and they tended to regard the Carolina as authoritative.

The Habsburg government implicitly referred to reconciliation in a decree issued in their Dutch dominions in 1544. It ordered local prosecutors always to make every effort to arrest a killer and bring him to trial. Furthermore, the decree insisted on the correct procedures in cases of remission, including the obligation of ratification by the provincial court and the opportunity for the victim's relatives to contest the decision.[45] Since then, the reconciliation ceremony, already more sober, was restricted to cases in which the killer intended to petition for pardon. Reconciliation, remission, and prosecution became intertwined, and the role of the first underwent a drastic reversal. Whereas for a long time it had been a guarantee against prosecution, it was now a necessary precondition for receiving a pardon. Reconciliation was no longer private and voluntary, but it remained relatively frequent as long as remission was common. The revolt of the northern provinces did not basically change the mesh of reconciliation, remission, and prosecution. Provincial authorities in the newly established Dutch Republic continued the policy of promoting the criminal handling of homicide.[46]

The Dutch revolt also brought the triumph of Protestantism, from which Calvinism emerged as the dominant doctrine. For more than half a century, synods of the Reformed Church promoted the criminalization of homicide much more actively than the secular authorities did.[47] Although keen on mediation between and consensus among their members, Calvinists hated the reconciliation ceremony. As it had often been held in a church with priests as witnesses, the Reformed laity expected to continue this practice in the presence of ministers. The synods, however, without explicitly designating reconciliation for homicide as Popish, vehemently denounced it. They forbade preachers to have anything to do with the practice and discouraged members from participating in it. The churchmen also believed that pardons were granted too lightly and too frequently, which hit back on their views of reconciliation. The principal reason for organizing the ceremony, they noted, was to facilitate receiving a pardon from the authorities, and homicide should lead to punishment, not pardon. Condemnations of the reconciliation ceremony recurred in synods' protocols until about 1630.

Simultaneously, the synods urged courts and prosecutors time and again to take care that no killer escaped punishment. A perpetrator's chances were greatest at the beginning of the Republican period, when Habsburg centralization was halted temporarily and local courts regained their privileges. They would pardon offenders or grant them a safe conduct, the churchmen complained, without even having that right. Such localism, however, soon gave way to renewed judicial centralization at the provincial level. From the 1620s, synods concentrated on demanding more severe placards against all kinds of violence, although they continued to complain about easy pardons from the Prince of Orange or the Estates during the 1630s and '40s. In 1650, however, the churchmen confirmed the authorities' opinion that the remission procedure was tightly controlled. Pardon ceased to be a major concern at the synods, as had happened to reconciliation 20 years earlier. Both procedures had become marginal in practice. The marginalization of reconciliation and remission by the mid-seventeenth century meant that Estates and courts had complied with the wishes of the Church. At the same time, magistrates had tightened the rules for self-defense, as evidenced by Amsterdam court practice after 1650.

Detailed information such as that provided by consecutive synod meetings is lacking for other European countries, which complicates any reconstruction of the trajectory of the criminalization of homicide. Scattered data are available for sixteenth-century Italy, where communes and city-states turned into, or were absorbed by, territorial principalities. In Tuscany, the peace settlement likewise had become a precondition for receiving a pardon for homicide.[48] The Venetian Republic, which had ended feuding in Friuli in 1568, followed this up in the 1570s in subordinate towns such as Brescia and Verona with the imposition of house arrest for clan leaders, so that they were unable to act on a feud that threatened to erupt.[49] Stuart Carroll found a number of reconciliation ceremonies between noble families in rural France in the sixteenth and early seventeenth centuries, especially in the unsettled times of the religious wars. These events were like their counterparts in the Low Countries, with

rituals of penance, the kiss of peace and a transfer of money. Most ceremonies seem to have been associated with the procedure of pardon ratification.[50] Everywhere, a firm link between reconciliation and pardon
meant that the first would become marginal as soon as criteria for self-
defense became more restrictive.

That applies to the Empire too. In Saxony, the number of recorded reconciliation settlements greatly diminished after a 1572 criminal law
reform.[51] Things were slightly different in Württemberg. A decree of 1515
tied reconciliation to pardon, without giving chronological primacy to the
first. A perpetrator who had not really meant to kill his adversary was
allowed to petition for pardon and, if the duke granted it, the petitioner
paid a fine to the treasury, whereupon he could negotiate a settlement with
the victim's kin. A few cases from the mid-sixteenth century show that
those who committed manslaughters, who had merely been provoked,
were eligible for remission. Until the 1580s, local burgomasters, clergymen, and distinguished citizens helped to negotiate settlements between
the parties. These settlements included the clause that the victim's kin
would refrain from revenge or incriminating talk, and that the money
transfer was intended as reparation for the victim's widow only.[52] In the
bishopric of Munster, remission became tied in particular to the procedure of granting safe conduct. Reconciliation settlements, coupled with
the payment of a fine to the authorities, were recorded until the 1610s. A
1608 ordinance, however, valid for Münster, Jülich, Cleves, and Berg
complained that reconciliation for homicide was also concluded secretly
out of court. The situation in Münster in the early seventeenth century
was further complicated because various lower courts obstructed the
prosecution of homicide. The territorial authorities ordered them several
times to arrest or turn in a killer. One small town, moreover, served as a
sanctuary, claiming that Charlemagne had bestowed this right on the
place. The magistrates could produce no document to substantiate their
claim, which was discarded in the 1640s.[53] In all these parts of the Empire,
obviously, full criminalization of homicide was not reached until at least
the mid-seventeenth century.

Scandinavian historians, finally, have documented a criminalization
of homicide taking place in the sixteenth and seventeenth centuries.
Throughout the Middle Ages, from Denmark to Iceland, the picture of
violence was similar to that in the rest of Europe. Revenge was common
and largely accepted, but it could be averted by reconciliation and financial compensation.[54] In the Swedish kingdom, which by then included
most of Finland, reconciliation became tied more closely to courts and the
state during the sixteenth century. Around 1550, the content of private
settlements for homicide and evidence about the case itself were reviewed
by local juries, while part of the financial compensation had to be paid to

the king. Among the victim's party, his widow played an independent role. In a case in 1573, for example, the victim's widow declared that she wished no settlement at all, only the killer's blood (to be spilled by the executioner). Thus, refusal of a settlement meant a criminal trial in which the defendant could be sentenced to death. Reconciliation settlements were common in Sweden and Finland until about 1620. Then they gradually gave way to a systematic prosecution of homicide.[55]

The Paradox of Criminalization

Processes of criminalization affect various types of behavior, not just interpersonal violence. These processes, moreover, are multifaceted, involving the targeting of certain activities as suitable for judicial punishment and its acceptance by broader groups in society. Historically, criminalization takes precedence over its counterpart, decriminalization. To label an activity as criminal presupposes the existence of at least a minimal judicial organization. In a stateless society, people suffer wrongs and are offended against in the general sense of the word, but all wrongs suffered are private grievances, to be redressed through private action. This state of affairs persisted for a large part throughout the Middle Ages, when courts mainly served as institutions of arbitration. Citizens were unafraid of and acquiesced in the fighting and killing that went on in their midst. Only heresy perhaps and, from the late fifteenth century, witchcraft counted as offenses that had to be punished in order to avert God's vengeance on the community as a whole. From the sixteenth century onward, a system of justice from above emerged, with courts increasingly taking the initiative. Most offenses were redefined as encroachments not only on the victim's rights but also on the larger community and the public peace, upheld by the state. The concept of crime surfaced, and soon extended to secular and victimless activities such as begging and smuggling. Homicide, too, was increasingly seen as a breach of the public peace.

Once the concept of crime as an offense to some larger body had become current, decriminalization became a possibility as well. The religious and moral offenses that had helped create the crime category were the first that ceased to be seen as proper targets for judicial punishment. At the same time, acts of appropriation that had long been viewed as traditional rights, such as gleaning and poaching, were increasingly prosecuted as crimes. Obviously, there never was a monolithic long-term process of criminalization. Since the seventeenth century, conjunctural processes of criminalization and decriminalization have occurred side by side, each necessarily affecting different behaviors. Moreover, when the law defines an activity as a crime and that definition gains widespread acceptance, this does not mean per se that the activity leads to the ultimate sanction. Eighteenth-century courts never imposed a death sentence for gleaning, but they regularly did so for manslaughter. In the case of homicide, the criminalization process comprised the disappearance of feuding and private reconciliation, the marginalization of pardon and sanctuary, and the extension of capital punishment to most cases of culpable killing. The death penalty for serious crimes was a common feature of European culture in the early modern period. When views of proper punishment changed, some homicides carried less severe penalties again, though rarely a fine as in the Middle Ages. Today, almost every industrialized country has abolished the death penalty, which means that even the most heinous murders are punished with imprisonment. This does not diminish the criminalization of murder and aggravated assault which, unlike in the case of some other activities, has continued unabated.

The paradox of the criminalization of homicide lies in its relatively late conclusion in the mid-seventeenth century (in Europe's core area, because feuding continued in some peripheral regions). By then, judicial prosecution and vigorous punishment for property offenses had been the rule for a long time, and beggars were routinely chased and committed to forced labor. Why did a greater tolerance for "accidental" and provoked killing prevail for a longer time? The consolidation of justice from above and the breakthrough of the concept of crime formed part of the process of state formation, whose overall tendency was increasing monopolization of violence. Hence, we might expect to find that the rulers of stronger states immediately attempted to get all private violence under control, but they did not. Why?

One answer, simple but important in itself, is that long-term historical processes are blind, never planned in advance by any person or group. Therefore, they seldom evolve on a step-by-step basis. Although the outcome, when viewed from a later point in time, consisted of heightened pacification, monopolization of violence by state agencies, and a system of punishment for murder and assault, there is no reason at all why this outcome should have come about in a "logical" sequence of events. Contemporaries were unaware of the ongoing development involving the criminalization of homicide, even though their very activities contributed to making it happen. Only the modern researcher, with the advantage of hindsight and a social scientific gaze, can overview the entire process. Long-term processes, moreover, are always many-sided. They result from the actions of millions of people, including humble people, over successive generations. Thus, the gradual establishment of a system of domination comes about by the interlocking behaviors of the groups that end up at both ends of the system. Processes of state formation, too, are top-down as well as bottom-up. They do not simply imply that smart rulers see new chances for extending their power and grab them. Medieval kings, dukes, and councils had no qualms about trying to extend their authority and control over others, but they did not envision a system of domination that would deprive people utterly of their right of vengeance. Originally perhaps, a few kings saw themselves as standing above all families and solidarity groups, so that they and their close advisors could deny everyone the satisfaction of honorable revenge. Very gradually, the number of such rulers expanded. Even then, however, the extensive use of remission perpetuated a fairly casual attitude toward homicide. Despite the ratification procedure, the monarch's message implied: "I provide a general measure of security for my subjects, but they don't have to fear that any quarrel with an unfortunate outcome will get them into trouble with my courts."

When viewed from another angle, there may after all be a measure of logic in the timing of the criminalization of homicide. The early phases of the state formation process comprised the gradual establishment of a dual monopoly, that of military force and that of taxation. Writing about France, Norbert Elias referred to them together as the formation of the royal mechanism. The two monopolies were a precondition for each other. A sufficient threat of military force enabled the king to levy taxes, and taxes enabled him to pay soldiers. Isolated murders and even petty feuds hardly posed a threat to the royal monopoly, but private armies did. Moreover, the size of the treasury's income depended on the country's economic prosperity. Robbery, burglary, and theft had a negative influence on trade and industry and able-bodied beggars came to be seen as a drain on the country's wealth too. Admittedly, statutes and ordinances routinely referred to legal criteria rather than economic considerations, but the latter probably had some influence. All this makes it understandable that powerful monarchs and republican elites first focused their attention on eliminating private armies and tightening the net of justice over serious property crime. The battle against interpersonal violence came later.

Finally, the prevalent conception of honor influenced the trajectory by which the full criminalization of homicide postdated that of ordinary property offenses. Originally, theft was infamous, whereas most acts of violence – when committed by men, which usually was the case – stayed within the domain of honor. There never was any significant opposition against the criminal handling of robbers, burglars, and thieves. Their punishment implied an infamous treatment for infamous persons. Some victims might have preferred to recover their goods themselves and perhaps beat up the thief, but such offenses seldom gave rise to feuding or reconciliation procedures. Thus, when processes of state formation entered a phase in which a system of justice had been established, it was relatively easy to extend the net of criminal prosecution over all property offenses. This was different in the case of violence. Physical punishment for a killer who had acted on provocation by his adversary implied infamous treatment of an honorable man. In the Middle Ages, the principal means of reducing violence was to try to prevent one murder from leading to further murders. Hence the authorities promoted private reconciliation and peacemaking. As an unintended consequence, official as well as popular attitudes toward homicide caused this offense, except in the case of devious murder, to be far from the center of the criminal sphere for a long time.

The decisive shift in official attitudes came after the Reformation and the Counter-Reformation. On a European scale, it remains to be investigated to what extent these movements pushed the secular authorities in the direction of full prosecution and caused the traditional concept of male honor to decline. There is something else, however. Both the Reformation and the Counter-Reformation made an indirect but crucial contribution to the decline of the private handling of homicide by promoting the nuclear family. Luther and other Protestant leaders shut down monasteries and convents and recommended marriage to everyone. Although Catholics maintained clerical celibacy and continued to see virtue in monastic life, they emphasized that these careers involved a calling and that few were called. Protestants as well as Catholics extolled the unit of father, mother, and children, where the father ruled, but treated his wife with affection and respect. Princes and city fathers reinforced this "micro-patriarchy" by proclaiming it a pillar of their own paternalistic rule. Moralistic writers were concerned primarily with marriage and paternalism, but their promotion of the nuclear family helped to weaken kinship bonds.[56] Vengeance and the reconciliation ceremony had been based on these bonds. The new emphasis on the nuclear family was reflected explicitly in the change whereby reconciliation money came to be viewed as compensation for the victim's widow rather than his kin. Calvinists accepted this as a valid purpose of payment, which did not preclude judicial prosecution. Finally, reconciliation gave way to criminalization.

In present-day society, a widespread sensitivity to violence prevails. Purposely causing a person's death or severe physical maltreatment count among the gravest of crimes. The criminalization of homicide stood at the beginning of this development. Changes in sensitivity often are slow to take root. Vestiges of the older view, according to which fighting was honorable and a lethal outcome excusable, persisted into the eighteenth century. The early modern period was characterized by a widening gulf between official and popular attitudes to violence.

3

Swords, Knives and Sticks: The Social Differentiation of Male Fighting

Warnaar Warnaarse worked as a gardener for burgomaster Nicolaes Witsen. Although Warnaar had a modest job, his employer was a leading Amsterdam patrician, a shipbuilder, scholar, and advisor to Russia's Peter the Great. That conferred on the gardener a higher status than that of an average working man. He turned up in the historical record because of a conflict in 1704, when his age remained unrecorded but his harassers considered him old. His enemy was 24-year-old Hendrik Block, alias cross-eyed Hein, who had worked in various trades and was now employed in the calico-printing industry. We don't know what caused the enmity, but perhaps the gardener had protected his master's property from the other. Whereas in the Middle Ages the clients of powerful men would actively pursue a vendetta, Warnaar stayed mostly passive. He was doing nothing in May of that year outside the city walls, where Hendrik, accompanied by six other men, hit him over the head with some dead seagulls, so hard that he fell into a ditch. The enemies met again in September at the Utrecht Gate, where Warnaar was chatting with a sergeant. Calling Warnaar an old rascal and a thief and accusing him of having stolen the burgomaster's pigeons, Hendrik searched his pocket for his knife. His companion encouraged him: "Stab your knife up to the handle into the skin of that old dog." But Hendrik was content to challenge Warnaar to come to the "stench mill" on Sunday with his son, where he would cut the faces of both. The gardener did not comply and another confrontation followed on Saturday, October 18, when he and his "little daughter" (which suggests that maybe he was not that old) were sheltering against the rain in a butcher's shop. His enemy repeated the challenge: "Tomorrow, on Sunday, I will cut your face at the stench mill, you old rascal." Warnaar felt sufficiently threatened to grab a stick in order to ward off his challenger, but the latter nevertheless drew his knife and cut Warnaar's chin and robe. It led to a judicial complaint and Hendrik's arrest at the beginning of November. Under torture, he confessed not only to harassing and attacking the burgomaster's gardener, but also to seven other incidents in which he had drawn a knife and injured people.[1]

The use of a stick as opposed to a knife marks Warnaar's social superiority. No case is representative for an entire era or even for a type of violence. The age difference probably enhanced the victim's passivity. When he finally acted, it was a little rash, because Amsterdamers who defended themselves with a stick usually did so when the other had already drawn a knife. Warnaar considered his adversary to be a dangerous man. Note that the story is essentially the former's version, since Hendrik only admitted to it under torture. The incident did not culminate in murder, but any confrontation in which one or both contestants swing a knife could easily go wrong. The significance of the case lies in the confrontation between men of different, though not widely diverging, social standing. The burgomaster's gardener was a respectable working man, who modeled himself on the peaceful values of his social superiors. His enemy lacked a steady job, was known by an alias typical of rough working men, and lived a life of violence. Thus, the case illustrates a major development with respect to male-on-male violence in early modern Europe: the social differentiation of attitudes and practices.

The early modern period can be approached in quantitative terms as well. The first vestiges of the great decline in homicide rates were visible toward 1600 and this process gained momentum, faster in some parts of Europe than in others, during the next two centuries. Much of it owed to a decrease in the incidence and seriousness of male fighting. The aggregated data might convey the impression that the history of murder after the Middle Ages is just the same thing over again with, at every stage, less of it. Luckily, there is more to say. The age of great vendettas was over, except in marginal zones, which gave murder a more individual character. The duel emerged as a stylized and highly regulated form of combat. It was embraced by elite men, in particular by aristocrats and the military and less so by merchants and intellectuals. Christian moralists condemned it, as they tried to soften the habits of their entire flocks. Dueling did not stay fashionable enough to prevent the gradual pacification of the upper and middle classes. The majority of them became calculating entrepreneurs, country estate-dwellers, and refined courtiers. In the eighteenth century a new concept of honor became visible, no longer based on physical bravery and violent defense. Many lower-class men, on the other hand, continued to cherish traditional notions of honor and stood ready to attack those who insulted or hindered them. Some fought their own kinds of duel, with knives rather than swords, and did so immediately when challenged. Hence, a widening social gulf separated segments of the population, between those who led a relatively peaceful and those who led a rather violent lifestyle.

As the Middle Ages extended until about 1550, this chapter picks up the story from then. It deals with fighting among men only, leaving violence in domestic or intimate relationships or with any women involved for the next.

The Persistence of Medieval Attitudes

Change was least visible, understandably, at the beginning of the early modern period. In many ways, interpersonal violence in the decades before 1600 implied a continuity with the Middle Ages. In France, the wave of centralization in the first half of the sixteenth century, which had brought the criminal ordinance of 1539, was followed in the second half by civil and religious wars with the 1572 St Bartholomew massacre as the most notorious incident. This instability was accompanied by a resurgence of non-political aristocratic conflict, leading to a series of feud-like *querelles*.[2] Thus, the incidence of interpersonal violence continued to coincide with the extent of general security that state institutions were able to provide. While France witnessed civil war, Spain and England went through a phase of further centralization, and in Denmark and Sweden royal absolutism developed too. On a European scale, the mid-seventeenth century, in particular the 1648 Peace of Westphalia, ended the period of uncertainty as to whether the modern state would be there to stay. After that, a large core area of Western, Central and Northern Europe was dominated by centralizing states, with the southern Netherlands and parts of the Holy Roman Empire, where most subsequent military campaigns took place, as the major exceptions. The authorities in the federalist Dutch Republic, too, increasingly cooperated in the pursuit of serious criminals.

Before that date, the medieval legacy was visible in the stories addressed to French and Habsburg sovereigns in pardon petitions, numerous into the early seventeenth century. All petitioners told similar stories of conflicts over women, drinking tabs, and economic transactions.[3] Literary evidence comes from the famous Florentine artist and autobiographer Benvenuto Cellini, who wrote his memoirs between 1558 and 1562. They contain an explosive mix of aggressiveness, professional rivalry, and impulsive action.[4] Throughout Italy, despite the invention of the duel, the behavior of elite men remained reminiscent of vendetta days. When insulted or called a liar, they often drew their swords immediately and did not always adhere to a code of fair fighting. Many violent incidents originated in family conflicts. That was the case in Tuscany, where the grand dukes attempted to pacify the upper strata by uniting them in the knightly order of Santo Stefano. Nevertheless, in 1578 two members of this order, leading citizens of Pistoia, confronted each other in a spontaneous sword fight, which left one of them with a slashed nose. Peace negotiations between the two families dragged on until the end of the year. Feud-like confrontations persisted in Rome too. High-ranking citizens hired so-called *sicari*, who helped them in beating up or killing their enemies. Ascanio della Cornea, a largely independent magnate of the papal state in the 1560s, employed two men who had been banished from Florence for murder. As late as 1618, hired assassins fought out a feud between leading families of Brescia. In England, too, retainers carried out surprise attacks against their patron's enemies until the end of the sixteenth century, while ambushes were common in the French Haute Auvergne.[5]

Real feuding continued in some parts of Europe, in particular its Mediterranean fringes. In mountainous coastal areas and on islands such as Corsica, vendettas persisted throughout the early modern period, or even beyond.[6] This persistence owed much to the relatively slow development of the modern state and the inability of its institutions to penetrate peripheral areas. Until the early seventeenth century, this applied to Scotland as well. Its clans were relatively autonomous and the royal court acted as a player in the power game rather than standing above the parties. Most feuds were local, but some extended to court circles. One notorious incident took place there in 1587. The eventual victim, Sir Walter Stewart, enjoyed royal favor, which made him reckless. During a quarrel with the fifth Earl of Bothwell, James V's bastard son, he uttered the classic insult "kiss my ass," whereupon his opponent swore that he would soon do so indeed. One day he had his chance, when he spotted Stewart in The Black Friar tavern. Bothwell approached his enemy from behind and announced: "Now I am going to kiss your ass." He immediately thrust his rapier into Stewart's bottom, piercing him all the way to his belly. Stewart did not survive this aggressive kiss.[7] Although his murder was revenge for an insult to individual honor, the attack from behind resembled the treachery that characterized the vendetta. Mutilating the victim's body after a murder was common too in acts of vengeance between clans. In the 1610s, in the wake of the Union of the Crowns, feuding waned in Scotland, though less so in the Highlands.

Even more tenacious than the feud was the traditional concept of male honor, which survived in peripheral areas as well as centralizing states. Around 1600, if we take that year once more as a checkpoint, the body-related view of honor, obliging a man to strike at his harassers, enemies, and challengers, held full sway among both Europe's elites and the lower classes. The only change concerned the slowly increasing condemnation of treachery and the concomitant value of a fair fight. In the nascent absolute monarchies, aristocrats tried to maintain an independent stance, as in Tudor England. In Mervyn James's classical analysis, aristocratic honor was bound up with the rebellious tradition among English nobles. Honor implied "the recurrence of personal and political situations in which conflict cannot be otherwise resolved than violently." In its turn, this mentality was linked to a heavy dose of fatalism. The dictates of honor could oblige a man, suddenly and unpredictably, to actions that might ruin him and cost him his life. Thus, fate ruled over human history. Preparedness to act, rather than success or failure, was the principal measure for assessing an aristocrat's reputation. Although it was honorable to serve one's master, a change of masters could be called for.[8]

Indications abound that the body-related concept of honor, without the status-specific elements, was equally prevalent among lower-class men. It played a major role in a ritual that has been termed "house-scorning." In its simplest form, this ritual had one man standing in front of another's home, calling upon him to leave it. The initiator stayed outside whether the other came out or not, because an unwanted intrusion of the house counted as dishonorable. When the inhabitant showed up, the implication was that the two would fight to avenge an insult or over whatever conflict they had. This ritual is mentioned as a peasant custom in local ordinances throughout the Empire from the end of the fifteenth century until the early seventeenth. Some of these ordinances distinguished between approaching the house of one's opponent with or without weapons.[9] Actual cases of German house-scorning are reported from the archive of Wilster, a coastal town in Holstein. It was mostly, but not exclusively, done by men against other men, in the evening or at night. The initiator would challenge the other with insults to leave his house, or he would just slam the doors and windows or throw stones. Men of all classes in this small town were involved in the custom. The reasons varied, but they always had to do with honor. Although the "scorner" was supposed to wait outside, there was at least one trial each year against a person who had actually intruded into his enemy's house.[10]

House-scorning also happened in a big city, Rome, with cases reported in the late sixteenth and early seventeenth centuries. There, the ritual appears to have been concentrated in a working-class milieu. Many poor people lived in sections of larger buildings, where it was often difficult to distinguish the exact boundary between one dwelling and the next. Nevertheless, each inhabitant attached a symbolic value to his *casa*. The initiator would take a few mates with him to the targeted home, where they called out insinuations or threats, threw stones against the wall or through the window, slammed the door, smeared the house with blood, ink, or excrement, or drew obscene pictures on the walls. In the papal city, the scorners were usually young men, but in the majority of cases the targets were women. It was considered an honorable task, though, for men associated with these women, to defend the house. As in Germany, the best time for scorning was during the hours of darkness, which facilitated the anonymity of the participants in this act of illegal shaming.[11] Although Roman house-scorning took place amongst the lower classes, the work of the Cohens amply demonstrates that all social strata in the papal city, and throughout Italy, shared the traditional code of honor.[12]

While all social classes shared the traditional code of honor and were still prone to violence, the clergy became the first visible group to be leading a peaceful lifestyle. In the Middle Ages, ordinary priests often mingled socially with their parishioners, taking part in the violent handling of conflicts. The first two generations of Reformed ministers in the Dutch Republic also included fighters and even killers. Provincial synods treated them as rotten apples. From the 1620s onward, Dutch synods no longer referred to violent ministers, indicating that the problem had been solved. Protestants regarded the "medieval" lifestyle as a remnant of Popery, but Catholic reformers equally repressed violent behavior and other sins among their clergy. The Counter-Reformation led to a greater separation of priests from the lay community than in the Middle Ages, while the taming of Protestant pastors occurred outside the Dutch Republic as well. Henceforth, the Catholic and Protestant clergy constituted a group of "men apart."[13] Records of Episcopal visitations in the southern Netherlands, for example, show a significant decline of complaints about the lifestyle of parish priests since the 1630s. These complaints, however, referred to drunkenness and failure to maintain celibacy, rather than violence.[14] The pacification of priests did not take place at the same pace everywhere. In the mountains of Haute Auvergne, they were still involved in violence by the mid-seventeenth century.[15]

Homicide rates around 1600 point at a relative continuity with the Middle Ages in some instances and at change in others. Again, we should consider only those figures that include cases in which killers escaped trial. In this period, Rome was the most violent town for which we have data, its rate averaging 47.3 between 1560 and 1585.[16] At Europe's other end, in Stockholm, homicide rates fluctuated between 20 and 36 during the period 1545–1625.[17] Amsterdam's rate averaged about 28 by the mid-sixteenth century and about 23 between 1560 and 1590.[18] The latter figure is half that of Rome in the same period and half that of Amsterdam itself in the mid-fifteenth century, but figures elsewhere were lower still. In Cologne, a nearly complete list of violent deaths during the period 1557–1620 yields a murder rate of 10.[19] The same rate can be estimated for the southern part of the bishopric of Münster in 1581–1600.[20] France is a notorious blank spot on the chart of reliable quantitative data, but a homicide count for Haute Auvergne, 1587–1664, based on reports from the *maréchaussée*, seems fairly complete. It yields a homicide rate of 15 (a rough estimate because of uncertainty about the population size).[21] It should be added that the Auvergne as a whole was considered an especially unruly province, which prompted the king to organize a special tribunal, the *Grands Jours d'Auvergne*, in 1665–6. By far the lowest of the reliable rates have been found for Elizabethan England: nearly 7 for Essex and just under 5 for Kent.[22] These figures point at an enormous decline of homicide in England since the fourteenth century, but as data are missing for the intermediate period, we cannot tell when the decline set in.

A unique Italian source, the *relazioni dei barbieri*, offers excellent possibilities for investigating the incidence of physical injury, but has hardly been studied yet. In Italian cities all barber-surgeons and doctors were obliged to report treatments for wounds caused by violence. At times, this extended to treatments for a slap in the face. Blastenbrei offers figures based on the Roman reports of the 1560s and early 1570s. The annual average comes at 1,260 physical injuries, which amounts to about 18 per 1,000 inhabitants.[23] Each year, 1.8 percent of Rome's entire population visited a doctor after suffering from violence. These visits peaked during carnival and, to a lesser extent, in the summer. Counts of prosecuted cases of assault usually tell us little, because we have no idea of the size of the dark number. If the result is considerable, however, the number of actual incidents must necessarily be at least that amount. Thus, in Augsburg in the 1590s fines were levied for just over 900 fights and brawls per year.[24] This amounts to an annual average of about 30 cases per 1,000 inhabitants, hence even higher than in the Roman reports. A large share of this violence, presumably, involved just fist fights.

The Rise of the Formal Duel

Dueling was responsible for some of the deaths and injuries implied in the figures just cited. Nevertheless, the rise of the duel deserves a separate heading. Although invented even before the mid-sixteenth century, dueling was not part of the medieval legacy. For one thing, many historians consider this custom as the successor to the vendetta and, moreover, it lasted until the First World War. As late as 1790, an anonymous Scotsman, an opponent of the custom, provided a clear definition, despite his antagonism: "A duel, I think, is a combat between two persons, with danger of their lives, entered into without any public authority for it, in consequence of a challenge given by one of the parties, who imagines that he himself, or some person dear to him, has been affronted by the other and intends by these means to wipe off the affront that is supposed to have been received."[25]

The words "imagines" and "supposed" betray the author's opinion that a man should not lightly feel insulted, but for the rest this is a neutral description. The clause "without any public authority" differentiates between the duel and medieval legal combats. However, the definition is silent about the elaborate rules of conduct which constitute the principal reason for speaking of a *formal* duel. They included issuing a written challenge, in which the proposed date was set at least a day later and the choice of weapons left to the opponent. Such rules distinguish the custom from all other one-on-one combats. In the first half of the sixteenth century, Italians invented the formal duel, establishing who should fight it and how it ought to be fought. From Italy, the custom spread to Spain, France, and England in the second half of that century, and a little later to the Empire and other countries. The terms "formal duel" and "elite duel" are often used interchangeably, even though at times lower social groups, ordinary soldiers in particular, were dueling. On the other hand, the formal duel did originate with the aristocracy, and throughout its history it continued to be associated with elite attitudes. This is understandable, since social rank was a major element in all dueling codes. The opponents in a combat had to be two men of approximately equal status. If, by any chance, a man received a challenge from a person of much lower standing, it was an act of prudence rather than cowardice to reject it. Conversely, to issue a challenge to a superior, in social status generally or in military rank, counted as an act of impertinent self-aggrandizement. When an ordinary man challenged or insulted a noble, the latter often ordered his male servants to beat up his harasser.[26]

In one sense, the duel represented a continuation of medieval violence. It was all about honor. The traditional male code of honor, associated with the body and obliging a man to react violently when insulted, was a crucial value in the world of duelists, as it had been in vendetta days. To a large extent, however, the duel represented a deviation from medieval violence. By the very meaning of the word, it was a one-on-one combat, stylized and bound to rules. The background could well be a pre-existing conflict, but the combat had to have an immediate cause in the form of some insult. In the vendetta, treachery, ambushes, and attacks on one person by several men, on old by young, had been commonplace. From now on, being called a liar, hence the reproach of treachery, was one of the most serious insults imaginable and thus a prime reason to issue a challenge.

The duel, then, represented a major innovation in violence. The delay between the challenge and the actual fight promoted the restraint of emotions. It was a step away from outright impulsiveness, in the direction of planned violence. Because of its stylized character, sixteenth-century aristocrats considered the duel to be part of the repertoire of polite behavior. Though violent, it was associated with the new court culture, as advocated in Castiglione's *Cortegiano*. This culture originated in the principalities and republics that grew out of the Italian city-states and spread a little later to Spain, France, England, and other monarchies. Thus, the spread of dueling and the new court culture largely followed the same route. Next to practicing it, noble or aristocratic-minded writers theorized about the duel and the "point of honor." Beginning with Girolamo Muzio's *Il Duello*, published in Venice in 1550, an endless stream of books appeared, whose authors praised the duel as a positive custom, explained the appropriate situations and reasons for issuing a challenge and laying down the rules of combat. This literature, in several European languages, accompanied the formal duel from its origins until its demise.

An anti-dueling literature soon emerged as well. The spread of the duel occurred when the criminalization of homicide was well under way throughout Europe. While monarchs and courts refused to equate the aristocratic protagonists with ordinary manslaughter, they did recognize the duel as a counter-force to their attempts to pacify the elites. The custom was an encroachment upon the ephemeral monopolies of violence in Europe. As much as national authorities wished the duel to die out, ambivalence reigned well into the nineteenth century. Its extent varied by country and by period. In France, Louis XIV was widely credited as an enemy of the duel, who had managed to make his courtiers refrain from engaging in it. In the German countries, on the other hand, much understanding for the point of honor prevailed and several statesmen themselves issued challenges. The duel's ideological critics, from a religious or a secular point of view, usually were uncompromising. They considered the violence of the duel a barbarity, unworthy of Christians and good citizens. Until the eve of the First World War, its defenders retorted that the duel actually promoted civility, because the prospect of a challenge ensured that men behaved politely in social intercourse. Those in favor and those against were united in love for their own nation. Whereas the former considered the duel to be expressing their nation's fundamental values, the latter regarded it without exception as a foreign importation.

Writing about Italy, and Friuli in particular, Edward Muir posits a neat transition from feuding to dueling, related to the rise of the new court culture. In the 1560s, the Milan court was already refined and Friulian nobles who frequented it would accept the duel there, while they employed all kinds of treachery at home. The peace of 1568 between the feuding factions constituted the turning point. It was preceded by an arranged duel between leading individuals from each faction, both of whom conveniently died. The "point of honor," still according to Muir, served as a subconscious affirmation of a courtier's truthfulness. In reality, the new culture required aristocrats to put on a mask, hiding their true feelings and making pretenses. Consequently, everyone became so obsessed with falsehood that "giving the lie" constituted the gravest insult. Justified or not, the accusation temporarily unmasked the collective fiction that all courtiers were truthful. The way to that insult often involved a measure of calculation. One man would say something that implied an offense to another's honor, perhaps that his wife was cheating on him. The offended man would not immediately challenge the other to a duel though. Instead, he replied "you lie," which left the one given the lie no choice but to issue the challenge himself. The advantage for the challenged man lay in the rule that put the choice of weapons in his hands.[27]

The sword, the aristocratic and military attribute, was the main weapon for dueling. In the early days this was a heavy weapon, but experts in arms were already developing a lighter type. It was known by the Spanish name of *espada ropera*, which became "rapier" in several European languages. The rapier demanded technical skill rather than muscular strength, but it was also more deadly than a common sword. One touch, quickly placed, could pierce an opponent's heart or other vital organ. The rapier's designers recommended it to the elite as a weapon that allowed them a quick and easy self-defense, in the street at night or when traveling in the countryside. In due course, the rapier became the dueling weapon *par excellence*.[28] Whether it was used for defense against an attacker or to fight a duel, fencing masters taught their pupils how to handle it. In England, the rapier and the art of fencing gained currency from the 1580s onward.[29] Contemporary terminology in several European languages did not always specify the type of sword used in a duel and, especially in France, the rapier was commonly referred to as an *épée*.

The level of style and emotional control inherent in the duel should not be exaggerated. Especially in its early years, the duel was more "civilized" in theory than in actual practice. For one thing, the popularity of the rapier did not preclude the use of side weapons. Many duelists were accustomed to handle a dagger in one hand and a sword in the other. Some thought that the code allowed them to wear a coat of mail around their chest. It protected them from the other's rapier and hence facilitated thrusting their dagger. As late as the mid-seventeenth century, Spaniards had the reputation of dueling in this way.[30] More important, the one-on-one rule that the name of "duel" implied was not always observed. Each combatant took two seconds with him, whose task was to help enforce the rules and ensure the fairness of the fight. In theory, they served as witnesses only and they might persuade the principals to stop because honor had been saved. It was also wise for the combatants to take a surgeon for the immediate treatment of wounds that could otherwise be fatal. Well into the seventeenth century and throughout Europe, however, the seconds often considered themselves as allies rather than witnesses. When they concluded that their patrons were in danger, they actively intervened in the combat. Only gradually did the rule gain acceptance that each opponent was allowed a single armed second, who could only intervene in the fight when he noticed a serious breach of the code that posed a threat to his patron.[31] This intermediate phase, in which the duel had replaced the feud but was still relatively wild, is in line with Elias's theory, which posits more gradual and long-term change rather than sudden reversals.

Indeed, whatever quick transition took place in Italy remained largely confined to the sixteenth century and, as the previous section showed, feud-like violence continued to exist alongside the duel. Although Italians had invented polite combat, it was practically absent from the peninsula throughout the seventeenth and eighteenth centuries. This is not to say that "wild" fighting took over again. Part of the existing energy of conflict was channeled into the peaceful custom of verbal dueling, which consisted of an exchange of incriminating notes.[32] Meanwhile, the real duel had established itself outside Italy.

Whereas the names of knife fighters have no other function than to enable the reader to distinguish the protagonists, those of many formal duelists adorned the equivalents of modern society columns. In 1556, for example, a conflict between two Habsburg courtiers, Richard de Mérode and Don Rodrigo de Benavidès, prompted the first to write a letter challenging the other to a duel just outside Brussels. Benavidès, however, was already on his way back to Spain and possibly never received the challenge. A year later Mérode sent another letter, challenging his opponent this time to come to Italy. Benavidès agreed, had the choice of weapons, and proposed, among other things, a protective coat of mail. Mérode found this Spanish custom unacceptable, not least because Benavidès was the better dagger fighter. The conflict over their armor, under the watchful eyes of assembled Italian nobles, lasted for an hour, until Mérode declared his opponent a coward and himself the winner.[33] A challenge within the English aristocracy was actually pursued. A widely publicized quarrel in 1613 opposed Edward Sackville, brother of the Earl of Dorset, to Lord Bruce of Kinloss, son of the king's advisor. They had been friends, but the friendship had turned to enmity. In January, they both wanted to sail from Dover, but bad weather kept Bruce in England. He did go to

France in May, in order to take fencing lessons, as the rumor went. Then he issued a challenge, which Sackville accepted. They fought in the border area between Flanders and the Dutch Republic and both were seriously wounded. Bruce died a few days later. Two years later, the Earl of Essex challenged his brother-in-law for questioning his virility. Both combatants arrived in Flanders, but at the last moment the king's envoy persuaded them to renounce the combat.[34] Throughout Europe, bourgeois men were less prone to dueling than the aristocracy and the military, but several high-ranking citizens of Malines, in the Spanish Netherlands, fought duels during the seventeenth century.[35]

Thus, kings gently persuaded their courtiers to be restrained. Dueling gained ground in Europe's new monarchies, but its incidence appears to have coincided with political instability. That was the case in France at least. The number of duels there peaked in the years before Henry IV's accession to the throne and again during the Fronde. Among the reported reasons, questions involving the honor of women stood out, with conflicts between rival factions in second place. The art of fencing was even more widespread. Bourgeois men learned it too, because it served as a more elegant form of self-defense. Fencing could be exercised also as a sport. As early as 1628, Girard Thibault d'Anvers distinguished between thrusts given *en rigueur*, which belonged to the duel, and those *en courtoisie*, which were at home in the sporting room.[36] In England, the number of duels reported in pamphlets rose to nearly 20 in the 1590s and to 33 in the 1610s. The actual number was much higher, since the Star Chamber tried about 200 duels, including those that went no further than the issue of challenges, during James I's reign.[37] Not much later, dueling reached Ireland, where Protestant as well as Catholic gentlemen practiced it. After William III's victories, however, Catholics were excluded from the circle of men who were allowed to use weapons to defend their honor. Despite this law, the authorities were tolerant in practice, which gave Ireland the reputation of being a dueling-prone country.[38]

In the Empire, dueling did not take off until the middle of the seventeenth century, but once they had adopted it, Germans remained eager duelists for a long time. The social compulsion surrounding the custom, moreover, was particularly intense. If a man had received an insult and refused to issue a challenge, arguing that the matter was not serious enough, he was derided as a coward. His friends would repeat the insult to him time and again and, if he persisted in his refusal to challenge, he suffered social ostracism. The compulsion to engage in a duel was so strong that differences in rank, if not too large, failed to serve as a counter-force. Elsewhere, the rejection of a challenge on grounds of superior social rank was a respectable way out. Duels were fought within a peer group. In the Empire, men uncertain of their status deliberately provoked duels in order to be accepted in the circles of their opponents. In 1707, Johann von Klettenberg, scion of a recently ennobled Frankfurt family, did just this. He behaved in such a way that a man from the established Von Stallburg family could not help making a derogatory remark, whereupon Klettenberg immediately challenged him to a pistol duel. When they had fired shots and Stallburg wanted to stop, Klettenberg insisted on continuing the combat with rapiers and finally killed his opponent. Just before the victim's death, both combatants shook hands and called each other brother. This confirmed Klettenberg's inclusion into the ranks of the elite – his real goal.[39]

At the other end of the spectrum was the Dutch Republic, where the official duel hardly took root, despite the adoption of aristocratic habits by the elites since the late seventeenth century. Volkert Teding van Berkhout, scion of a leading patrician family who had followed his patron, the French duc de Guise, to Rome, created a scandal in 1628 by fighting a duel with another Dutchman, who died a week later. The family in Holland expressed their dismay in several letters, even though physicians at Rome determined that the victim had died of diarrhea caused by heavy drinking.[40] Amsterdam court records, while containing much evidence for lower-class knife fights, are almost completely silent about the official duel. In line with their indifference to this custom, the Dutch civilian elites seldom carried a rapier as a mark of status. An Amsterdam ordinance of 1668 even prohibited the carrying of any type of sword during the daytime, unless the person in question was in active military service. The document explicitly noted that Amsterdam was such a safe place that having such a weapon at hand was to no one's advantage.[41] References to rapiers in the Amsterdam judicial records often involve foreigners. In 1713, the court questioned a 30-year-old wig-maker, born in Copenhagen, who had drawn his rapier when a bouncer had kicked him out of a night bar and hit him with a stick. The judges explicitly asked why he was carrying this weapon even though this did not suit his profession of wig-maker.[42] All this was different in most of Europe. In Rome, for example, every man who thought himself important carried a *spada*. In the German countries, simple craftsmen attempted to look better by having a rapier at their side, often against official laws.

With monarchs still ambivalent, the formal duel received heavy criticism from church people. The Council of Trent forbade it to Catholics and its eradication was part of the Counter-Reformation program. Anti-dueling treatises were soon published in Italy, while Spanish writers followed a little later. Most of them rejected traditional male honor even for nobles, or considered it secondary to Christian morality.[43] Calling revenge God's prerogative, Catholic theorists equated the duel with the vendetta, and, in addition, with judicial combat, which the Church had condemned for a long time.[44] The Counter-Reformation attack on dueling appears to have had its greatest effect in Italy, and the least in France. Because the duel came to Protestant countries a little later, the criticism of the Reformation also started later, but Protestant clergy and moralists were equally stern. By 1600, English preachers had included dueling among the vices to be warned against in sermons, while French anti-dueling books were translated into English. The critics associated dueling with other aristocratic vices such as drinking, sports, and smoking.[45] This was also the case in the Dutch Republic, despite the lesser prevalence of dueling there. A famous issue, in Protestant as well as Catholic countries, concerned the question whether the Old Testament combat between David and Goliath had been a duel. The defenders said yes, but the moralists indignantly disagreed.[46]

Secular authorities turned severe, if not in actual practice, at least in legislation. In 1557, Philip II issued an edict prohibiting the duel in his province of Brabant, threatening capital punishment as well as declaring offenders infamous.[47] In France, repression started in between the peak periods. In 1599, the Paris Parliament defined the duel as a form of lese-majesty and the first royal edict against it followed three years later. In 1651, a minority of French aristocrats founded a brotherhood whose members swore to refrain from dueling. They took the injunctions of the Council of Trent seriously. The cultural climate changed only slowly, and even under Louis XIV repression was mild in practice. The king successfully persuaded members of his court to refrain from dueling and he tried to redefine the point of honor as consisting primarily of pleasing him. Many aristocrats, however, distinguished between "honors," which included favors, goods, and offices obtained from the sovereign, and "honor" in the singular, which inhered to the person and depended only on the opinion of one's peers.[48] In England, an attempt at redirecting aristocratic honor to the sovereign had already been made under James I by the chancellor Francis Bacon, who wrote: "The fountaine of honour is the king, and his aspect, and to be banished from his presence is one of the greatest eclipses of honour that can bee."[49] The failure of absolutism in England eventually frustrated such attempts to focus nobles on the royal court, but even French nobles essentially refused to comply. A more widespread renunciation of dueling among Europe's elites had to wait for the eighteenth-century breakthrough of the spiritualization of honor.

Scandinavian monarchs issued prohibitions of dueling between the 1660s and 1680s.[50] Dutch legislators, on the other hand, refused to consider it as a distinct offense. Provincial placards referring to the duel usually did so in connection with fighting and assault generally. Moralists and Reformed synods associated the custom with the military, urging the stadtholder, as captain of the army, to issue a general prohibition. William

Figure 3.1: A duel watched by the devil. From *Gulden-Spiegel*, Jacob Coenraeds Mayvogel, 1680. Reproduced with permission. © Leiden University Library

III finally complied in 1682.[51] The ambivalence of the authorities in the Empire produced a half-hearted repression, in small territories and city-states no less than in larger principalities such as the rising state of Prussia. The strong military tradition in Prussia prevented a direct attack on dueling. Throughout the Empire, princes failed to commit their nobles to a code which defined the ruler as the sole source of honor. Whether they were courtiers, officers, or bureaucrats, nobles retained a large measure of independence.[52]

Outside the Empire the last peaks in aristocratic dueling occurred in the mid-seventeenth century. On a European scale the pacification of the elites had definitely progressed by then. Aristocrats, whose ancestors had been warriors, became courtiers and even provincial nobles became quiet estate-dwellers. Merchants no longer found that defense of their masculinity necessitated a violent attack. In Augsburg, violent conflicts in which men drew their daggers repeatedly broke out in the socially exclusive taverns reserved for patricians and rich merchants until the 1610s. Thereafter, the town's elite became more peaceful.[53] In France, in the second half of the seventeenth century, upper-class participation in violent conflict was limited to local elites in small provincial towns. Respected family chiefs of Agen and Clairac, for example, at times failed to restrain their younger compatriots from fighting in rival bands.[54] Dutch urban patricians, by contrast, were solidly pacified. Scandinavian historians have documented a withdrawal of the upper and middle classes from interpersonal violence, which started in the early seventeenth century.[55] The quantitative evidence for the pacification of the elites is still patchy, but Cooney as well as Eisner argue that a decline of elite homicide set in during the early modern period.[56] Persons with a status above that of shopkeeper made up a mere 12 percent of the victims and 8 percent of the defendants in tavern brawls in eighteenth-century Paris.[57]

By the mid-seventeenth century, murder within an upper-class setting, except in a duel, had become a sensational rarity. Two such murders took place near each other, geographically and chronologically. In 1638, a judge from the Burgundy Parliament in Dijon killed his cousin, former president of the royal financial court, with whose wife he had had an affair. Eleven years later, the two sons of Nicolas Guyot, royal prosecutor in the small town of Beaune in Burgundy, were accused, on largely circumstantial evidence, of having killed their uncle and his female servant with the complicity of their father. The male victim, Guyot's brother-in-law, was a magistrate for the surrounding bailiwick and had been mayor of Beaune before that. He and his servant were found in their house bathed in blood, still alive but unable to speak. They died soon afterwards. The murderers had clubbed them with a hammer and forced and emptied the victim's safe, perhaps in order to make it look like a robbery.

Everyone in the small town knew about the tensions between Nicolas Guyot and his family, on the one hand, and his mother, his sisters, and their husbands, on the other. Guyot accused his mother of handling his father's inheritance to his disadvantage. In the course of this conflict, one of the sisters had died, making the future murder victim a widower. The murderer in the 1638 incident, not arrested until two years later, had the higher status. He was decapitated, whereas Guyot was hanged and his sons were broken on the wheel.[58] Both cases are very different from traditional upper-class violence; they were not for honor and neither swords nor similarly honorable weapons were used.

Like every long-term process, the pacification of the elites had no end point of zero homicide. For each period of history, cases can be added, like that of the notorious Lord Ferrers, hanged at Tyburn for killing his steward in 1760.[59] From the mid-seventeenth century, however, it is no longer common to find murderous upper- or middle-class men in judicial records.

The Popular Duel

The principal characteristic of any duel is implied in its name: there were just two combatants. The early elite duels in which seconds from each side joined in the fight at least maintained an equality of numbers. From the mid-sixteenth century on, unequal fights were increasingly considered as unfair and hence dishonorable. This change of values did not remain restricted to the upper classes. Or rather, we are ignorant as to whether the equation of equality in numbers with fair fighting even originated with them. Because lower-class fighting lacked written codes, we can only infer the codes from actual practice. The fact that popular duelists had to learn about the proper rituals through direct contact with like-minded men, whereas their elite counterparts could consult books, constitutes the main difference between the two customs.

It is possible that popular duels originated in imitation of the formal duel, but the positive valuing of equality of numbers pre-dated it. This idea underlay many cases of house-scorning, in which it was implied that the scorner challenged the other man to leave his house and have a fight. In an incident in 1545, recorded in a pardon letter registered by the court of Holland, a homicide victim had first given a knife to his unarmed opponent and then challenged him.[60] The only non-peaceful illustration in a 1618 booklet with agricultural and recreational scenes is unmistakably a popular duel. Outside a tavern, two peasants are fighting with knives, while people inside and two passers-by watch the outcome.[61] In the seventeenth and eighteenth centuries, the popular duel was widespread in Europe, but evidence for its circumstances and codes is much better for Amsterdam than for anywhere else. This makes it important that we concentrate on this city; an evaluation of the evidence for the rest of Europe will follow at the section's end.

In the court records of Amsterdam, a relatively uniform type of popular duel becomes visible. In the overwhelming majority of cases it was fought with knives rather than swords. Yet knife fights resembled official duels in several respects. A previous history of conflict sometimes lay behind them, but often the disagreement arose on the spot. One party, at least, had to perceive an encroachment upon his honor. A disagreement accompanied by strong language or just a sudden insult often started the incident. For a combat to ensue, one party had to challenge the other. In line with an implicit code to avoid fighting indoors, the challenge often consisted of an invitation to leave for the street together. When tempers turned hot in a tavern, the words "come, follow me outside" could hardly be misunderstood. In the street the fight did not always start immediately. The protagonists might continue their quarrel verbally. Alternatively, they agreed to retire to some quiet area, a back street or a courtyard. One December night, for example, two men coming out of the bar in which they had had an argument drew their knives but realized it was utterly dark. "Come here, under the lantern," one said to the other, who followed him.[62] Thus, a duel began with mutual agreement. Whatever the preliminaries, the yell "*sta vast*" ("stand your ground") was the point of no return. If third parties were present, they served as witnesses. Their role was comparable to the seconds in the official duel, but their presence had not been prearranged.

That the code required a one-on-one combat becomes especially clear in cases where third persons declined to intervene. In December 1690, Antwerp-born Claas Abrams fought with Abram Smit, while the latter's friend, Freek Spanjaart, just watched. He did hand over his knife to Abram, because his broke in the middle of the fight. Apparently, Claas granted his adversary a time-out for the exchange. It did not help Abram. He was fatally stabbed and taken to the bandage house, where he died later that night.[63] As it happens, the records of another trial reveal that Freek Spanjaart, the friend who declined to intervene but provided his knife, was a famous *voorvechter*, the contemporary term for "knife fighter." The defendant in that trial, Hermanus de Bruijn, was at least as famous. A female friend of his recalled a conversation, in his absence, at a place they often frequented. According to the innkeeper, Hermanus was a *voorvechter* whom no one could beat, even better than Harmen Hoedemaker or Freek Spanjaart.[64] From this conversation, we learn that knife fights and their protagonists were talked about in taverns and that

Rustica turba madens stricto dat vulnera cultro Ebrius hæc illis porrigit arma Furor

Figure 3.2: Possibly the oldest surviving representation of a knife fight in Europe. From *Deliciae Batavicae*, Jacobus Marcus, 1618. Reproduced with permission. © Universiteitsbibliotheek Amsterdam (UvA) Bijzondere Collecties

many people admired skilled fighters. The clerks filing body inspection reports also noted from several homicide victims that they had the reputation of skilled fighters.

Intervention was not entirely anathema. If the combat was to remain within the confines of the code, it could take two forms. First, a third person might jump in to take the place of a comrade no longer able to fight. In 1698, two brothers, Coenraat and Antonie, were sitting in a tavern when an enemy of the latter entered the place. Soon after, Antonie and his enemy went outside for a combat. At the point when Antonie stumbled and fell to the ground, Coenraat intervened, apparently thinking that he could take his brother's place. Stabbed in the belly, the other man died the next day.[65] The second type of intervention was more common. Many accounts of knife fights mention a third man stepping in between the combatants in order to persuade them to stop. The records routinely refer to this as separating the fighters. Sometimes this was successful with everybody being recorded as satisfied afterwards. On other occasions, the quarrel flared up a little later and a new fight ensued. In cases of homicide, from which much of the detailed evidence comes, this had to happen by definition. Intervention with the purpose of separation had its risks. Many knife fighters were so much focused on their opponent that they failed to give proper attention. Several third persons accidentally suffered wounds themselves, sometimes serious. It was noted of a man whose body was inspected in 1721 that he had died in Leiden Square the previous night while trying to separate two knife fighters. The duelists themselves were not caught.[66]

Only an equal fight, it must be concluded, counted as honorable. Everybody might be involved in the preliminaries, but once a combat had developed between just two men, the others stepped aside. These others could well be friends of one or both of the protagonists. According to the traditional code of honor, a man's honor was more precious than his life. Consequently, by not interfering, the friends were doing what was best for their comrades. To turn the incident into an infamous fracas of two against one would be the worst solution. On this point, the popular and the official duel converged. This equally applied to their setting in the open air. The instantaneous character of the popular duel left room for the combatants to retire when a conflict arose in a tavern. That is why an invitation to go outside was understood as a challenge to fight. Cases in which a tavern customer drew a knife indoors were not usually duels. The principal difference between the two forms of dueling lay in the greater directness of the popular type. Rituals there were, but they were attuned to an instantaneous settlement once a conflict had arisen. Popular duelists never issued written challenges; many were illiterate anyway. Among the cases examined in the Amsterdam judicial archive, only one referred to a non-instantaneous settlement that occurred in a popular setting. The prosecutor charged a 25-year-old wig-maker with having challenged an Englishman to fight with him in the park in the east part of town the next day. As a sign, he had torn his handkerchief in two, giving one half to his opponent. The defendant turned the accusation around: the Englishman had been the challenger asking for a sign. They had indeed met the next day, but instead of proceeding to fight, they had reconciled their differences and drunk together. There is no record of which weapon would have been used.[67]

Many knife fights started because one man insulted another or a person dear to him. The Amsterdam repertoire of insults was similar to that found everywhere in Europe. An angry man called his opponent a rogue or scoundrel, or more particularly a thief. To call a man's female friend a whore could equally give rise to a fight. Insults that included labels of animals, such as a dog, were thrown at both sexes. Young fighters felt insulted at being called a boy or "little brother." One man replied to another who claimed to know him "then you won't blow into my ass unacquainted."[68] Such insults also led to attacks that ignored the popular dueling code. Other cases handled by the Amsterdam court, of homicide as well as assault, originated from disagreements about gambling debts or alleged false play.

Occasionally there was talk of special rituals surrounding the victim's death, as on a Wednesday night in July 1681, when four young men took a 15-year-old boy, known to one of them, out with them. A quarrel arose first because the boy's acquaintance had made fun of him. After some teasing and a few blows, the boy and one of the others, Simon, tested their skills with knives. "*Sta vast*," Simon said, "now it's you or me that gets a cut in his face." Simon was stabbed, put his hand on his chest, exclaimed "I am hurt," and lay down. Then the boy said to him: "Think about your sins and pray to God for forgiveness." The victim was no longer able to speak and the whole group remained sitting around him until he died. Then the killer took the victim's handkerchief from his pocket and placed it on his chest.[69]

Gender was a factor in the knife culture in various ways. The ritual repertoire and the code of honor its practitioners adhered to belonged to a male world. Through fighting, each combatant built up a self-image of a tough, non-effeminate man. Popular duelists felt that testing each other's skill in the game meant testing each other's manhood. The sources contain few explicit references supporting this contention, so we have to be content with indirect evidence. One homicidal incident, for example, originated in a quarrel in a music hall, when the owner's brother wanted to dance with one of the women accompanying two male clients. In the ensuing fracas, the landlord's brother was stabbed to death. The killer's comrade, a 34-year-old sailor, vehemently denied that his alias was David the *lolder*, a term referring to homosexual activities. Interestingly, the trial of these two comrades took place in the summer of 1729, a year before the great wave of sodomy prosecutions.[70]

Chivalry, if we may use this exalted word, can be taken as another piece of indirect evidence. A number of knife fights originated in the defense of a woman against a man by another man, often not her husband or lover. Although it was common for men in the tavern milieu to beat women when they were angry with them, this did not always go unchallenged. The duel between Claas Abrams and Abram Smit, referred to earlier, was fought because of the latter's sister-in-law, Jets. Claas first met her in a bar, where they got into a quarrel. Wanting to pursue her, he was stopped at the door by other male customers, but later he caught up with her on a bridge. When Jets's brother-in-law, Abram, came by, he defended her. Other chivalrous men defended a woman from the danger of theft. In the early summer of 1715 a company of three men met three women, all known by nicknames. The men invited the women for a drink in a bar upstairs in the nearby alley. Everyone had a good time and when they left the bar, one of the women was so drunk that she fell asleep on the threshold of a chapel. She carried her money, half visible, in her bosom. One of the men took it and handed it over to his comrade, which infuriated the third: "Dog's breed, why are you taking this woman's money? I don't want you to rob her." It resulted into a knife fight between the woman's defender and the thief, who died five days later.[71] More often, however, the chivalrous defense was from harassment or violence.

Women whose defenders were friends often encouraged them. When a passer-by called the two women walking with a man whores, one of them said "Come on, Toon, give him something." Toon obliged her and stabbed the man.[72] Fights in defense of a woman were not always equal duels. About an incident for which several people were interrogated, so much is clear: Frans, the eventual killer, went out with his maid, a separated woman. They drank and danced, met other men and, deep in the night, the company encountered a fish vendor. Frans jokingly said that if he wanted to kiss his sister it would cost him a pound of fish each time. This led to a conflict in which the unarmed fish vendor was slashed to death with a dagger.[73] Another unequal fight took place after the rejection of a duel. Philip Braek and his mate were playing backgammon in a bar and, because of Philip's inexperience at the game, they lost two pitchers of beer. A quarrel ensued. The landlady physically restrained Philip three times, whereupon he beat her and she fell down. Philip then drew his knife, challenging every man prepared to defend the landlady. There were no other braves in the room, and after four glasses of brandy Philip left the bar, persuaded just verbally by the other customers. Dismayed that no one had accepted his challenge, Philip returned the next day, put his knife on the chest of the landlady's husband, said that he did not want to stab him after all, but then cut his face. The surgeon who treated the victim declared that it was a wound from the corner of the mouth to the nose, deep to the bone and cut like a water current.[74]

As in the official duel, in the popular variant there was always a fair chance that both combatants would suffer injuries or would even cause each other's death. Amsterdam's body inspection reports refer to three incidents in which both knife fighters died. A number of killers tried had serious injuries and one was obliged to sit in a chair when the executioner beheaded him.

The fact that almost all knife fights cited were fatal follows from the nature of the sources. Detailed evidence comes overwhelmingly from homicide trials. When the authorities discovered a slain corpse, they wanted to arrest a perpetrator and sometimes they succeeded. When two men just wounded each other and then went their separate ways, few people learned about it. Knife fighters did not publish accounts of their duels and no newspapers reported them. Non-fatal popular duels only came to light in passing in later trials, when the principal charge might be a property crime or still another offense. The prosecutor would level an additional accusation of wounding someone. Sometimes the accused replied that this had occurred during a fight and that the other had drawn a knife too. Sometimes the court added automatically "while fighting." In a few cases it was explicitly said that the accused had cut his opponent's cheek, nose, or face. Furthermore, the court records contain numerous cases, none very informative, of men sentenced to a minor punishment for drawing a knife. They usually declared that they had done it in a quarrel in order to defend their bodies, adding that they had injured no one. These cases can be considered as incidents that just did not lead to a duel. By piecing these fragments together, we can conclude that the popular duel was primarily a test of skill, which could be over when one man had cut the other or obtained a clear advantage. It is even quite plausible that the most skilled fighters routinely managed to cut their opponent's face and went home satisfied. The less experienced ones had a greater chance of inadvertently stabbing their opponent's chest or belly, which would explain why these stabbings predominate in homicide trials.

Some knife fighters wished to test their skills even without an argument or insult. The evidence is scant but indicative. Thus, one of three young men going out together threw his knife to the ground exclaiming "whoever wants to fight with me must pick it up." One of the others did and they started fighting. It only became a court case because the third, a twenty-year-old hat maker who watched them with his knife in his hand, stabbed a stranger who intervened to separate the duelists.[75] Some other men were sentenced because they had scraped their knives on the pavement or a stone, which counted as a challenge to whomever wanted to respond. One man, charged with wounding a passer-by in the street, had made his intentions clear while drinking in a bar. He had ostentatiously stuck his knife into the table and asked "who dares to take it?"[76]

The techniques of knife fighting are seldom specified. Once it was said that two men, on their way to a tavern, decided to postpone the duel until one of them could drop his black coat there. He had been to a funeral earlier that day.[77] The weapons on the illustration in a 1618 booklet look like kitchen knives for cutting grass, but we don't know how realistic the artist was. A fighter portrayed in a 1633 collection of idle and licentious scenes sticks up a thinner knife.[78] Popular duelists always held the knife with the blade pointing out, which was essential for defense against another knife, but which carried a greater risk of having it kicked from the hand. The illustrations in Nicolaes Petter's *Art of Wrestling* (1674) – of which, see more below – in which an unarmed man surprises a knife-drawer, suggest that fighters pointed the blade out even when confronted with an opponent who did not respond likewise. To start with, this is how the attacker draws his knife from the sheath.[79] In real life, many knives were identifiable. After a fight with a fatal outcome, the killer would usually throw his weapon into a canal or some dark alley. Watchmen and witnesses routinely recognized these knives, after they had been dredged up and brought to court, as the perpetrator's property. Admittedly, though, the court never actually organized a line-up of different knives.

Many popular duels were characterized by a high level of impulsiveness. The comments made in chapter 1 equally pertain here. The fact that duelists followed a ritual script by itself tells us nothing about the degree of impulsiveness. The script, with several variants, was in people's heads and they did not have to pause and think about it. In many cases, it appears, there was no prior conflict or enmity. Sometimes the duelists had quarreled earlier in the day and resumed hostilities later. In a few cases, the court did record the existence of a longer-lasting enmity. A certain Black Toon, for example, came all the way from Haarlem by barge to confront his enemy at the Texel wharf. When he spotted him, he exclaimed: "Well, here I am!" Toon first hit him on the head, then said *"sta vast,"* and both then drew their knives. It was not recorded what had caused the enmity.[80] We can take the court's silence about long-lasting conflicts in most of the other cases as evidence for their absence. The observation that knife fights were characterized by a relatively high degree of spontaneity should suffice. There is no point in trying to establish whether fights in early modern times were a little less impulsive than medieval violence. The long-term trend, rather, consisted of some groups gradually learning to handle conflict and dissatisfaction without resorting to fighting.

The popular duel resembled the vendetta to the extent that reconciliation could end hostilities. Dutch sources often refer to *afdrinken*, which literally means that the enemies "drink their conflict away." When the conflict had started in a bar, they usually drank beer or wine at the spot, sometimes after any necessary medical treatment. Two men, Lambert and Fredrick, quarreled in a tavern over a prostitute and in a first fight Fredrick stabbed Lambert's arm. He visited a surgeon in the company of the innkeeper and returned to the tavern to drink the conflict away with his attacker. At 1 a.m., however, hostilities flared up again and Fredrick challenged Lambert to go outside. During the knife fight, Lambert cut Fredrick's left cheek, allowed him to pick up his knife when it dropped, and then stabbed him in the belly. Fredrick died the next day.[81] Obviously, the peace they had concluded earlier did not hold. In terms of reconciliation, too, most of the evidence comes from homicide stories, in which one of the protagonists has obviously died in the end. We are ignorant about how many times the drinking ritual was effective, although we do know that reconciliation by drinking together was widespread in Europe. It was common in Germany, where, after exchanging no more than verbal insults, men often drank together to make up. Nevertheless, as happened in Amsterdam, the conflict could flare up anew with actual violence following. In Augsburg in 1643 three butchers insulted a carter in a tavern. The carter approached their table and suggested that they should pay for a round of beer, which they refused to do. Renewed insults followed and the butchers beat up the carter. The next day, the incident was finally settled with a reconciliation drink at which the tavern keeper was present. He even agreed to pay the butchers' fine should the authorities get word of the incident.[82] This example illustrates that the ritual of "drinking away" was not restricted to series of events involving a duel.

The Frankfurt authorities, obviously, were bent on repression rather than reconciliation. This was also plain in Amsterdam, whose court refused to acknowledge the honor culture. The magistrates were reluctant to acknowledge a plea of self-defense, telling some popular duelists that they could have fled the scene when their opponent dropped his knife. Many ordinary citizens, on the other hand, continued to view the death of a knife fighter as an accident, despite the criminalization of homicide. They were prepared to assist the unfortunate perpetrator, with advice, activities, and sometimes money, in his escape from town. Significantly, the public tended to excuse knife fighters, but not men who had attacked decent or unarmed citizens. A fracas in July 1674 began after two gentlemen reproached two other men for beating the women with them. These two men then attacked the gentlemen with their knives, even though one of the victims was carrying a rapier. With blood on their hands, the attackers retired to a bar, where a woman washed away the blood with gin water. To make the other customers believe that everything was all right, she told them that these two had been fighting each other.[83]

The knife-fighting culture in Amsterdam can be located in a specific social milieu. It was obviously gendered. The only role for women was to make an occasion of some of these fights. Next, the dueling culture was associated with youth, though not so much with early adolescence. Most homicide defendants were in their 20s. Among men convicted for wounding or assault in Amsterdam in the period 1650–1750, the share of the 20–29 age group fluctuated between 40 and 60 percent. This was more or less the same for all criminals in this period, while the average age of convicted thieves was even slightly lower than that of attackers. This was because, in large part, juvenile delinquents tended to be thieves rather than aggressors. Defendants under the age of 20 made up some 40–50 percent of those convicted for simple theft and only 10 percent or less of those convicted for assault.[84] The difference was due mainly to prosecution preferences. The court's interest in teenagers primarily concerned their participation in the company of thieves, for whom they performed assistance tasks. The judiciary was not particularly interested in youthful fights, which occurred frequently nevertheless. The concept of juvenile delinquency did not yet exist.

Juvenile fighting surfaced in the records when someone was arrested at a later age and witnesses or fellow delinquents told stories from his past. As an example, let us consider the intriguing criminal career of Jacob Manuels, alias Co Bale of Wool, from Amsterdam. The only time he was ever arrested, in March 1711, he was 20 years old and was put on trial for petty extortions, pick-pocketing, and theft from unlocked houses. Several prisoners, however, already knew him to be a knife fighter from when he was younger. They remembered that, five years previously, the defendant had belonged to the group of boys hanging around at the Butter Market who habitually fought the boys from the nearby almshouse. In one of these fights 15-year-old Co had stabbed an almshouse boy in the buttock. At about the same time, also at the Butter Market, he and Little Piet had fought with knives, and Piet's leg had been injured. At the age of 17, Co had fought with Jan Dik, who got a cut in his face but who retaliated by cutting Co on the temple. A few months later, once more at the Butter Market, Co had intended to throw his knife at his enemy Meindert, but, according to his own version, he accidentally hit a girl's buttock. His mother gave the girl a ducat for the necessary bandages. The judges sentenced Co to be whipped with a knife hanging above his head, 10 years in the rasphouse (the prison in Amsterdam), and a banishment of 12 years for the various offenses that they considered him guilty of. While in the rasphouse, a prisoner's term was usually shortened and upon release Co continued his criminal career. In April 1717, the clerk filing the autopsy report of Arie Cornelisz wrote on it that Co Bale of Wool was said to be the killer. This case came up anew at the trial of one of his mates in January of the next year. Two witnesses testified that three men had attacked Arie, but the defendant insisted that he had been absent from the scene and that Co Bale of Wool and another friend had done it. The judges apparently believed this defendant, since they only sentenced him for a few other offenses.[85] Co, now 27, did not turn up in the record again. The significance of his knife-fighting career is that it started when he was 15, at the latest. Around 1700, such fights among teenagers were recorded in London as well.[86]

Social stratification is the third important factor after gender and age. That Amsterdam knife fighters were lower-class men is no surprise. This was true for practically all defendants sentenced by the city's court in an inquisitorial procedure. Many, moreover, belonged to the floating population bordering on the underworld or to the disreputable segment of the urban lower classes. Established workingmen like guild members usually had the privilege of an accusatory trial without detention. Although a large number of these trials were for assault, they almost always involved minor violence only.[87] Established residents, members of the Reformed Church, had been censured for violence, some involving knives, in the early seventeenth century, but since the 1630s this had no longer been necessary.[88] Thus, the flourishing of the popular duel around 1700 exemplified the process whereby instantaneous and serious fighting among males became unacceptable, not only for elites but also for a broad, "respectable" segment of the population. This was a European-wide process, also apparent in the further regulation of the official duel. By 1700, no formal duelist any longer used a dagger alongside his rapier.

When we consider specific occupations in Amsterdam, that of the sailor stands out. This is of course peculiar to large seaports. Sailors were equally prominent in the violent subcultures of other European ports, such as Seville in Spain.[89] Whether sailors or not, many Amsterdam knife fighters supplemented their income with theft and robbery. Among all those tried for homicide, the proportion of recidivists was 29.7 percent between 1650 and 1700, 24.3 percent between 1700 and 1750, and 10.8 percent between 1750 and 1810, when knife fighting had gone out of fashion. Many recidivists had committed property crimes. In trials for non-homicidal violence, minor property offenses were frequently mentioned as additional charges and, conversely, many men who received a scaffold punishment for street robbery or theft were also charged with wounding another man or woman.

The association of knife fighting with disreputability is highlighted by the observation that respectable men refused to get involved in it. This chapter began with an illustration of this social distinction. Sometimes a knife fighter wanted to attack the wrong person, as it were, who refrained from drawing a knife and instead defended himself with a stick. A long stick allowed the defender to keep just enough distance from his attacker to avoid being cut. The intention was either to smash the attacker's weapon from his hand or to hit him so hard that he backed away. In court cases, two groups of stick handlers stand out: respectable citizens on a walk and the personnel of public places. The second group wanted, in the first instance, to secure peace in their establishment. Thus, in July 1699, when a man, angry at not being served, drew his knife and uttered threats, the tavern keeper immediately exclaimed: "We must have sticks!" His brother hit the attacker on the head so hard that the stick broke.[90]

On a Saturday night in August 1736, one stick handler appears to have acted. Two cousins, both diamond cutters, and two journeymen had been out all night when a conflict arose in the bar of Willem Soldier. One of the diamond cutters challenged an East India man to come outside, but while the challenger was waiting there, the landlady persuaded the sailor not to respond. The diamond cutter came back in and the enemies drank away the conflict. The landlord was already in bed during all this, but when his wife again had to persuade the sailor not to follow the other outside as the quarrel flared up anew, Willem awoke. Angrily, the sailor asked him if he was no master in his own house. Interestingly, Willem declared in court that he had then gone outside with three of his men, all armed with sticks, in order to chase the diamond cutter away. Two neighbors and a customer, however, testified that only the fiddler had gone outside with a stick to confront the diamond cutter's knife. The fiddler was fatally stabbed in the belly.[91] Willem's seemingly false testimony was meant to show his determination and masculinity, which had been challenged as well. It served to ease his conscience, as he made himself believe that he had not let his fiddler die alone. To the court, in no way bothered by his statement, it counted as a steadfast example of private law-enforcement. Indeed, the stick was the standard weapon of nightwatchmen, and the judicial records also contain examples of them using it to disarm knife-drawing offenders.

A few stick handlers managed to injure knife fighters, as in a case when the defender was a citizen attacked in the street. He was walking with his family, when a Frenchman threatened him with a knife for calling him a rascal. The citizen had his walking stick ready and gave the Frenchman a head injury which had to be bandaged.[92] But stick-handling citizens, too, sometimes got killed. After visiting several bars, Servaas van der Tas made a remark to three men he met in the street. They refused his company: "We don't speak to you, little friend." Thereupon, Servaas drew his knife and attacked two of them. One was stabbed and later died, while the other warded off his assailant with a stick.[93] Still other citizens, attacked on their doorstep or near their home, quickly went inside to find a stick. In a stick versus knife confrontation, there was always the possibility that both contenders might lose their lives. Of two male corpses inspected in November 1705, it was noted that one had stabbed the other to death, while the stabbing victim had hit his opponent to death.[94] Once more, it is the nature of the evidence that leads to the apparent preponderance of cases of unsuccessful defense. When a stick handler made a knife drawer back off, it was unlikely to become a court case, unless the former filed a complaint. In the sources examined, no ordinary stick handler turned up as a defendant himself, but one man, who had hit the knife from a friend's hand with a *janbroer* (a stick with a leaden end), was condemned to a fine of 15 guilders and payment of his friend's surgeon's fee.[95] In Amsterdam around 1700, violent lifestyles were sinking downward along the social scale, but violence was not yet contained. It was frequent enough to reach respectable people at times, who had to rely on their own resources in order to protect themselves and their property. Whereas people with knives belonged to the disreputable segment of the lower class, people with sticks belonged to its respectable segment or were lower-middle class.

An interesting booklet, published in 1674, further illustrates the social distinctions in male fighting. Its author, Nicolaes Petter, was a German born in Hessen who had come to Amsterdam as a wine trader, and who later opened a wrestling school. He died in 1672 at the age of 48 and his master-pupil, Robbert Cors, took care of the manuscript's publication. The main part of it consisted of some 70 illustrations by the famous engraver Romeyn de Hooghe, a protégé of stadtholder William III. Romeyn de Hooghe may have practiced in Petter's school. The wrestlers are clearly represented as middle to upper class. They wear Louis XIV-style wigs and fine clothing. Although their opponents, too, are decently dressed, the title page recommends the art taught in the book as "very useful and advantageous against all quarrelsome persons prone to beating or those who threaten someone with a knife or try to injure him." The preface speaks of "fight-craving malefactors." The knife fighters, cleverly disarmed by the unarmed wrestlers, wear shabby clothes and typically lower-class hats. They are termed "the most unreasonable and unrestrained scoundrels, whose hot-boiled brains cannot be tempered by reason." Wrestling is obviously recommended as an alternative to self-defense against a knife with a stick. To foreigners, the art taught in the book served as an alternative to defense with a rapier. Petter's work was published in German translation in the same year and in French in 1712. With William III, who was to become king of England, indirectly involved, the book had a truly international dimension.[96]

Quite probably, knife fighting was an international pastime too. One reason to assume this is contained in the Amsterdam judicial records

Figure 3.3: From *Klare Onderrichtinge der Voortreffelijcke Worstel-Konst*, Nicolaes Petter, 1674. Reproduced with permission. © National Library of the Netherlands

themselves. Foreign immigrants routinely participated in the popular dueling culture. Thus, two Walloon cloth workers, the father born in Lille and his son in Leiden, were involved in a homicidal incident in 1682. The son had called upon his father for help, with the words: "*Mon père, mon père, on me frappe.*" In addition, each was also charged with having engaged in earlier knife fights that had no fatal consequences.[97] Another reason lies in the fact that knife fighting has been attested for during the nineteenth century in such distant countries as Italy, Greece, and Finland. It seems reasonable to assume that it had already been practiced there in the early modern period.

The available literature on early modern violence yields scant references. Taken together, they suggest that a continuum existed from the formal duel, through instantaneous sword fights, through knife fights as just described, and then to duels settled by boxing. The latter variant has been recorded in Paris and several parts of England, mostly in the eighteenth century. In the French capital, in particular, the apparent preponderance of fist fights may be due to the nature of the available evidence. Historians of Paris usually rely on the extensive police archives, according to which the lowest 10 percent of the city's population, a largely transient group, never filed a complaint. Brennan, who claims that these people had no money to spend in taverns, admits that many of them supplemented their income by stealing. So they may have spent this income on drinks and settled tavern disputes with knives without this being recorded. The men who do turn up in the Paris police records were somewhat higher up the social scale, on average, than Amsterdam inquisitorial defendants. These Parisians mainly fought popular duels in the form of fist fights. Significantly, the insults which most often gave rise to duels consisted of expressing doubts about a man's economic trustworthiness. The head was the target in more than half of the cases, in taverns or in the street, as it is in fist fights everywhere.[98]

In England, popular duels often consisted of boxing matches. These contests were not recreational but were fought over insults and arguments. Boxing matches were rarely fatal, but there were exceptions. In Yorkshire in 1659, two men quarreled and one demanded satisfaction, whereupon they agreed to fight each other in front of witnesses. Although both were unarmed, one later died of his wounds.[99] Here, too, settlement in the form of a fight was instantaneous. A Frenchman observed in the 1720s that lower-class Londoners often settled a dispute with a fist fight. They retired to some quiet place, stripped from the waist up, and preceded the match with a handshake. A German visitor confirmed this, adding that a code of fair fighting was always observed in such matches. A few cases in which one combatant had died despite the absence of weapons were prosecuted at the assizes of rural Surrey in the second quarter of the eighteenth century. One man challenged his opponent to a boxing match after an accusation of unfair play in a game of cricket. Two others had an argument in a tavern, were reunited, but resumed the quarrel at night. They retired to the yard and when they came back asking for a candle, the innkeeper held the light for them and watched the rest of the fight. One combatant ran his head into the belly of the other, who was dragged home on a wheelbarrow and died the next day.[100] This and other incidents confirm that, throughout Europe, it was common to settle a conflict that had arisen in a bar by going outside.

In some parts of Europe, several variants of the popular duel were practiced alongside each other. Tavern clients in Augsburg, for example, reacted to an affront to their honor with a challenge to go outside, where they would fight with fists or knives. In 1591, two members of the city guard fought with swords, after one had called the other a dog's cunt. The insulter died of his wounds.[101] This incident resembled an official duel, except for the instantaneous settlement. A number of homicides in seventeenth- and early eighteenth-century Stockholm appear to have resulted from a popular duel, in which one man challenged the other and the two fought with swords or knives.[102]

Knives were common in Southern Europe too. The popular duel, known by names such as *desafío*, was common in Spain, where foreign visitors credited ordinary laborers with an acute sense of honor, to be defended with a knife.[103] In France, outside Paris, the sword was the weapon used most frequently in popular duels. Frenchmen referred to instantaneous fights as *rencontres*, to differentiate them from the official duel. By 1600, provincial nobles, too, engaged in *rencontres*, but later these became truly popular. Many peasants of the Languedoc knew how to handle a sword and their duels could be deadly if the insult or issue was serious enough. Fairness required an equality of weapons. When a man carrying a sword got into a conflict in the street with an unarmed man, the former threatened the other with his sword but he would only beat him with its flat side or with a stick.[104] Intervention in order to stop the combatants was recorded as well. In a village inn in the Auvergne, two guests continued to gamble deep into the night, after the landlord had gone to bed. He woke up because the gamblers had started a fight. He jumped in between them and received a sword cut in his thigh which pierced a vital artery. As the innkeeper lay dying, the combatants apologized to him, accused each other of the fatal strike, and fled.[105]

The Limits of Fair Fighting

Male fighting was not restricted to the duel, official or popular. It would be surprising if all men in early modern times had always adhered to the code of a one-on-one combat. A knife versus stick confrontation was clearly not a duel, but it retained a precarious balance of chance. For the rest, non-dueling violence among men was characterized by an inequality either in the number of opponents on each side or in the weapons used. In such incidents, too, honor and ritual often played a role. If a man stabbed an unarmed opponent because of wounded pride, insult, or provocation, this did not adhere to any dueling code, but it did nevertheless vindicate the attacker's honor. For that person at that moment, his reputation required him to act immediately. In almost every case, we will never know whether the attacker refused to wait for the opportunity of an equal fight or did not hold this to be important in the first place.

Just like popular duels, many one-sided attacks originated in tavern disputes. Public places are referred to as hot spots in every study of violence everywhere in early modern Europe. Fights occurred in English alehouses, French *cabarets*, and German *Bierstuben*, in big cities, small towns, and villages. This violence was rarely premeditated. When it had a fatal outcome, this was almost always because the fight got out of hand. A specific type of drunken violence was to attack the landlord of a public house. Whereas popular duels were often fought because of an argument between two drinking men, the refusal to serve a customer was a common cause for a one-sided attack. In Amsterdam, where women often managed bars, most recorded victims were female. Paris had a larger share of male innkeepers. About two-thirds of the tavern brawls there were between customers, but the other third consisted of attacks on proprietors and personnel. In the German countries, soldiers had a reputation for not paying bills in taverns and attacking landlords because of alleged poor treatment.[106] Attacks on innkeepers only rarely resulted in the victim's death, so that a trial for assault, not homicide, usually followed. The non-fatal character of this violence can be explained in terms of ritual and impulsiveness. The discontented customer facing an unarmed landlord just wanted to vent his anger. There was no serious impediment against aiming at parts of the victim's body that would ritually speak to this anger, such as the face or an arm raised in defense of it. Two duelists, on the other hand, who had to attack each other and defend themselves at the same time, had a greater chance of accidentally stabbing a vital organ.

Whereas the ritual course of the popular duel often had the effect of mitigating violence, unequal confrontations, by definition, lacked a code of fair fighting. Consequently, the rituals visible in these incidents more often than not added humiliation to attack. One humiliating ritual was to stab someone's buttock. Since most victims in Amsterdam were women, in the few cases that men received this treatment they experienced it as doubly degrading. Buttock-stabbing was an old and widespread custom, recorded in fifteenth-century Bologna and sixteenth-century Zeeland.[107] A ritual of humiliation that could reasonably be performed on men only was to attack them while they were urinating. In December 1718, while two sailors quarreled in Amsterdam's East India House, one threw away the other's drink. He retaliated a few days later in the early evening, when he saw his harasser urinating against a tree near the place where the East India men were embarking. The victim must have turned around, because he was stabbed in the chest. When he fell down, he was stabbed again, now in his back.[108] This type of ritual violence, too, usually amounted to assault rather than homicide.

Some men who harassed and humiliated people in the streets were after their hats. The symbolic value of a man's headwear has been attested for in the Middle Ages. It was no different in early modern Europe, even though pointed hats were no longer fashionable. It still was widely understood that tampering with a man's headwear stood for challenging his masculinity. Meddling with men's hats, from playful teasing to serious attacks, is mentioned in studies of early modern violence throughout Europe. In eighteenth-century Paris, enemies' hats were paraded as trophies and one of two pork sellers who had a conflict grabbed the other's hat and urinated on it.[109] In the hilly Eifel region of western Germany, young men customarily grabbed each other's hats and did not return them until they received drinking money.[110] In England, it counted as a heavy insult to strike the hat off a man's head.[111] An Amsterdam case involved two Hamburg-born sailors, who were out all night, grabbing the hats of passers-by, especially new hats, and exchanging them for old trash. In the early morning, when one of the sailors drew a knife against a skipper who tried to get his hat back, citizens overpowered him.[112]

To some extent, the populousness of cities such as Amsterdam, London, and Paris facilitated peculiar types of violence not found in small towns and villages. Although urban neighborhoods functioned as communities providing a collective identity for their inhabitants, metropolitan centers as a whole also provided a measure of anonymity. You could be attacked by a total stranger, which was unlikely to happen within a rural community. Nevertheless, villages experienced violence too. Many scholars emphasize that the fact that people know each other well does not preclude conflict and that face-to-face communities often were back-to-back communities. This was the case in Zell (Württemberg) in the 1730s, when the two brothers Drohmann intimidated and terrorized the inhabitants, especially into silence after the murder of the village pastor.[113] The physical domination of an entire residential area by a few violent men, clearly impossible in a large conglomeration, may have been exceptional. For the rest, villages witnessed homicide and assault as a result of insults, provocation, drink, and gambling, just as towns did. The frequency of such incidents tended, of course, to be lower in these smaller communities. When we look at the causes for violent incidents that were found less frequently in towns than in rural regions, the available literature yields at least two: conflicts over property rights or land use and encounters between local inhabitants and soldiers.

These two categories figure among the types of frequent conflict, sometimes fatal, mentioned for rural areas in England, France, the German regions, and Finland.[114] Soldiers could serve in the army of their own nation or of a foreign power during a war, but in both cases they were usually strangers in the local community. Several countries had a system of quartering them in civilian homes. Violent confrontations between soldiers and local inhabitants were as numerous in the country-side of Namur in the southern Netherlands as they were in the Swedish capital in the seventeenth century.[115] Hence, such confrontations were not entirely absent from cities. Another urban/rural difference derived from family structure. In villages and small towns, large family groups often lived near each other, which could be a source of violent conflict.[116] There is no reason to assume that the relative number of seriously aggres-sive incidents during conflicts in villages and small towns was lower than in large cities. Studies of rural violence often find that innocent fights, without knives or swords, predominated, and that homicides were few. This is not surprising, because the population of the area studied is also often of modest size. London prosecutors, the Paris police, and the Amsterdam court concentrated on serious attacks simply because they had more of them in absolute numbers. With court systems and prose-cution policies varying throughout Europe, the percentages of diverging types and contexts of violence, mentioned in the literature, have a very limited value. It must be repeated that honor played a role in almost every type of male-on-male fight, whether it concerned property rights, the defense of a woman, or still something else. Studies that single out honor as a separate motive for violence miss the point.

In villages as well as cities, "sneaky" murder continued to be infamous, as it had been for a long time. One particular type was the contract murder, already witnessed in medieval and Renaissance Italy. It remained a rarity among the total of violent deaths in most of Europe throughout the early modern period. In 1664, when a hired killer shot a Jew at the request of another Jew, with a pistol furnished by his contractor, the Amsterdam court noted that such a crime had never been heard of before.[117] It is unclear whether this qualification referred to the contract or to the shoot-ing. Another paid killer, hired by a dancing master to eliminate a man somehow involved in his divorce case, simply made the victim drunk and hit him on the head.[118] In most of Europe, methods of detection and proof in cases of hidden murders slowly improved. At the beginning of the early modern period, many people still placed their hopes in magical or super-natural devices. It was not until the eighteenth century that medical tech-niques of gathering evidence became more sophisticated.[119]

The use of a pistol in one of the contract murders raises the issue of the weapons employed in all violent incidents. Again, percentages are influ-enced by the longer or shorter reach of the particular court for which we have evidence. If the dataset contains a wide array of cases from serious to mild, fist fights and attacks with all kinds of objects dominate numer-ically. Where the dataset consists of aggravated assault and homicide only, it includes a larger share of dangerous weapons. Therefore, body inspection reports, also the best source for calculating homicide rates, are the most reliable documents when it comes to establishing trends in the use of weapons. Data are available, in the order of series length, for Kent, Geneva, Amsterdam, and Paris.

Kent, the only rural area of this quartet, recorded the highest percentage of firearms. Their share increased from 2 percent between 1560 and 1649 to 8 percent, 14 percent, and 21 percent in the next three half centuries. It dropped to 15 percent in the period 1800–50. Correspondingly, the share of sharp instruments decreased: 34 percent (1560–99), 28 percent (1600–49), and 19 percent (1650–99); and 14 percent, 13 percent, 12 percent in the next three half centuries, respectively. The share of the other categories (blunt instrument; beating and kicking; strangling/suffocating; other) fluctuated, but together they were always in the majority.[120] Sharp instruments predominated in the three cities. Stabbings in Geneva fluctuated between 40 and 60 percent from the 1530s until 1798. There was no correlation with the overall homicide rate.[121] In Amsterdam, however, there was. There, the share of stabbings peaked (75 percent to 83 percent) during a temporary rise in homicide from the 1690s to the mid-1720s; it stood at 49 percent in the 1660s and 1670s, when the homicide rate was relatively low, and it fluctuated between 17 and 29 percent between 1752 and 1816, when the overall rates were still lower.[122] Swords predominated in eighteenth-century Paris, representing no less than 49 percent. The overwhelming majority of the victims in question had been stabbed in the chest with a rapier. The prevalence of swords in Paris ensured that deaths from knife wounds amounted to little more than zero. The other categories were skull fracture (28 percent), strangulation (10 percent), firearms (7 percent), fist beatings (6 percent), and poisoning (0.4 percent).[123]

One firm conclusion is that, except in some parts of Europe, the age of shootings had not yet commenced. In cities at least, knives and swords far outnumbered firearms as murder weapons. Firearms had been relatively widespread in England since the Restoration. In the Kent data, they outnumbered sharp instruments after the middle of the eighteenth century, but they continued to be used in only a minority of murder cases. Many of the incidents in question involved farmers who had shot a burglar.[124] The inhabitants of rural regions throughout Europe often had hunting guns. They took these with them when they went poaching and some shot at law-enforcement agents who tried to stop them. Guns used to kill were common in some of Europe's feuding fringes like Corsica. Bandits routinely owned pistols, but often they primarily employed them just to frighten their victims. Indeed, early modern pistols required elaborate loading procedures, and even then they were imprecise. The relative ineffectiveness of firearms is attested by a few Amsterdam cases. In December

1654, when nightwatchmen entered a bar because two men were making trouble, one of them fired from a hailshot pistol, apparently without hitting anyone. He confessed to have taken it with him for want of a knife.[125] In 1698, in three violent incidents on one day, the motives of which remain unclear, a group of three men had used pistols with little effect. Once, when the leader saw that the powder burned without firing the bullet, he switched to his knife. After the third incident, chased by several citizens, the three fired their pistols again in vain, whereupon one of the citizens received a cut in his face from the leader.[126]

Up to this point, the emphasis has been on individual fights, whether duels or unequal confrontations. Yet a large share of male violence in early modern Europe was group violence. Collective fights are a favorite theme in the historiography of popular culture. They were ritual in several senses, for one thing because the participants often fought on specific occasions. Combats took place between the men of two neighboring villages, adjacent urban neighborhoods, and rival guilds, or just between the married and unmarried men of one place. The latter possibility, in particular, reveals that neither social distinctions nor population density is necessary for there to be opposing camps. Throughout Europe, such events were rarely fatal, but there were exceptions. In the Roussillon in southeast France, for example, neighboring villages were in constant conflict throughout the eighteenth century. Youths from one place watched their opponents from a stronghold on a hill before attacking. Inhabitants of Saint-Laurent considered their village more important than Saint-Hyppolite. One night in May 1774, the young men from Saint-Laurent managed to tear down Saint-Hyppolite's maypole. They were chased away after the act, but returned with about 100 men armed with sabers, guns, and other weapons. No casualties ensued. Four years later, however, when an inhabitant of Estagel visiting Rivesaltes dared to meddle in a dispute about a cat, the Rivesaltais turned on him. In the ensuing fracas, the man from Estagel was stabbed to death. To be sure, these villages witnessed internal violence as well, which at times was at least as ferocious.[127] Some territorial fights evolved into staged happenings. That was the case with the famous summer battles on the bridges of Venice, which visitors from afar came to watch. Once more, casualties did occur, but they were the exception rather than the rule.[128]

The friendly and recreational atmosphere of territorial fights usually precluded serious injury, but it was different with the newer phenomenon of urban gangs giving themselves a name. We hear of them in the larger cities. One of the first such gangs, the Amsterdam Laberlots of 1685, may have been entirely imagined, but the magistrates took them seriously enough to publish a warning.[129] A similar scare took hold of London in 1712. Its gang was named after an Amerindian nation, inaugurating a fashion that would catch on in several countries. Newspaper and pamphlet writers created a veritable moral panic that year. The Mohocks were corrupt and dangerous youths from the highest circles, these writers claimed, who had the bad taste to adopt the name of a barbarian tribe. They cut every passer-by with their swords and rolled old women in a ton from a hill. In this case, court records have been found which corroborate, if not the gang's name, certainly the existence of a violent youth group. Many adolescents arrested in the spring of 1712 had assaulted and injured passers-by, men as well as women, in ways suggested by the newspapers. In two cases, a number of youths from elite circles were involved; one group had attacked a watchman, while the second had cut a servant's nose with their swords. Nightwatchmen, amateur law-enforcers with a social status lower than their harassers, constituted the Mohocks' favorite victims. Watchmen also were much older, which gave the confrontation an element of generational struggle. Only a few contemporaries refused to partake of the moral panic, speaking of a partly excusable youthful excess.[130]

Violence between Jews and Christians certainly was real. In the second half of the seventeenth century, the Jewish community in Amsterdam became a visible group, though still relatively small. In 1682, eight adolescents approached the synagogue and attacked Jewish men and women in the streets with knives, injuring a young man.[131] The influx of Yiddish-speaking immigrants from Germany and Poland continued unabated, so that after 1700 Jews had become numerous enough to be more than just victims. After that, fights between Jews and Christians occurred on a more or less regular basis. In October 1716, the Amsterdam court considered the matter serious enough to publish a special ordinance, which mentioned that *smousen* and Christian boys often came together to fight each other with sticks, stones, knives, and daggers. This regularly caused serious injuries to participants, the ordinance continued, while passers-by got hurt and horses ran wild. Henceforth a person's mere presence in such a fighting group would be sufficient to merit a sentence of whipping. Bystanders refusing an order to leave from the scene would be fined. Significantly, the court called this an elaboration of a 1627 ordinance, which just mentioned fights between "many boys and also men."[132]

The court's emphasis on boys appears justified, because many of the offenders tried for Jewish/Christian fights were teenagers. For example, 14-year-old Abram Isaacqs was arrested in June 1718 after his group had withdrawn from a fight and jumped on a boat when constables arrived. Citizens who had watched the fight told the constables that Abram had been the principal combatant, carrying a dagger.[133] A Christian, appropriately named Christiaan Christiaansz, tried in 1729, was 22. Arrested along the Amstel river on a Sunday, he claimed that he just happened to be going that way and noticed a fight between Christians and Jews. When he saw two little boys being beaten by two Jews carrying knives, he had to draw his knife against them. Christiaan, however, was charged with having fought Jews on the preceding Saturday too, carrying a dagger, and he had already been banished for participation in Jewish/Christian fights the previous year.[134] The ritual element in all these confrontations is plain, since many of them took place on either a Sabbath or a Sunday. Obviously, the religious and ethnic differences were an important background, but the antagonism had a territorial aspect as well. The large majority of the Jewish community in Amsterdam lived in the north-eastern part of the city and the Blue Bridge over the Amstel river formed the border between "Christian" and "Jewish" territory. Fights often took place on this bridge. Participants who had drawn a knife or dagger, when caught, usually received a whipping sentence, but the majority probably used blunt weapons or just their fists. Two casualties, both Christian, were reported: an orphan boy in 1720 and an Englishman in 1724. After the first murder, the court published the 1716 ordinance anew, but in both cases no perpetrator was ever caught.[135]

Next to religious and ethnic solidarities, occupational bonds played a role in violence. In this case, too, confrontations were rarely serious. In Frankfurt, for example, journeymen of different trades, distinguishable by their clothing, often fought each other in groups of several dozen, but normally with fists only. German journeymen's ordinances usually recognized the "right of the fist."[136] In Amsterdam in 1661, a group of cloth workers was attacked by several other men during a lunch break. One of the attackers, a cobbler, was injured in the fracas and died of his wounds. Witnesses declared "that the cloth workers had done it," but it was never established which of them.[137] Ethnic solidarities again were involved in a stabbing outside an Amsterdam bar in August 1807, the result of a fight between Portuguese and American sailors serving on the same ship.[138]

The solidarity amongst bandits was plainly illegal. For a band to survive, its members had to stick together and keep silent about planned operations. More than that is needed for a group of brigands to be successful and prolong their collective existence. The longevity of many bands, in early modern Europe and beyond, constituted a central element in a discussion between Eric Hobsbawm and Anton Blok in the early 1970s. They agreed that a band could only be successful over a longer period if it enjoyed outside support – but from whom? From peasants, Hobsbawm replied, in a study that covered rural societies within and outside Europe.[139] He interpreted brigandage within a model of class struggle. Although pre-modern bandits were no conscious revolutionaries, he argued, they acted as primitive rebels in opposition to the existing power structure. The peasant population acknowledged bandits as their own kind. In popular literature, figures like Robin Hood were usually portrayed as heroes. Although few bandits, if any, distributed their booty to the poor, peasants sympathized with them. Blok, by contrast, emphasized that large bands always operated in niches left free by the developing states.[140] Brigands retired to inaccessible places or thrived in border areas between states. Peasants formed the weakest party in the game, while robbers often had itinerant occupations such as skinner or peddler, which made them familiar with a larger region than just one village. They got support more often from regional elites, threatened by the advancing modern state. Indeed, classical banditry disappeared from Western and Central Europe in the nineteenth century. In France, the turbulent revolutionary years, just before Napoleon's takeover, witnessed the last successful bands.[141]

The Hobsbawm–Blok discussion extends beyond the subject of murder but is relevant to it. The more callous and ruthless that bandits appear to be, the less they look like primitive rebels articulating archaic social protest. An examination of this aspect should begin with distinguishing bands of smugglers from robber bands. The first enjoyed a large measure of popular support, because their activities lowered the price of subsistence goods. Smugglers employed violence primarily against the law-enforcement agents who hunted them. Groups who brought untaxed flour or meat into a town were usually of a modest size. The larger bands of smugglers were most often rural. They operated in coastal areas, of England and Spain among others, or along internal tariff barriers, as in France.[142] Robber bands were much more likely to employ violence. Of course their victims owned some wealth, not because they were enemies in a class struggle but because the enterprise had to be worthwhile. Isolated farmsteads, whose inhabitants kept their capital at home in a safe place, they thought, and churches, with devotional objects full of gold and jewels, were favorite targets. The robbers involved in such enterprises carried on the violent tradition of medieval bands. When they broke into a farmstead, they would tie the inhabitants to a chair and torture them, by holding a burning candle under their bare feet for example, in order to make them reveal the hiding place of their fortune. Bandits had no qualms about shooting their victims. Sometimes they ritually feasted while watching their hostages being tortured.

The activities of robber bands, then, conformed more to Blok's model than to Hobsbawm's. An element of social protest may have played a part in the formation of a few of them, such as the Morisco bands in Spain.[143] In some other cases, accomplices who were not full members enjoyed popular support. Most robber bands, however, if they could count on any such support, received it instead from powerful men with an agenda of their own. Moreover, most studies find that former peasants formed a tiny minority among robber bands and that many members were ex-soldiers or originated from marginalized groups. Some notorious band-leaders were nevertheless credited with political ambitions or remembered afterwards as popular heroes. These included Mandrin and Cartouche in France, Dick Turpin in England, and Schinderhannes in Germany.[144] Robber bands, often numbering more than 50 members, were active in Mediterranean regions, most provinces of France, parts of rural England, throughout the Empire, and in border areas such as those between the northern and southern Netherlands and the Danish–Swedish border, which for a time lay in present-day southern Sweden.[145] To some extent, their activities defy the chapter scheme of this book, because women often actively participated. Some bands even constituted mini-communities, with men, women, and children living together in a remote area. Murdering victims, on the other hand, was usually a task for the male bandits.

Next to organized bands, groups consisting of two to five men went out robbing or stealing. Women typically served as accomplices, providing assistance, not least in selling the spoils. This type of crime, while not unknown in the countryside, was predominantly urban. Street robbery was a frequent occurrence, plaguing the inhabitants of the larger cities of early modern Europe. The perpetrators' activities, taken together, produce a fairly uniform story of either overpowering the victim, often female, and grabbing a purse or threatening her or him with a knife and getting the valuables. In the majority of such cases in Amsterdam, the victim offered no resistance. This was different in rural regions in France and England, where farmers, robbed on the way to market, often chased their assailants for hours and sometimes managed to recover their goods.[146] Occasionally, this could lead to the robber's death. Street robbery in cities was rarely fatal, also because the booty was often of modest value. The Amsterdam court tried few cases of robbery with murder, except in the 1710s when its agents had rounded up a notorious band led by Hamburg-born Jaco. This band defied the urban/rural distinction, because its 20 or more members performed raids in the countryside but had their base in the city.

As the great majority of homicides in Amsterdam were not committed to facilitate a property crime, trials for wounding and assault, too, outnumbered those for non-fatal robbery. They outnumbered them by no less than 14:1 in the period 1650–1700 and just over 4:1 during the next half century. This may be taken as indicative for a trend whereby total violence moved away from the ritual pole in the direction of the instrumental pole. However, the difference was due entirely to a decline in the prosecution of less serious assault. If we take trials leading to public punishment only, wounding slightly outnumbers robbery in the second period, while the relationship is equal in the first.[147] With respect to the impulsive–planned axis, it should be noted that several of the robberies accompanied by murder in Amsterdam were of a decidedly impulsive nature. Almost all of them, however, fall outside the theme of this chapter, because a woman was involved, as perpetrator, victim, or both. There were two cases of clearly impulsive robbery in the male-on-male category, the first in the summer of 1660. A man who had recently arrived from Emden in Germany, and found employment in digging canals, had been drinking with a compatriot for a while when he noticed that his mate had six ducats. He immediately decided to take them. With a sharp spade he hit the other, who fled, received another blow, tumbled into a ditch, and drowned.[148]

The Decline of Interpersonal Violence

The total volume of the violence just described dropped drastically during the seventeenth and eighteenth centuries, with the timing varying between regions. In any society with a high incidence of (non-infant) homicide, this high level is due, to an overwhelming degree, to killings in which men are the victims as well as the perpetrators. The evidence for this is so clear that a detailed discussion of the statistics is best left for the coming chapters. Because a considerable part of the early modern decline in homicide is the result of a decrease in male-on-male fighting, the most suitable place to discuss the overall rates is here.

Amsterdam's homicide rates, above 20 at the end of the sixteenth century, dropped to a very low 3.1 between 1667 and 1679, but here a measure of underreporting probably played its part. The rates of 9.6 (1693–1709) and 8.7 (1710–26) nevertheless represent a temporary peak, coinciding with the heyday of knife fighting. After another gap in the records, the rates again dropped significantly: 2.1 (1752–67), 2.7 (1768–83), 2.0 (1784–99), and 1.4 (1800–16).[149] Figure 3.4 renders the general European trends calculated by Eisner. The surprisingly low figure for Scandinavia is based primarily on nationwide medical statistics, available since the 1750s, which Swedish historians consider reliable.[150] A massive decline between 1600 and 1800 characterized all regions, despite the variance in the starting and end levels. Since Europe's population did not increase by a comparable factor during these two centuries, the decline of homicide occurred even in absolute numbers.

Individual towns and regions rarely deviated from this trend. Geneva is one exception, its rate rising again to 6.8 in the second half of the eighteenth century.[151] Outside the five regions, Dublin had a relatively high rate of 8 between 1780 and 1795.[152] Madrid's homicide rate, on the other

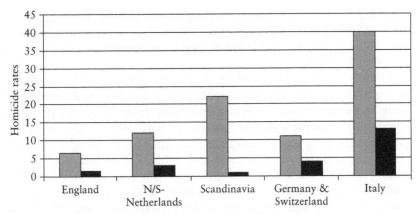

Figure 3.4: Annual average of homicides per 100,000 inhabitants in five European regions around 1600 and around 1800
Source: Eisner 2001 and 2003

hand, while peaking around 15 between 1650 and 1720, dropped to below 5 in the second half of the eighteenth century. The rates in rural Cantabria were surprisingly low, between 1.2 and 1.8 throughout the period 1660–1830.[153] The figures for Paris are important because of the relative lack of research in France. Brioist, Drévillon, and Serna are the only French scholars ever to have done quantitative research in body inspection reports of the early modern period. They examined the records of the Paris morgue, complete for 25 years between 1692 and 1791. The number of bodies that had suffered a violent death in these years was 251, giving an annual average of 10. The second largest city of Europe, Paris had between 500,000 and 600,000 inhabitants during the eighteenth century, but, allowing for the fact that bodies directly identified did not end up in the records, it is reasonable to round off the homicide rate at 2.[154] To compare this with the figure of 15, cited earlier for Haute Auvergne, is like comparing apples and oranges, but it is all we have for France. Whatever else they mean, the two rates do not run counter to the general European trend.

The incidence of non-homicidal violence is always difficult to ascertain, as trends in prosecution rates, the only ones available, are difficult to interpret. A rise in prosecuted cases of assault, for example, could mean that the population in question really became more violent or, alternatively, that sensitivity to violence increased, which led to intensified action against offenders. The best estimates weighing all possible factors are for England, in particular London, Surrey, and Sussex. Both Beattie and Shoemaker argue that a pacification of social relations took place. Homicide as well as assault declined from the Restoration onward, with the biggest drop in the course of the eighteenth century. Shoemaker connects this trend with changing notions of masculinity as well as honor. It became increasingly possible for all men to be respected as men without resorting to violence.[155]

As daily life turned less violent, on average, ideas about honor slowly began to change. Its association with outer appearance and the physical body weakened, while it became tied more strongly to moral values. Although this transformation touched on female honor too, it had its principal effect on the self-image of men. Fewer men thought that their status among their peers depended on toughness or a capacity physically to protect themselves, their property, and their dependents. Alternative sources of honor, such as economic solidity, gradually came to the fore. Theft, to be sure, had always been considered infamous and "thief" was a traditional word of abuse. Originally, however, to be called a thief implied that the person so dubbed belonged to an underclass of outcasts. From the seventeenth century onward, men from the settled population took pride in a general reputation of trustworthiness in economic affairs. Bankruptcy equally became something to be ashamed about. In seventeenth-century Dijon, for example, economic solidity was the principal source of honor for men, and "thief," "*banqueroutier*," and "receiver" were common words of insult. The latter word was used also for a master who hired another's runaway journeyman. Even sexual propriety became a source of honor for men, as it had long been for women.[156] Mohrmann, whose study of conflict in Wilster ranges from the late sixteenth century to the mid-nineteenth, concludes that during this period, "love of truth and honesty, discipline and an unblemished ancestry" had become the principal sources of honor, "whereas piety and courage had lost their originally decisive significance for honor."[157]

Notions of civility increasingly centered around peacefulness in social intercourse. Originally, the ideal of the graceful courtier had included being ready to fight a stylish duel when necessary. From the end of the seventeenth century, civility and politeness increasingly constituted a counter-model against the traditional concept of male honor. An English author wrote in 1673 that civility consisted of three elements: "not expressing by actions or speeches any injury, disesteem, offence or under-valuing any other; receiving no injuries or offences from others; being ready to do all good offices and ordinary kindness for another." The second element implied that a person should not take everything as an insult or a derogatory act that could possibly be interpreted as such. A truly polite man ignored some remarks as unimportant, instead of always insisting on his *point d'honneur*. In the eighteenth century, this kind of attitude spread, not only among the English elites, but also in countries such as France and Italy. As civilized behavior came to include restraint in demanding satisfaction, this contributed to the shift in notions of male honor away from an association with physical courage.[158]

Paradoxically, the Christian attack on the traditional male code of honor contributed to change by becoming less rigorous. Just after 1700, some theologians and religiously oriented moralists started to use a different tone. Their predecessors had rejected honor outright and condemned dueling in particular. Their attack was so uncompromising that it had effect only upon godly laymen. The rest largely ignored the moralists' warnings. A few Christian philosophers of the early eighteenth century, however, partly rehabilitated honor. They still condemned physical violence, but they allowed men to defend their honor and rights by peaceful means, thereby reinforcing the spiritualization of the honor concept.[159]

For London, Robert Shoemaker demonstrates the breakthrough of the spiritualization of honor in a detailed study of insult. There was a brief upsurge of insults, handled by various agencies, just before 1700, which Shoemaker links to the beginning of the decline in violence. This temporarily prompted more men to react to a breach of their honor with a counter-insult instead of an attack. From the 1720s onward, however, the incidence of insult as well as violence started to decline. He demonstrates this with quantitative as well as qualitative evidence. The functions of insult, moreover, were changing too. First of all, insult became less public. According to the traditional notion of honor, if a person wanted to damage another's reputation, he should take care that many people knew about it. An insult had to be public in order to be effective. During the eighteenth century, insults were increasingly uttered in a person's home or in shops or pubs instead of in the street. At the same time, the social power of abusive words was declining. In the past, people could lose clients or friends because of insults, which need not be verified. Their very utterance damaged a person's reputation and might induce others to avoid contact. In the eighteenth century, defamatory words had at least to be true in order to damage reputations. Finally, from the mid-century on, complaints about insult increasingly focused on the accompanying threats, spitting, beating, and the like, instead of on the words themselves. By the end of the century, male as well as female honor came to be seen as a private matter, unfit for public discussion, and scolding as an archaic and rural activity. By the early nineteenth century, defamation declined in the provinces as well. Increasingly, people saw themselves as individuals whose identity was determined by their inner, "true" selves.[160]

Literature constitutes another important source. In the second half of the eighteenth century, the breakthrough of a new concept of male honor is visible in elevated as well as popular genres. Dutch hack writers of the 1770s, for example, made it a sport to unmask seemingly decent citizens as cheats who secretly visited prostitutes or charged their clients too much. They ferociously attacked each other in print as well. A colleague was always a "thief of honor," wrecking the reputations of his fellow men for his own financial gain. The model of honor which these writers cherished was that of the unblemished husband who supported his family by legal means. It stood far away from the macho ideal of a man who commanded respect because of his ability to employ or enlist violence.[161] German novelists and philosophers of the later eighteenth century equated honor with inner virtue, recognizing that all decent men, ordinary and great, possessed it. Personal honor was all-important to Fichte, but he added: "I by no means place this honor in the judgment of others about my actions . . . but rather in the judgment which I myself can form about them."[162] Fichte imagined that he could determine the extent of his honor totally by himself, whereas modern social scientists know that honor always includes the judgment of others. But the criteria for judging increasingly depended on a person's moral and cultural accomplishments.

As a cultural movement, the Enlightenment both reinforced the process of spiritualization and contributed to the democratization of honor. In the seventeenth century, the propagation of the idea that honor derived solely from the prince had weakened its association with the body but maintained its elitist character. Montesquieu still argued that a monarchy was best off if the subjects were allowed to play out their desire for honor by serving the sovereign. Writers in the second half of the eighteenth century replaced pleasing the king with a devotion to one's duties as a citizen and partaking in honest commerce as the principal sources of honor. And everyone was a citizen in principle. Since the soul was the true seat of a man's honor, it could never be diminished by harassment of his body. Nor could assaulting the body of the harasser restore the attacker's honor. Several entries in the *Encyclopédie* advocate the new sense of honor, reject violence, and ridicule the duel.[163]

Thus, the spiritualization of honor and the spread of a peaceful lifestyle were intimately associated, but the evidence for an explicit connection with the quantitative decline of interpersonal violence is largely indirect. We do know that people's readiness to offer cases of insult, libel, and conflict to courts and arbiters increased, as in Sweden for example.[164] This transformation affected not only ordinary people, but also the elites, in particular in relation to the official duel. At the same time, princes and governments instituted special honor courts for the aristocracy. Aristocrats were encouraged to let their conflicts be judged and their reputations saved, instead of fighting duels over them. In France the *Maréchaux de France* acted as such a special tribunal, for all conflicts pertaining to honor and reputation, since 1651. Whereas the institution of the French honor court was accompanied by a formal prohibition of dueling, the English Parliament did not adopt an anti-dueling bill until 1819.[165]

The extent of elite dueling during the eighteenth century is debated among scholars. No doubt it continued to be common among German aristocrats. The Irish, too, remained eager duelists, but the mortality rate from these encounters gradually decreased. It was not until the Act of Union of 1800 and the ensuing abolition of the Irish Parliament that a major source of conflict disappeared and dueling went out of fashion.[166] In France, there were waves of heightened prosecution at the beginning of the eighteenth century and in the period 1730–50. Because of the large proportion of people killed by swords, as reported in the Paris body inspection reports, Brioist et al. believe that the prosecution figures reflect real behavior and that many men, also aristocrats, continued to practice the duel in secret.[167] England witnessed a notorious aristocratic duel in 1712, when the Duke of Hamilton and Lord Mohun fought each other in Hyde Park and both ended up dead. Opposition to dueling, on the other hand, intensified in the eighteenth century. In line with the new emphasis on peaceful social relations, a growing number of people argued that dueling was incompatible with civility. True civility, they said, is based on innate benevolence instead of external appearance, fashion, theatrical politeness, and the opinion of others.[168] A severe repression of dueling took place from the 1730s onward in Geneva, an independent republic allied with the Swiss confederation. The practitioners were branded as serious criminals, deserving capital punishment when they killed their opponents. If the duel was not fatal, it was a good idea to impose an infamous penalty, so that the combatants would, after all, lose the honor they had been trying to save. Prosecutors found the duel an archaic custom, contrary to the social contract and republican mores generally.[169]

Similar uncertainties remain with respect to the incidence, during the eighteenth century, of the popular duel with knives. The only thing we are sure about concerns the regional variation in its persistence or demise. It was alive and well in some parts of Europe even in the nineteenth century. In Amsterdam, the popular duel flourished especially between 1690 and 1720, which coincided with a temporary rise in the city's homicide rate, the peak period of sailors' involvement in violence, and the heyday of the music hall. Since then, one-on-one knife fights quickly became infrequent in the city's records, presumably because they largely disappeared from street and tavern life. Concomitantly, references to assistance in the escape of killers practically ceased. After a decade or two, moreover, references to citizens handling a stick against a knife fighter became rare. It appears that, in the second half of the eighteenth century, only the relatively marginal Ashkenazi Jews engaged in popular duels. Two of them fought with lethal consequences over the spoils of a theft in 1768. The killer fled as far away as Paris, but after six months he was arrested in Bruges, in the Austrian Netherlands, and extradited, which suggests increasing international cooperation in the capture of serious criminals.[170]

Throughout the early modern period, there were no traces of any great fear of interpersonal male violence. Knife fighting was hardly represented at all in contemporary visual art. Cheap prints dealt mostly with exceptional cases of murder within the family or in other surprising circumstances. The representation of violence by painters concentrated on the horrors of war and the dangers from deserters or disbanded soldiers.[171] Notorious bandits were regularly depicted on broadsheets or in chapbooks, but much of the nuisance of brigandage consisted of theft rather than violence. On the whole, early modern people were more afraid of losing their property than of suffering physical injury. The fear of crime that existed was primarily a fear of property crime.

That the great decline in homicide rates was overwhelmingly due to a decrease in male aggression is easily established. Behind this lay not just one factor but several interdependent developments, which is congruent with Elias's theory. The social differentiation of male fighting constituted a crucial, intermediate process. The upper strata of all countries believed that only dueling befitted a gentleman. They refused to consider a knife fight as a duel, ranking it with common brawls as an unworthy pursuit for lower persons. This attitude trickled down, so that by 1700 even the respectable upper layer of Amsterdam's working class avoided knife fights and, if necessary, resorted to defending themselves with a stick. During the eighteenth century, the official duel, too, partially lost its grip on upper-class men, though less so in the German regions or, possibly, in Paris. Upper- and middle-class criticism of dueling also became more vociferous. In the eighteenth century, the elites, on average, were more strongly pacified, which reinforced the peaceful tendencies of other groups.

The pacification of the elites, which introduced the cultural model of a non-violent lifestyle, in its turn owed much to processes of state formation. Nobles and high-ranking bureaucrats became tied to national centers such as princely courts, where they had to exhibit restrained behavior. This process began in the new monarchies and gained momentum after the consolidation of the European state system. The presence of this system also influenced life in the smaller and less centralized territories. Along with state formation, urbanization was an equally crucial factor. Dutch urban patricians, for example, cherished a relatively peaceful lifestyle from the Revolt on, hence before the consolidation of the European state system. The total number of towns grew during the early modern period and most cities increased in size. Living in larger conglomerations possibly had a pacifying effect, although this is hard to determine exactly, and knife fighting was at home in towns too. Toward the end of the eighteenth century, however, with the exception of Southern Europe, serious violence involving knives appears to have become more characteristic of the countryside.

There is no reason to accord primacy to urbanization over state formation processes. The early decline of homicide in England, for example, manifested itself in rural regions like Kent and Essex. Amsterdam's rise to economic prominence began in the 1540s and, by 1590, with its homicide rate still over 20, the town already had a population of about 60,000. Furthermore, the lack of reliable rates for France hampers any assessment of the contribution of bureaucratic centralization as against the growth of cities. The first rather than the second characterized Scandinavia, which witnessed the steepest decline, a twentyfold decrease between 1600 and 1800. A cultural factor, finally, the spiritualization of honor, was intertwined with the decline in male violence. Both processes probably reinforced each other, again with neither of them having primacy. In their turn, these processes produced new models of masculinity. Whereas around 1650, boys were taught toughness and it was expected that they would fight sometimes with fists or sticks, around 1750 this was no longer self-evident.[172] The decline of male fighting, then, formed part of the overall integration and differentiation of society, in which cultural, demographic, and political developments worked interdependently.

4

Patriarchy and its Discontents: Women and the Domestic Sphere

Emilie Breil lived with her parents, who had a coffee house in Carouge, a popular resort west of Geneva City. The Genevan Republic boasted such famous inhabitants as Jean Calvin, who arrived there to establish his theocracy, and Jean-Jacques Rousseau, who left it to write his books. Emilie's fame had more modest proportions. Her first name was mentioned on two occasions only, because almost everyone just called her *la fille Breil*. It was in 1760 that she enjoyed her moment of notoriety. The incident became public knowledge on a Sunday, when a group of six young men, among them a journeyman surgeon, got together for supper in one of Carouge's many inns and afterwards visited the coffee house. When they asked the landlady how her daughter was, they were told that she lay sick in bed. The journeyman surgeon kindly offered his services and, after an initial hesitation, her mother led him upstairs. He learned that Emilie had injured her arm in a duel with a man.

The combat had taken place on the preceding Wednesday, November 19, but what exactly had happened? There were no eye witnesses and the court apparently had insufficient ground for questioning the suspect, whose wounded arm would have constituted no impediment to a trial. Testimonies were based on hearsay, with only two witnesses – the journeyman surgeon and another young man – who declared that they had heard the story from Emilie herself. Obviously, the company who visited her parents' coffee house that Sunday did so because rumors were already in circulation. Some thought that she had challenged her opponent to appear at the city's ramparts, others that she had accidentally met him there. This much recurred in all testimonies: a *monsieur* had bragged about his exploits, telling everyone that he had slept with Emilie and her friend Rosalie. This lie prompted Emilie to demand satisfaction. She possessed a silver-colored sword, which several witnesses had seen before. One man claimed it was his, stating that he had left it with her father three weeks earlier. At the ramparts, Emilie first slapped her opponent's face. Then she drew her sword, exclaiming: "Defend yourself and then you can get to know Emilie." He hesitated, but finally drew his sword too. Perhaps not taking the matter seriously enough, he was injured and fell to the ground. She knelt down to look after him, but at that very moment he struck at her arm, causing a serious wound. This treacherous act made her so furious that she plunged her sword into his body. Believing that a surgeon could take care of him, she left the scene and returned home in a carriage which Rosalie had ordered for her.

Perhaps it was all a fake. The alleged opponent never showed up, and witnesses disagreed about his identity. He was certainly a Frenchman, named Burnay, Beurlin, or Beranger, names that look alike, but he was also known as Deschamps. Some said he had just arrived from Paris. The prosecutor's agents desperately tried to find the male duelist, dead or alive. While they were searching, gossip in the town continued and many were convinced that he had died. The prosecutor's agents inquired into all names mentioned in the protocol and finally found a certain Jacob Beranger, who was 20 years old and a citizen of Geneva. He gave a brief testimony, stating that he had seen the Breil girl only once in her parents' coffee house and that he thought the whole story was made up. The court temporarily closed the dossier with a "*plus amplement informé*," which meant that the case was left open until further information was forthcoming.[1] So we cannot be sure about the truth of the matter. But either way, whether Emilie Breil made up the story or whether she actually fought a duel, the whole thing was equally exceptional. And the public's fascination retains the same meaning in both scenarios, because they believed in it.

Why should such an unusual story serve as the opening to this chapter? The answer is simple. When it comes to women and intimates as victims and perpetrators of homicide and assault, there is no standard case. So often, the scholarly discourse about women and violence revolves around female victimization. There is no doubt that the statistics justify this. Nevertheless, some women were more than just victims and did fight. When they resorted to violence outside the domestic sphere, it was most often in an attack against other women. That makes the case of Emilie Breil doubly exceptional: she belonged to a minority within a minority. Her motive was quite traditional though. She defended her chaste reputation, which for ages had been considered as a woman's most precious asset. The public was fascinated by the sensational rumor of a duel with a female combatant, identifying her all the while as someone's daughter, rather than as an individual person. More than anything else, the exclamation "you can get to know Emilie" justifies us in comparing her case with violence carried out by men. Again, since only one of the people questioned attributed these words to her, we cannot be sure that she spoke them, but they illustrate a contemporary line of thought. In one version of the story, the man had slept with two other women but said it was Emilie and Rosalie. When Emilie actually stood in front of him, she mentioned their names, asked whether he knew them, and he replied "yes." She then said "I am Emilie. Get to know me." In the past, "to know" had a second meaning, with the implicit addition of "carnally," hence to have sexual relations. Emilie implied: "You have spread the rumor that you knew me, but now you will really get to know me." Her reaction was much like that of the Earl of Bothwell, as we saw in the previous chapter: she symbolically repeated the insult in a violent manner.

Female honor, then, played a role in almost every act of violence that involved one or more women, which makes it the central theme of this chapter. At first thought, this may be puzzling. Honor was highly gendered. Whereas male honor, before spiritualization broke through, depended on a reputation for physical bravery and protection, women's honor was linked closely to their sexuality. The reputation of a woman depended on an absence, first of all, of any rumors of impropriety and, second, of sorcery, as long as magical beliefs were prevalent. By contrast, the seduction of a woman, married or single, enhanced rather than diminished a man's reputation, while it was a blow to the honor of the man under whose authority she resorted. Ridicule befell the cheated husband in particular. The distinction between sources of honor paralleled the overall division of gender roles, which had it that men should be active and women passive. A man counted as honorable when talked about and a woman when not talked about. However, while the passivity required from women reinforced the social expectation that they refrained from violence, the interaction between men and women, particularly between male and female honor, was a source of frequent conflict, and hence violence. The incidents resulting from this entanglement, even though they constituted a minority among all cases of homicide and assault well into the eighteenth century, add to our understanding of the social context of these crimes.

The quantitative preponderance of men's fights, which most often were inter-familial, justifies us in taking the incidents that fall outside this pattern together and regarding them as a unity. This includes just a few male-on-male cases: those that took place within the nuclear family.

Violent Women

The case of Emilie Breil appears to be unique. There are occasional exam-ples of fights between women in a manner that resembles the male dueling code, but the references are all untrustworthy. A Paris almanac listing events in 1665 mentioned that on May 25, "two ladies, whose names were not revealed, have fought a duel with pistols three miles from Paris. One is dead."[2] Two inmates of Amsterdam's spinhouse swore that, upon their release, they would stage a combat with their lives at stake, the sign being the same as in a case mentioned in the previous chapter: they tore a handkerchief and each woman took one half.[3] In 1636 Jusepe de Ribera painted a duel between two women, which contemporaries believed had taken place in Naples 80 years earlier.[4]

The European homicide and assault record has always included female perpetrators. Since they continue to form a small minority to the present day, it is futile to look for trends. This is different from women's involve-ment in overall crime, which exhibits a greater variation over time than their involvement in violence. In the seventeenth century, the share of female crime lay between 30 and 40 percent, and sometimes even higher. It decreased somewhat during the eighteenth century and further after 1800, until it reached the modern figure of about 10 percent by the early twentieth century.[5] Women's involvement in serious violence, on the other hand, has been relatively impervious to change. Eisner concludes that from the Middle Ages until the twentieth century, the normal range of female perpetrators – of homicide, assault, and robbery combined – lay between 5 and 12 percent. The approximate upper limit was 15 percent.[6] A plausible hypothesis considers the level of female violence to be a func-tion of the power balance between men and women. This balance has con-sistently been uneven throughout the centuries and it has changed only slightly in recent times.

Nose-slitting is among the few examples of violence that was both serious and typically female. It was a customary revenge by a married woman against her husband's lover. Although the chastity of the perpe-trator herself, strictly speaking, was not involved, the act nevertheless implied an aggressive defense of her sexual reputation. By marking her rival as an infamous person, the avenger posed as an honest wife. Significantly, she blamed the other woman rather than her adulterous husband. The term "nose-slitting" refers to the median result, as some perpetrators merely caused injury to their victim's nose, whereas a few managed to cut it off entirely. The victim might be married as well. In 1486, residents of Nuremberg eagerly followed the news about the neigh-boring town of Schwabach's coin master, who was having an affair with

Figure 4.1: *The Duel of Isabella de Carazzi and Diambra de Pottinella*, Jusepe de Ribera, 1636. Reproduced with permission. © Museo Nacional del Prado

the wife of a Nuremberg citizen. Although the council forbade the adulterous couple to see one another, they continued to meet publicly in the city. On October 3, the coin master's wife traveled from Schwabach to Nuremberg, ambushed her rival in an alley, and attacked her with a knife. She did not quite manage to cut off her nose. The council ordered the arrest of the perpetrator, together with her husband. They were released after a short time through the intervention of Schwabach's margrave. The magistrates told the coin master to stay away from Nuremberg altogether. It is unclear whether he was arrested for adultery or because of his wife's revenge, but there were certainly instances in which the woman acted with her husband's connivance. Understandably that happened when he wanted to end or had ended the affair, as in another Nuremberg case in 1506. A citizen who had made his maid pregnant agreed to pay her off with 10 guilders. He asked his wife and a male relative to accompany him for the money's transfer, but after handing it over they attacked her. While the men held the servant in grip, the wife cut her nose.[7]

Most reported cases of nose-slitting are from southern Germany and Switzerland around 1500, but the custom was more widespread both geographically and chronologically. In fifteenth-century Paris, a woman named Jeanne Albiz managed to perform the act on her rival. She ambushed her with a pruning-knife, jumped forward, and cut her nose.[8] In early seventeenth-century London, a few women threatened to slit the nose of their husband's mistress, but actual violence only amounted to a scratch in the face. Significantly, this was called the "whore's mark." Nose injury as the characteristic revenge of a cheated wife on her rival also figures in old English ballads.[9] By the seventeenth century, however, the association with female revenge had weakened, since a few cases were reported of a man calling his wife a whore and threatening to slit her nose.[10] The fact that the custom was so widespread, probably less in actual practice than in representation, suggests that this revenge was acceptable to many women. It also proves that there were exceptions to the code that denied women the right to use violence in order to defend their honor. Finally, it underlines the fact that women's honor, too, originally was associated with the body. The nose had a highly symbolic value, linked to the sexuality of men and women. With men, the nose stood for their genital member, the size of the one indicating that of the other, while cutting off a man's nose symbolized castration. For women, a heavily injured nose meant less beauty, and hence a diminished sexual attractiveness.

It is no coincidence that the target of revenge was the other woman. Although some women did attack a man, especially in or near their home, this was uncommon outside the domestic sphere. Studies of various parts of Europe find that, when women became violent, they tended to direct themselves at other women rather than at men.[11] Exceptions gave rise to comment. When the wife of a Cologne regiment leader intended to assist her husband during a nightly conflict with his dissatisfied men, the soldiers said to her, "If you want to do a man's job, you must expect a man's payment," meaning blows.[12] The only female defendant tried for injuring a man with a knife in Amsterdam had victimized him by accident. In the street at midnight, she had intended to stab her female companion, but a young man passing by intervened. While trying to wrestle the knife from her hand, he was injured. The prosecutor was surprised that she walked the street that late carrying a knife.[13] Indeed, as some authors believe, women were as aggressive as men and their underrepresentation

Figure 4.2: *Women Arguing in Rome*, Bartolomeo Pinelli, 1809

in trials for serious violence is due solely to the strong taboo on the use of knives.

Female-on-female violence, although statistically more common than female-on-male, was either dismissed as unimportant or stereotypically portrayed as comical. Popular books and plays of the early modern period invariably satirized the subject. Men laughed about women who scratched, pulled hair, or threw household utensils at each other. Even wife-beating was considered comical, at least until the seventeenth century.[14] The denigrating attitude to female-on-female violence did not remain confined to literary sources. A Paris police officer of the eighteenth century remarked: "A dispute among women interests no one."[15]

Nevertheless, female violence and its male counterpart shared an important component: that of honor. When motives for female fighting were recorded, they often involved the preservation of the attacker's honor. That was the case in the only prosecuted murder case in Amsterdam in which an insult led an adult woman to attack another. The scene was semi-domestic. The victim, Maria Borman, had an upstairs room in the same lodging-house in which the killer, Jannetie Fagelaar, and her 14-year-old daughter also rented. People living in such rooms, although unrelated, nevertheless shared their lives to a large extent. Because Jannetie had a fever, she asked her daughter to get her some beer.

On her return, the landlady reproached the girl for staying away too long, to which she replied with rough words. Then Maria intervened from the stairs: "How can you be so rude to the old woman?" The mother, no longer that ill, failed to appreciate the tone of instructive reproach in the remark by her fellow lodger, and retorted: "What do you care? It is none of your business!" Various insults from both sides followed. Then Maria walked up to Jannetie, pulled her hair, and called her a married men's whore. This was a grave insult. Even prostitutes themselves looked down upon colleagues who accepted married men as clients. Jannetie returned the same words and when Maria tried to slap her, she took the knife with which she had been cutting bread and sausages and plunged it into Maria's chest. The victim fell down and died shortly afterwards.[16]

Some women, on the other hand, killed for financial gain. The Amsterdam court tried no fewer than five women for murder committed in the course of an impulsive robbery or in order instantly to solve a financial problem. In all instances, the victims were also female. These cases belong to the category of violence that was both primarily instrumental and highly impulsive. This category comprised more female-on-female murders than male-on-male ones, but the overall number in Amsterdam is too low for us to draw a firm conclusion and the European literature seldom specifies such cases.

Examples of fatal female violence for honor or financial gain remain few. Yet, women routinely used knives for preparing food and these sometimes served as weapons, despite the heavy cultural taboo. In metropolitan centers, many women visited bars. Most likely, female violence as well as women's abstention from violence resulted from a learning process. Many women conformed to the cultural stereotype of passivity, and when they did attack or defend themselves, they primarily targeted their own sex. Possibly, this group of passive women was somewhat less large than it appears, because female defendants and witnesses were reluctant to admit their active roles in court. The other group, the minority of women accustomed to some measure of violence, was present especially in Europe's larger cities. They associated more frequently with lower-class men and learned to be aggressive in their company. They probably developed this aggressiveness through imitation rather than conscious male teaching. This conclusion equally applies to violent prostitutes and brothel-keepers. Notably, Paris and Amsterdam had a large number of female brothel-keepers. Many of these were strong women who employed tough men whose main task was to protect the whores from assault and persuade unwilling clients to pay. In both cities, moreover, the public helped prostitutes to escape arrest. In Paris in 1785, a man attacked the guards who were bringing in several women, which enabled them to escape. Thereupon a few policemen, considering the attacker a pimp, arrested him, but he was liberated in his turn by a large crowd.[17]

Female Victimization by Strangers and Acquaintances

The category of prostitution-related violence bridges the gap between women's aggression and female victimization. In spite of all protective measures, prostitutes frequently suffered, as has been noted for the Middle Ages. Much of this was casual violence, but it extended to Roman house-scorning. The targets of this ritual attack included prostitutes who had rejected a special client. Roman men considered being a preferred visitor as akin to a personal relationship, so the attackers felt like jilted lovers.[18] Elsewhere, the targeted woman may not have been a prostitute, but her assailant called her a whore by way of insult or to underline that it was a sexual attack. In seventeenth-century England, house-scorning involved breaking windows, and even some married women became victims in such attacks. More characteristically, the victim was a widow, as in the case of Jane Minshull. Thomas Cowdell went as far as breaking through two doors and intruding into her house at night. She fled from her bedroom through the back door, wearing only her smock, and took refuge in a neighbor's house. Thomas left her terrified children alone, just repeating that Jane was a whore and that he would ruin her.[19]

Clearly, this widow was victimized in her own home, but other women suffered from violence in brothels, in the street, and in taverns. Even attacks by intimates were not confined to the home. With female-on-female violence already treated, this section deals with homicide and assault on women by male friends, acquaintances, and strangers. Quantitative studies usually do not differentiate between female victimization by intimates and by non-intimates. Moreover, in body inspection reports we do not usually find enough information about the perpetrator. The reports do, however, constitute the most reliable source when it comes to quantifying the victim's sex. In this case, too, Eisner's database offers the most comprehensive information. He concludes that the share of female homicide victims was about 7 percent in the thirteenth through sixteenth centuries, 13 percent in the seventeenth century, and 27 percent in the eighteenth.[20] It is likely, however, that the increase is due mostly to a concomitant rise in the proportion of domestic homicides. Female murder victims accounted for just under 10 percent in early modern Geneva.[21] In the Amsterdam body inspection reports of the late seventeenth and eighteenth centuries, the share of female victims is one-fifth. Another crucial finding is that the percentage of female victims went further down when total homicide went up. During the heyday of knife fighting in the 1690s to 1720s, with a homicide rate around 9, the percentage of female victims was a mere 13. Female victims accounted for 22 percent during the trough in homicide of the 1660s and 1670s and for about a third between 1752 and 1816, when the overall rates were even lower. The total homicide rate also correlated negatively with the percentage of non-infant children and adolescents among the victims and positively with the percentage of stabbing as a cause of death.[22]

The homicide statistics are indicative only of serious violence. Casual violence by men against women, either their wives or strangers, may have been as frequent as that against other men, but it was less often prosecuted. The lack of a code in such cases often made a man's attack on a woman more random and callous. In eighteenth-century London, male-on-female violence involved mostly one-sided assaults.[23] On the other hand, violence against female acquaintances and strangers was less often fatal than attacks against wives or lovers. This is suggested by the frequency of both categories among Amsterdam homicide trials. The highest incidence of casual violence against women by non-intimate men was in the larger towns, where they enjoyed a relative anonymity and where there was a sizeable group of independent women. In small towns and villages, men were more likely to think twice, because the woman's husband, father, or another male relative, if not present at the scene, would soon hear about it. To be sure, as the previous chapter showed, strangers too defended women.

In accordance with the lack of a fighting code, rituals such as a script to establish fair combat or that of "drinking the conflict away" were absent from male-on-female violence. The ritual elements that we observe mostly belonged to the repertoire of humiliation. Dutch men preferred buttock-stabbing, suffered by a few male opponents as well, but mostly by women. This degrading treatment crossed the intimate/non-intimate boundary, because lower-class men lavished it on their wives and sweethearts as well as on female acquaintances. As well as being degrading, it certainly wasn't fatal, since that part of the body contains no vital arteries. Amsterdam court records mention the stabbing of a woman's buttock on a routine basis, almost always as an additional charge without further information. An untypical case of premeditated revenge, however, plainly illustrates the ritual significance of this part of the female body. For undisclosed reasons, two men intruded into a woman's house and attacked her. While his mate pushed her down, the other man stabbed her twice in the right buttock, twice in the left one and once just above in her back.[24] A ritual attack that entailed more dangerous consequences consisted of kicking a pregnant woman in the belly. It was an act of symbolic abortion, but it could easily turn into a real one. Such attacks have been reported for France and England. A Parisian said of a lady he respected that she was not the kind of woman that one kicks in the belly.[25]

Occasionally a woman became a victim of violence in a situation similar to male victimization, for example when a released convict took revenge on her for testifying at his trial. More often, women were at risk because of their occupation, in particular that of landlady. Drunken men attacked female innkeepers for refusing to serve them or if they requested payment. In some cases, the victims were married women, who, like Emilie Breil's mother, worked in a public place together with their husbands. A chivalrous customer might vent his anger on the husband, but many men directly assaulted the wife for a perceived injustice. Her husband might not be around to help her. Other female innkeepers suffering attack were single or widowed. Even when male defenders were around, things could get out of hand. In a rural tavern in Haute-Auvergne, the landlady, Anne Guion, asked Bernard de Conquans to pay his check. Deciding that she had made the request in an impolite manner, he reacted with verbal insult. He had already paid her, he claimed, and would kill her if she did not leave him in peace. Before he could put his threat into practice, some of the male customers pushed him outside. He continued to shout insults, returned with his sword drawn, was kicked out again, and turned his anger on the servant girl who stood there. Although he intended to beat her with the flat side of his sword only, she raised her arm in defense and was mutilated.[26]

Like men, women were confronted with violent offenses against their property. Bandits, who had an infamous reputation to begin with, indiscriminately attacked both sexes. Street robbers, too, often found women easy prey: they were even more ready than men to part with their possessions when threatened with a knife. As in every situation, there were exceptions. Going out with two mates on a January night, Jan Kijser saw three women walking in the street. One carried a raincoat under her arm. Jan's mates encouraged him: "This raincoat is for the taking." Jan approached her from behind and grabbed the coat's tail, but she held on to it. Trying to get it, he dragged her over a distance of three houses, but she still held on to it. Thereupon Jan drew his knife. The victim received shallow cuts through various layers of clothing and into her straw hat and a deep one on her face.[27]

Removing a woman's cap or headdress involved no serious physical injury, but it was highly significant within the symbolic vocabulary of honor and infamy. "Uncoiffing," as James Farr terms it, has been reported from all over Europe. The meanings of dishonor for men and women converged in the act. As a male hat stood for prowess and virility, it was shameful for the owner if another man took it. Women's caps symbolized chastity, so removing them stood for impropriety. The perpetrator was either making a statement to the effect that the victim was already unchaste, or the act was meant to make a respectable woman look unchaste. In either case, the woman's reputation suffered. Cases in Burgundy usually involved other women as perpetrators. They accompanied the act with verbal abuse or dragged the victim's headwear through the mud. A married woman, suspected of being a *seigneur*'s lover, demonstratively put on her bonnet in the street.[28] "Uncoiffers" in the north German town of Wilster were women as well as men. One man admitted that he had beaten a woman but not that he had gone as far as removing her cap.[29] An Amsterdam case had a male perpetrator. He brought home a woman with whom he had been drinking and attempted to rape her on the way, but she yelled loudly. Then he cut her cap loose with his knife. He intended to show the cap to the tavern keeper as a sign that he had slept with her but was arrested before he could do so.[30]

Rape and sexual assault exclusively concern female victimization, because the historical evidence for homosexual violence is too scant. Over time, rape has been conceived of as falling within one of three offense categories: property, morality, or violence. The third view is relatively recent. For a long time, rape was considered as a kind of property crime. The victim was the woman's protector – her husband, father, or other male relative – rather the assaulted woman herself. This was the logic of an extremely patriarchal culture that denied any woman an identity of her own. A sexual assault meant that her protector had failed in his task and hence suffered in his honor. The rapist had robbed a man of his symbolic capital, which had repercussions on his economic capital. If the act was viewed as seduction, where the woman had given in voluntarily, it amounted to the same thing, because protection and control were two sides of one coin. At the same time, women had no independent honor – only a status which derived from their husbands or fathers. In Europe, this situation began to change by the late Middle Ages. Women acquired a partial responsibility for their own honor, which meant, first of all, that they themselves should guard their sexual reputation. Yet the idea that rape was an economic loss lingered on. If the perpetrator robbed a young woman of her virginity, this, in particular, significantly lowered her value on the marriage market. The morality view broke through after the Reformation. Rape became caught up in the ensuing civilization offensives which condemned all forms of extramarital sex. For moralists, the crime primarily consisted of forbidden sex, and only secondarily of assault. Throughout the early modern period, the property and morality view coexisted.[31]

The absence of a victim-oriented approach to rape, well into the twentieth century, influenced the types of case that were prosecuted and that are hence known to us. In accordance with the mechanism of blaming the victim, rapists and defense witnesses argued that the woman had provoked the act or at least had enjoyed it. In the early modern period, the belief that a subsequent pregnancy precluded a rape charge was widespread. Writing in 1776, the physician Johann Gottlieb Walter went against it, distinguishing moral virginity from physical virginity. After an act of rape, the first remained intact, even though the hymen had been violated. Walter took a giant step in the direction of the spiritualization of female honor, but his ideas were slow to take root.[32] References from all over Europe show that rapists considered themselves excused when they knew or thought they knew that a woman was no longer a virgin. Especially when a woman had had casual sex, for money or not, other men would consider themselves entitled to force her to let them have his way. The French glazier Jacques-Louis Ménétra recounted that, while traveling in a forest, he and his mate spotted a young man and a girl who were just about to have a sexual rendez-vous. The man had stuck his sword into the ground next to him, but Ménétra's mate managed to grab it. In turn, the two raped the girl, while the other held off her boyfriend with his own sword. Ménétra treated this as a cunning joke, not at all unpleasant for the victim. After all, she had been ready for intercourse.[33]

To a large extent, French judges shared this glazier's attitude. The prosecution rate for rape was low throughout the early modern period and heavy punishment was even more rare. Courts imposed it when aggravating circumstances applied or if additional offenses had been committed. In 1606, for example, three soldiers, who had raped the daughter of an aristocrat, wounded her valet, and strangled the woman afterwards, were broken on the wheel. The Parlement of Provence accused a man who had raped a married woman of adultery committed by force, thus treating most seriously the offense to her husband.[34] A case in the Auvergne in 1664 was conclusive only because the accused escaped from jail and fled. Perpetrator and victim knew each other as servants in the household of a provincial aristocrat. According to her statement, he had forced her into sexual intercourse against her will and promised to marry her if she remained silent. Now she claimed she was pregnant, although a midwife could find no signs of this. He denied everything. The accusations and counter-accusations revolved around honor at several levels. The man alleged that she had worked as a prostitute and that even her origins were obscure, while he was of good repute. To the contrary, she retorted, their native villages lay close together, she had a highly esteemed job in the aristocratic household, and she had always been honorably employed before this. She attacked his honor by pointing out that he worked in the lowest rank of domestic service. After the rapist's escape, the midwife finally concluded that the victim was pregnant. At least the judges refrained from considering this a sign of her consent. They granted the victim 60 *livres* from the fugitive's confiscated property and ordered his capture.[35]

Under the English accusatory system, it was just as difficult to get a rapist convicted. In order to be credible, women declared that they had lost consciousness because of the attack or emphasized their vain attempts at escape. London women, servants in particular, found it hard to make juries believe a rape charge.[36] Female servants and maids were vulnerable everywhere. A case in the Spanish town of Manganeses in 1649 involved an official of the Inquisition, Gabriel Temprano. He had taken his niece, the 18-year-old Lorenza Lozana, into his house as a servant. There were rumors that the uncle required services of a sexual nature as well. Neighbors knew that his wife had suspicions and that she behaved in an increasingly hostile manner toward the young woman. To prevent further gossip, the couple expelled their niece, now 20, to an adjacent building where they kept cattle. One day, they found her dead in the stable. It was concluded that she had committed suicide, which started another round of public rumors. Some neighbors thought that the jealous aunt, with her enmity, had driven her to the deed, others that she had been ashamed because of the contact with her uncle. Still others gossiped that Gabriel had even planned to kill his wife before his niece had committed suicide. The case remained inconclusive, but the rape charges were never investigated.[37]

Courts were more eager to act in cases of enforced sex with very young girls. Even victims from humble social backgrounds received the satisfaction of having their assailants prosecuted. Yet, the crime consisted primarily of depriving a girl of her virginity. The Florentine magistrates tried such a case in 1487. The weaver Giovanni Francisci had kept Ginevra Angeli, a poor girl aged about 10 years, in his house, where he allowed several other men to rape her, also anally. The magistrates sentenced Francisci to a whipping and 10 years in jail, and he had to deposit an amount of 100 *lire* in Santa Maria Nuova as a dowry for the girl. She was placed in the Convent for Converted Women.[38] In 1700, the supervisor of the Reformed children's poorhouse in Rotterdam admitted to having raped five of the girls entrusted to him. He had been charged with raping twelve since 1698, upon the testimony of the victims only. Apparently, he did not consider his offense to be assault, since he pleaded with his wife to forgive him for his adultery. He received a death sentence.[39]

The half-hearted prosecution of the rape of adult women continued beyond the early modern period. In England, in the first half of the nineteenth century, there were few trials for rape, which was often settled out of court. In order to avoid having to testify against their assailants, many women refused to file a complaint. Out-of-court arrangements were equally common in Belgium at this time. Magistrates and other males professionally dealing with the subject continued to believe that women often provoked the act.[40] Throughout Europe, marital rape was never prosecuted, except in occasional trials for incest. It was not until the end of the twentieth century that penal law recognized the possibility of rape within marriage. In England, for example, marital immunity was not abolished until 1991.[41]

The Enigma of Poisoning

Poisoning takes us close to the home. Lethal food and drinks were usually prepared in the kitchen, but might be offered to victims outside. This crime forms a special case for several reasons. The perpetrators included men eliminating men, but it would be inadvisable to split this discussion over two chapters. Secondly, poisoning is a special case because it involves no overt aggression. Yet it unmistakably falls within the overall subject of murder. The absence of aggression has led to the stereotypical notion that women, in particular, were prone to this crime. They tended to kill their enemies with poisonous substances, whereas men would use weapons. This stereotype goes back to Ancient Rome at least. In pre-industrial Europe, many people saw poisoning as akin to harmful sorcery, since both activities were performed in secret and seemed to work equally mysteriously.

In Franck Collard's database of medieval cases, however, only 18 percent had exclusively female perpetrators and another 7 percent consisted of women acting together with men. Collard emphasizes that this can be read in two ways. Women clearly constituted a minority among poisoners, but they were overrepresented in comparison with the proportion of female killers overall. Another conclusion from his database is even more important. Three-quarters of all poison victims in the Middle Ages were from the upper classes. Among this sector of society, this crime was a favorite means of liquidating an enemy or rival. This fact explains all other statistics. The murders in question were usually commissioned by people of equally high rank and were executed by their servants. The households of nobles and magnates, including their kitchens, employed men as well as women. Female victims, too, accounting for 11 percent in the entire database and 20 percent among instances prosecuted, were overrepresented compared with their share in medieval murder. This is largely explained by those incidents in which a prince or count, if not a bishop, was poisoned together with his wife. All statistics, finally, are based on cases that were handled by courts or reported by chroniclers. The bias of the latter toward the elites is also reflected in the figures.[42]

In body inspection reports and causes of death statistics, cases of poisoning have always constituted a tiny minority among all murders. In eighteenth-century Amsterdam, for example, the inspection committee found poisoning to be the cause of death only about once every three years.[43] Some historians believe that such figures imply an undercount in an otherwise reliable type of source. When people discovered a corpse with cuts or bruises, it was an obvious task for the surgeons, but if a person's death raised no suspicion, the body was buried right away. Hence, an unknown number of murders by poison were listed as natural deaths and, even if a medical examination followed, doctors did not always recognize the unnatural cause. Supposedly, this situation prevailed until the mid-twentieth century. On the other hand, in the past, Europeans were quick to gossip about suspicious deaths, especially if a seemingly healthy person suddenly died after heavy vomiting. Sometimes the suspicion turned out to be unfounded. So is the argument about a massive undercount plausible? Whatever the dark number of cases of poisoning, we can say with confidence that fighting on impulse declined after the Middle Ages. We also know for sure that in the majority of ordinary homes in the past women did the cooking. If future research could somehow prove that a large number of these women who cooked routinely poisoned household members and guests, we would have to revise our standard theories of murder. Then the conclusion would be that women had been as murderous as men for centuries, that they were even more murderous than men between about 1750 and 1950, and that they suddenly stopped their criminal activities as methods of detection improved. This seems an unlikely scenario. Poisoning obviously implies premeditation. In the overwhelming majority of male-on-male murders, except in feuding, no premeditation was involved. If murderous intentions were relatively rare among men, why should they have been common among women?

A variety of poisons was already known about in the Middle Ages. They were not all widely available, but arsenic, often called rat poison, and powder against flies were standard ingredients in rural as well as urban households. Whereas some historians think that unhappy wives got rid of their husbands along with the rats, contemporary rumors most often concerned remarriage. The prototypical cause for gossip was when the spouses of a man and a woman died within a short space of time and the survivors then married each other. The Kent Justice of the Peace William Lambarde investigated such a case in the 1580s. On February 23, 1583, he noted in his diary that he and a colleague had interrogated several people in Sevenoaks because there was suspicion that Mrs Parnel, together with her second husband Thomas Heyward, had poisoned her first husband. Five days later, he and two colleagues interrogated still more people, because of a suspicion that Heyward's late wife had been poisoned as well.[44]

The detection of murder by poison entailed a mixture of popular knowledge, legal reasoning, and medical expertise. For centuries, it necessarily started with the first, because doctors were expensive and not present at every deathbed or illness. In eighteenth-century Germany, symptoms such as stomachache or headache, dizziness, fever, and vomiting served as indications, in combination with existing conflicts within a family or between neighbors. After a suspicious death, villagers fed the remains of the meal to a chicken or dog. For their part, lawyers insisted that a permission for torture in a poisoning trial required clear indications of malicious intent.[45] Confidence in torture decreased during the Enlightenment. In a 1772 treatise, the Dutch lawyer Johan Jacob van Hasselt argued for the need to inspect bodies in all suspicious deaths, devoting a separate paragraph to "the bodies about which a rumor circulates that they have been killed by poison."[46] Autopsies in such cases became common in France and England during the early modern period. All over Europe, methods of detection gradually improved during the nineteenth century, while control over the sale of poison increased as well.[47]

Case studies of criminal trials sometimes confirm the stereotype of poisoning as a female crime, and sometimes not. The statistics depend on the prosecution policy and the methods of detection practiced in each respective region or town. In early modern England, the stereotype influenced court practice as well as popular literature. Thus, just over a third of all poisoning defendants in Cheshire were male – a considerable underrepresentation compared with total murder. Men had an excellent opportunity, though, to commit this offense during a wife's illness or childbirth, when they temporarily directed the household. English crime pamphlets of the first half of the seventeenth century concentrated on wives poisoning their husbands, but in the second half they treated this offense as one of both spouses. On the other hand, some English husbands, suspected of having poisoned their wives, used the prevailing stereotype to their advantage. Asserting that they lacked knowledge of such things, they were acquitted or not tried in the first place. A few men tried to divert suspicion to a female servant.[48] Seventeenth-century England also witnessed a few scandals whose offenders have been termed the first serial killers. Men and women were among the perpetrators, most of whom used poison. In 1671, for example, a man employed arsenic to murder his wife, his father-in-law, five other family members, and a servant.[49] A similar case came to light in the Dutch town of Brielle, where a woman poisoned seven adults and eight children.

German studies mostly confirm the supposition that poisoning is mainly a female crime. In small towns in the south, wives constituted the majority of offenders in cases of attempted or successful poisoning. The reasons lay either in insoluble marital conflict or in the desire to facilitate marriage with a lover. Most of the poisoning incidents of the first category occurred shortly after the wedding. The spouses in question had gone through with an arranged marriage before really getting to know each other. One woman, tried for attempted poisoning, said she had only wanted to weaken her husband. Eighteenth-century Württemberg, on the other hand, did witness a few men who experimented in the kitchen. Again, it was mostly wives who were tried in relatively steady numbers in Schleswig-Holstein during the eighteenth century. In this rural region, many women worked in domestic service until their late 20s, which diminished their chances on the marriage market. Several of them married an older widower, often after just a brief period of acquaintance, in the hope of being materially well off for the rest of their lives. Some were disappointed, realizing that they had made the wrong choice. Their husband maltreated them or they felt that caring for the stepchildren was too heavy a burden.[50]

Statistics about perpetrators and victims as well as recorded motives after 1800 continued the early modern pattern. Poisoners were men as well as women, but the latter were overrepresented compared to their share among all killers. A quarter of English victims in the period 1750–1914 were spouses, and a fifth were parents, including step-parents and in-laws. Conversely, a French study of parent murder found that poison had been used in no more than 11 percent of all cases. Despite this low percentage, French farmers called arsenic "the powder of succession," and it had a similar reputation in England.[51] Belgian poisoners mostly belonged to the poorer classes, using this method to get rid of a relative; just over half the offenders were women.[52] The nineteenth century also brought a resurgence of the phenomenon of multiple killing by arsenic, this time for financial gain. Poisoners in England as well as the Netherlands obtained money from their victims' funeral or life insurances. There was a woman living in Leiden during the 1880s known as Good Mie. By then, a doctor's certificate was obligatory for all deaths, but this law was only lightly enforced in poor neighborhoods. Mie owed her nickname to the great care she ostensibly lavished on her neighbors. In particular, she signed them up for funeral insurances, often paying the dues herself. When these neighbors died without anyone suspecting a crime, most of the money went to Mie. She was exposed when three family members died simultaneously.[53]

Domestic Violence

A terminological question must come first. Domestic violence is a common expression, used with reference to the past as well as today. As in the section on female victimization by acquaintances and strangers, the relationship constitutes the criterion rather than the location of the crime. Consequently, domestic violence includes cases in which the offender attacked someone well known to him or her outside the home. But what do we mean by an intimate relationship? In the historical literature on homicide, this category is often confused with that of the family, whereas the two do not entirely match. While we can make our own judgment in individual cases, the confusion has repercussions for a statistical study. Some authors quantify family homicides rather than intimate homicides. However, the intensity of one's relationship with a relative outside the nuclear family can be compared to the ties a person has with a friend or neighbor. Conversely, unmarried partners, while strictly speaking not family, are certainly intimates. In modern times many couples live together for years without being married. In pre-industrial cities, this was common among the lower classes, often with the partners officially married to someone else. The moral condemnation these unions received from respectable contemporaries should not prevent us from classifying them as partnerships. Courtships, too, must be considered in this group. Finally, the intimate category includes gay and lesbian partnerships, but past evidence about domestic violence among them is too scarce. As in many of the poisoning cases just discussed, this section is about people who often loved, and yet attacked and sometimes killed, each other.

Perhaps these remarks are less pertinent for the period before the seventeenth century. The further back we go in time, the more we find that relations of blood had primacy over relations of intimacy. The rise of domestic violence as a problem, and its changing faces, should be explained with reference to long-term developments regarding the family as well as personal relationships. Without going too deep into the great unsolved debate about spousal and parental affection, a few things can be stated with confidence. The decline of the vendetta in Europe, as well as the sobering of the reconciliation ceremony, owed much to the weakening of wider kinship ties. As long as large and allied groups of relatives were powerful players on the socio-political scene, secular and ecclesiastical authorities often saw them as parties to be confronted. By the mid-sixteenth century, the struggle was largely over. When family came to stand for the nuclear unit, church and state began to support it. The result was an increased emphasis on patriarchy, but this concerned the "micro-patriarchy" of a father leading his wife, children, and a few servants.

Kings and magistrates considered this a reflection of their own benevolent rule. Protestant as well as Catholic moralists defined marriage as an affective partnership in which the husband ruled.[54] This micro-patriarchy was supposed to be paternalistic rather than dictatorial, but it possibly led to increased tensions within the home. In this way, the rise of domestic violence was indirectly related to the decline of the vendetta.

Patriarchy did not preclude affection. The assertion of earlier historians that marital and parent–child relationships in the past were loveless and that courtships were merely instrumental in setting up an economic unit has been rightly criticized. Nevertheless, the nature of love changed over the course of the early modern period. The physical discipline exercised by husbands over wives gradually lost its legitimacy, which influenced the nature of spousal violence. In the eighteenth century, it became more common for husbands and wives to spend leisure time with each other. Family life moved to the center stage of the cultural scene. A new romanticism emphasized the psychological dimension of love, while heartache and loss were bemoaned in sentimental novels. This change affected married couples as well as unofficial, engaged, adulterous, and casual couples. A psychological type of bond often implied a peaceful exploration of each other's feelings, but close ties could give rise to peculiar tensions that might suddenly erupt. Alternatively, they increased the pressure to eliminate a third person who was in the way. The ensuing love dramas were increasingly characteristic of most cases of murder, and this continues to be the case today.

The available statistics are unambiguous. The proportion of intimate murder victims has steadily increased from the Middle Ages through modern times. Next to the great decline in the overall rates, this is the second important long-term trend in homicide. Of course, our information is necessarily restricted to cases in which the perpetrator of the crime can be identified, in other words in those cases that led to a prosecution. It may be objected that the figures are biased because intimate killers are less likely to flee, but this is far from self-evident. At least until the late-eighteenth century, when tension-related violence came to the fore, wife killers fled just as much as knife fighters did. Data from English, Dutch, and German studies show that, until the sixteenth century, the proportion of intimate homicide victims was well below 10 percent, with 5 percent as the median. It rose to about 16 percent in the seventeenth century and 30 percent in the eighteenth, while 40 percent or more was common after 1800.[55] In Amsterdam, the shift came by the mid-eighteenth century. Between 1700 and 1750, victimization by strangers accounted for 44 percent and by intimates for 14.7 percent. During the next 60 years this ratio had reversed: 17.5 percent to 42.5 percent (with the last dataset probably a little biased).[56] A similar trend, but less pronounced, was visible in Germany's hilly Eifel region. There, the increase in the share of intimate perpetrators, of homicide and assault, set in earlier and continued more gradually.[57] Stockholm witnessed a gradual development, too, with intimate killers accounting for 10 percent in the sixteenth century, 14 percent in the early seventeenth, 24 percent in the eighteenth, and just over 50 percent in the twentieth century.[58]

Thus, the long-term trend clearly is away from male fighting. The opposite conclusion is more ambiguous. The share of domestic homicide increased dramatically, but since the overall rates declined by a much larger factor, the rate of intimate victimization declined as well. A rough estimate, based on a combination of all available European data, comes at 2 homicides on intimates per 100,000 total population in the Middle Ages and 0.5 after 1800. Thus, it will not do to consider intimate homicide simply as being residual in society, impervious to change. It is true that, whenever and wherever homicide rates are high, male-on-male fighting largely accounts for it. It is not true that the only change implied in the long-term decline of homicide was the drastic reduction of male-on-male fighting, causing the proportion of intimate victims to increase automatically. Scripts of intimate victimization changed as well.

Moving gradually to the heart of the home, we must begin with conflicts that were the result of a terminated courtship. Amsterdam defendants included jilted male lovers who attacked their former sweethearts. Incidents around 1700 usually involved disfiguring the woman's face with a knife – a type of revenge still practiced in some countries today. One man visited his ex-fiancée in her room to demand back the ring he had given her. She thought that they were still friends and that he was leaning over to kiss her. Instead, he cut her face and neck. According to a surgeon, the scarf she was wearing, folded into eight layers, had saved her life.[59] In a well-publicized case in 1775, Johannes van Gogh, a romantic dreamer, stabbed his beloved, an ex-prostitute, to death. He was charged with premeditated revenge, although he claimed that he had in fact wanted to commit suicide.[60] Other men were glad to terminate a courtship. The appeal court of Württemberg tried a number of young men for getting rid of their pregnant girlfriends. The body of 23-year-old Barbara Kuhn, who had died from a severe head injury, was found in a forest, six months pregnant. The authorities immediately arrested her lover, the 19-year-old carpenter's apprentice Johann Haldenwanger, who had courted her without her parents' consent. Under torture, he confessed that he had clubbed her to death while they were on their way to the annual fair, because she had confronted him with his coming fatherhood.[61]

Almost every example of spouse murder can be situated within the three-sided relationship between hierarchy, honor, and love. Wife murder in particular often had a prehistory of aggression, which makes it necessary to consider routine marital violence first. For a long time, the authorities considered this to be an essentially private matter. Husbands and fathers should solve their own problems. The authorities intervened in marital disputes as mediators only. Intra-familial conflict – other than homicide – was of no concern to outside agencies.[62] In the ideal situation, according to preindustrial values, all members of a household willingly accepted the lead of the husband and father, causing an absence of physical aggression. Actual practice, as expected, was different. Throughout Europe, the confrontation between assertive wives and husbands trying to maintain their dominance was a source of potentially serious violence.

For England, we can trace the development of legal opinion with some precision. Sixteenth-century lawyers confirmed the right of a husband to beat his wife, in moderation, as a punishment for misbehavior. A 1619 manual for Justices of the Peace specified that a wife could only complain about this treatment if her husband threatened to kill her or beat her "outrageously." The definition of "outrageous" was a constant point of debate. Although in the second half of the seventeenth century some lawyers questioned the legality of wife-beating, the doctrine of reasonable chastisement remained influential until the mid-nineteenth century. By then, most legal scholars considered it a thing of the past, agreeing that even when a husband threatened to use violence, this fell within the definition of cruelty.[63] In line with such standards, an early modern wife who dared to complain in court about her husband's excessive violence routinely argued that she feared for her life or at least for severe bodily harm. Continental wives argued in a similar manner. Battered wives could either submit a complaint to a criminal court or a church institution, or file a civil suit to request separation.

Husbands who declined to assert their authority, on the other hand, stood at risk of becoming the focus of a "shivaree" (or "charivari" in the original French). This mocking ritual has been amply analyzed in the literature on popular culture. Neighbors publicly shamed a husband or a couple by making rough music on their doorstep or riding the man around on a donkey, horse, or wooden pole. This happened in particular when a couple inverted the "natural order" – i.e. when the wife beat her husband. According to popular tradition, a man had to refrain from beating his wife in May. If he did so anyway, he could also become a victim of the shaming ritual. The next step was to subject to a shivaree husbands who abused their traditional right of chastisement by indulging in excessive beating. This use of the shivaree occurred more frequently in the eighteenth century, and by the nineteenth it was happening even more often, in particular in England. Thus, a ritual which started off as an informal sanction in support of patriarchy turned into a custom that put cruel husbands to shame.[64] The cultural appreciation of wife-beating switched

180 degrees between the sixteenth and the twentieth centuries. Once an accepted tool of informal social control, it is a crime in modern times. Schwerhoff views this historical shift as part of a broader development by which interpersonal violence began to be seen simply as a suitable object of social control, whereas formerly, within local communities, it was both a means of and an object of control.[65]

Examining a German village, David Sabean distinguishes between systematic and reactive violence by husbands. The first occurred when a man appeared to have acted from a belief that he had a right to mete out punishment to his wife. In such a case, he had slapped her face or beaten her shoulder or back with a paddle or a rope. Around 1800, a decisive shift occurred toward reactive violence: anger rather than a belief in the right of chastisement was the primary factor.[66] Sabean's categories form a starting point for distinguishing types of spousal murder. The systematic violence of wife-beating can get out of hand. If it goes as far as murder, we can categorize the case as "punishment-related." Reactive violence leading to the death of a spouse is termed "anger-related." A third category is necessary, which has no clear match in non-fatal violence. It is associated with the emergence of romanticism and sentimentalism, constituting its darker side. The modern emphasis on psychological exploration means that possible tensions between a couple often remain submerged and explode only when triggered. Spouse murders resulting from such a configuration are called "tension-related." This category is the most "democratic" of the three, since, whatever the statistics, the script is more or less the same for husband- and wife-killers. The anger-related category comes closest to male-on-male violence and appears characteristic for husbands in particular. Punishment-related murder has a parallel in wives who opposed and then drastically ended the marital hierarchy. The data on anger-related spouse murders are insufficient to show a pattern over time, although it is justified to hypothesize that, like male-on-male fighting, it was subject to civilizing tendencies. The great historical shift occurred in the move from the first to the third category.

Wife-killers usually outnumbered husband-killers, although some historians believe that this is an artefact of prosecution policies. Let us nevertheless begin with the first group. They turn up in the pardon petitions of the fifteenth and sixteenth centuries. We saw that this type of source usually contains embellished stories, in which the petitioner always protested his relative innocence. It is no surprise, therefore, that wife murder was almost always anger-related. The petitioner described it as an unfortunate accident, unintended, just like in male-on-male fighting. A butcher from Picardy, whose main business consisted of making deliveries to the local garrison, emphasized that he and his wife had been living in perfect harmony for a long time. One night in 1524, they had some soldiers as guests. The company was happily drinking wine and the butcher told the visitors that he and his wife had been married for 12 years. She intervened "no, it is 13." He accused her of lying, she stormed at him, and he threw a knife at her which accidentally killed her.[67]

Nolde's study of the Parlement of Paris, which had appeal jurisdiction over two-thirds of France, covers the years 1580–1620 – the earliest period ever to have been subjected to systematic study. Among spouse murders by men, the punishment-related type clearly predominated. This reflected a change in legal opinion, because medieval customary law had exempted husbands whose castigation got out of hand from a homicide charge. By the late sixteenth century, even local courts no longer accepted such an excuse. The majority of the husbands tried by the Parlement were charged with a previous history of violence against their wives. Most of the accused men tried to belittle their aggression. One admitted to have beaten his wife, but not for at least two or three years. Another, charged with beating his wife to death with a stick, said he had only used his fists. A third admitted that he had slapped and clubbed his wife but denied that he had threatened to kill her. Still others denied that the violence to which they had subjected the victim had been the cause of her death. She had suffered from plague or epilepsy, these men claimed.[68]

The punishment-related type of wife murder equally predominated in early modern England and the northern Spanish province of Cantabria. A notorious crime in the village of Canales in 1799 had a previous history of systematic violence. The victim, Antonia Isabel Sánchez, was the local cacique's sister-in-law. After an arranged marriage that lasted for 19 years, her neighbors found Antonia bathed in blood, stabbed 10 times. Her husband, Don Domingo García, was a wealthy local proprietor. He had threatened her with a knife several times before, as both servants and neighbors testified. They had also heard him say that he would rather sleep with all the monks in the world than with his wife. Instead, his relationship with a female servant was more than friendly, causing a scandal for which the priest reprimanded him. While Domingo was away on a business trip to Andalucia, Antonia increasingly confided to her sister's husband, the cacique, who was a ruthless man and respected, but the two brothers-in-law did not get along well. When Domingo returned to Canales, he was even more furious with his wife, with fatal consequences.[69]

Anger-related wife murders resembled male-on-male killing in several ways. They could be termed accidents, as in eighteenth-century London.[70] Between the attack and the victim's death, they often involved an episode in which the husband offered his apology and the wife forgave him, as in an incident in the village of Rosenfeld in Württemberg. One morning, Hans Jakob Schlagenhausen ordered his maid to spray dung on the meadow. His wife, whose name we do not learn, protested: this was the time when the maid did the spinning. Her husband insisted: the weather was good and the job would not take long, so their servant could spin afterwards. The wife became infuriated and, after an exchange of verbal abuse, she exclaimed: "You want to be the master, but you drink up all our income." He proceeded to slap her, but a neighbor prevented him, and further scolding followed. "For God's sake, shut up!" Hans cried, threatening her with her own distaff. She retorted: "I wish that the dung would stick into your shirt and I was the only one who could get it out." Then Hans beat her heavily with the distaff and she fell down. The final scene took place when she lay in bed, half dizzy. "God, have pity on us; don't let her die," he said, and she to him: "I forgive you a thousand times." At her autopsy, it turned out that she had been seven months pregnant.[71]

Murder trials of wives were influenced to a greater extent by cultural stereotypes than those of husbands. As Laura Gowing comments, violence carried out by wives was laughed about so much, in literature, on stage, and in reality, that it had to be fatal in order to be taken seriously.[72] English law defined husband-killing as petty treason, perfectly in line with the parallel between political rule and family rule. Officially, it carried the penalty of being burnt to death, whereas wife-killing led to hanging. Petty treason also included cases in which servants killed their masters or ecclesiastics their prelates.[73] Hierarchical perspectives equally prevailed on the Continent. As Nolde explains, contemporaries had a dichotomous view of marital power, thinking solely in terms of the dominators and the dominated, with little room for anything in between. Hence, every attempt by a wife to alter the circumstances of her subjection was understood as a challenge to the husband's authority. It turned the world "upside down." Such views loomed large in the perception of magistrates and influenced the outcome of trials for spousal homicide. For their part, moralists warned against unequal partnerships. They advised men against marrying a richer woman, for example, because she might refuse to accept her husband's authority and murder could be the result.[74] The actual reality was more complex. In an overview of Europe, Olwen Hufton lists as motives for husband murder: repossessing the dowry and having financial assets as a widow, often with an eye on remarriage with a partner of her own choice, and, alternatively, revenge for the man's adultery or violence.[75]

Magistrates of the Paris Parlement in around 1600 considered a woman's rebellion primarily in relation to her own adultery. They routinely suspected the woman of having an affair and, consequently, always inquired about it. Whether this was true or not, a much larger share of female than of male defendants had acted with an accomplice. Partly, this reflected the reality of the situations, but in addition these statistics amounted to a judicial artefact. The magistrates always questioned female defendants about male accomplices, whether they were lovers or not, whereas, in the case of a male defendant, they did not particularly insist on this point. Sometimes the helper's role underwent a complete turn-around during the trial. At her first interrogation, the magistrates accused Felizon Bourgoing of "killing him," then suggested that "she and her son-in-law had killed her husband," and, on the third occasion, that "her son-in-law had beaten him to death in her presence."[76] Conversely, when a soldier shot the master of the house in which he was quartered, the testimony of the perpetrator's comrade served to implicate the wife, Perrette Trillet. The two soldiers shared a room and the witness had seen Perrette joining his comrade in bed and taking his member in her hand.[77]

In seventeenth-century England, too, wives often received assistance from men as accomplices or main perpetrators. Popular opinion always assumed that the helper was her lover, because no one, it was thought, would commit murder out of mere friendship. An extramarital affair also served as the most frequent motive for husband-killing in the pamphlet literature.[78] The situation was no different in Germany. Many murders of husbands involved an affair in which the male lover provided assistance, as an accomplice or by committing the act himself. In most cases, the lover was a servant in the house, which made that of Johann Hunn's wife excep-tional. Johann was much older and his wife fell in love with the young son of the town secretary. Witnesses told colorful tales of the secretary's son sucking the milk from her breasts. Once, for the sake of a bet, he had drunk her "chamber water." The old man's wealth meant that divorce was out of the question.[79] The frequency with which female adultery in cases of husband murder appears in the historical literature makes it hard to believe that only cultural stereotypes were at work.

Some wives, on the other hand, commissioned their husband's murder for money or otherwise. On October 29, 1728, the body of Jean Boiveau, a rural gentleman from Burgundy, was found along the road between Toulon-sur-Arroux and Rozier. The people who discovered the corpse immediately saw that he had been shot, probably with two bullets in the back. The next day, the curé of Rozier reported the case to the authori-ties. Although Boiveau and his wife belonged to the lower aristocracy, the couple had been friendly with a number of their social inferiors. Two local men were soon arrested, while a few other suspects fled. It turned out that Magdelaine Boiveau had been unhappy for a long time. Her mother had arranged for her marriage, and Magdelaine hated her husband. Witnesses at her trial declared that she had expressed the wish that her husband would drown, saying that she would gladly pay for his funeral 10 times over. Jean suspected his wife of an affair with one of their friends, Barthélémy Bérard, and refused to let him into his house any more. Threats and actual violence escalated, with Jean beating Magdelaine and her threatening him, asking by which method he wanted to die. Not waiting for the answer, she mixed a brown drug through the dough of the bread she baked for him, but he only got sick. Two other attempts failed as well. Then she asked help from several men, among them Barthélémy. It remains unknown who actually fired the shots, because there were no witnesses and we, as modern observers, cannot trust the confessions made under torture. Magdelaine and the two men caught were executed, the other conspirators were sentenced by default. Whether or not the fugitive Barthélémy was her lover remains undetermined.[80]

The motif of a male lover eliminating his rival with the complicity, or at the instigation, of his wife clearly pre-dated the rise of romanticism, but this cultural movement gave the crime a sentimental twist. We first observe it in an Amsterdam case at the turn of the eighteenth century. At the time of the murder, Hiddo Grittinga, a master surgeon, was 44 years old and his lover, Helena Knoop, was 25. Hiddo had married Amarentia Nolting at a young age; she had borne him seven children, two of whom were still alive at the time of Hiddo's trial. Helena moved into their home, as a servant or a lodger, in the mid-1690s. After her marriage to Gerrit Avares, a ship's clerk, she remained friends with the couple she had worked for, who frequently came by for a cup of coffee. She enjoyed their company, because her husband was at sea most of the time. He was away for a whole year in 1698, when Helena got pregnant, which suggests that Hiddo also visited her alone. The records do not disclose whether this affair had already started before Helena's marriage. When Amarentia suddenly died in December 1698, rumor had it that she had been sick for two weeks after drinking wine with Helena. During Helena's trial, the court briefly interrogated her about the poison charge, but dropped it, apparently finding it doubtful. In February 1699, Helena gave birth to a daughter. Mother and father had the child baptized under a false name, but it died after seven months. In the meantime, Gerrit had returned home. What did he say about the child? Or were the parents able to hide it from him?

The stage was set for a dramatic finale. Now that Hiddo's wife had died, Helena's husband must die, too. There was no other choice. Then the lovers could marry each other and be happy for the rest of their lives. It was a premeditated murder. On the night of April 17, 1699, Helena told Gerrit that an acquaintance had asked to see him. When he stood in the door, she kissed him goodbye. She knew that Hiddo was hiding along the route with a knife, which he had threatened to plunge into his own chest if Helena refused to cooperate. But she did. From his ambush, Hiddo took Gerrit by surprise and stabbed him in the back. With no suspicion falling on them yet, the killer and his accomplice went to the victim's funeral. Helena and Hiddo then moved to The Hague, where they published their marriage banns in November. They did not marry until a year and a half later, when Helena was pregnant again. Another year later, the couple was arrested and handed over to the Amsterdam court. She broke down first and urged Hiddo to confess too. He did, but at first he wanted the court to believe that it had been a conflict over money, in which there had been a challenge and each of them had fought with a knife. At the rack, he confessed to premeditation, admitting that the victim was unarmed. The crime resounded in popular literature. The author of a pamphlet, published shortly after the couple's execution, took it for a fact that Helena had poisoned Hiddo's first wife. The pamphlet gloomily describes the Judas kiss she gave her husband going off to meet a violent death, and supposes a parallel on the scaffold. When the executioner led Hiddo to the cross on which he was to be broken, they passed the garrotte at which Helena had just been strangled. Hiddo asked permission to give her one last kiss, which the directing magistrate refused.[81]

Romanticism also affected marital conflict when adultery was not involved. The new ideal that husband and wife spend much of their time together gave rise to tension-related spouse murders, but not many typical examples were witnessed in the eighteenth century. Next to spouses and lovers, the intimate category includes the parent–child and sibling relationships. Before modern times, the reported murders of brothers or sisters are too few for us discern any patterns. The parental right of castigation was unchallenged well into the twentieth century, but excesses rarely led to a criminal trial. No doubt, cases were covered up as natural deaths. Most parents who recorded having killed their own young or adolescent children did so in a context of mental disturbance or extreme despair about poverty. They belong more properly to the next chapter.

A View Toward the Present

The female share in preindustrial murder, as perpetrators and victims, continued to be modest. Women more often killed someone close to them than they did a mere acquaintance or stranger. Female honor played a role in almost every incident in which a woman was involved. In cases of intimate victimization, however, emotions were an equally prominent ingredient. Subtle changes regarding the family and marriage influenced the character of male-on-female as well as female-on-male violence. The spiritualization of female honor affected female-on-female violence, to the extent that it deprived women of the few acceptable methods for aggressively defending their reputation.

The proportion of female killers in total homicide figures remains low to the present day. Murders within an intimate relationship, on the other hand, are highly characteristic of modern fatal violence. Today, they usually belong to the tension-related category. Excesses from aggressive husbands have not died out, but anything like a socially accepted right of punishment by the master of the house has disappeared. All physical aggression against one's partner, on occasion also against a male partner, is now defined as domestic violence and is actively combated. The right of chastisement by school teachers and other authority figures has been abolished, and that of parents severely limited. Hierarchy and economic cooperation have ceased to be constitutive elements of family life. In modern Europe, the ties between partners living together and the bonds between parents and children are largely of a psychological nature. At times, they give rise to peculiar problems, to which the modern frequency of divorce has contributed. Tension-related killings of intimates, which gradually emerged during the eighteenth century, have grown considerably in importance since then.

5

Marks of Innocence: Babies and the Insane

Upon entering the courtroom, Effie Deans "shaded back from her face her luxuriant locks, and showed to the whole court . . . a countenance, which, though pale and emaciated, was so lovely amid its agony, that it called forth a universal murmur of compassion and sympathy." Within a moment, the counsel for the crown had regained his composure and explained her legal situation: "According to the stern, but necessary severity of this statute, she who should conceal her pregnancy, who should omit to call that assistance which is most necessary on such occasions, was held already to have meditated the death of her offspring. . . . If, under such circumstances, she could not alternatively show by proof that the infant had died a natural death, or produce it still in life, she must, under the construction of the law, be held to have murdered it, and suffer death accordingly." Unable to prove her innocence, Effie received a capital sentence. In anticipation of her execution, she went back to jail, which the citizens of Edinburgh called the Heart of Mid-Lothian. But then her sister Jeanie undertook the long and difficult journey from Scotland to London. At the recommendation of the Duke of Argyle, she procured a royal pardon for Effie. It saved the condemned from the gallows. Effie moved to London in her turn, married an aristocrat, and became a popular lady in court circles.

These fictionalized events are situated in the 1730s. In 1817, the Edinburgh authorities ordered the demolition of the city's old jail. This inspired Sir Walter Scott (1771–1832) to write *The Heart of Mid-Lothian*, which was published the following year. The novelist's sympathetic depiction of Effie is characteristic for the romanticism of his days. Many people laid the blame on the man who had seduced an unmarried woman. Scott believed a true mother incapable of killing her baby and suggested that a vagabond had done it instead. He vehemently denounced the law which

Figure 5.1: The Heart of Mid-Lothian, Edinburgh, marking the location of the old jail. Reproduced with permission. © Ruth Corrigan

put a presumption of guilt on the woman who had given birth out of wedlock. But the novel's true heroine is the sister, Jeanie. In the preface of the 1830 edition, the author explained that her real name was Helen Walker and the next year he wrote an epitaph that was inscribed on her tombstone.[1]

Babies, although born with original sin, according to theologians, were innocent. This chapter unites murder's youngest victims with a group of innocent killers. Throughout history, some homicides have been considered as falling outside the realm of moral responsibility, because the perpetrator had acted out of sheer madness. Such a killer, innocent but dangerous, was usually committed to an institution. Thus, the theme of innocence connects disturbed killing with infanticide. The association is more than just one of convenience. After a long historical process, mothers who killed their newborn babies were eventually defined as disturbed too. Supposedly, they suffered from puerperal insanity or, as it is now known more generally, from postnatal depression. Moreover, neither type of murder discussed in the following pages stems from everyday aggressive tendencies. They do reflect socio-cultural change. For killings as a result of madness, no reliable statistics exist before recent times. The history of such killings is part of the overall history of attitudes to insanity. Infanticide is associated primarily with attitudes to extramarital sex. For this crime, a few statistics are available. Its incidence peaked when the disadvantages attached to having an illegitimate child were highest and at places with the greatest risk of bastards being born.

Throwaway Babies

The title of this section sounds cynical perhaps, but it conveys the essence of the crime. After killing her offspring, the mother had to dispose of it in order to save her own life. No DNA-tests existed then. When the body was discovered at some distance from her home, few clues pointed at the perpetrator. For the killing of a baby, "infanticide" is the common expression. Some historians prefer "neonaticide" or "newborn child murder," which have equivalents in other European languages as well. The second term has the advantage of conforming to early modern usage, but it is tediously long. Hoffer and Hull, on the other hand, make use of the word "infanticide" but extend its meaning too far. They include in this category all murders of children up to the age of 9, even by non-parents. Other scholars understand infanticide to be the killing of a baby, at birth or shortly after, by the mother, or at least with her active complicity.[2] The word is used in this sense here.

James Cockburn is the only historian to argue that infanticide should be ranked with cases of intimate victimization.[3] Such a procedure would cause the proportion of intimate murder victims in the seventeenth century to approach the modern one and the eighteenth-century proportion would probably exceed that of today. But the intimacy of an unwanted pregnancy is quite different from that of a personal relationship. Moreover, inclusion of infanticide cases, however categorized, into the homicide rate would alter the long-term graph, with considerable differences for the seventeenth and eighteenth centuries; the early modern decrease in murder would become less pronounced, with a new decline setting in at some point after 1800. There is no need to do this. When someone slays a newborn child, it is a victim, not an opponent. In most murders of adults, by contrast, the victim is also an opponent. Therefore, many scholars, including this author, prefer the calculation of entirely separate rates for infanticide and homicide (the latter defined as the killing of persons older than a few days).[4]

One more reason for the construction of such separate rates lies in the scarcity of reliable statistics for infanticide. Before the seventeenth century, few magistrates found it necessary to have corpses of babies inspected. Moreover, for a married couple of one mind, the crime is relatively easy to cover up. Any estimate of the incidence of infanticide must begin with assessing the likelihood of its occurrence within marriage. A child's handicap, the parents' poverty, or preference for a son constituted possible motives. Nevertheless, most historians believe that infanticide within marriage was as uncommon in the Middle Ages as it was in the early modern period. In medieval England, this crime was handled by the Church courts, which considered it to be a sin that required penance. The clerical judges at Canterbury, for example, ordered Joan Rose in 1470 to "go before the procession in the parish church of Hythe on three Sundays with a wax candle of half a pound in her right hand and the knife with which she killed the boy in her left." She was to repeat this act of penance at the markets of Canterbury and two nearby villages.[5]

The Reformation and Counter-Reformation brought an increased condemnation of extramarital sex. Whereas the sexuality of married couples was ideologically upgraded from a necessary evil to a means of showing affection, moralists associated sex on all other occasions with abhorrence.[6] They rejected the traditional double standard, warning men that their adultery was as sinful as that of women. Consistories and ecclesiastical courts even started to reprimand couples who had a baby less than nine months after the wedding. Such prenuptial pregnancies, as demographers call them, had been less of a concern before. In the popular mind they were perfectly compatible with honor, and this view continued to be prevalent for some time. For many people, the making of a marriage constituted a series of events, in which it did not matter much whether intercourse or the ceremony in church came first. But it did matter to the clergy, whose views gradually prevailed. Moreover, the increasing emphasis on decency affected the less decent too. Employers and masters sought to control the sexuality of their apprentices and servants. A female servant who got pregnant faced immediate dismissal. Thus, ancient notions of honor and the intensified religious and moral campaign against extramarital sex reinforced each other. Welfare legislation had an influence as well, notably in England. The 1576 Poor Law was meant to prevent bastard children from becoming a financial burden on their parishes. This often induced the man who had made a poor girl pregnant to flee.[7]

These developments significantly lowered the threshold when it came to infanticide. Although the state of preservation of medieval records leaves a degree of uncertainty, all indications point to an increase in the incidence of this crime from the mid-sixteenth century onward. Prosecutions in England started to rise during Elizabeth I's reign.[8] Trials in Germany, too, became more frequent after the mid-sixteenth century. Of course, infanticide was never an automatic response to pregnancy outside marriage. The overwhelming majority of single mothers kept and raised their children. Since we have no records on this majority other than some brief notes in baptism registers, it is difficult to compare the emotional and social situation of the women whose decision or impulse was to kill the child with those who kept it. We only know that the stakes were highest between the middle of the sixteenth century and the beginning of the nineteenth. Prosecution rates, however, reflect the concerns of the authorities as much as the incidence of the crime. Registers referring to all murdered infants found constitute the best source; that is, if we can be confident that most throwaway babies were in fact discovered.

Evidence about the disposal and discovery of murdered infants comes from various countries. Dead babies in Amsterdam were almost invariably found floating in one of the city's canals, which could mean that they had arrived there by way of a toilet. Delivery and disposal in a privy have also been recorded in Germany and England. English mothers sometimes burned their baby's corpse in the fire or in hot ashes, but rivers and wells were more common, as well as burial in a dunghill. For the eighteenth century, trunks, pails, haystacks, stairwells, vaults, and coalbins are mentioned too. Some historians believe that the ignominy of many places of disposal indicates that the mothers considered their offspring likewise, but the smell of a privy or dunghill was instrumental in helping to conceal that of the decomposing corpse.[9] It can be concluded that some form of semi-covert disposal of the body was common, but that many were easily discovered. A counter-example of a chance discovery after a long concealment dates from 1721, after a fire had ravaged the French town of Rennes. The rebuilding project required the opening up of drains, in which the workers found the skeletons of some 80 infants who, by all appearances, had been killed in the first hours of life.[10] The fact that this is the only spectacular discovery on record, repeated over and over again in the historical literature, suggests that normally the dark number of undiscovered infant corpses was not that high.

Extant registers referring to the discovery of dead babies regardless of information about the mother are few. A particularly long series, running from 1484 to 1803, is available for the city of Nuremberg. The rate per 100,000 inhabitants has to be calculated from a graph with absolute totals over 10-year periods provided by Richard van Dülmen. Until 1524, the infanticide rate stood between 0.6 and 1. It fluctuated between 2 and 3 during the next 50 years and climbed to around 4 between 1574 and 1624. Then the infanticide rate fluctuated heavily, until it reached a peak of no fewer than 6 in the decades around 1700. It stood between 1 and 3 during most of the eighteenth century and climbed again to 4.5 at the end of the register's period.[11] Figures for Stockholm cover an even longer term, but they contain large gaps. Its infanticide rate stood at 1.5 in both the sixteenth and the eighteenth centuries. Whereas this represented a tiny fraction of all killings in the former period, in the latter it amounted to two-thirds of the non-infant homicide rate. Stockholm's infanticide rate was insignificant in the twentieth century.[12] The available Amsterdam rates begin with a mere 0.3 in the 1670s, but by then the inspection committee was probably not investigating dead babies on a routine basis. Infanticide rates increased to 1.2 and 1.9 in the 1690s through 1720s and reached peaks of 2.8 and 3.3 in the 1750s through 1770s. Then they declined again to 0.5 (1784–99) and 0.6 (1800–16).[13]

Whereas the Stockholm infanticide rate, aggregated per century, never rose above the city's regular homicide rate, in Amsterdam this did happen during the years 1752–83. Coroner's records for the English Palatinate of Chester show the number of infanticides, without population estimates being taken into account, to be equal to that of homicides in the 1690s and 1700s.[14] No homicide rates are available for Nuremberg. These few reliable figures suggest that infanticide was much more widespread than prosecution figures indicate and that its incidence did not follow the homicide trend. To draw more conclusions would amount to speculation. Yet the Amsterdam evidence contains one more crucial piece of information. In almost every case, the inspection report reveals the baby's sex. Of the corpses which, according to the conclusions of the committee, had not been stillborn, 51.6 percent were boys and 48.4 percent girls; of all infant corpses found, the figures were 51.4 percent and 48.6 percent respectively. In Geneva, girls were slightly overrepresented among cases of certain infanticide and boys among all cases of questionable infant death.[15] Thus, the baby's sex rarely was a factor in the decision to kill it. This observation is consistent with the hypothesis that almost all these babies were the fruit of illegitimate relations and the claim that fear of the consequences rather than the victim's characteristics played the primary role in the process of killing and disposal.

Yet the consequences for the mother could be worse when the discovery was linked to a suspect. Throughout Europe, relatively modest prosecution rates were coupled with harsh penalties. German courts sometimes had the executioner tear pieces of flesh from the culprit's body with hot pincers, before putting her to death.[16] A defendant might get away with it, on the other hand, because of the difficulty of distinguishing stillbirth from murder. The lung test was the principal method available. A physician cut the lungs out of the child's body and laid them in water. If they swam, they were supposed to contain air, which counted as evidence of a live birth. In England, the lung test was not introduced until 1720 and in the north not until the 1760s. The validity of the test results remained subject to controversy. By the mid-eighteenth century, German and Dutch physicians were beginning to express doubt. The lung test was common in Germany from the late seventeenth century onward; until then, midwives or physicians had merely examined the dead baby for outward signs. The Amsterdam inspection committee routinely applied the lung test until the early nineteenth century.[17]

The problem of proving murder, coupled with an anxiety about extramarital sex, led to special laws in several countries. France was first. Henry II's law of 1556 obliged every pregnant single woman to register at a local office, where a magistrate should question her about how long she had been in this condition, who had caused it, and where the act had occurred. The principal aim was to discover the identity of the father, in order to force him to marry the woman. Failure to register carried a relatively light penalty, but if the illegitimate child was apparently stillborn or died within a short time, this raised the suspicion of murder. Courts began to entertain a presumption of guilt in such cases. The judges found it unnecessary to inquire whether the child had been stillborn. If the mother had concealed her pregnancy and the baby was dead, this counted as proof that she had killed it. That interpretation was codified in its turn. Any woman who had "been silent about, concealed and made secret her pregnancy and confinement, without having provided sufficient testimony to the one or the other, will be taken to have slain her child and, as a satisfaction, will be punished by death." All priests were required to read this law aloud to their parish every three months before mass.[18] Protestant England followed Catholic France after some delay. The issue was debated in Parliament from the beginning of the seventeenth century, finally resulting in the Act to Prevent the Destroying and Murthering of Bastard Children of 1624.[19] Technically, the presumption of guilt applied to hiding the baby's death, not the pregnancy, but for a successful cover-up, it was as well to conceal the pregnancy too.

Note that, in both countries, the presumption of guilt upon concealment applied to unmarried mothers only. The legislators reserved their moral indignation for any woman who sealed her lack of chastity with murder. By implication, they viewed the father's unchaste behavior with less severity, in conformity with the double standard. A modern commentator might argue that, in order to combat infanticide, it would be useful to try to diminish the social rejection of illegitimacy and make facilities for single mothers, but that was not the way seventeenth-century politicians and moralists thought. For them, evil bred evil. Extramarital sex was a sin as well as an offense, and it could induce the offender to commit an even worse crime. Both had to be combated rigorously. Women whose pregnancy was the result of sinful and impure lust were supposed to lack the maternal instinct that automatically induced all other mothers to overrule their doubts and accept and nurture the child.

Laws meant to counter the claim of stillbirth were enacted in other countries as well. In Denmark and Norway, then united, giving birth in secret was made a capital offense in 1635.[20] The Scottish Parliament acted 17 years before its dissolution: a 1690 law presumed infanticide even in cases where a single woman's child was just missing.[21] This was the law that Walter Scott denounced. Legislation in some other countries was less explicit on the issue, but concealment of birth often served as an indication that justified judicial torture. Dutch courts, on the other hand, clearly distinguished between the proven killing of a child and concealment of birth. If a woman had refrained from calling a midwife, giving birth alone, and the child had died, the mother was publicly whipped for failing to take the necessary precautions. Courts designated this offense as death through neglect, not infanticide.[22] That practice kept the number of executions of mothers low throughout the early modern period. In 1788, a 24-year-old domestic servant confessed that she had deliberately suffocated her baby with a cloth. The clerk filing the child's autopsy report noted that the mother was the first to be executed for infanticide during his 36 years of office.[23] These years coincided with the highest peak in the actual incidence of the offense.

For all of Europe, information about the people, social circumstances, and judicial handling of the mothers who killed their babies can be obtained from trial records only. Most of the research so far pertains to England and Germany. The overwhelming majority of infanticide defendants were single women, more often than not servants and workers who had not yet married rather than widows. A few were married but lived separately from their husbands. Most defendants who made up the minority of men and married women were charged as accessories to the murder of a bastard. Some bias is involved here, because law and public opinion targeted single mothers, but it is unlikely that these figures are entirely an artefact. Most historians believe that few married parents actively killed their babies, as opposed to the grey zone of more or less conscious neglect.

Almost all these single women belonged to the lower classes, which limited their range of occupations. Domestic servants and farm workers predominated. Understandably, the first were especially numerous in the larger towns and the second in rural areas. Women accused of infanticide in northern England performed jobs such as spinning, picking crops, guarding and caring for animals, and making cheese and other dairy products.[24] Trials in Amsterdam, by contrast, involved domestic servants almost without exception.[25] That is no surprise for this city, but elsewhere they appear to have been overrepresented. In Prussia, 70 percent of infanticide defendants were domestic servants, whereas about 50 percent of all single women between the ages of 20 and 30 worked in this occupation.

Kerstin Michalik believes that domestic servants engaged in sexual activities more often than other young women, both voluntarily and because they were forced to give in to their masters' wishes. Of all known fathers in Prussia, 30–40 percent occupied a social position higher than that of the mother.[26] Olwen Hufton, on the other hand, emphasizes the disadvantages for domestic servants in comparison with a third group, that of female cloth workers employed under a putting-out system. Whereas the former faced instant dismissal when pregnant, the latter often were able to continue working with a child.[27] Yet in the South of France, there were many cloth workers among the perpetrators.[28]

In regions of the Empire where there were frequent military operations, still another group stands out. During the Thirty Years War, in particular, many women tried for infanticide had conceived from soldiers, who had either raped them or talked them into intercourse with a promise of marriage. In the second case, too, the fathers quickly disappeared and the women invariably came to be called soldiers' whores.[29] In all parts of Germany, women performing household tasks or doing farm work predominated among infanticide defendants. Most of them were in their 20s, at an age at which other women would get married. The fathers, when mentioned, unlike the situation in Prussia, overwhelmingly came from the same social class. In rural areas they belonged to the bottom stratum of agricultural workers and in towns they were journeymen or male servants.[30] A study of Scotland, 1661–1821, comes up with similar results. The defendants were young single women, mostly farmers' daughters and agricultural servants. Sometimes they received assistance from their mothers and occasionally from the child's father. Deborah Symonds's conclusion is the opposite of Michalik's for Prussia: the extant evidence about the fathers suggests that situations of exploitation, rape, or prostitution were rare. Even if the father was the woman's master, he wasn't usually particularly wealthy.[31]

Magistrates and neighbors often were of one mind in their wish to detect cases of actual or intended infanticide. Evidence from the English Northern Circuit, investigated independently by two historians, provides an excellent illustration.[32] Everything began with forcing a single woman to admit that she was pregnant. Women who were rumored to have concealed their pregnancy and killed their baby on an earlier occasion were especially suspect, but suspicion also fell on alleged first offenders. Female neighbors called in midwives or conducted investigations themselves, sometimes against the will of the woman they were targeting. One winter, around New Year, four women of Isabel Barton's village visited her at her mother's house, demanding to see her breasts. She refused to show them, saying it was none of their business. Then she agreed to show one, but barely revealed it, so that the women remained unsatisfied. One, noting that her nipples were black and purple, demanded to be allowed to pull them. Isabel showed her full breast very quickly, but allowed no one to touch her. The next day she was gone, and when she returned after two months, she admitted to having had a miscarriage on the day prior to the visit. When questioned further, she explained that around midsummer, when she was coming from Scarborough market, a man had pulled her off her horse and raped her. She had miscarried, but the fetus had had no shape.[33] Older spinsters and widows felt more self-confident, often refusing to allow such searches altogether. Other women invented a variety of diseases to explain their swollen bellies.

In the eighteenth century, overseers of the poor often induced single women suspected of pregnancy to comply with the searches of female neighbors and to answer their questions. This was in violation of a 1733 law that denied even justices of the peace the right to force women to answer such questions until a month after the alleged delivery. The swollen belly continued to be the surest sign. In 1744, Jane Barnes of Cumberland visited the apothecary Henry Hall twice, complaining about a violent cough and pains in her breast and stomach. Henry questioned her suspiciously, asking her in particular whether she had her period at the regular time. She replied affirmatively. Later she was tried nevertheless on suspicion of having concealed the birth of a baby. Henry testified that he had never seen Jane without her cloak.[34] Other women wore hoop petticoats or wide dresses in order to hide their condition. Toward the end of the eighteenth century, the role of male medical practitioners in detecting pregnancies became more pronounced.

Neighbors and local officials also cooperated in other parts of Europe. French women were accustomed to accusing outright another woman and to challenging her to show that her breasts contained no milk. Sometimes they called upon the local priest, who would summon a midwife to check the suspect.[35] In a village near Geneva, several women rudely attacked a single woman, touching her breasts to see if they contained milk.[36] In Württemberg, neighbors and sometimes even relatives denounced women to the authorities. When Dorothea Mengler was working in the field with some others, she began to feel contractions. She absented herself, intending to return quickly, but she remained in labor longer than expected, so that the others went looking for her. They found her beside a small river and noticed a patch of blood-stained grass there. Soon they discovered her dead baby. They took her to the village, where four men guarded her until constables from the nearby town came to pick her up.[37]

Despite such efforts, there is also evidence of assistance being given to help these pregnant women conceal their condition. In Cheshire, several women drew on support networks of relatives and friends. These provided assistance with childbirth and helped to conceal the dead baby.

In 1656, John, Richard, and Elizabeth Hancocke helped Amy Hancocke deliver a baby in secret, which they then buried in John's house. Elizabeth Fisbie shared a house in Aldford with at least one family. In July 1732, when she was about to give birth, she asked a co-tenant, a laborer's wife, to call for her brother and sister who lived a few blocks away. Family solidarity often overruled feelings of horror at the crime of infanticide. Although this evidence is mentioned in passing in court records, Dickinson and Sharpe assume that baby killers who could draw on assistance networks often managed to conceal both the birth and the corpse successfully. Consequently, the mothers who were caught and prosecuted were disproportionately drawn from groups unable to marshal such support.[38] Similar cases of help by family and friends were reported from German cities and the Dutch province of Friesland. Agnes Schönen, a resident of Frankfurt, got pregnant from a married soldier. Her sister and the soldier's wife tried at first to induce an abortion, using special drinks, bathing, and blood-letting, but to no avail. Then Agnes's sister recommended killing the baby and helped her to accomplish this. Afterwards, the soldier's wife smuggled the body out of their house and hid it.[39]

Notably, German historians have drawn attention to the strategies that women employed to escape conviction when caught. In the sixteenth and seventeenth centuries, during the height of the witch craze, many defendants claimed that Satan had whispered in their ears, which was of little help.[40] In the eighteenth century, they came up with more elaborate strategies of defense. On the discovery of a baby's corpse, the suspect was provisionally detained at her home, which usually meant the household where she served. At that point, she requested to speak with her mother, which her employer often granted, even though the judges became suspicious when they found out about it. Usually, there is no record of the two women's discussions, but presumably they made plans for the defense. One defendant admitted that her mother had told her about a maid in Lübeck who had gotten away with murder by denying everything. Most often, they settled for the claim of stillbirth. The defendant substantiated this with the argument that she had never noticed the child move in the womb – or at least not during the last few weeks. Others claimed a serious fever, which must have caused the fetus to die. When the corpse showed signs of head injury, the woman stated that she had been obliged to give birth while standing or sitting on the fireplace, which had caused the baby to drop on its head and die accidentally. Ten percent of the defendants had entirely repressed their memory of the pregnancy and delivery, but when confronted with the facts, this was hardly an effective strategy. In most cases, the mothers appear not to have considered their deed as an act of violence. For them, it was an offense far less serious than murder.[41]

Research all over Europe shows that murdered babies had usually been suffocated or strangled and marks of serious violence were uncommon. There were exceptions. Occasionally, we hear that the baby's throat had been slit. In northern England a few infants were found with their mouths bound, their heads covered, with wounds on their throats or chests and one with the tongue cut out.[42] Swine were rooting up the ground near the house of Mary Stockton, a Cheshire woman. The animals dug up something that looked like a baby, with two feet and a round head, showing serious wounds. Mary eventually admitted to her pregnancy and delivery, saying that she had not made clothes because she thought it was eight weeks before her expected time and, moreover, she had not noticed the baby stirring in the womb for quite a wile. The swine, she added, must have caused its wounds. Mary received a death sentence.[43]

Together, the available evidence confirms the strong link between infanticide and illegitimate birth. Demographic and cultural historians have established that bastardy in early modern Europe resulted, in the large majority of cases, from courtships gone wrong. Prenuptial pregnancies, sometimes amounting to a third of all first births within marriage, were much more common than illegitimate births. According to the popular norm, it was acceptable if a young man and a young woman had intercourse, as long as they themselves, their families, and the neighbors could entertain a reasonable expectation that they would eventually marry. If their relationship went awry and the woman did not get pregnant, she retained her honor for as long as the man remained single. If he announced his plan to marry someone else, the rejected fiancée often sued him in order to force him to keep to his original promise. If a courtship went wrong and the woman was pregnant, she certainly risked losing her honor. In its turn, a woman was more likely to decide to bring up a bastard child than to commit infanticide. Despite honor's crucial role in most murder cases, the evidence suggests that poverty was the decisive factor in tilting the balance from raising a baby to killing it. The threat of instant dismissal explains the overrepresentation of domestic servants among the perpetrators. Whereas moralists and authorities considered infanticide an extremely sinful crime, the mothers themselves may have justified the act with the thought that a non-baptized baby was not yet fully human.

Insane Killers

A mad dog is dangerous and unpredictable: it bites people indiscriminately, even its own master and his children, making it unreliable against thieves too. By contrast, a good dog comforts its owners and attacks all intruders. Anyone bitten by a mad dog will become mad himself, but some people exhibit similar symptoms without being bitten. The parallel was obvious to Europeans of the past. In several languages, the (original) words for animal rabies and human aggressive insanity are the same. Scholars have examined the history of insanity from various angles, but here it is relevant only to the extent that it intersects with that of murder.

Preindustrial Europe knew two prototypes of insane conduct. One category involved people described as simple or innocent, who were unable or less capable of performing ordinary tasks. They need not concern us. The other prototype concerned dangerous madness, producing aggressive behavior that no one could understand. A sane man acted like a good dog. He attacked his enemies and protected and cherished his loved ones. Even if a husband killed his wife as a result of a punishment that got out of hand, there was method in it. Likewise, any homicide that followed a provocation, insult, or quarrel, although criminally punishable, could be comprehended. A man counted as insane if he killed a stranger, a neighbor, or, more often, an intimate without any apparent reason. A woman might act from madness too, for example if she killed not her less-than-human newborn baby, but the child she had been nurturing for a while. The insane murderer derives no discernible advantage, material or immaterial, from his or her deed. In such cases, whatever the standard of punishment at the time, it did not apply. In 1270, for example, the Norwich court determined that a man who had murdered his wife and children was insane and committed him to the local hospital. The first Dutch madhouses, established in the fifteenth century, were designated explicitly for inmates whose families had been obliged to keep them in chains.[44]

Whereas the insanity defense is a regular topic in legal history, few historians, of madness or murder, have systematically examined the circumstances of insane killing. Helga Schnabel-Schüle, who discusses a number of Württemberg cases, concludes that crimes committed within a context of religious sensibilities increased in frequency in the eighteenth century.[45] Nevertheless, the religious controversies and the proliferation of sects in the sixteenth and seventeenth centuries already confused some people's minds. Martín López de Séneca, a Burgos shoemaker, was a devout Catholic. One morning in March 1643, he was praying, not yet fully clothed, in front of a picture of the Holy Virgin that hung in his bedroom. To his wife, he announced his intention to attend a religious service in the convent of Nuestra Señora de la Victoria just outside the city walls, but he wished to have breakfast first. She brought him the pastry that his sister had made for him the other day. He took a long knife, but instead of cutting the pastry he went to the apprentices' room, where Francisco de la Peña was still asleep. Martín's wife heard a grizzly scream and the next moment she saw Francisco drop dead. Martín was sentenced to death, but he claimed to have been possessed by evil spirits who had induced him to commit the act. After several conversations with him, two exorcists concluded that the devil was responsible for his crime. Eventually, the shoemaker received a royal pardon.[46]

The exorcists' conclusion suggests that religiously inspired murders of the sixteenth and seventeenth centuries were often evaluated within a religious context. Hence, the apparent increase in the incidence of such murders in the eighteenth century was probably due to the rise of a secular view that considered them more readily as symptoms of insanity. Most of the Württemberg cases, though, concerned trials in which law professors discussed the killer's sanity but eventually concluded toward criminal responsibility. Another shoemaker, 26 and deaf, always became very agitated by the priest's sermons, despite the fact that he could not hear them. When villagers explained to him in writing that his 33-year-old wife expected twins, he was convinced that another man had made her pregnant, since he had lost too much semen through youthful masturbation. He decided to murder her.[47]

From elsewhere in Germany, a variety of cases was reported in which the mental state of a killer was the subject of debate. A 24-year-old journeyman tanner had concluded from the Bible and some books by "fanatics" that all women were hellish snakes who had brought sin into the world and deserved to die. He acted on that conviction in 1724 by killing a woman unknown to him and splashing in her blood. After two years of expert debate, he was declared a melancholic. His opinions were ascribed to his dominant mother and manipulating mistresses, not to his contacts with various sects. In a similar case in 1731, the defendant, who had stabbed to death a heavily pregnant woman, was also declared melancholic. He stated that he became furious whenever he saw a woman, but also that he had acted because of disappointment in love. Toward the end of the eighteenth century, medical advice in trials of seemingly disturbed killers became increasingly common. Physicians exhaustively questioned two fathers who had slit the throats of their daughters, aged 9 years and 9 weeks respectively. In both cases the conclusion was melancholia again. Magistrates asked medical advice during the trial of a musketeer who had killed a little boy in the street, induced by voices in his head.[48]

Intimate victimization, mostly of young children, by a number of insane or disturbed killers can be traced in Amsterdam from the mid-seventeenth century onward. Some of the mothers were depressed because of poverty, which the judges refused to take as an excuse. The defendant's mental state was not taken into consideration until a trial in 1736. Sara Abiatar, a Jewish widow of 31, had a 3-year-old boy from her late husband, and a girl of 9 months. The girl, according to her statement, was the fruit of enforced sex with the son of the house in which she lived. When interrogated, Sara admitted right away that she had killed both children with a knife at 3.30 a.m. Asked about the reason for such a horrible act, she replied: because of poverty, sadness, and debts. A Jewish man living in a back room of the same house testified that someone had knocked on his door in the early morning, crying "Murder! murder!" He found one child bathed in blood on the floor and the other with its head hanging from the bedstead. Sara explained that she herself had warned the neighbor and that she had intended to turn herself in immediately, but it was too early. Her trial dossier contains two anonymous comments, presumably by members of the court. The first starts: "I like to admit that as soon as I saw the confession of this prisoner, I could only conclude that she was entirely robbed of her senses. Otherwise it is unthinkable that a mother can be so degenerate as to murder her two children in an inhuman way without any reason." Despite this conclusion, the commentator stated that all homicides, certainly those by a mother, should be punished by death. The other declared without further ado that the defendant's sanity had been amply demonstrated. Her excuses of poverty, sadness, and debts were insufficient for a remission from the death sentence.[49]

The next recorded case of disturbed intimate victimization took place in 1783, and this time the Amsterdam court acknowledged insanity. Maria Meijbeek, 45 years old, and her husband had five children altogether, four of whom died a natural death. Now 11-year-old Harmanus, deaf, dumb, and simple, was dead too. As external symptom, the medical examiners found just a scratch, but the boy's lungs were full of blood, which they considered the cause of death. The mother stated that this was best for him, even though, as her husband declared, she had always treated this one unfortunate child left to them very lovingly. But it turned out that three years earlier, following a petition from her husband, Maria had spent twelve months in the pesthouse, as insane. She appeared confused during her trial as well. They had threatened to harm her boy with sulphur, she said, and either she, her husband, or the Princess should kill him. She was a Catholic, but now she could die blessedly, without torture from the Pope. The judges concluded that Maria was out of her senses and committed her to the secret ward of the spinhouse for 50 years.[50] Despite this precedent, after the Batavian Revolution the newly appointed magistrates hailed a similar judgment of a man who had slashed the throats of his two daughters as an expression of the new spirit of progress.[51]

We can conclude that the readiness of courts to consider the mental state of murderers was on the increase toward the end of the Ancien Régime. In the Genevan Republic and England, too, insanity defenses and medical intervention in trials of mad murderers became more common during the course of the eighteenth century.[52] Nevertheless, England witnessed two notorious murders whose seemingly disturbed perpetrators were quickly executed. In both cases, the motive and state of mind of the killer have remained a matter of debate until today. In 1743, John Breads, a butcher and innkeeper from Rye in Sussex, stabbed to death Allen Grebell, a scion of one of the town's leading merchant families. Breads had meant to kill Grebell's brother-in-law, mayor James Lamb. The intended victim had been invited to a dinner, but, feeling unwell, he had asked his relative to go in his place, lending him the mayoral cloak. As Grebell passed through the churchyard on his way back, after a copious meal and much wine, he was taken by surprise. The perpetrator drew attention to himself the next day by parading through town, yelling "Butchers should kill lambs!" Breads hated the mayor, who had fined him a few years earlier, but according to many, the killer was raving mad. Whereas this incident was remembered at the local level only, in 1779, the murder of Martha Ray, mistress of the Earl of Sandwich, inspired writers all over the country well into the nineteenth century. In this case, public opinion wavered between an attribution to romanticism and madness. James Hackman, a young man who had just been ordained a minister of the Anglican Church, shot the victim, twice his age, on the steps of Covent Garden theater in London. The killer also shot himself, but he survived – that is, until his hanging two weeks later. It was certain that James and Martha knew each other. According to some, they had a secret affair, while others believed that he was insane, only imagining that she was his lover.[53]

Suicide: Indirect and Direct

Suicide comes next, first because this act became increasingly associated with insanity and, second, because of the intriguing possibility of indirect suicide. Some disturbed offenders were perfectly content with the prospect of dying on the scaffold. The application of capital punishment offered those who were tired of living an opportunity to arrange for a spectacular end. Under the inquisitorial procedure that prevailed on the Continent, a defendant might even invent an offense, although the authorities usually doubted such spontaneous confessions.[54] For the successful completion of indirect suicide it was much more effective actually to commit a capital crime. In the past, religious objections against direct suicide prompted some people with a death wish to kill someone else.

Indirect suicide for religious reasons was especially frequent in Sweden. From the late seventeenth century until the 1770s, Arne Jansson found 62 cases: 40 in which the murderer confirmed the suicidal motive, 13 probable cases, and 9 attempts. Almost all perpetrators were women. Margareta Höök, for example, had a daughter from a soldier she had been engaged to during her stay in Riga. He had died just before their wedding, whereupon she had returned to Stockholm. Her situation was precarious. After a few years she became acquainted with the constable Petter Barck. She hoped to marry him after testifying against his wife in an adultery trial. Under Protestant law, the constable was free to remarry once his wife had been convicted. Meanwhile, many of Margareta's neighbors considered her to be a whore. One night, when Petter brought her home, he was obliged to fight a duel with a man who thought he could solicit her sexual services. Alone again, Margareta felt very depressed, taking the knife that Petter had given her from her pocket. If she used it against herself or jumped into the water, she knew she would be damned. So, instead, she cut her daughter's throat with such force that she separated the head from the body. The case was untypical only to the extent that most perpetrators of suicidal murder slit the throat of someone else's child. They chose such a victim, not only because it offered least resistance, but also because they believed it to be free from sin and hence destined for heaven. That knowledge eased the killer's conscience at taking a second person with her to the other world.

Thus, murderers such as these didn't actually want to hurt anyone, but they had religious objections against direct suicide. Death by execution would save them from eternal damnation. To the modern observer, one conclusion is inescapable: this crime could have been prevented if it were not punishable by death. The Swedish authorities, however, tried to prevent it by introducing elaborate pre-execution tortures. Only in the nineteenth century did they substitute imprisonment for the death penalty.[55] In Schlesswig-Holstein, on the other hand, a 1767 law introduced life imprisonment for this crime.[56] The few similar cases known outside Sweden are confined to Denmark and northern Germany. One woman threw a boatman's child into the canal that encircled the town walls and turned herself in, declaring she wished to die. Before the deed, she had ordered festive clothes from a tailor for her execution.[57] Historians attribute the religious scruples against direct suicide to the strong Pietist movements in Northern Europe rather than to Lutheranism.[58]

Rates of recorded suicides in the strict sense underwent a massive increase in England and Germany during the sixteenth century. After a careful assessment of the evidence, Alexander Murray concludes that part of this rise was real. He considers the religious responsibilities conferred

upon lay people by the Reformation as the decisive factor.[59] The concomitant decline in homicide meant that the ratio of the one to the other
underwent a complete about-turn. Suicides began to outnumber homicides, in some places by the mid-seventeenth century, and elsewhere, such
as in Sweden, during the eighteenth. In eighteenth-century Geneva the
incidence of both suicide and homicide increased, but the former rose
more sharply. In the English town of Hull, suicide rates fluctuated
between 11 and 20 per 100,000 inhabitants during the years 1840–1900.
For the whole of the German Empire, they were practically stable at
around 20 between 1880 and 1910.[60] Men's suicide rates in France
increased from about 10 in 1835 to nearly 40 in 1900; for women, the
rate went from about 4 to about 10.[61] Studies comparing countries or
regions in the twentieth century often, but not always, find an inverse relationship between the incidence of homicide and that of suicide, but almost
everywhere the second is more common.[62]

Views of suicide started to change toward the end of the early modern
period. The demise of witch persecutions contributed to a lessening role
for the devil, even in religious thought, and Satan was no longer the great
instigator of self-murder. Everywhere, suicide ceased to be treated as a
crime during the course of the eighteenth century. Popular attitudes were
slower to change. Ordinary people in northern Germany, including survivors of a suicide attempt, continued to ascribe the act to the devil.[63] The
elites, on the other hand, considered suicide to be the ultimate consequence of melancholia or spleen, which counted as fashionable maladies.
Enlightened writers such as Montesquieu, Voltaire, and, posthumously,
David Hume gave a theoretical justification to the right of suicide, while
Goethe and Rousseau romanticized the act in their novels. While an artis-
tic tradition had always praised raped women who committed suicide in
order to avoid shame on them and their families, the spiritualization of
male honor made the act less reprehensible for men. It was understood
that, in some cases, a man decided to leave the world instead of literally
fighting back to save his honor.[64]

These developments never led to a complete social acceptance of
suicide. Ambivalence prevailed throughout the nineteenth century. In
1818, many Englishmen sympathized with Sir Samuel Romilly, who had
made great efforts to combat the country's "bloody code," but who cut
his own throat out of grief over the death of his beloved wife.[65] At
the same time, conservative German writers blamed Goethe and the
Enlightenment for causing suicide rates to increase. Yet, in the first half of
the nineteenth century the debate was less intense. The issue of a decent
burial for suicides had been settled everywhere, although their bodies
ended up disproportionately in anatomy rooms. At the end of the nineteenth century, Emile Durkheim dealt with suicide as a social fact, pushing

aside any moral judgment. Psychiatrists, on the other hand, continued to consider the act as pathological. Throughout the twentieth century, the appreciation of suicide was a major issue in the continuous debates between the representatives of various political and religious movements. The issue became linked, moreover, with that of euthanasia.[66]

Convergence of Infanticide and Madness

The laws that placed the burden of proving stillbirth after a secret delivery on the single mother were never rigorously enforced. Few English women suffered execution for concealment alone. Reluctance to enforce the statute led to its dissolution in practice from the 1720s. Courts started to employ the same standards as in murder trials, requiring proof that the mother had actually killed her baby and had intended to do so. Evidence of preparation for birth, such as collecting linen or making a bed, counted as decisive against such an intention. Doubts about the reliability of the lung test reinforced these new judicial attitudes.[67] Cultural change affected them too. Dana Rabin argues that the eighteenth-century culture of sensibility fostered a climate in which greater leniency toward infanticidal mothers could arise. Defendants and witnesses increasingly focused on the accused's emotional and mental state. A claim of temporary insanity replaced the traditional defense based on having made preparations to care for the baby. The women in question, while admitting the act, stated that they had been overwhelmed by emotion.[68]

After a failed attempt in the 1770s, the English law about concealment was formally repealed in 1803. Some other countries had acted earlier. In Sweden, Gustav III's "decree on infanticide" of 1778 explicitly allowed women to give birth anonymously and forbade magistrates to interrogate them about the father's name. France abolished the crime of concealment of birth at the beginning of the revolutionary period. The reform was followed by a wave of trials for infanticide, which suggests that, in this country too, legislative severity had made courts reluctant to prosecute. The harsh Scottish law faced its Waterloo in 1809, nine years before Walter Scott gave it a leading role in his novel. Similar reforms took place in Prussia and the Habsburg Empire. German legal historians have credited Frederick the Great with a change of heart, but the transformation of infanticide into a special offense in Prussia took place in the early nineteenth century.[69]

These legal reforms reflected a broader cultural transformation, in which views of motherhood and extramarital sex played a prominent role. The result was not unlike what happened to suicide. Writers, lawyers, politicians, and physicians discussed infanticide in terms of either romanticism or madness. Scots of the Enlightenment believed that even single mothers were incapable of killing their babies, and the typical heroine of a Scottish ballad lamented that although she was forced to kill the sweet babe, she was not really a murderess. German novelists and poets of the Sturm und Drang in the 1770s and 1780s treated infanticide in a manner similar to Walter Scott a few decades later. They represented single mothers who killed their babies as the victims of seduction, in particular by ruthless noblemen. The father, who could not even be brought to trial, was really the guilty party. At the same time, some scholars began to argue that the physical pain and mental anguish of childbirth were the real causes, denying that the women in question had any intention of killing.[70]

However much romantic compassion for seduced women there was, a plea of insanity remained a necessary prerequisite for an acquittal. This became increasingly common in the nineteenth century, when physicians described a specific disorder that caused the mother to kill her baby. In 1820, the London obstetrician Robert Gooch published an account of so-called puerperal insanity (named after the first, or puerperal, period after giving birth). It was a derivative of the general weakness and susceptibility to disease that for ages had been believed to characterize the female constitution. Gooch's colleague John Reid specified in 1848 that in puerperal insanity the baby usually was the target, although it could lead to suicide instead. "The mother is urged on by some unaccountable impulse to commit violence on herself or on her offspring," while at the same time she is "impressed with horror and aversion at the crime." Puerperal insanity became the standard defense in infanticide trials in England, despite this disorder's elusive nature. Yet in the 1860s, most English defendants in infanticide trials still were, overwhelmingly, unmarried female servants who had concealed their pregnancies. Psychiatrists of the later nineteenth century extended puerperal insanity to include disorders during pregnancy and breast-feeding. The sufferers escaped the death penalty, but they were often committed to a lunatic asylum.[71]

In France, the medicalization of infanticide did not set in before the Third Republic. A study of Brittany, covering 1825–65, found that, in a tiny minority of cases, lawyers had pleaded insanity or sought medical advice. Although the law prescribed the death penalty, juries routinely took mitigating circumstances into account. They sentenced just under 2 percent of the women to death, while 38 percent were acquitted. In Brittany, too, the traditional suspects predominated.[72] The Dutch king withheld his pardon from only one mother, who had buried her baby alive in 1822. The medicalization of the offense did not emerge until the early twentieth century; the psychiatric report in an Amsterdam case in 1912 constituted a breakthrough. The defendant's engagement to a man other than the father of her child and the fear of her parents' reaction, the psychiatrist argued, had caused a pathological state that intensified as she approached the moment of delivery.[73] In Belgium, where the painter Antoine Wiertz represented young mothers who had killed their babies as victims of seduction and abandonment, juries acquitted them on grounds of doubts about the evidence or temporary insanity.[74] Poor farm servants constituted the great majority of infanticidal mothers in Upper Bavaria in 1878–1910. Superior courts in Munich and Traunstein judged them, almost always ordering a psychiatric report and sentencing the woman to prison.[75]

Thus, the convergence of infanticide and madness began in England and developed most fully there. The English situation also serves to illustrate what happened next. The beginnings of welfare legislation constituted an important factor. This eased the financial burden of single mothers, even before the social rejection of bastardy started to diminish. An 1872 law considerably raised the maximum support the fathers were obliged to provide. The 1922 Infanticide Act made the offense a form of manslaughter, while another law in 1938 defined it as any willful act or omission that caused the death of a child under the age of 12 months, specifically attributable to a disturbed state of mind after giving birth or during lactation.[76] The decline of domestic service reduced the size of the highest-risk group. This happened in most of Europe, especially after World War Two. The introduction of the contraceptive pill in the 1960s and the subsequent removal of restrictions on abortion in many countries led to a further decline in (completed) pregnancies out of wedlock. Since the 1970s, moreover, the distinction between illegitimate and legitimate birth has lost its meaning, with the spread of unmarried cohabitation, quick divorce, and consciously single mothers. Julie Wheelwright, conducting interviews with British women who had killed their babies in the 1990s, concluded that infanticide was no longer associated with poverty. She provides an estimate of 20 cases, including abandonment of a baby, per year in England and Wales – that is, even if we count abandonment with murder, a rate of less than 0.05 per 100,000 population.[77] Amsterdam medical statistics of the 1980s list homicide victims under one year of age together, which also exceeds the strict definition of infanticide. Over a period of 11 years, there was only one case in this category.[78]

From the early nineteenth century onward, madness was more often taken into account even in cases of ordinary murder. In 1819 the French psychiatrist Jean-Etienne Esquirol introduced the concept of "monomania," which was further developed by successive colleagues. This theory implied that a person could behave normally most of the time, but that one particular part of his mind was deranged. A kleptomaniac, for example, had an irresistible urge to steal, but for the rest he was normal and law-abiding. Some people suffered from homicidal monomania. They were decent, even respected, citizens, but they were compelled to kill occasionally.[79] This idea never caught on in society as a whole, but it contributed to making the image of murder much more disturbing. These developments belong to the next chapter.

6

M for Less: The Marginalization of Murder, 1800–1970

While Frau Beckmann worries about Elsie, who is late home from school, younger children, playing at the inner court of a block of houses, form a ring round a little girl in the middle. She is chanting a rhyme about a man who will hack you to meat – the child she points at on the last word is out. The rhyme is a variant on a song about the infamous murderer Haarmann. Now a new killer is in town. Seven children are missing already, says the placard against which Elsie bounces her ball. The nice man she meets buys her a balloon and her mother will never see her again. Newspaper vendors eagerly announce that the unknown murderer has taken his eighth victim. The police are in despair. They have no clues whatsoever, in spite of a search for fingerprints and an analysis of the handwriting on a letter that the culprit sends to the press. Dogs find no trace either. The police can only increase their surveillance of the usual suspects, rounding up professional thieves, prostitutes, and gambling operators. This is to the chagrin of the *Ringvereine*, Berlin's criminal organizations. By causing the intensification of police activity, the serial murderer is frustrating their business. Representatives of the various organizations discuss the situation under the chairmanship of Schränker, an internationally renowned criminal who has fooled even Scotland Yard. At the end of the meeting he presents his conclusion: "We must catch the beast ourselves." Beggars and haberdashers, who can go anywhere without raising the killer's suspicion, should be able to find him.

In the company of a prospective new victim, the murderer passes a blind man selling balloons. This girl will get a different present, but the pedlar recognizes the tune that the man is whistling: the same as when he bought a balloon for Elsie Beckmann on the day she disappeared. Quickly, the blind man makes a signal to one of the beggar-detectives, who smartly chalks the letter "M" into the palm of his hand. As if by accident, he bumps into the guy and touches the back of his coat, marking him as a murderer. The suspect is obliged to take refuge in an office building, but the underworld catches him and takes him to a deserted factory. There, he faces a huge tribunal of "experts in legal matters," presided over by Schränker. The defendant implicitly admits his guilt when he exclaims "But I cannot help it!" The president concludes that if he has a compulsion to kill, no rehabilitation is possible, so he must be eliminated. All the men and women in the room make their agreement known. Only the "defense lawyer" pleads that the defendant is sick and should be handed over to a doctor, but the audience noisily objects. At the very moment when the crowd rushes forward to lynch the offender, everyone raises their hands, because the police has discovered the location. The murderer's ultimate fate remains undisclosed.

This is, of course, M, a movie released in 1931.[1] Apart from its aim as a commentary on murder and professional crime, M links up with the political events of its day as well as with film history. The two principal people involved shared their country of origin with the man who would soon alter the face of Europe. Director Fritz Lang (1890–1976) was born in Vienna, worked in Germany, left the country after Hitler's takeover, and eventually moved to the United States. Leading actor Peter Lorre, originally László Löwenstein, was also a native of Austria-Hungary. His Jewish descent obliged him to flee Nazi Germany right away and, after working in France and England, he moved to Hollywood. Gustaf Gründgens, who plays Schränker, started off with leftist sympathies, but he advanced his career after 1933 by pleasing the Nazis. Klaus Mann critically portrayed him in his 1936 novel Mephisto, filmed in its turn by István Szabó in 1981. According to Lang's unverifiable statement, Joseph Goebbels, while explaining that he was going to ban his newest movie, had invited him to become head of the UFA film studio. Earlier, some of the Nazis criticized M too, interpreting its title as "murderers are among us" and a reference to them.

Lang's script was powerful enough to become a template for local variants – a French connection. In April 1932 the Paris correspondent of the Dutch newspaper De Telegraaf wove a fictional report around the correct observation that professional criminals in Marseilles were called nervis. It follows exactly the theme of M, including the underworld's chase because the killer has not yet been caught. The reporter gave the murdered girls local names and he invented a new detail: the crossed knives that the serial killer left behind, without fingerprints. The article drew the attention of the Marseilles chief of police, who was not amused. It was a complete fantasy, he wrote, that could seriously damage the city's reputation.[2]

In various ways, M illustrates the trends in murder from the age of Napoleon to the 1960s. As even lower-class fighting resulted, on average, in fewer fatalities, the image of residual murder darkened. Serial killers, appearing after the mid-nineteenth century, exemplified this sinister image. The law-abiding public also feared youth gangs, violent robbers, and the underworld. Yet the criminal organizations of the interwar period, although Lang's portrayal makes them too benign, were less active in liquidating competitors than were late twentieth-century drug syndicates. Homicide rates, too, increased markedly after 1970, which is why this chapter ends there. At the other end of the spectrum of fear were the disillusioned lovers committing *crimes passionnels*, visible especially around the turn of the century. Many people could understand and excuse them. Generally, the expansion of the jury trial over Continental Europe in the wake of the French Revolution ensured that some killers, with whose plight jurors sympathized for one reason or another, got off lightly. That also applied to the official duel, which first underwent a revival and then disappeared. Many contemporaries, finally, believed that the world wars in the first half of the twentieth century carried over into peacetime a brutalizing effect, but in reality these wars had little lasting impact on personal behavior.

One more factor providing unity to the period 1800–1970 concerns the absence of victimization surveys. They were conducted systematically by criminologists from the 1970s. Before then, murder rates continue to be the only reliable quantitative measures for violence. More recently, even these came under fire, especially in England. Howard Taylor argues that budgetary limitations caused an under-investigation of murders and other crimes by coroners and the police during much of the nineteenth century and beyond. Consequently, murders were also under-reported, although this applies mostly to cases involving children and the elderly as victims and hence affects the incidence of male fighting only marginally. Several scholars, however, have contested Taylor's arguments.[3] On the Continent, body inspection records from local courts either disappeared after the Napoleonic period or have been left uninvestigated, with few exceptions. Most of the quantitative research into homicide has made use of national statistics, which were quickly assembled. In most countries, such judicial statistics are based on prosecuted cases, sometimes on convictions only, so a dark number remains. On the other hand, they may include attempted murder, which makes the homicide count higher than the actual number of killings. Medical statistics on the causes of death are more reliable, but, except for Sweden, they were not assembled until the end of the nineteenth or the beginning of the twentieth century.

The very least we can say with certainty is that, Europe-wide, the declining trend continued after 1800 but the lion's share of this decline had already occurred before that date. Eisner's overall averages for the five European regions he studied show a homicide rate of 3.2 for the eighteenth century, 2.6 for the nineteenth, and 1.4 for the twentieth century, as always measured per 100,000 inhabitants per year.[4] Understandably, these highly aggregated rates obscure all kinds of fluctuation and geographic differences. In England, based on judicial records, the nineteenth century started with a modest rise: from 1.4 before 1800 to 1.7 in the period 1825–50.[5] In causes-of-death statistics for England and Wales, the homicide rate declined from about 2 around 1870 to about 0.5 around 1930.[6] French statistics are important because of the near lack of reliable quantitative evidence for the early modern period. Extrapolating from a comparison of judicial and causes-of-death statistics, Jean-Claude Chesnais estimated the real French homicide rates from 1826 onward. They stood somewhat above 1 until 1855 and then fluctuated between about 0.7 and 0.9. From 1906 until World War One they were just above 1 again.[7] Eric Johnson presents the best figures for Germany, based on body inspection reports from Prussia, i.e. about half the Empire. The rate was 2.1 in the years 1873–5 and declined, measured in five year averages, until it reached 1.2 in 1886–90. Then it rose again, arriving back at 2 in 1911–13. Apart from one period, the Berlin rates were always lower.[8] Swiss causes-of-death statistics show a continuous decline from 3.5 in 1880 to 1.2 in 1940.[9]

The most conspicuous development, however, concerns the division of Europe into an inner and an outer zone. In the outer zone, murder remained relatively frequent throughout the nineteenth century. This zone constituted a ring from Ireland to the Mediterranean, over the Balkans and Eastern Europe to Finland. We have good rates for several countries and regions in this zone. Finland followed the common Scandinavian development of declining homicide in the early modern period, but it began to deviate from this path. Homicide rates went up from about 2 in the eighteenth century to about 3 in the nineteenth, and they rose even higher during much of the twentieth century. In Ireland, with elevated rates in the eighteenth century and the beginning of the nineteenth, it was the other way around. The homicide rate for victims over one year stood at just over 3 in the late 1830s and again around 1850. Then decline set in and the rate was around 1 at the beginning of the twentieth century, when Ireland ceased to belong to the outer zone. Even higher rates prevailed in Mediterranean areas. On Corfu and Cephalonia, off the western coast of Greece, the homicide rate was 12.4 in the first half of the nineteenth century. Italian rates were always higher the more one went southward. Those of Rome stood between 10 and 12 from the 1850s to 1880s, around 8 until 1910, and just under 5 on the eve of the Great War. Throughout the nineteenth century, Corsica was probably the most violent region of Europe. Its homicide rate, coming from 45 around 1700, fluctuated between 26 and 64, measured by five-year averages, between 1800 and 1850, then declined, went up again after 1875, and still stood at 14 in the 1890s.[10]

Judicial statistics for non-fatal violence are merely indicative.[11] Nevertheless, a number of scholars maintain that the real incidence of assault as well as theft declined in England from the mid-nineteenth century until about 1920.[12] In Germany and the Netherlands, such a decline was also visible, but it did not occur before the advent of the twentieth century. German convictions for serious assault and battery fluctuated between 140 and 240 per 100,000 of the population aged 12 years and older between 1882 and 1914. After World War One, this rate stood at around 60. Dutch convictions for physical maltreatment fluctuated between 70 and 100 per 100,000 inhabitants from 1850 to 1905, then dropped to below 60, fluctuating between 35 and 55 until 1970.[13]

New Police and New Fears

As previously, the decline of violence resulted from a complex interplay of state growth and cultural competition between social classes. Several innovations originated in England, but the country had to catch up first. Within its accusatory trial system, non-fatal violence had been considered more of a private matter than on the Continent, and even manslaughter often carried a lenient punishment. Between 1780 and 1820, a shift occurred in the punishment of assault from fines to imprisonment.[14]

The "new police" constituted the most important innovation in law-enforcement in the first half of the nineteenth century. This agency was termed new because it replaced traditional constables and servants of justice, whose numbers had always been low, specialized forces that hunted only beggars or smugglers and amateur nightwatchmen. Note, however, that Paris had had a sizeable police force since the late seventeenth century. The formation of the Metropolitan Police Force in England in 1829, consisting of 3,000 men for Greater London, was comparable to the Parisian force, but English governments followed it up by ordering other towns and counties to establish a police force, especially after 1856. British historians speak of a thorough, expensive, and efficient machinery for the detection of crimes and the apprehension of suspects. Although it was aimed primarily at property offenses, violence received increased attention too. In addition, the spread of street gaslights proved more effective than earlier systems in ensuring safety at night. After setting up an urban police force, most Continental countries introduced special forces for the countryside. These were usually semi-military corps, called *gendarmerie* in France and countries influenced by French institutions and *carabinieri* in Italy. Law-enforcement with political overtones was common everywhere. Throughout Europe, and well into the twentieth century, the police saw it as their task not only to combat crime, but also to maintain the existing social order and uphold the regime in power. These goals came together in the supervision of the working classes.[15]

In the most developed parts of Europe, the growth of state power put an end to classical banditry, which had been a plague for centuries. Its demise was no simple consequence of the introduction of the new police. In England, France, the Netherlands, and Prussia the retreat of bandits appears to have predated the coming of the new police. The disappearance of large bands was part and parcel of the advance of the modern nation-state. The influence of all its institutions increased, leaving robber groups with fewer loopholes and hiding places. Banditry continued to be rampant, on the other hand, in southern Italy, Corsica, and many parts of Spain, where state institutions had less influence.[16] Elsewhere, we hear of smaller groups of highwaymen, but even these fell upon hard times, and gradually the countryside became more safe. In the region west of Paris, for example, hold-ups of coaches and armed attacks of travelers became less frequent after 1830.[17]

A second important innovation in law-enforcement followed at the end of the century. Experts like Alphonse Bertillon in France developed various systems for identifying criminals, but the adoption of fingerprint analysis had the most lasting effect. For the first time, unwitnessed crimes could be linked to specific perpetrators. The technique of identifying people by their fingerprints had been used for centuries in Asia. Reported on by a Bengal colonial official, it attracted the attention of European forensic scientists. At first, this technique served to convict thieves, burglars, and robbers, but it was potentially useful in all murder cases without eyewitnesses. At the Berlin trial of the pimp Hugo Guthmann, suspected of having killed the prostitute Bertha Singer in 1899, a chemist and four handwriting specialists were present. The chemist showed the jury photographs that explained the uniqueness of the lines of the finger in every individual, but the jurors acquitted the defendant nevertheless. England boasted a breakthrough for fingerprints and murder convictions. One morning in 1905, the brothers Alfred and Albert Stratton broke into a shop near London, searching it for cash and valuables. The manager, who lived upstairs with his wife, caught them in the act, whereupon the robbers clubbed the couple to death. An apprentice discovered the victims a little later in a pool of blood. The Stratton brothers thought they had got away with their crime, but a woman who had seen two men running down the street believed that one of them was the older of the brothers, so the police arrested him. It turned out that the thumbprint found on the shop's cash-box matched his. Found guilty by the jury, the Strattons were hanged the same year. This well-publicized case paved the way for the routine adoption of the fingerprint technique.[18]

Among the socio-cultural reforms that underpinned the forces of order, we can include the rise of modern sports. Sports underwent a massive change from violent and sometimes homicidal confrontations to regulated spectacles. The bourgeoisie were the first to embrace modern sports and it was only in the interwar period that working-class players came to dominate. The reform primarily was an English movement that spread over Continental Europe as its inhabitants began playing British games. In previous centuries, sports like English "folk" football and French *soule* had been rather uncontrolled. The participants played in the streets, or on a square or field outside their village. National competitions were unknown; most games were associated with festival days and pitted two groups from the same location, their size unlimited, against each other. Most important, there were few restrictive rules, which meant that physical aggression made the difference. Although the slaying of a participant was not supposed to occur, this was always a possibility. Guilds and corporations had charity boxes for compensation to the families of deceased players. "Civil play" meant that only wrestling and kicking, no boxing, was allowed in order to conquer the ball.[19]

Beginning in the 1840s, sport became increasingly regulated and "civilized." As a result, violence decreased, while different games became more clearly distinguished from each other. Each had its own number of players, and the ball was propelled either with hands, feet, or an instrument. The creation of the British Football Association in 1863 was a landmark. Its new rules banned players from running with the ball in their hands and from obstructing opponents by kicking their shins. Rugby had its origins in the minority who refused to accept these rules. After 1871, association football, or "soccer," was distinguished from "rugger" football, but in the latter sport the ban on kicking was introduced later. Such reforms did not put an end to all injuries, and the playing of many games involved a tougher physicality than today. Even cricketers tried to intimidate opponents by purposely bowling the ball in such a way that it bounced up at the batman's body. By 1900, British games like football had spread over most countries of Continental Europe, as well as to Argentina. The French added cycling to the canon of sports, and also from France came Pierre de Coubertin, the father of the modern Olympic games. Reformed sports, engaged in by the middle classes in particular, counted as manly. They were an integral part of the new masculinity, according to which men no longer fought (although dueling had not completely vanished) but they still displayed their manhood in a tough and physical way.[20]

Boxing forms a special case. In England, it was a popular sport throughout the nineteenth century, as it had been in the eighteenth. Its rules entailed few restrictions and occasional deaths and severe injuries occurred. Courts sometimes reacted with criminal prosecution, notably after the death of the famous prizefighter Brighton Bill in 1838. In 1845 it was established that when a prizefight ended in the death of a participant, everyone who had provided assistance in the event was guilty of manslaughter. Judges and juries, however, continued to impose moderate sentences. Restrictive regulations came about in the mid-1860s, drawn up by the eighth Marquess of Queensberry. An elaborated version of these rules 10 years later laid the groundwork for modern professional boxing. Since then, commercial boxing, on raised platforms with admission restricted to paying spectators, has been clearly distinguished from spontaneous fighting by men over their differences.[21]

Paradoxically, while actual violence diminished, fears among the general public increased. Before 1800, wealthy citizens had been more afraid of property crime than of violence, and many victims counterattacked thieves to get back their belongings. During the nineteenth century, respectable people's fears of crime began to concentrate on violence and insecurity. They were afraid of robbers or gangs and their anxiety mainly concerned the threat of physical attack. Exaggerated media attention occasioned a number of collective panics, especially after the middle of the century when the English feared so-called "garotters." It began in January 1851 with a report in *The Times* about a robbery in Manchester. The robbers had attacked their victim from behind as he walked out of Victoria Station, grabbing him by the throat, suffocating him, and taking money and valuables. Similar cases were identified in other cities in the course of that year, and soon it was reported that the aggressors used special cords to facilitate their threat of strangling. In 1856, the magazine *Punch* satirized the panic with the design of an anti-garotting collar, with which respectable citizens could safely walk the streets again. By the end of the decade "garotter" had become a common word for street robber, regardless of the method used. One night in July 1862, a few men threw to the ground James Pilkington, a Member of Parliament who was returning home late from his duties, causing a bleeding wound, and robbed him of his gold watch. The next day an enraged House of Commons demanded action, and eventually it passed a bill authorizing flogging sentences for street robbers. The garotting panic of the second half of 1862 had the whole country in its grip and similar but less intensive panics recurred during the remainder of the century.[22]

The press also aroused the public's concern over youth gangs, although they more often fought each other. In Manchester and its suburbs, these gangs were called "scuttlers" – a collective epithet, since individual gangs styled themselves with names such as Bengal Tigers. Most members were in their mid- to late teens, living with their parents but enjoying a measure of independence because they earned wages. Their customary weapon was the thick leather belt, but sometimes they used bricks, stones, and even knives. Defense of one's territory was the major issue. Special clothing, underlining the increasing importance of consumer goods, distinguished one gang from another. For these juveniles, traditional male honor still mattered. Apart from fighting each other, they attacked policemen and intimidated witnesses, but their exploits were rarely fatal. In the entire Manchester area, in the period 1870–1900, Andrew Davies found no more than five homicides which he could attribute to scuttling activities. A new element in these late nineteenth-century gangs concerns the participation of young women, whose passivity the courts and the press overstated. In reality, girls actively engaged in threatening witnesses who could provide evidence against the gang. But they hardly ever used belts, which they did not wear, or knives.[23]

From France we also hear about gang names as well as collective epithets. Lyons had its Kangaroos, while all youth gangs in Marseilles designated themselves as *nerfs*. Here, too, different gangs were recognizable by their own style of clothing.[24] During the Belle Époque, Paris journalists revived the custom of calling gangs after Indian tribes, designating youth gangs collectively as Apaches. Reports concerning these youths mixed myth with reality. Supposedly, they numbered 20–30,000 altogether in the Paris metropolitan area, but in fact they were divided into a number of neighborhood gangs, each with its own territory. Most members were aged between 15 and 20, and included boys as well as girls. Rival gangs fought each other, preferably with knives, but, here too, few deaths were reported. Apaches hated the police and bourgeois residents, but they valued distinctive clothing, in this case for them all: a short vest, "elephant" pants, a cap with a large brim, pointed boots with gold buttons, and a brightly colored shawl. Tattoos distinguished gangs from one another. Broken-hearted young men from the bourgeoisie, they said, purposely went to dark alleys at night to commit "suicide by Apache." Fearful citizens associated Apaches with robbery, and in 1910 there was a lively debate in the press as to whether or not flogging should be reinstituted for violent attacks aimed at persons or property. France did not follow Britain in this. All Apaches vanished into the army in 1914.[25]

Concern over robbers and youth gangs coincided with a general increase in sensibilities toward violence, which extended to state violence exemplified by the scaffold. Almost everywhere, executions were removed indoors between 1850 and 1870. Although duelists still took pride in their scars, many Europeans wanted to beautify their bodies and aesthetic surgery developed to help make their wishes come true.

Sensitivity also increased against pain, which lost its positive association with Christian suffering. Becoming unacceptable, pain was associated with obscenity, which culminated in the introduction of the terms "sadism" and "masochism" by Richard von Krafft-Ebing in the 1880s. While opiates had been used for a long time to alleviate pain, the nineteenth century witnessed two medical breakthroughs. The first was the introduction of anesthesia during operations in 1846. The second was the Bayer company's invention of aspirin in 1899, which the British feverishly sought to copy. At their surrender in 1918, the Germans were obliged to reveal the secret of making aspirin.[26]

Yet we should not exaggerate the fear of crime, gangs, and violence that prevailed among Europe's respectable citizens at the turn of the twentieth century. A study of Berlin in 1900–14 found 36 cases in which passers-by turned against an offender. Often this was to prevent serious assault, in particular when the attacker had drawn a knife. Crowds would even attempt to disarm a criminal carrying a revolver by encircling him in a threatening way. They also acted against carriage drivers who endangered the public by their recklessness. In most cases, these private law-enforcers were unarmed themselves, not even carrying sticks. Nevertheless, they often beat up and injured their target. Sometimes the police had to rescue the offender in such incidents, but they took no action against his assailants. A similar attitude prevailed in Paris at the time. Unafraid, crowds would jump on suspected offenders, also killers, and deliver them to the police or beat them up.[27]

Male Fighting and the Working Classes

Whereas the fear of robbers and gangs gradually increased, attitudes to individual fighting were less straightforward. As a trivial consequence of the low homicide level, the literature on post-1800 violence contains few murders or cases of near-fatal assault. It is worthwhile, nevertheless, to examine the patterns of male fighting that have been observed. All scholars agree that after 1800 it was largely confined to the working classes, urban as well as rural. This sealed the social differentiation which had begun in the early modern period. Nineteenth-century Germany, for example, has not been extensively studied yet, but the literature so far confirms the working-class nature of fighting.[28] For England, John Carter Wood argues that although lower-class people were subjected to the civilizing pressures of police and social workers, violence remained an integral part of their daily lives. Since they had few opportunities to exert power in any other way, the use of physical strength constituted a significant resource, in particular for men. For them, newer ideals of masculinity, based on a spiritualized sense of honor, had less significance. In addition, elite men at times enjoyed watching a fist fight between two of their social inferiors.[29]

Such fist fights were ritual events that continued the tradition reported by eighteenth-century visitors to London, but their formality increased after 1800. Each combatant was supported by one or two seconds and there were distinct rounds, just as in a prize fight. The opponents shook hands before they began and the spectators formed a ring. The fight ended when one combatant gave up or was unable to continue. The location, all kinds of pubs, and the reason, an insult or degrading remark, were no different from confrontations in earlier periods. A fight between men of considerably unequal size counted as unfair though – a feature that applied much less to knife duels. Toward the end of the nineteenth century, one-on-one street fights among young working-class women, around whom spectators also formed a ring, were reported as well. Whether between women or men, these fights were rarely fatal. One exception was the combat between John King and a man named Griffiths, a ploughman, in 1830 at a summer fair in Hertfordshire. At night, some 30 men gathered in the Leather Bottle public house. Earlier, there had been a race for a whip, which a certain Kitchener had won. Some men murmured that he had not run fairly and a few, among them Griffiths, grabbed the whip from him. It became an affray in which John King apparently defended the winner and at a certain point everyone agreed that King and Griffiths should settle the matter by fighting. The spectators formed a ring and both men took a second. There were to be three rounds. Although after round two a few bystanders thought that they should stop, as John King was not looking well, most considered the fight to be fair and that they should continue. At the end of the third round Griffiths dealt a hard blow into King's neck and the latter fell down. They laid him in the pub's stable, but he never regained consciousness and died the next morning.[30]

Popular duelists themselves appear to have shared the growing conviction that it was non-English to fight with anything other than bare hands. Englishmen of this period did carry knives, but, as long as they were not gang members, these were mostly small penknives or tobacco knives. In the 1840s, courts turned more severe against knife fighters, often charging those who had killed their opponents with intentional murder. Only foreign sailors, if their victims were also foreigners, got off lightly, because they did not know any better. In 1874, a Liverpool magistrate judging a non-fatal stabbing case among natives, explained to the defendant and the victim: "If you fellows would confine yourselves to the use of your fists, it would be a good thing for the town. . . . If you had used your fists I might have discharged you; but I wish all you fellows to understand that as soon as ever you use a knife you shall be dealt with according to the law." In other male-on-male fights weapons at hand were used, such as shovels, hammers, bottles, glasses, and cotton hooks, depending on the location or workplace.[31]

French historians of nineteenth-century violence have dealt with rural areas in particular. François Ploux's 2002 study of Haut-Quercy is exemplary. Among its villagers, the ancient male code of honor was alive and well. Any man who declined to respond to an insult with assault suffered a loss of face. Conflicts were routinely settled by fighting and even some revenge murders were considered as falling within the confines of honor. At least until the 1860s, a wide gap existed between public opinion and the law. The inhabitants excused any ferocious homicide that occurred during an inter-village fight, but they despised murder for personal gain. Inter-village fights involved dozens, sometimes hundreds, of men, usually single men in their 20s. Honor conflicts between men of the same village concerned the sexuality of female family members, but also the male sociability of the cabaret, where things like toppling a glass could lead to a challenge. Popular duels generally took place after church at the end of mass, with the rest of the village watching. The weapons in these cases were stones, fists, or unloaded guns used for striking. Individuals and parties then made up by drinking wine together.

Such inter-village fights were not confined to southern parts of the country. For much of the nineteenth century, rows and collective boxing confrontations regularly occurred all over rural France. Only on rare occasions did the combatants use knives or guns. A village doctor not far from Paris noted in his report for July 1838 that he had taken care of two men. One had a bleeding wound near his ear and several broken bones, and he was unable to speak because of a heavy concussion. The other had only a bad eye. French historians disagree about the extent to which rural violence decreased as the nineteenth century wore on. Some follow up on the classic study by Eugen Weber (1976), who describes the massive campaign, in the four decades preceding the Great War, of establishing schools and building roads, which served to modernize the French countryside and change the ways of the peasantry. Fréderic Chauvaud additionally points at the decline of agrarian protest and the fact that revenge increasingly took the form of taking an opponent to court. By 1900, he concludes, urban residents had ceased to consider the countryside as a hotbed of violence and dangers. Ploux, on the other hand, in a recent re-examination, maintains that it was primarily the collective fights that declined, a trend that began as early as the 1860s. The level of overall violence in the countryside was as high on the eve of the Great War as just after the era of Napoleon.[32]

All French historians do agree that arson, not physical attack, was the most common form of vengeance in rural settings. Villagers with a grudge purposely set fire to the farm or barn of their enemies. This was equally the case outside France. Arson as revenge was a common occurrence in rural parts of England and Germany throughout the nineteenth century. Bavarian incendiaries carefully took note of the direction of the wind, in order to hit nothing else but their enemy's property.[33] Detailed information about arson in the Dutch countryside is not available, but it underwent an overall process of pacification in the course of the nineteenth century. Until the 1860s, Brabant witnessed inter-village fights, usually with sticks, as well as a persistence of ritual knife duels coupled with the custom of reconciliation by drinking together.[34] In rural parts of other Dutch provinces, around the turn of the century, assault with knives had become a rarity too.[35]

The pacification of cities is best illustrated with the example of Paris. Its working class became less prone to fighting as the nineteenth century progressed, as evidenced in a study of café violence. In the first half of the century, popular duels over affairs of honor were still reported, as were the chaotic fracases in which everyone fought each other. By 1870, however, this had all changed. Parisian working-class café life of the Third Republic was governed by an ethos of good humor and play, in which it was understood that conversation revolved around jokes and laughter instead of challenges to one's reputation. The conflicts that erupted were often subject to arbitration by customers and bartenders. Individuals who felt easily affronted and wanted to fight, whom others attempted to avoid, were thought of as troublesome.[36]

Thus, both urban workers and the peasantry in the core countries of Europe gradually became more peaceful. Nevertheless, the quantitative work that has been done suggests that, on average, the level of violence was lower in cities. After examining a mass of local and regional statistics in England, Chassaigne concludes that most of the larger cities, including London, were less violence-prone than the countryside.[37] In the German Empire, 1883–97, conviction rates for assault and battery amounted to 177 per 100,000 in urban districts and 190 in rural districts. The corresponding figures for the years 1903–12 were 207 and 240. Throughout this period, the rates for Berlin alone were significantly lower than the urban average.[38] In France and Italy around 1900, the incidence of violent crime equally was lower in the urbanized regions than in the countryside. A detailed study of murder in the industrialized département du Nord of France shows that its homicide prosecution rate was always well under the national average in the period 1826–1914.[39]

Evidence concerning male fighting in Europe's inner zone of low homicide rates is consistent with the quantitative data. Fighting was even more socially exclusive and less lethal than in the previous century. Among men prepared to use violence, many shared an understanding that a confrontation should not become too dangerous, refraining from handling knives in particular. Spatial segregation enhanced the social exclusiveness of fighting. Whereas in the early eighteenth century respectable men had often been obliged to defend themselves, after 1800 they were less likely to meet their social inferiors. Physical confrontations were confined even more strictly to working-class neighborhoods and rural villages. Unlike in the United States, moreover, these developments took place in the absence of a spread of handguns. A Dutch study of probate inventories shows that throughout the nineteenth century, 18 percent of households in highly rural areas owned firearms and only 4 percent in urbanized areas. The difference indicates that the weapons in question were mostly hunting guns. In England, firearms were available, but rarely used in interpersonal violence. Prohibitive legislation was introduced in 1920.[40]

Two background factors to the further decline of serious violence after 1800 can be singled out. The first, the preventive effect of the new police and improved detection methods, has been discussed. The second consisted of the persistent civilization campaigns by moral entrepreneurs and charity organizations. Toward the end of the century, the influence of such campaigns was even stronger because they came from the working-class leadership too. Amsterdam's first socialist movement, for example, from the 1850s to the 1880s, had a populist character, with traditional male honor as a constitutive element. Physical aggression was channeled into strikes, riots, and fighting class enemies. The second generation of working-class leaders substituted the semantics of political ideology for that of honor.[41] Throughout Europe, the social-democratic branch of the workers' movement, which came to the fore in the 1890s, propagated a bourgeois lifestyle, in which masculine values were restricted to the aspiration of husbands to earn enough wages to allow their wives to remain at home. Quite another background factor stemmed from the age's imperialism. As a number of scholars emphasize, the level of pacification reached in many parts of Europe was accompanied by, and probably dependent on, a high level of violence against non-Europeans, because of the slave trade at the beginning of the nineteenth century and later through the expansion of colonialism.[42]

A closer examination of Europe's outer zone serves to underpin these conclusions. Ireland belonged to that zone during the first half of the nineteenth century. Although the decline of homicide did not follow immediately upon the famine, this disaster probably had a delayed influence. Many men who would otherwise have been violent were starving, and many others emigrated to the United States. Intriguingly, the traditional culture of honor remained prevalent until the end of the nineteenth century. Men continued to challenge each other, fighting over insults or slights, and if a fatality ensued, it was reckoned by bystanders to be an accident. Carolyn Conley elucidates the problem of this culture's coincidence, in the second half of the century, with lower homicide rates: people fought with fists or stones instead of knives. In just 11.4 percent of homicides, a knife was the weapon and a man who stabbed another to death was considered dishonorable. Guns accounted for 1.8 percent of homicide deaths.[43] Firearms were common, on the other hand, among the Orangemen of Ulster. The character of sectarian clashes there was halfway between ordinary territorial fights, as in the south of France, and collective political violence. In a ritual vocabulary of challenge and defiance, Orangemen would march demonstratively through Catholic territory, while both sides were sure to take long sticks with them to horse races. Each party's calendar counted plenty of holidays, which were just so many occasions for mutual violence.[44]

In Finland, especially in the province of Ostrobothnia, men continued to prefer knives as weapons. Inter-village fights were frequent too, even becoming increasingly ferocious. Regions with elevated homicide rates also were regions where special fighting knives were widespread. At the end of the nineteenth century, lethal violence was concentrated in industrializing areas, which in this country were forested frontier regions rather than towns. Aggressive masculinity was still very much alive in Finland in the interwar period.[45] At the other end of Europe, the elevated homicide rates of Corsica were due to a persistence of banditry as well as feuding. On this island, traditional male honor held full sway, including among local elites. Vendettas continued unabated, as if the Middle Ages had never ended. A few had their roots in the previous century and lasted more than 100 years. The French state, of course, disapproved of feuding under any conditions, but there was little that it could do. Even in 1900, most villages in Corsica could only be reached by mule tracks. The widespread use of guns constituted the principal difference with medieval times, although daggers were common too.[46]

Revenge killing also occurred elsewhere in the Mediterranean, but the most conspicuous form of violence on the Ionian Islands was knife fighting. Between 1817 and 1864 the islands were formally independent, but remained under a British protectorate that in practice was indistinguishable from colonialism. Records reveal that the popular duel on these islands was similar in several ways to that in early modern Europe. As ever, masculine honor was the key element. Knife fights began with words that damaged the reputation of the other party if he refused to react. These words often had to do with the sexuality of women. A wine shop was the most common scene. In the villages on the islands, the protagonists often knew each other and many incidents had a prehistory of conflict, but some popular duels pitted strangers against each other.

Remarkably, the majority of non-fatal fights also ended up in court, so that we have detailed evidence for them too. Spectators usually intervened when they considered the fight to be over, most often when one man had given the other a huge cut in the face. The most conspicuous difference from earlier periods was the apparent readiness of knife fighters to face arrest after a non-fatal combat. The public trial instituted by the British offered the defendant, the victim, and the witnesses an excellent opportunity to re-enact the drama of the conflict and to comment on the merits, bravery or cowardice, state of intoxication, and skill of the protagonists. This readiness to face trial was enhanced by relatively light penalties, although they turned more severe toward the end of British rule. In Greece as a whole, murders for honor continued to meet with understanding until the early 1960s.[47]

In Italy knives remained common throughout the nineteenth century. The evidence for Rome also derives mostly from fatal cases. Many incidents originated for apparently trivial reasons that had to do with matters of honor. Homicides occurred in tavern fights and street brawls and as a consequence of tensions in the neighborhood, at the workplace or within the family. As in early modern Amsterdam, many knife fighters had a previous criminal record. They were more or less ostracized within the working class. It would be a stain on the honor of other, more self-controlled working people to associate with them.[48]

Italy is even better known for its mafia. Mafia activities differed from banditry and they cannot be described simply as private or criminal violence. As in medieval Europe, the weakness of the state was a key factor, but with the crucial difference that mafiosi exploited the ephemeral institutions of the Italian state rather than looking for its niches. In Sicily, at the turn of the nineteenth and twentieth centuries, mafia cliques and regional elites wielded real authority. No overarching mafia existed, only a number of local cliques, called *cosche*. Each *cosca* supported its own candidate in local elections, for example, who was then supposed to further their interests. Mafiosi acted as middlemen. They served landlords both in their struggles with rivals and by intimidating peasants with the purpose of keeping them subordinated. Finally, locally based mafia cliques struggled for power among themselves, in conflicts that often entailed the elimination of a key figure of a rival *cosca*. Courts had hardly any grip on mafia murders. When two rivals met at the crowded square of a provincial town, the place would almost instantly become deserted. Everybody knew, but no one saw. Thus, the presence of mafia continued a de facto fragmentation of the monopoly of violence.[49] Although mafiosi differed from bandits, their training in violence and intimidation was a valuable asset when they emigrated to engage in criminal activities elsewhere. From the early twentieth century onward, some mafiosi and related experts in violence moved from Southern Europe to the cities of the north, and the USA, to contribute to the formation of a new underworld.

The examination of Europe's outer zone sheds further light on events in the core area. It is perhaps not surprising that we observe the persistence of feuding and banditry in regions of the outer zone. Its most remarkable feature is the prevalence of knife fighting in many parts. This is in flagrant contrast to the inner zone, where we observe the relative absence or marginalization of this weapon during the 100 years preceding the Great War. After 1800, knife fighting was not so much un-English as unlike the ways of core Europe. The continuing decline of homicide rates in the inner zone was straightforwardly related to the retreat of the knife as an ordinary weapon.

The Upper Classes and the Formal Duel

Violence never was confined just to the lower strata. The middle and upper classes had their share of domestic disputes too. Non-domestic murders in the higher social milieus continued to draw wide attention; a case in the Rhineland just after the Congress of Vienna reverberated throughout Prussia. It is not certain, though, if it had a middle-class perpetrator, since the suspect, 36-year-old Peter Fonk, was cleared of the charges in the end. A scion of a well-respected merchant family from Goch, he moved to Cologne in 1815, where he set up a brandy-trading business with Franz Schröder from Krefeld. A year later, Franz suspected his partner of withholding information about the size of the profits and he demanded that a third party check his books. For this he chose another Krefeld merchant, 28-year-old Wilhelm Cönen, who arrived in Cologne on October 31. As yet unable to detect outright wrongdoing, he did not trust Peter Fonk either, and after a few days the two men were seen quarreling in public. Wilhelm's assistant, who accompanied him to his guesthouse on the night of November 9, was the last to see him alive. On December 19, after a frantic search and several newspaper advertisements, they found Wilhelm's body floating in the Rhine near Friemersheim. His golden watch was in his pocket but his money was missing. The examining physicians, who discovered severe head injury as well as symptoms of strangling, concluded that he had died before being thrown into the river. The case against Peter Fonk remained inconclusive throughout appeal trials in Trier and Berlin, until it reached the Prussian king in July 1823. By rejecting the Supreme Court's guilty verdict, the king made Peter a free man again.[50]

Potentially lethal violence within the upper strata meant, first of all, dueling. The nineteenth century witnessed a resurgence of the official duel. Whereas for some countries, notably Germany, this meant continuity with a few new features, for others, like Italy, it was an outright revival. In both countries and in France, elite duelists enjoyed special treatment from both the law and judicial practice. This was different in England, where dueling became another target in the period's campaign against male violence. The practitioners were mainly bourgeois officers, who aspired to rise socially by embracing aristocratic habits. They preferred pistols, but it counted as very unmannered to consciously aim at your opponent. The death rate has been estimated at 15 percent. In 1838 a jury found two seconds guilty of murder. Although they eventually served twelve months, public opinion quickly shifted. In the mid-1840s the authorities threatened with a court martial officers who even encouraged a duel, and withheld army pensions from the widows of deceased duelists. In 1852, two Frenchmen fought the last known official duel in England that ended with a casualty. Until the end of the century, the London *Times* continued to comment unfavorably on foreign duels.[51]

It is perhaps no coincidence that England led the way in the suppression of dueling and the reform of sports. To play a really manly game constituted an acceptable alternative to the courage displayed in a duel. Dutch elites, who in the nineteenth century often took England for a model, maintained their negative attitude to the custom. Even here there were exceptions. In 1844 a civilian professor at the Breda military academy challenged an officer, whose inexperience with pistols made him kill his opponent, although he had meant to aim at his leg. Two years later, a national representative challenged the minister of finance for calling him a liar, but the appointed seconds reconciled the parties without a fight.[52] In the later nineteenth century, on the other hand, several Dutchmen published treatises about dueling, which were against it almost without exception.[53]

Other countries witnessed recurrent duels up to World War One. France's *Compte Générale* listed 189 fatal duels and 331 non-fatal ones between 1827 and 1834, an annual average of 65 in all. The high death rate of 36 percent is no doubt biased because of the judicial origin of these statistics. An estimate for the period 1875–1900 comes at 200 – of which only one was fatal – each year. The figures for Italy, 1879–94, collected by the journalist Iacopo Gelli mostly from newspaper reports, amount to an annual average of 269 duels.[54] Gelli did not provide a fatality percentage, but throughout Europe the duels of this period rarely ended in death, and this for an obvious reason. The custom was to fight "at first blood."[55] As soon as the sword or saber had drawn blood from whatever vein, the fight was over. In Germany, where pistols were common, dueling codes no longer obliged the combatants passively to wait for each other's shots. Willingness to risk one's life was a more important element than a possible victory. The duel supposedly established a fraternal bond between the combatants, which had the greatest chance of success if both survived. Thus, the revived official duel of the nineteenth century was decidedly less violent than its seventeenth-century predecessor.

Despite the lesser violence, the revival obviously constituted a counter-trend to the spiritualization of honor. Elite men again considered ritualized violence as an appropriate response to an insult, and for the first time the proponents included bourgeois men. Disregarding their leftist ideology, even a few socialists had fought a duel in their student days and the socialist leader Ferdinand Lassalle ended his life in one in 1864. The French bourgeoisie adapted the aristocratic code of honor to include an emphasis on sexual propriety and personal hygiene and in the Third Republic civilians rather than the military embraced the duel. In unified Italy, journalists were eager participants, next to military men of mostly middle-class origin. According to Gelli, who did not even identify nobles as a separate group in his statistics, a loosely defined class of gentlemen could lay claim to honor. The duel was at home in the north and center of the country, rather than the *Mezzogiorno* with its mafia cliques. Challenges in Italy, where parliamentarianism was a novelty, for a large part concerned politics. The challenger took criticism in a newspaper or unkind words from a member of a rival party as an insult. One politician, upon his election to parliament, confided to his daughter that he must now take fencing lessons.

Occasionally, we find people from lower social ranks practicing the formal duel. In the region west of Paris, the office of forest guard descended from father to son and a semi-friendly rivalry existed between these law-enforcers and residents who liked poaching. In the summer of 1856, a worker challenged the local guard several times in the café. If the guard tried to prevent him from hunting, the worker said, he might well shoot a lead bullet into his body. "Poachers are thieves," the guard replied, whereupon the other retorted that all guards were worth nothing. Finally, the guard challenged the worker to a pistol duel the next day at a distance of one handkerchief from each other. It was half serious, and the prospective seconds first had to unload a grain cart. The guard won the duel by firing a shot that caused his opponent to need medical assistance.[56] Elite men, however, were unlikely to recognize such a confrontation as a real duel. As before, the practice of the official duel was socially exclusive and published dueling codes defined the exact boundaries of the circles "entitled to satisfaction." An elite man could simply ignore an affront from an outsider or his inappropriate challenge.

An intriguing feature of the bourgeois duel and its underlying honor code concerns the intimate association with nationalism. An affront to the nation could easily be taken as a personal affront that would lead someone to issue a challenge. In 1826, for example, the Neapolitan general Gabriele Pepe fought a well-publicized duel with the French poet and diplomat Alphonse de Lamartine over the latter's denigration of the Italians in a poem. The general's compatriots rejoiced over the bleeding wound that he caused to his opponent's arm, because it meant punishment for the hand with which Lamartine had written. Patriots in Lombardy in the 1850s issued challenges to anyone prepared to frequent the court of the Austrian governor. After the Italian army's humiliating defeat by the Ethiopians in 1895, the count of Turin challenged the Prince of Orléans for writing a derogatory article about the event, and killed him in the Boulogne forest near Paris. Frenchmen preferred to fight each other, in order to wash away military defeat. They viewed their duels as a sign of courage, showing to the rest of Europe that the German victory of 1870–1 had been a mistake. For their part, the Germans underlined their newly won national self-consciousness by dueling. Thus, honor was not simply personal, but was tied to the nation as well. Perhaps, Britannia's success story explains the lesser need of the English for duels.

The great catastrophe, sparked by Europe's nationalisms, that closed the long nineteenth century also ended the official duel. It died in the trenches. A general feeling arose that the exalted tales about courage displayed, honor regained, and fraternal bond created were a lie. The horrors of war represented the reality of violence. Nevertheless, there was an effort during the war, especially in France, to democratize the official duel. According to Georges Breittmayer's revised code, written in the winter of 1917–18, anyone of draft age was allowed to issue a challenge or be challenged and hence belonged to the same honor group. Breittmayer only excluded men who had avoided military service or disreputably profited from the war. This code came too late. After 1918, France and other European nations witnessed only a handful of duels. Only Italians, who had all agreed to postpone their personal grievances in order to concentrate on the war effort, went through a brief phase of catching up. The duel disappeared in Italy with Mussolini's takeover, partly because this put an end to the political discussion that had fostered the custom. By ignoring standards of legal proof, the Fascist régime also dealt a blow to the mafia, thereby tightening the state's monopoly of violence.

Women and the *Crime Passionnel*

The interaction between gender, the family, and violence was traced in chapter 4 up to the mid-nineteenth century. Trends since then imply continuity as well as change. As far as sexual assault is concerned, English scholars come out on one side or the other. Shani D'Cruze emphasizes women's vulnerability, for example, in cases in which men took their friendliness for a sexual invitation. By 1900, narratives in the press still revolved around the question whether the woman had provoked the assault, with too little resistance implying consent. Victims' concern over the publication of indecent details was as high as ever.[57] Martin Wiener, on the other hand, emphasizes the subtle changes in legal attitudes and court practices that, by the later Victorian period, produced an improvement of prosecution chances for sexual violence. The abolition of the death penalty for rape actually removed a significant barrier. It became possible, moreover, to prove the victim's resistance without visible marks of injury and it was recognized that prostitutes could be raped. Previous consensual sex with the perpetrator, however, continued to reduce the chances for a successful prosecution to practically zero. The number of trials for sexual violence increased, indeed, in particular between 1870 and 1890.[58]

French women were equally reluctant to reveal indecent details, or even the entire incident. A young daughter in the Loire region, lying in her room with a broken leg in 1889, first denied that she had been raped. Later she admitted: "I was ashamed that I had been the victim of such an assault and I didn't want my name to come up in an affair like that." Women seldom filed a complaint when they could show no signs of injury and witnesses were lacking. The situation was similar, throughout the nineteenth century, in the rural region west of Paris. Men often assumed that single women were available and, after enforced sex, they claimed that the victim had consented.[59]

The legal treatment of domestic violence and spouse murder underwent a reverse development for male and female perpetrators. English courts started to reproach husbands for abusing their physical strength against the weaker sex. A member of Parliament, who in 1856 proposed harsher penalties for the maltreatment of wives, spoke of "unmanly assaults" and explained that "the character of our own sex" was in need of reform. Ancient excuses for wife murder, such as nagging words, drunkenness of the victim or the perpetrator, squandering, or adultery, ceased to count as mitigating circumstances. By contrast, women were more easily considered insane or not fully responsible. This reverse development extended to extramarital intimates. The press depicted several men who had murdered their lovers or mistresses as ruthless seducers, especially if they had taken a financial advantage from the affair. The opposite happened in November 1902, when Kitty Byron stabbed to death her partner, Reggie Baker, of middle-class background and officially married to another. He had refused to pay for a telegram she sent, but it turned out that he had often beaten her when drunk. The newspapers dramatized the case and many readers sympathized with beautiful Kitty, who served seven years in prison.[60]

Laws enacted in Belgium in the course of the nineteenth century implied a growing intolerance for violence against both women and children. A case study of East Flanders, however, found that juries continued to lend a sympathetic ear to husbands who claimed that their wives had provoked them. They took such arguments into account, even when the victim had died.[61] In England, legislation that was meant to protect women continued to be enacted in the interwar period, but Clive Emsley believes that actual practice lagged behind. He speaks of a widening "gap between a growing body of legislation . . . and the fact that widespread violence continued to be prevalent and unpoliced."[62]

Even less change was visible in France. A study of trials for the killing of partners in the Rouen region, 1811–1900, found a persistence of traditional attitudes. As perpetrators, husbands and male lovers met with greater understanding from juries than did wives and female lovers. Prosecutors charged women more frequently with assassination, as opposed to the "voluntary homicide" of which they accused men. Partly this reflected actual behavior, because wives often compensated their lack of physical strength by the use of knives or guns. Courts also accused wives more often of having acted with the help of an accomplice, as the Parlement of Paris had done three centuries earlier. Change occurred, however, with respect to the actual motives. A study of northern France found a definite shift in the nature of intra-familial murders around 1870. Whereas conflicts about inheritances and material interests had occasioned them earlier, after that date it was the emotional ties between spouses. Not adultery, but an independent decision by a wife or girlfriend to leave a man became the most frequent cause of partner murder. Instead of following the script of honor and hierarchy, a man more often became obsessed when his partner left him, stalking her for days.[63]

Evidence concerning violence against children is patchy, at best. In Victorian Kent, nearly a quarter of homicide victims, infanticides excluded, were under the age of 12. This mostly concerned excessive parental punishment. The corresponding figure for London, 1861–1900, was just under 10 percent. In the Swiss canton of Uri, throughout the nineteenth century, children under 16 were the victims in one-fifth of all cases of physical injury and murder, but only a small minority suffered it at the hands of their parents. In France toward 1900, physical maltreatment of children by their parents was more frequent in the urban and industrial north than in rural districts, but this conclusion refers to a much broader range of abuse than potentially fatal treatment.[64]

As in the early modern period, some women killed their small children in circumstances of disturbance, poverty, and distress. In England, such cases usually led to a verdict of not guilty. In 1888, when Emma Aston was tried at the Old Bailey for murdering her two children after her husband had deserted her, she was found insane. *The Times* published an editorial applauding this judgment, confirming her madness, and blaming the runaway husband for what happened.[65] Three years earlier, a murder had shocked Geneva. The 32-year-old Jeanne Lombardi had cut the throats of her daughter and three sons, aged between 4 and 7, on the rainy night of May 1, while their father was working late in his tailor's shop. Contemplating suicide, the mother was struck by fear that after her death her husband would starve the children and let vermin beset them. After covering their beds with white lilies, she fell asleep and forgot to kill herself. Her lawyer, a future Swiss president, pleaded insanity and solicited several forensic experts, among whom Von Krafft-Ebing. The verdict was hung on the question of criminal responsibility, which meant that the most favorable option for the defendant, incarceration in a lunatic asylum, applied. Jeanne was declared cured and released in 1894.[66]

At the other end of the spectrum are those children, usually grown up, who killed their often aging parents. A recent study analyzes parricide, legally defined as the killing of any legitimate male or female ancestor, in nineteenth-century France.[67] Until 1832, the offender had his or her right fist cut off before execution. The family reputation still was a precious asset, but in this case, honor would be violated by violence. To avoid shame, families tried to keep the murder silent, or, if this was impossible, they claimed that the perpetrator was insane. The victim often died from a head injury, in line with the age-old ritual significance of this part of the body. The parental head, in particular, symbolized authority. The murder weapon, on the other hand, was rarely chosen for its ritual significance. The killers took whatever was close at hand: a kitchen knife, an axe, or any farm utensil that would smash the victim's skull. It was an impulsive moment, despite the fact that the decision to kill had often been taken long before and that threats to that end had been uttered many times. Parricide occurred most often in rural areas. The motives reflected all possible conflicts in this village world: revenge for maltreatment, parental veto of a marriage partner, strain within the family economy, disputes over the succession as head of a farm, and many more.

The type of gendered murder that was most distinctive at the turn of the century was the *crime passionnel*. Even in its home country, France, the term was a popular, not a legal, concept. From 1832 onward, French law allowed juries to take mitigating circumstances into account. *Crime passionnel* was a compound resulting from the sympathies of juries as well as the growing importance of forensic experts. According to popular understanding, it meant killing for love, more specifically out of jealousy or disappointment. While juries never pronounced automatic acquittals, they tended to excuse the defendant's deed, because they could imagine themselves in her or his shoes. The just-for-once character of the event and the unlikelihood of recidivism ensured that the public had no great fear of this type of murder. For their part, psychiatrists concluded toward temporary insanity, induced by blind love, jealousy, or furious hatred. Biologically oriented criminologists considered the passionate killer as a normal person, in contrast with the degenerate or born criminal. The confluence of these legal and scientific developments produced the powerful image of *crime passionnel*, especially influential between 1870 and 1930.

In the public mind, women – elegant ladies, indeed – were especially prone to the *crime passionnel*. The woman would stalk and take revenge on the man who had deserted her, his mistress, or both. As so often is the case, the statistics fail to bear this out. Most passionate killers had a working-class background and, more important, the majority did not consist of women. Statistics of "crimes of passion," compiled in France in the 1870s, showed that men had committed 82 percent of them. However, this still means an over-representation of female offenders compared to the total criminality of the period, certainly for overall violent crime. The same over-representation emerges from studies of trials in the Paris area between 1870 and 1910.[68] The offense had other exceptional characteristics. Passionate criminals were relatively old; two-thirds were aged between 25 and 40. This is understandable, since a relationship of some duration often preceded the crime. Compared to all murderers, a relatively large share of passionate criminals used a revolver, which made them unexpected partners in crime with the men of the emerging underworld. Yet, the *crime passionnel* was not straightforwardly modern, since old honor lurked in the background. The demands of patriarchy and reputation for ages had obliged men, in case of adultery, to act against their rivals and wives. On the other hand, the act itself did not restore a man's honor; his good reputation, according to spiritualized notions of honor, along with proof that he had shown loyalty, devotion, or romantic attachment to his partner beforehand, were preconditions for a light sentence. A woman's anger was especially aroused when the first man with whom she ever slept then left her, which echoes ancient notions of female chastity. On the other hand, *criminelles passionnelles* re-enacted the romantic dramas that abounded in the theaters of the period.

Not all passionate crimes involved a gun. A special method consisted of throwing vitriol (sulphuric acid) into the victim's face. This act was meant to maim rather than kill. If done well, it severely disfigured the target, symbolically robbing the person of his or her individuality. Throwing vitriol appears to have been a female crime in particular, and the women committing it were appropriately termed *vitrioleuses*. In 1883, Rose Chervey's cowardly lover asked his friend to notify her that he intended to break off their relationship. The messenger explicitly added: "Above all, no scandal; no vitriol!"[69] The acid's targets were unfaithful husbands and ex-lovers as well as their mistresses or new sweethearts, sometimes caught together in the act. The extant descriptions and photos, however, leave the impression that the new woman was more often targeted than the man who had deceived or deserted the offender. Thus, the *vitrioleuses* remind us of the women who slit their rivals' noses a few centuries earlier. Here, too, traditional female honor played its part.

Reports about assault with vitriol are confined to fin-de-siècle France, the country that invented the *crime passionnel*, but other nations had their share of murders resulting from desertion or a romantic triangle. In Wilhelmine Germany, mitigating circumstances were routinely taken into account and few killers were executed. A Berlin case drew great media attention because of the perpetrator's extreme attractiveness. Hedwig Müller, a bookstore clerk, was not only beautiful but also intelligent and handy, having worked for a dentist and a lawyer before. In the summer of 1911, at age 18, she met the Jewish physician Leo Sternberg, whose lover she became. Early in 1912, her employer hired Georg Reimann, one year her junior, as a messenger. Hedwig and Georg liked each other; he bought her fruit and candy and soon they became intimate. When Georg found out that his beloved was also having an affair with a richer and older man, he became understandably jealous. He intercepted Hedwig's letters and threatened to reveal the affair to the bookstore owner. Then he promised to remain silent in exchange for one more night of blissful sex in his apartment. So it happened, but the troubles were not over because, for unrevealed reasons, it was Georg who was fired. He began stalking his former lover and when he saw her leaving Sternberg's house, he wrestled the keys from her hand. In despair, Hedwig invited Georg by letter to meet her in the Tiergarten, Berlin's big park, on March 7, 1913 at 10 p.m. Perhaps Georg thought they would have sex once more in exchange for the keys. Only Hedwig, standing near his body with a pistol lying on the ground, was left to tell what exactly happened. Georg's head contained two bullets. A lawyer hired by Sternberg adduced evidence of abnormality in her family and pleaded temporary hysteria. Hedwig got off with a sentence of 30 months.[70]

For a long time, the Dutch had the reputation of being an unromantic, decently middle-class nation. Perhaps that is why one notorious *crime passionnel* has been remembered there for decades. The principal victim, born in 1880, was a native, but his French name fitted the international flavor of his career and romances. Jean-Louis Pisuisse first worked as a journalist and Dutch correspondent in London, then toured The Netherlands as

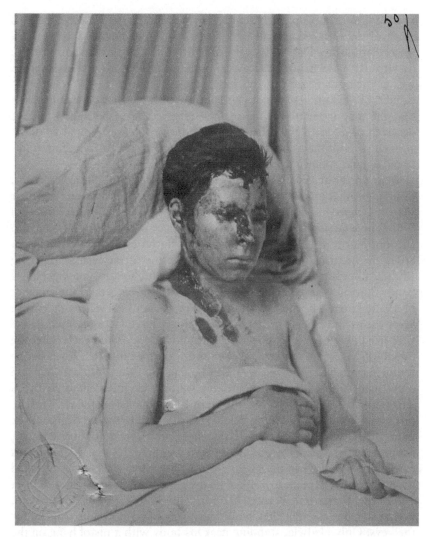

Figure 6.1(a): Victims of vitriol attacks, from legal proceedings, Paris 1885

a bohemian singer; from 1908 he led a cabaret company influenced by French popular culture. After divorcing his first wife, he married the actress Fie Carelsen, with whom he entertained the troops mobilized at the borders during World War One. Shortly after introducing the Belgian singer Jenny Gilliams to his company in 1919, he began an affair with her. Their daughter was born the next year, but Jean-Louis remained fond of his wife as well. She left him, but did not initiate divorce proceedings until 1925, and the final document included the note "temporarily dissolved."

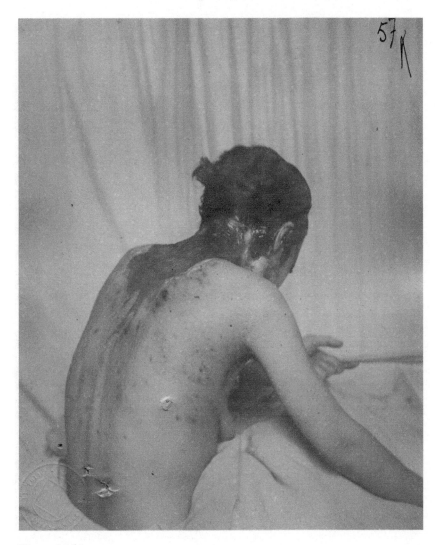

Figure 6.1(b)

Jean-Louis and Jenny toured Indonesia for two years and married in July 1927. Around the same time, Jenny had a brief affair with Tjakko Kuiper, the company's guitarist, but she soon returned to her husband again. Her lover had hoped for more. On November 26, 1927, Tjakko shot the couple and himself in Rembrandt Square, the center of Amsterdam's theater district. Pisuisse's rich love life had repercussions after his death, since Jenny's body was removed from their common grave the following year and Fie's was laid into it after her death in 1975.[71]

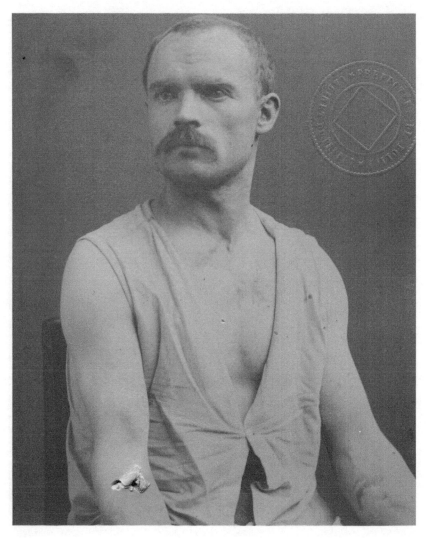

Figure 6.1(c)

After 1930 the age of the *crime passionnel* was largely over. Murders resulting from romantic triangles still occurred, but their appreciation by magistrates, behavioral experts, and the public changed. Some commentators had always considered the treatment of such crimes as being disrespectful of the law and the offenders as selfish persons with unseemly sexual appetites. After 1930, French criminologists, too, changed their opinion. Henceforth, crimes of passion were viewed as dangerous and as testifying to a bloodthirsty temperament.[72]

Monsters and Fanatics

Everyone – and no one – knows Jack the Ripper. Everyone knows him for his notoriety, which follows him down the generations, and no one knows him because his identity remains a mystery to this very day. But was Jack the Ripper the first serial killer? Most historians routinely answer "no" to the "first" in this question because they always find antecedents. Individuals with multiple victims were mentioned in passing in earlier chapters. They included classic bandits and a number of poisoners. Almost all these offenders killed for financial gain, which also applied to the Edinburgh duo William Burke and William Hare, who in 1828 took the lives of 16 people in order to sell their bodies to an anatomist.[73] Seven years later, the Normandy peasant Pierre Rivière committed a more common type of murder: he bloodily slaughtered his mother, sister, and brother, wrote his own account of the deed, and gained posthumous notoriety when Michel Foucault devoted a book to his case.[74]

None of these murderers easily matches the modern image of a serial killer. The instrumental element of financial gain is certainly foreign to that image. Following modern analyses, Philippe Chassaigne distinguishes between mass murderers and serial killers. The latter, to deserve that name, have to meet at least one of three criteria: the systematic selection of the same type of victim on each occasion, a sexual element in their crime, and sadistic rituals in conducting it. In my view, the term mass murder is misleading. It usually connotes orchestrated campaigns like the St Bartholomew massacre, or the elimination of the Kulaks at Stalin's orders. By replacing it with "multiple murder," which can accommodate all cases since the Middle Ages with more than a few victims, we avoid confusion. With that minor correction, Chassaigne's distinction appears relevant. Serial killers, he maintains, appeared on the European scene in the second half of the nineteenth century and first in France rather than in England.[75]

Debate is possible in each case about the applicability of any one of the three criteria, while future research may disclose forgotten incidents. One of the candidates for the first serial killer is an inconspicuous villager named Martin Dumollard, who lived with his wife in a hamlet near Lyons. He was in his mid-40s when he embarked upon his criminal career, which stretched from at least 1855 to 1861. Clad in a blue shirt, a grey hat with a large brim, and big shoes, he used to visit the city, approaching young women in the streets. Pretending to be a gardener looking for a servant and promising high wages, he lured his victims into some deserted place in the countryside, never the same, intending to kill them there. Five of these women, however, managed to escape before he could hurt them. The police linked their cases to the same perpetrator, together with that of a young woman whose nude body was found in the woods with traces of rape in 1855. Martin had tried to rob some of the escaped victims, which fits less easily into the profile of the modern serial killer. After his arrest in May 1861, the investigators accused him of attempts at rape and robbery of several other young women and suspected him of having killed three girls whose bodies had been fished from the Rhône in 1852–3. These accusations may be unsubstantiated, but we cannot get around the unidentifiable skeleton buried in the woods and the corpse of yet another woman thrown into a ravine, because both were discovered with the help of Martin's wife. He declared that he had killed no one, but delivered all the women to some bearded men from Lyons at their command. Martin Dumollard was guillotined in front of an immense crowd in March 1862.[76]

The next criminals of the serial killer type included the Frenchmen Joseph Philippe, who murdered several prostitutes in 1866, and Eusèbe Pieydagnelle, who allegedly derived immense sexual pleasure from boxing six young girls to death in 1871.[77] Spain shuddered at the crimes of a certain Garayo, a native of Alava living in Madrid, who between 1870 and 1879 strangled six women and afterwards raped them.[78] An Italian precursor was of the more traditional type: a simple cartwright from the small Tuscan town of Incisa, Callisto Grandi. He strangled or beat to death four boys, between 4 and 9 years old, between 1873 and 1875, and buried their remains under the floor of his workshop. Neighbors finally caught him while he was attempting to murder a fifth. Callisto declared that he had done it out of hatred for the town's children, who often mocked him for his physical deformities.[79]

The Ripper's crimes are often called the Whitechapel murders, after the part of London's East End where they occurred. It was a dark slum area where prostitutes walked the streets hoping to attract clients. Between August 31 and September 30, 1888, four women were found partly undressed with their throats cut and their bodies, except in one case, severely mutilated. All four victims were in their mid-40s. Then a news agency received a letter and a postcard signed by "Jack the Ripper" who explained that he was "down on whores." Jack remained inactive until November 9, when the police discovered an Irish-born prostitute disemboweled in her slum dwelling. Unlike the other four, she was 25 and attractive. The rest of the story consists of more than 100 years of speculation. It included an affair that took place only three and a half years later, when four prostitutes in the Lambeth quarter of south London were found poisoned by strychnine. It turned out that the perpetrator, a doctor who had also committed crimes in Canada and the United States, had approached them with the suggestion that they try his special pills for improving their complexion. The media linked the two series of murders and many thought that this doctor and the Ripper were one and the same person. Journalists were as yet unaffected by the modern understanding that a serial killer is unlikely to change his method so drastically.[80]

The fact that reports of many of the post-1900 serial killers can be found with ease on the internet testifies to the continuous fascination they elicit. A few were made the subject of historical study. The twentieth century opened with Henri Vidal, a 34-year-old hotel keeper about whom two French scholars wrote a biography.[81] In December 1901, on the French Riviera, he attacked two prostitutes and managed to kill a third with a kitchen knife. After stabbing to death a young Swiss woman and throwing her out of the train on which he met her, he was arrested for traveling without a ticket. Vidal died in the Guyana penal colony in 1906. The crimes of Henri Landru had even more resonance. During World War One, when he was in his mid- to late 40s, he preyed on the widows that his fallen compatriots had left behind. He would put an ad in the lonely hearts section of a newspaper, win their confidence in his Paris mansion, persuade them to entrust their valuables to him, and then burn them in his oven. After the war, the police finally linked him to the missing women whose cases they had investigated without success, and he was guillotined in 1922. Landru's notoriety extended to the Netherlands, where people sang a song about his case.[82]

Songs were equally prominent, as Fritz Lang's *M* indicates, in the public's recollection of a set of serial killers whose exploits shocked Weimar Germany. The first was the most notorious of all. Fritz Haarmann from Hanover had already served several prison terms for burglary when he started on his murder career in 1918, at the age of 39. The police now used him as an informer and unofficial detective, which allowed him freely to inspect the papers of male adolescents at the railway station. Haarmann persuaded them to come with him, had sex with them and, at his orgasm, bit through their throats. He disposed of their body parts in the nearby river, but popular imagination afterwards had it that he made meat out of his victims and sold it. His murders continued until 1924, when he was caught, which led to his execution the next year. In *M*, the authorities briefly discuss his case and that of his colleague Grossmann, while still another serial murderer, the "Düsseldorf Vampire," whose victims were girls as well as men, was on trial as Lang was shooting the film, so that some accused him of exploiting that case.[83] With the intermediate period better known for mass murder, the German Federal Republic witnessed serial killing too. At his arrest in 1966, the Rhinelander Jürgen Bartsch was just 20. In the previous four years, he had raped and dismembered four boys in an abandoned air-raid shelter. His various trials lasted until 1971, leading to much publicity in the German media. Numerous people wrote letters to the police, the court, or the press. This writing is noteworthy for showing the prevalence of deep-seated feelings of retaliation even in a period of relative tolerance, a democratic spirit, and anti-authoritarianism. Many writers called for the reinstitution of the death penalty. Some tried to explain the offender's career, for example by his adoption and his overly caring mother. Bartsch died on the operation table during a voluntary castration in 1976.[84]

These few cases show that, even within the strict definition of the act, serial murderers were, in the past, a mixed bag. This applies to their age and sexual preference, among other things. Modern serial killers are continually profiled, laid on a symbolic couch, and their media impact analyzed, but these exercises are insufficient to explain why their type didn't appear until the second half of the nineteenth century. The role of publicity suggests that the expansion of the media had something to do with it, but newspapers, and broadsides before them, had been devoting their attention to sensational crimes for ages. An explanation for the appearance of serial murder in terms of Victorian sexuality would fail to account for its persistence through to today. A skeptic might maintain that there have always been serial killers, but that for a long time their crimes remained undetected. That would run counter to the observation that serial killers thrive on the publicity that their deeds and victims elicit. Moreover, the breakthrough of serial killing occurred several decades after the introduction of the new police but before the application of fingerprints, which makes an argument based on increased chances of detection even more unlikely. To the contrary, because all pre-industrial people frequently spied on their neighbors and scrutinized strangers even more intensely, it would have required superhuman cunning to lure, unobserved, a succession of victims into one's home or to a deserted place, or to dismember them in the streets.

A plausible historical explanation must take the emergence of serial killing as an integral part of the long-term history of murder.[85] This emergence is roughly coterminous with the demise of the official duel and the rise to prominence of the *crime passionnel*. As traditional male honor became further discredited, the overall incidence of violence declined, and psychiatric defenses became more common, so the image of murder was associated more firmly with the dark realm of overwhelming passion or sadistic preferences. The serial murderer, in particular, with a combination of secrecy, twisted sexuality, and lust for torture, was the anti-model to civilization. There is no reason to assume that a raise in the standards of behavioral control automatically calls forth their antithesis in some individuals. However, the theory of civilizing processes may help to explain the modern fascination with serial killers, which is perhaps related to the equally modern quest for mimetic excitement.[86]

Politics and government were transformed from the secretive and private to a more public and open matter. At the same time, this development promoted murder. Whereas princes like Louis XIV had been unapproachable, the demands of democratic representation and elections led to a greater visibility of politicians in the streets. Hence, it happened more often that an ordinary person, out of deep conviction or confused ideas, made an attempt to kill a political leader – and sometimes succeeded. The perpetrator usually had a gun and often the nationality of murderer and victim differed. Thus, two presidents of the French Third Republic were murdered. On a visit to an exposition in Lyons in 1894, Sadi Carnot was assassinated by the Italian anarchist Santo Caserio. The Russian *émigré* Paul Gorguloff shot Paul Doumer with a revolver in 1932. The first assassination had the greatest impact, especially when we take into account the fact that Carnot was in office for much longer than Doumer. The media treated the act as akin to the regicide of former days, whereas by 1932 everyone seemed to have become familiar with the phenomenon of political murder.[87] In almost all cases, the perpetrators were men, but there was the remarkable case of Violet Gibson, an Irish woman of nearly 50, who shot at Mussolini from a crowd in Rome in April 1926. She managed only to injure his nose. Her lawyer, Enrico Ferri, student of none other than the criminologist Cesare Lombroso, successfully pleaded insanity on her behalf, which satisfied the Fascist leadership. The Italian authorities extradited Violet to England, where she spent the rest of her life in an asylum. After unsuccessful requests for her release to Winston Churchill in 1940 and at the wedding of Queen Elizabeth and Prince Philip in 1947, she died there in 1956.[88]

Anti-Semitism is intimately related to politics. Eastern Europe's pogroms and the Holocaust were its most fateful consequences, but a few individual murders drew attention as well. Toward 1900, after some 100 years of emancipation, the Jews of Western and Central Europe met with renewed anti-Semitism, of which the Dreyfus Affair in France in the 1890s is the best-known example. In London, during the Ripper scare, some people had suggested that the killer was a Jew driven by a desire for ritual bloodshed. According to an ancient belief, Jewish men were obliged to kill any gentile woman with whom they had engaged in sex. The police arrested one Jewish man, but he was quickly released. On a wall near the site where Catherine Eddowes, the fourth victim, lay, either the Ripper or some other person, in any case a bad speller, had written "The Juwes are the men That Will not be Blamed for nothing."[89] Unfounded accusations occurred elsewhere too. In April 1899, when the corpse of the seamstress Agnes Hruza was found in the woods near the Bohemian town of Polna, people believed it to be bloodless. The inhabitants, recalling the old story about ritual murder, suspected a Jewish apprentice of being involved. The district court sentenced him to death as an accomplice, but because of an imperial pardon he only served a prison term.

The murder of another Christian who was reputed to have been robbed of his blood for ritual purposes shook the west Prussian town of Konitz (Chojnice) a year later. In the nearby lake, his own father discovered the torso of Ernst Winter, an 18-year-old gymnasium pupil, who had been missing for a few days. His other remains were subsequently recovered in several places around town. The body had been severed in parts very neatly, as if done by a butcher. When a detective from Berlin arrived, many of the inhabitants already suspected the Jewish butcher, Adolph Lewy. Nevertheless, the detective started to interrogate the suspect's Lutheran colleague Gustav Hoffmann, a respected citizen. Since the victim's reputation as a womanizer and visitor of prostitutes was well known, the investigator's theory had it that Ernst had attempted to seduce Gustav's 15-year-old daughter and that the father had caught and killed him. In response to this supposition, Christian inhabitants vented their anger on the town's 300 Jews during several months of rioting that led to army intervention. Gustav Hoffmann published his account of the murder, explaining that the cut in the victim's throat was a typically kosher one, but the case of Ernst Winter remained unsolved.[90]

Next to the Jews, other minority groups suffered from riots as well as individual murders in which national or religious differences exacerbated personal grievances. England witnessed recurrent violence between natives and the Irish, sometimes also between Anglicans and English Catholics. Incidents were especially frequent in Liverpool.[91] In France, Italian immigrants bore the brunt of xenophobia. There were nearly 300,000 of them in the south-east of the country, where they constituted a badly paid underclass, branded in the press as uncouth and dirty. Natives designated all Italians as "Neapolitans." The most serious incident, which led to the death of 8 Italians and serious injury for 50 others, took place in Aigues-Mortes in 1893.[92]

Two World Wars and Their Aftermaths

Measured in absolute numbers, the destructiveness of the years 1914–18 was unprecedented. At the Western front, the net result of massive death was often no more than the gain and loss of 100 meters. For the first time, Europeans realized that, whereas the internal pacification of states had progressed, the destructive potential of interstate conflict had immensely increased. Did World War One bring a reversal of the civilizing process, in the sense that overall self-control declined? No doubt life in the trenches was degrading, and, afterwards, many Europeans realized what state violence could entail. Here we are concerned with the question of a lasting effect in everyday life.

Contemporary fears are much in evidence. Many thought that the experience in the trenches had removed restraints on aggression from former soldiers, that the slaughter and misery they had witnessed made them unable to adapt to civilian life. British newspapers carried reports on returned servicemen who savagely raped women or committed excessively violent robberies. In the opinion of some, this aggressive mentality not only characterized ex-soldiers, but also infected broader sectors of society. Writers included comments about reprisals against Irish revolutionaries and the massacre of unarmed civilians in colonial India. Conservatives feared an export of the Bolshevik Revolution, considering each political riot, strike, or leftist demonstration as a sign of brutalization. Similar anxieties, focusing on political unrest and the reported killing of wives and their wartime lovers, were widespread in France, Germany, and Italy.[93]

Based on selective impressions, these fears were predestined to be discredited by later historians. For Belgium, Rousseaux et al. systematically assessed the effect of both world wars on homicide rates. The authors used medical statistics for an analysis in which they examined separate regions in detail. Even though the data are missing for the years 1914–18, they are revealing. Homicide rates fluctuated at just over 2 between 1901 and 1913 and stood at 5 when the series resumed in 1919. However, the rates had already returned to the pre-war level by 1922, and during the 1930s they were even lower. World War Two brought peaks of about 8 in 1943 and more than 20 in 1944. Once more, the rates quickly returned to normal, standing at 5 in 1945, at 3 in 1946–7, and about 1 in 1950. Thus, whereas the homicide rate increased in the aftermath of World War One, the peak came during the later phase of World War Two. The regional analysis, combined with qualitative evidence, shows why. The 1919 peak was most pronounced in rural areas, which witnessed a resurgence of traditional banditry in the wake of the breakdown of the state apparatus. Since this breakdown began during the war, the authors assume that the concomitant rise in murders also started earlier. Homicides during World War Two were concentrated in places with the strongest resistance movement. Hence, these murders mainly involved the elimination of political opponents, while the delay until 1943 was consistent with the polarization process that gradually took shape. Banditry also accounted to a certain extent for the peak.[94]

For our inquiry into the lasting effects of the two world wars, the quick return to normality constitutes the most relevant observation. In France also, the start of the Great War inflamed passions, as is indicated by a lynching in the village of Vandélicourt. In the first few days of the invasion, after the Germans had retreated from the area, the mayor's barn, stored to the roof with corn, caught fire. The inhabitants suspected a former employer, who, at his dismissal, had threatened the mayor. They seized the suspect, mutilated him, and threw him into the fire alive. French homicide rates showed some aftermath effect, with an average of 1.3 in the years 1920–5, but since then they were less than 1 until 1933. Fluctuations occurred after that date, with the lowest five-year average (0.6) in 1951–5. The short-term effect of World War Two was similar to that in Belgium: 2 in 1943, then 17.7 in 1944, and 2 again in 1945. France, moreover, witnessed a new peak between 1957 and 1962 at the height of the Algerian war, with an average of about 2.[95]

This last French peak was exceptional in Europe west of the Iron Curtain. Throughout this area, homicide rates converged, which meant a slight rise for some countries. Thus, the rate for England and Wales stood at 0.7 during the 1950s and 1960s, whereas Italian homicide rates decreased from 1.9 in 1948–55 to 0.9 in 1966–70. This followed upon nearly 10,000 (estimated) political murders at the collapse of the Fascist regime and a peak in robberies in 1946. The Netherlands witnessed very low homicide rates for much of the twentieth century. Measured in five-year averages from 1911 to 1969, they reached their lowest point (0.23) in 1920–4 and their highest point (0.44) in 1935–9; that is, with the exception of World War Two. With only five-year averages reported, this war influenced the periods 1940–4 (1.7) and 1945–9 (1.5).[96] Together, the cited figures prove that, as far as aggressive tendencies were concerned, the two world wars did not bring about a reversal of the civilizing process in everyday life.

Research on non-fatal violence confirms this conclusion. In the absence of reliable evidence from victimization surveys, newspapers constitute an alternative source. A team led by Eric Dunning investigated disturbances, involving three or more people, in England, Wales, and Scotland in 1900–75. In scale and substance, most incidents were comparable with the inter-village and inter-faith fights of earlier periods. The authors distinguish four types, belonging to the spheres of sport and organized leisure, politics, industry, and a residual category that they call "community." This latter category included gang activities as well as working-class street fighting with or without the police. These were classic forms of physical aggression, much in evidence for the nineteenth century as well. Political violence involved fighting at elections as well as attacks on suffragettes and the women's counter-attacks. The evidence reveals that middle-class people, too, were involved in political violence. The trend was clearly downward in three of the categories distinguished. Only violence connected to sport exhibited a rise toward the end of the period investigated. This did not prevent the overall trend from showing a marked decline, with the highest peaks in the first two decades of the twentieth century. Probably, these decades represented a continuation from earlier times. Qualitative evidence about pre-1900 political violence, for example, shows its extent to have been considerable. During the 1868 election, schools were temporarily turned into hospitals, in order to accommodate the injured.[97]

The further decline of violence between 1920 and the 1960s owed something to the intensified civilization campaigns aimed at the rougher sections of the urban working classes, with housing reform programs at the center. These programs originated in late nineteenth-century England and spread to Continental Europe after 1900.[98] In the Netherlands, a 1902 law facilitated the demolition and rebuilding of decrepit dwellings and introduced female supervisors of living spaces. The movement gathered momentum after 1918, when it was aimed at a specific group of families called "inadmissible" or "asocial." The main criteria for earning such a label were alcohol consumption and a lack of cleanliness, but neglect of one's children, sexual immorality, prostitution, and criminality came next. The criminal behavior in question primarily concerned theft and swindle. Thus, fighting habits constituted just a minor target of the housing projects. Nevertheless, these were part of a campaign to instill middle-class values, which included the renunciation of violence, into the rough sections of the working classes. The records of the supervising agencies regularly contain complaints about aggressive men, who intimidated neighbors or beat their wives. The nucleus of the various programs consisted of the removal of families deemed inadmissible to specially built neighborhoods, where they received regular visits from the supervisors. Such re-education projects continued until the early 1960s. By 1970, they had been abandoned everywhere and denounced as paternalistic and degrading.[99]

While the pacification of the working-class majority proceeded, the underworld slowly developed. It had begun to take shape, in Europe's principal cities, by the end of the nineteenth century. The concentration of prostitution, gambling, and the homes of habitual criminals all in a few neighborhoods fostered violence there. Berlin, expanding with great rapidity after becoming unified Germany's capital in 1870, forms an example. In 1887 the murder of a nightwatchman, a representative of the "old police" determined to combat the underworld, shook the city. A suspicious couple was arrested a few years later and convicted of physical injury with deadly result. It led to Berlin's first moral panic, with outcries against professional crime and new laws arranging for stricter regulation. In England, the term "underworld" itself appeared around the turn of the century. Formerly, people had spoken of "rookeries" or "dens" and the conversion to the singular implied a more powerful counter-image to the visible or upper world of law-abiding citizens.[100]

The underworld was firmly established in the interwar years. England had race-course gangs, who vigorously defended their turf and tried to conquer that of competitors. Some had Italian names, like the Sabini gang. They fought each other by boxing and kicking, but also with knives and iron bars and sometimes with pistols. Convictions included assaulting the police, wounding, and manslaughter. There were more gangs with a nucleus of foreigners, such as that of the five Messina brothers born of a Sicilian father and a mother from Malta. They operated in prostitution and gambling in London's Soho district, and were known for the violence with which they conducted their business. Contemporaries liked to attribute all gang violence to foreigners, but there were native syndicates as well. Within France, Marseilles boasted a reputation as a town of cutthroats. By the 1920s, the youth gangs called *nerfs* had evolved into an underworld of *nervis*. Illegal trading and the sex business took the place of property crime. Assassinations and fights between rival organizations were reported, as well as violence by men against women within the organizations. Several syndicates, such as that of the Guerini, were led by Corsicans.[101]

Weimar Berlin had gangs of unemployed youths between the ages of 16 and 25, as well as the *Ringvereine*, composed of experienced criminals, that figure in *M*. Illegal clubs with names like *Immertreu* (Always Loyal), whose main business was organized prostitution, each guarded their own turf. Male members helped each other when a prostitute threatened to leave her pimp or a fellow ran into trouble in a bar, identifying themselves by their insignia before striking. The police viewed these clubs as a "lesser evil," ensuring at least some order, but the newspapers complained about "American conditions." Sometimes things got out of hand. When two groups of pimps, each claiming the same territory, fought a battle involving some 200 men at the Silesia station in December 1928, one participant was left dead. The media were especially outraged a few days later, when a host of club members escorted the victim to his funeral – in cars! The rich feared that, since the underworld appeared to be motorized, they could easily come and burglarize fancy neighborhoods. The English, too, were quick to speak of American methods when the underworld seemed too powerful or when guns were in play. In 1938, two British deserters, armed with revolvers, hijacked a car and robbed several people, until unarmed bobbies managed to overcome them by causing their car to crash. Supposedly, they had acted under the influence of marijuana, almost unknown in Britain, it was said. The judge who presided over their trial stated: "It cannot be too clearly understood in this country that the methods of the gangster and the gunman are not going to be tolerated."[102]

In the interwar period, politically inspired street fighting, especially characteristic of Weimar Germany, constituted one more visible form of aggression. Much of it must be categorized as revolutionary rather than interpersonal violence, but in the "quiet years" of 1924–8 the battle for the streets assumed a more traditional, territorial character. Scholars describe these confrontations, between communists and national socialists in particular, as ritual clashes not unlike earlier neighborhood fights. The recruiters appealed to ancient notions of strong masculinity, as did the communists, despite their commitment to female emancipation. Casualties did result from these battles. Between 1924 and 1928, 66 fatalities were counted, and 266 injured. Thereafter, the situation worsened and the state partly relinquished its monopoly on violence. There were 155 fatalities and 426 injured in 1929–31 and another 155 dead in the "bloody year" of 1932.[103] Outside Germany, there were fewer such political battles and also fewer fatalities. The British Union of Fascists, led by Oswald Mosley, occasioned some of these. Their violence, and the counter-violence from Jewish and leftist groups, was especially fierce in 1936.[104]

The Trough of Violence

In Europe west of the Iron Curtain, the 1950s were, on average, the least violent period in history. This decade had the lowest homicide rates ever, and in most countries prosecution rates for assault were down as well. It was an ebbing tide even in the United States, although the level there was considerably higher. In some European countries, homicide and assault slightly rose in the 1960s, but on the whole this decade was comparable to the preceding one. Contemporaries might have been afraid of the prospect of nuclear war, but interpersonal violence, it seemed, was disappearing. In 1953, a Dutch criminologist, observing that violent crime was typically rural, predicted that it would decrease even further as urbanization progressed.[105]

The fighting that did take place was largely confined to young males – the group that had always been most prone to violence. Concern was high in several countries in the 1950s about "wild" youths and juvenile delinquency. Juvenile institutions in Britain inculcated in their inmates a sense of strong masculinity, which excluded, however, all aggressive tendencies. A 1999 study, in which three generations of Londoners were interviewed, provides a picture of social realities. For the generation that grew up in the 1930s, notably for roughs, fist fights were still an accepted means of solving conflicts. Women sometimes fought too. Men of the second generation, young in the 1950s and early '60s, reported fights that broke out near dance halls, but many added that they tried to avoid such trouble.[106]

Once more, it should be added that this fighting hardly contributed to the homicide rate. Almost everywhere by the mid-twentieth century, even though the fascination with the *crime passionnel* had faded, conflicts in intimate relationships accounted for nearly half of all homicides.

The use of knives as well as guns was uncommon in these years. Murder weapons in France in 1950–70 included a great variety of objects that are difficult to classify, which were always in the majority except during the Algerian war. Firearms accounted for 20–25 percent among male victims and 20–30 percent among female ones. Only during the Algerian war did just over half the male victims fall to gunfire. Sharp instruments accounted for 15–25 percent of the killings of women and 15–20 percent of those of men, again with the exception of the years 1957–62, when their share was lower. Because this period represented a peak in the total homicide rate, it meant that the incidence of stabbings remained relatively constant. A German study covering the years 1963–74, while not providing percentages of stabbings among all murders, yet indicates the relative marginality of the knife. It was largely the weapon of foreigners. In a sample of 40 lethal stabbers examined by psychiatrists, 23 were German, 7 Italian, and 6 Turkish. In this period, the two foreign groups consisted mostly of young single male guest workers. Nevertheless, traditional male honor played a negligible role; the investigator attributed four cases to it. Out of a total of 84 wounds suffered by the victims, only 11 were in the face or head. These stabbings conformed to the general murder trend, to the extent that half of them occurred in an intimate relationship. Half the victims, but only three perpetrators, were female.[107]

The relative marginality of the knife among murder weapons during much of the twentieth century indicates that any downward effect of increased medical expertise on homicide rates remained modest. Past victims who might have been saved, had they lived in modern times, mostly died after suffering stab wounds. Their wounds became infected or they perished from blood loss that the availability of ambulances and advanced operations might have prevented. A skeptic could argue that knives accounted for so few homicides precisely because most stabbing victims were saved in hospitals, but the qualitative evidence about fighting habits runs counter to that supposition. Eric Monkkonen (2001) proposed the measurement of the time between attack and death as an indication of the chances of survival. Such an exercise will no doubt make our assessment of the effects of medical expertise more precise and hence improve our estimate of the comparability of homicide rates from various ages, but this factor has not yet been systematically investigated. The evidence we have so far suggests that the low level that European homicide rates had reached by the 1950s was real.

The hippie movement of the second half of the 1960s was the cultural corollary to the trough in violence. The word "hippie," at first a derogatory term employed by the older generation of beatniks, originated in San Francisco. The encompassing youth culture, however, had firm roots in 1960s Europe too. Its most important characteristic, from the point of view of our subject, was its peaceful character, applying to male and female adolescents alike. For ages, physical violence had been the preserve of young males in particular. By contrast, hippies expressed physical love and a return to nature. On them, unlike the 1938 robbers, marijuana had a calming effect. Many channeled their energies into social and political protest, in particular against the Vietnam War. Precursors there were, such as some idealistic youth groups around 1900, but they consisted overwhelmingly of young men and women from a middle-class background. The hippie movement was the first to attract a significant group of working-class youths.[108] Toward 1970, it seemed as if violence would be further discredited. But some political activists wondered whether peaceful demonstrations were enough, and others, instead of sticking to marijuana, turned to opiates.

7

The Tables Turned: 1970 to the Present

In the early 1990s, David Lepoutre worked as a teacher in the *banlieue*, the ring of satellite towns around Paris that non-residents usually avoid. For his anthropology thesis, he decided to investigate the world in which he taught, with an eye on violence and the culture of inner-city youths. His school was in La Courneuve, but most of his pupils came from nearby Quatre-Mille, where he moved in 1992. He saw the inhabitants routinely throwing their waste from the windows; despite frequent cleaning, by the end of the weekend the streets were always full of rubbish. Even worse was the penetrating smell of urine that invaded his nostrils each time when he entered his condo or used the elevator. He often wondered what kind of uncouth people were responsible for this. As he came home one night from his judo club in the company of three informants, bright adolescents with excellent school results and good at sports, he invited them in for a drink. In the hall of the building they suggested to each other that they should "re-assume the habits of the city." Continuing their lively conversation, all three urinated against the wall.[1]

Several comments are possible. Perhaps the informants considered the prospect of having to use their teacher's bathroom as the greater incivility. On the other hand, they were conscious of reverting to ways that many comrades found normal. Lepoutre included the episode in his book to illustrate that some habits offensive to him were more widespread than he had at first thought. Whatever our interpretation, the combination of indoor-urinating adolescents and a teacher investigating violence raises the question of the relationship between levels of aggression and of hygiene. As the previous chapter showed, neither of the two world wars brought a reversal of civilized standards into daily life, even though many contemporaries thought they would. Stereotypical images equally abound with respect to present-day cities. Is this an age of de-civilization? Scholars following the approach of Norbert Elias and related theorists seldom use such an either/or formula. Instead, they attempt to assess the balance between civilizing and de-civilizing tendencies in modern society. From that angle, the question becomes whether we are observing a – possibly temporary – rise in homicide and assault or something more fundamental and lasting.

Determining whether a contemporary development will last into the future is always a hazardous enterprise. Historians, moreover, find it problematic to analyze the recent past, because it is hard to tell the main trends from sidelines and dead ends. Although it is feasible to frame a continuing story about successive governments in France and Italy, the disintegration of the Communist system, and the reunification of Germany, this applies much less to the social and cultural history of which interpersonal violence is a part. The literature on modern violence is vast, but much of it consists of studies lacking a time perspective. The attempt to mold all this into a framework of long-term change requires a concentration on the principal trends. The modest aim of this chapter, dealing with three and a half decades, is to make sense of the evidence on recent murder and assault against the background of the long-term developments that the preceding chapters illuminated.

Despite the turning point in the overall rates, murder since the 1970s does feature some continuities. The proportion of intimate victims, for example, maintained the relatively high level that it had reached by 1900. It declined somewhat only in countries that witnessed the largest increase in homicide. The public's and the media's fascination with serial killing persisted, as did its quantitative insignificance among all fatal crimes. The pacification of the elites, sealed with the demise of the formal duel, remained a fact. Someone who aspires to rise socially and who entertains aggressive habits is obliged to renounce them. Fighting still concentrates in the lower social milieus, which in many countries consist, for a large part, of non-European immigrants. This immigration, which has taken off since the 1970s, constitutes one of the principal new trends. Together with de-industrialization and the growing importance of nighttime recreation, it has changed the face of cities in particular. Accompanying developments include the increase of ethnic and religious divisions within neighborhoods, a measure of de-pacification in some of them, and a partial revival of traditional macho honor. The diminution of power differentials between social strata, in itself a continuing trend, has turned into a positive influence on the level of violence. In particular, it led to a slackening of civilization campaigns, now considered as paternalistic, and a decline in deference toward social superiors and representatives of institutions, such as teachers or civil servants. The most crucial change since 1970 consists of the twin trends of an expanding market for illegal drugs and the proliferation of organized crime on a global scale, coupled with intensified counter-activity by law-enforcement agencies.

The Incidence of Murder

Figure 7.1 shows homicide rates, based on medical statistics and aggregated for seven European countries, 1950–95. While the level fluctuated between 0.8 and 1 per 100,000 in the 1950s and '60s, it subsequently started to rise, reaching 1.4 in the 1990s. In combination with the preceding decline, some scholars speak of a U-curve, but that is only appropriate if we do not look back beyond the mid-nineteenth century. The homicide rates of the 1990s are insignificant when compared to the incidence of murder in the Middle Ages, or even around 1700. Nevertheless, an increase of over 50 percent within a quarter of a century calls for an explanation. Since the mid-1990s homicide rates have stabilized and even gone down again in some countries, but they are far from returning to the pre-1970 level. The average per decade for 17 European states combined was 0.7 in the 1960s and 1.0, 1.3, and 1.3 in the next three decades; between 2000 and 2004, it was 1.2.[2] If the rates were now to drop, we will have witnessed only a temporary upsurge, comparable in duration to the Amsterdam peak between the 1690s and 1720s. In the past, however, such counter-trends were usually local or regional, whereas the recent rise is more or less European-wide. That makes it a structural phenomenon.

Yet marked differences between individual countries exist. First of all, the Soviet Bloc, which disintegrated from the middle of the period under discussion, underwent an entirely separate development, but throughout this book Eastern Europe has been left out of consideration. The post-1970 rise manifested itself in an especially steep manner in Great Britain and Ireland, where it did not stop by the mid-1990s. Between 1970 and 2000 the rates more than doubled in England and tripled in Ireland. France and Germany, on the other hand, witnessed hardly any increase. In between were countries like Italy, Spain, and Sweden, which hovered around the mean rise of about 50 percent. These geographic differences imply a complete reversal of the age-old pattern by which the rates were lowest in England and highest in Southern Europe. Indeed, Rome, once Europe's leader in murder, now ranks in the lower echelon of the national capitals.

The analysis of recent medical statistics should always be supplemented by an examination of police counts, which are now performed systematically. Few homicides escape their reach, no more than the number that escapes the attention of doctors. Moreover, the location of

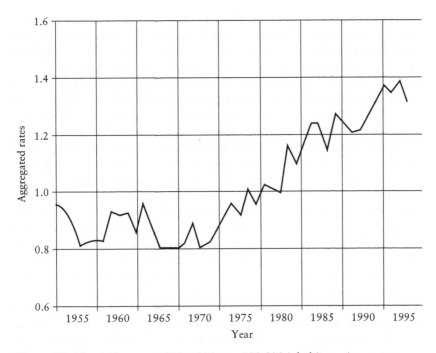

Figure 7.1: Homicide rates, 1950–1995, per 100,000 inhabitants in seven
European countries
Source: Presentation by Helmut Thome, based on data from Manuel Eisner, at
the seminar on violence, Ferrara, September 2003

the crime, as evidenced by the victim's body, forms the basis for police
counts. Medical statistics, by contrast, list victims by the criterion of residence in the country concerned. The effect of this classification difference
is clearly visible in The Netherlands. Whereas its homicide rates, calculated from medical statistics, rose from about 0.5 in 1970 to around 1.3
in the 1990s, when based on police registration, the 1990s homicide rate
comes at 1.7. Since the compilers of medical statistics aim to include all
Dutch residents who die abroad, it means that the national territory has
a surplus of murder victims. The number of Dutch residents who suffer a
violent death in a foreign country is lower than that of foreigners who
meet with the same fate in The Netherlands. It is unclear whether the
medical statistics of other European countries include residents who die
abroad, but almost everywhere, since the mid-1990s, the police-based
homicide rate is higher than the doctor-based one.[3] This points, if at
nothing else, at the increasingly border-crossing nature of murder.

Doctors play another crucial role by saving the lives of crime victims.
Since the proportion of those killed by firearms and, to a lesser extent, by

knives has increased, medical advances must have an effect on the rates. This effect would be to underestimate the scale of the rise in homicide, but we have no idea by how much. Since 1980, when historical research into murder started, scholars have noted the growing influence of medical intervention on the proportion of life-threatening injuries that become homicides – notably the twin components of stopping blood loss from penetrating wounds and quick transport to hospitals. Little systematic research has been done yet in order to estimate the effect. Investigating three European countries, Thome and Birkel (2007) just cite an American study. Its authors estimate that the 1999 US homicide rate would have been at least three times higher had trauma care and its infrastructure remained at the level of 1960. There are reasons to assume, however, that this estimate is an exaggeration, since the authors base it on statistics of aggravated assault and lightly pass over the possibility that the definition of this offense has become inflated. At the medical side of the equation, moreover, an increase in the countryside's density of hospitals is the decisive factor, which makes it hazardous to extrapolate the results of this study to Europe.[4] Its importance, rather, lies in drawing attention to a third component of the fatality risk: the speed of communication with emergency agencies. As it happens, the stabilization and partially downward trend of Western European homicide rates since 1995 coincides with the spread of cell phones. Research is needed to determine whether this is more than a spurious correlation.

The perception of a modern world full of aggression has been fostered by trends in non-fatal violence. The rates in question are based either on registration by the police or prosecution by courts. Assault rates, for example, rose significantly in England, Germany, and Sweden between 1950 and 1995, with the largest increase, from an annual 100–200 per 100,000 inhabitants to 400–600, since the mid-1970s. Figures for rape went up as well in England and Sweden, but not in Germany, which even witnessed a slightly downward trend. Robbery rates increased significantly in all three countries, especially since the mid-1980s and most dramatically in England, where they went further upward in the period 1995–2004. A steep rise in robbery rates since 1970 also characterized Denmark, Switzerland, and Italy. France witnessed an upward trend in all violent offenses recorded by the police. Their lowest point (120 per 100,000) was in 1963, followed by a very gradual increase to 200 in 1982. A spectacular rise started at the end of the 1980s, reaching a rate of 560 in 2004.[5]

The crucial question is whether the modern explosion of registered non-fatal violence reflects actual behavior. For robbery, this must at least partly be the case, because the rise is so steep. Robbery is of course as much a property crime as a violent offense and there is some evidence that many contemporary street robbers need calculated threats only. In some instances, moreover, the definition of robbery was subject to inflation. In The Netherlands in the 1980s, courts started to charge offenders who had grabbed a person's bag or purse from his or her hands or shoulders with violent theft, whereas such acts had been considered as simple theft earlier. In France in the early 2000s, grabbing a cell phone from a person's hands became classified as robbery. As far as rape is concerned, there is a broad consensus that the modern campaign against the age-old mechanism of blaming the victim has led to an increase in its being reported.

Figures for common assault, too, are subject to the influence of a heightened sensitivity to domestic as well as street violence. Victims and the public show a greater willingness to report cases and, more important, police and magistrates tend to regard violent incidents more seriously than they had done previously and to classify accomplices along with the principal suspects. German scholars add that people increasingly call the police to end simple conflicts among youths, especially when natives feel threatened by foreigners or members of ethnic minorities. Margarethe Egelkamp, who compared court dossiers in The Netherlands and Germany in 1986 and 1996, found unequivocal evidence of a "violence inflation." In the latter year, similar cases had moved up one level on the legal scale of seriousness: severe injury automatically led to a charge of attempted manslaughter; what had been simple assault became aggravated assault; and incidents not considered worth prosecuting before streamed in at the bottom. Because of legal peculiarities, this inflation was less pronounced in Germany, but still clearly visible.[6] Hence, there is good reason to assume that a large part of the rise in registered non-fatal violence reflects increasing sensitivities rather than actual behavior.

The systematic comparison of victimization surveys, from the 1980s onward, lends support to this conclusion. The French survey of 1994 showed a significant rise, compared to ten years earlier, in the reporting of serious assault, but there were fluctuations after that, and in 2001 the reported rate was back at just above the 1984 level. By contrast, less serious violence continued its upward trend in France. Dutch victimization surveys show an increase in assaults and threats in the early 1980s, followed by a decrease in the 1990s. A recent EU-wide comparison of victimization surveys since 1988 shows a variegated pattern for assault with force. National differences were more marked than change over time; the rates went up in some countries, down in others, and showed a U-curve in still others.[7]

Great certainty prevails about the return of violence in urban areas. After one or two centuries of higher levels in the countryside, homicide and assault are now concentrated in cities. Whereas the nineteenth century witnessed a division between outer and inner zones, Europe's high homicide zone is now dispersed over its metropolitan centers. The effect is most marked when large cities are isolated from remaining areas. Thus, a French study that divided each region into municipalities with fewer than or more than 50,000 inhabitants found the urban concentration to be only modestly confirmed for the homicide rates of 1989–91. A Dutch study covering the years 1990–3 distinguished five groups of municipalities; with each increase in their size, homicide victimization was higher. Most of Europe's capital cities have homicide rates ranging between 2.5 and 5.5 per 100,000 inhabitants – much above the national average.[8] The urban return is only partially due to fighting and lethal robbery in "bad neighborhoods." It probably owes as much to the recreational function of metropolitan centers and the concentration of organized crime activities there. Both factors make it increasingly meaningless to compute separate homicide or assault rates for individual cities. Especially when it comes to recreation-related violence, in dancing and drinking places, potential perpetrators live in a wider area than that represented by the city and its number of inhabitants.[9]

Other available statistical data anticipate the discussion of the nature of violence. It can be concluded that the homicide rise since 1970 is due overwhelmingly to an increase in male victimization. In the medical statistics of Germany, Sweden, and England, the trend in the victimization of women was nearly flat, whereas the victimization of men increased more than threefold in England and about twofold in Sweden, but not at all in Germany. The English rise in male victimization was especially marked in the 20–40 age group. Judicial statistics for attempted and completed killings in 1955–95 show an increase in the number of male suspects, notably in Sweden, but also in Germany. Statistics of the British Home Office on victim–offender relationships since 1969 show a moderate decline in intimate homicides, a moderate rise for the killing of acquaintances and an eightfold increase in the killing of strangers. Dutch data for the years 1992–2001 reveal a share of 91 percent male killers, 71 percent male victims, and 35 percent of homicides in the intimate sphere.[10]

Scholars have proposed a variety of explanations for the trend in aggregated rates since 1970. After an elaborate quantitative analysis of socioeconomic and cultural variables, Helmut Thome concludes that egoistic and disintegrative individualism, in the sense of Durkheim, is on the rise and that the trend of increased violence is with us to stay.[11] Sebastian Roché (1998) equally finds that increased levels of physical aggression are inherent to modern society. According to him, the very forces that generated the long-term decline of violence now promote its rise. In his study of Switzerland, Manuel Eisner allows for de-industrialization, which led to a greater marginalization of risk groups and decreased their chances for conforming to the modern ideal of the self-conscious and autonomous individual, but in a re-examination for the whole of Europe, he lays different accents.[12] Ian O'Donnell, speaking of Ireland from 1995 to 2004, makes these links: "[R]apid prosperity, full employment, soaring alcohol use and a concomitant increase in violent deaths."[13] These explanations may all be pieces of the puzzle, but any convincing theory must be based on a supplementary body of evidence next to national statistics.

The Nature of Violence

Since the aggregated homicide rates point at the involvement of young men, an obvious question is whether the modern world is witnessing a resurgence of male-on-male fighting, similar to the type that was so prominent in the past. In order to arrive at an answer, we must examine qualitative evidence. Lepoutre's study of the Paris *banlieue* in the 1990s contains a model description.

His research contacts were 10–16-year-olds, but he received additional information on older youths. The Paris *banlieue* is one of the most heavily mixed metropolitan areas of Europe. When Lepoutre lived there, the inhabitants themselves distinguished six broad groups: Arabs, Blacks, the French, Hindus, the Chinese, and Jews. Neither racism nor mutual respect characterized everyday reality. Members of each group regularly made derogatory remarks about all the others and stereotypical images were current, but the neighborhood was the primary unit to be defended. Next to territorial battles, there were spontaneous fights lasting a few seconds, as well as duels fought before a large audience of boys and girls. Such duels were usually held after school, following a challenge in the morning or the previous day. Pupils would eagerly discuss the coming event during breaks and lessons. At the end of such a fight, the participants often had a broken nose or their faces cut open. Girls fought too, but less seriously. This violence occurred within an honor culture not unlike that of early modern Europe, although the word itself was hardly used. Male honor depended on a capacity to defend oneself, personally or by mobilizing a revenge group. An attack at one's face was the prime insult that required repair. Female honor, related to sexual reputation, was defended by fathers and brothers. Boys could also earn respect by treating others from the spoils of stolen goods. Under the influence of American movies and clips of rap performers, everyone hoped to impress his comrades by wearing clothes and accessories with expensive trademarks.

The role of weapons in all this was ambiguous. Pupils usually fought with their bare hands, but when a group fight escalated, the participants got hold of stones and sticks. Many possessed a tear gas spray, which they also used for fun in the classroom. Possession of stabbing weapons, too, was common, but these were for showing off rather than for use in a fight. The school's collection of confiscated knives, razors, and similar weapons increased annually. Firearms were even more rare, but the investigator heard about two incidents, one at the school exit and one in town, in which a person threatened another with a pistol without actually shooting. Older adolescents, however, no longer at school and involved in the drug scene, usually owned firearms, which they proudly showed to the junior boys. One boy told the investigator that he once inadvertently kicked a ball in the direction of such a drug dealer, whereupon the guy put his pistol to the boy's forehead in order to frighten him. These older adolescents, to be sure, formed a minority among all youths. Most boys dropped out of the street culture at about age 17, when they had to enter an advanced school. A small group moved on to more serious criminal business, centering around the drug trade. Shootings, in which the police intervened, regularly occurred in the school's area.

Thus, whereas the violence of the majority of schoolboys was real but relatively innocuous, that of a minority of older adolescents was serious but concentrated in the drug scene. Other French cities are also encircled by *banlieues*, except Marseilles and Strasbourg where the underprivileged quarters are located within the town's borders. The media were accustomed to describing all these areas as hotbeds of aggression and rebellion. Journalists and politicians referred to practically all offenses of urban youths, as well as to resistance to the police and rebellion against institutions, under the heading of *violences urbaines*. Reported incidents quadrupled between 1993 and 1997, but they were not all that serious. Sophie Body-Gendrot distinguished eight categories, from vandalism to rioting. In particular, she observed an increase of aggression in public transport, against passengers as well as personnel.[14]

London, too, witnessed renewed aggression, as reported in the interview study cited in the previous chapter. The generation that grew up in the 1990s saw more crime around them than their predecessors, and attributed this to drug use. Youths exhibited consciously aggressive behavior in order to sustain a violent reputation, which in its turn served to protect the valuables they had on them against robbery. Blacks as well as whites, between whom tensions existed, underlined the importance of such a tough reputation.[15] Throughout England, since the end of the 1980s, the late-hours leisure economy has greatly expanded, involving the laying-out of special night strips with clubs and bars. Consequently, alcohol-fueled street violence increased during the 1990s, most of it non-fatal.[16] Quite another perspective emerges from the gangs with political labels that were common in Norway in the late 1990s and early 2000s. They have been studied in depth for Kristiansand. Two antagonistic youth groups operated in this town, styling themselves Nazis and anti-racists and dressed in skinhead and hip-hop styles, respectively. Although youths with non-European backgrounds understandably favored the latter group, membership was determined primarily by ties of friendship and trivial conflicts with representatives of the other side, rather than political conviction. Individuals regularly switched allegiances. Fights, usually following upon ritual provocations, were about issues of respect, revenge, and the reputation of girls. These fights were usually unarmed and only a few boys moved on to a career of robbery or drug trading.[17] Of course, in a town of 75,000 we can expect no more than one murder per year.

In Dutch cities, schools are sites of violence, but most of it unarmed. As in the Paris area, possession of a knife is more common than its actual use. In the 1990s, a quarter of secondary school pupils owned one and 10 percent took one with them on a night out, but only 2 percent reported to have stabbed someone or been stabbed.[18] Urban life in The Netherlands, too, is marked by the presence of communities of non-European origin. A study of Berber-Moroccan youths in Rotterdam in the late 1980s and early '90s found many of them active in the drug trade, selling to French visitors in particular. The income from this trade gave them the status of successful businessmen. Honor, related primarily to the standing within their own community, was an important cultural commodity.[19] An interview study of Antillian adolescents in the mid-1990s also found that honor was a key element in their culture. Most of the respondents, 14–17-year-olds, had emigrated in their early youth and lived with just their mother. These mothers tended to allow their sons to carry a knife, because they considered their neighborhood a dangerous place, and some of the mothers themselves had a tear gas spray. Since the study purposely contrasted subgroups with and without police contacts, the group interviewed overall was not entirely representative of the community. The boys' criminal behavior was largely instrumental, consisting of petty theft, street robbery, and cocaine dealing. Their sense of honor became manifest especially when someone insulted their mothers. A boy readily stabbed another when he felt his honor to be at stake and a bad look from someone was considered a challenge. Obviously, this was traditional male honor: "In certain situations a man is required to demonstrate his capacity for physical defense and stabbing is considered obligatory then."[20]

The qualitative evidence about urban youths suggests that a part of the increase in homicide rates since 1970 is due to a resurgence of male fighting. As in the past, this fighting usually was non-fatal, but casualties occurred. To some extent, the situation resembles that of West European countries in the nineteenth century, when the homicide rate often was comparable too. But some groups today are more prone to use knives than their counterparts among the nineteenth-century working classes. Today's underprivileged strata consist for the most part of ethnic and racial minorities, whose members have taken the traditional male – and female – code of honor from their countries of origin. This concept of honor, now often called respect, has influenced native youths as well. International performance, TV clips, and movie scenes give rise to a powerful influence of rap musicians and African-American culture. Yet significant differences remain between underprivileged quarters in Europe and American inner-city neighborhoods. To a much lesser extent, the former can be characterized as unpacified islands or no-go-areas. The lesser prevalence of guns in Europe's inner cities ensures that showing off courage and toughness is not a necessity for survival, as Elijah Anderson (1999) describes for American inner cities. In Europe, only a small minority of adolescents moves on from the youth culture to engage in the drug trade and possess guns. Whereas the US hip-hop scene is rooted in the precarious conditions of the ghetto, in Europe it is imported as entertainment. Willem de Haan argues that one may speak of "pockets of poverty" or "ethnic concentrations" in French, English, and Dutch cities, but certainly not of ghettoes. The degree of segregation of all ethnic minorities is lower than that of African Americans. Unlike in Europe, US inner-city neighborhoods witness a breakdown of state agencies and public institutions.[21]

Statistics of murder weapons confirm that the prevalence of guns has increased since 1970, but their use remains far below the American level. In the 1990s, the average European share of murder by firearms was about one-third, as against two-thirds in the US. Within Europe, however, there was great national variation, from 14 percent in Sweden to 74 percent in Italy.[22] Counter-violence by the police remained modest. The Netherlands, Germany, and France, in the 1980s and '90s, annually witnessed one death through police bullets per five to seven million inhabitants.[23] More ambiguous are the statistics showing the nationality or ethnic origin of perpetrators and victims. Since the 1980s, nearly all European countries have witnessed an over-involvement of minorities and non-nationals in murder, which can be due to various causes. In view of the fact that, for several centuries, violence was concentrated in the lower social milieus, the computation of separate homicide rates per ethnicity is a biased enterprise. It would be more realistic to compare ethnic minorities with the underprivileged sections of the ethnic majority. The involvement of minorities and non-nationals in murder, moreover, points at the immigrant population and its subcultures, as well as to transnational organized crime.

Organized crime often means illegal drugs. The 1970 turning point in homicide coincides with the wholesale introduction of heroin on European markets and the spread of drug addiction. Here, too, there is a difference with the US, whose inner-city neighborhoods witness a violent competition for turf on almost every street corner. In many European countries the consumption and the retail trade of drugs are associated with petty theft and hustling rather than with lethal violence. Wholesale trade, on the other hand, subject to vigorous police scrutiny and judicial prosecution everywhere, normally is an organizational activity. Thus, the expanding market for illegal drugs has fostered organized crime, which, in its turn, came to focus also on human trafficking, the smuggling of weapons, and still other specialties. As the qualitative evidence about violence and crime among young males in European cities suggests, there was a fluid continuum from youth culture to juvenile delinquency, to regular drug trading, and finally to hardened professional crime. The networks at the criminal end of this continuum constituted a more complex system than the interwar underworld that thrived on local prostitution and gambling, let alone the world of classical brigandage, where separate bands seldom operated in each other's vicinity. Infused by globalization, today's underworld has an international dimension, with cooperation as well as competition extending over long distances. The weak level of coordination among Europe's police forces allows them too little space to cope with this situation.

Organized crime affects the profile of homicide through lethal conflicts among professional criminals. The presence of this category within overall murder is often obscured in studies that focus on nationally aggregated rates. Scholars studying crime-related murder usually define it by a broad criterion: perpetrator and victim are both involved in criminal activities and the killing is related to these activities. Not all such murders involve the calculated eliminations of competitors or punishments of cheaters that the public imagines them to be. A Dutch study of cases in the mid-1990s found that many did not convey a picture of cold-blooded violence. Here, too, honor and revenge were key elements. Even more crucial, given the increasingly international character of organized crime, was the offenders' experience of having to do business with people they did not know well and could not quite trust. On a methodological note, the investigator stresses the relative non-transparency of the process by which the police came to classify certain murders as liquidations and others not.[24] We should take into consideration, though, that this study was based on dossiers with known suspects. It is quite possible that another share of crime-related murders, executed by experienced professionals who leave no traces, involves calculated, rational killing indeed.

As studies of killer/victim relationships are necessarily based on dossiers with at least some information about the protagonists, they are likely to underestimate the proportion of crime-related murders. Examining a sample of French homicides in the 1990s, Laurent Mucchielli compares cleared cases with unsolved incidents, the latter nevertheless attributed, like the former, to either one of four categories. Whereas the clearance rates of three of these categories ranged between 75 and 96 percent, that of crime-related murders was a mere 43 percent.[25] In the Dutch study just cited, the proportion of crime-related murders stands at 16 percent, of which nearly a third occurred in or near Amsterdam.[26] The compilers of an extensive database of murders in The Netherlands in 1992–2001 distinguish killer/victim relationships for cleared cases only. They count 278 solved crime-related cases and 510 unsolved murders altogether.[27] If we extrapolate from Mucchielli's findings and assume that the 510 unsolved murders include another 278 crime-related cases, the figure stands at 21.8 percent. For Ireland, Ian O'Donnell arrives at an even higher share – one-third of all homicides in the early 2000s – attributed to "gangland feuding," whereas this phenomenon had been relatively insignificant in the 1970s and '80s. The gangland category is described as incidents relating to drug disputes, involving abduction preceded by torture and followed by a shot in the head either in a public place such as a bar or a raid and hit at the victim's home.[28]

To conclude, there is sufficient evidence to assume that another significant part of the post-1970 rise in homicide rates was due to the expansion of organized crime and the drug trade. The further criminalization of illegal market activities and the ensuing "war" on drugs and organized crime in the 1990s led to an intensified violent competition among the actors involved.[29]

The Modern Anxiety

On February 12, 1993, in the Liverpool area, two 10-year-old boys abducted and murdered nearly 3-year-old Jamie Bulger. Tabloids and television carried the story as breaking news, eagerly picked up by media outside England. In shock and grief, many observers complained about worsening times and called for severe punishments. The youthful killers eventually served eight years each, getting release for good behavior in June 2001. Like mafia witnesses, they were each given a new identity in order to prevent reprisals from members of the public. Clive Emsley compares this case to two similar ones in the 1850s and '60s, which were just regional news and whose much lighter sentences drew no comment.[30] On August 15, 1996, the Belgian nation rejoiced in the liberation of two girls, aged 12 and 14 and still alive, from the dungeon of serial killer Marc Dutroux. At least five other victims were dead. A public outcry against the shortcomings of the investigation followed, culminating in the "white march" of 300,000 people in Brussels in October.[31] In the night of August 16 of the same year, four friends, who had been out drinking and dancing until the early hours, attacked and chased fellow customers for fun at a snack bar in the center of Amsterdam. When 26-year-old Joes Kloppenburg said "*kappen nou*" (stop it now), they turned toward him, one of the quartet dealing such severe punches that Joes died the next morning. This murder started off the movement against "senseless violence" in The Netherlands. Joes's father established the foundation "Kappen Nou," and at the anniversary commemoration a sign saying "Help" was erected at the spot.[32]

These are three examples of the intense anxiety over violence, extending to individual murders, that emerged in Europe during the 1990s. It was a new and highly visible spurt in the process of increasing sensitivity that we saw reflected in the rising prosecution rates for non-fatal assault. This process first revolved around female victims, as a function of a decrease in power differences between men and women. The second feminist movement, starting in 1970, focused on the issue of abortion, but after 1980, female victimization, in domestic violence and rape, received increasing attention. At about the same time, sensitivity toward violence against children increased.[33] The Bulger case was exceptional because the perpetrators were children too. The anxiety emerging after 1990 extended to murder in male-on-male confrontations, especially those considered somehow unnecessary. Individual homicides gave rise to an acutely felt need to express indignation and a desire to commemorate. Public concern is equally high about murders related to sexual honor within communities of Turkish or South-Asian descent.

This modern anxiety takes various forms in the countries of Europe, but it accelerated everywhere in the 1990s.[34] In The Netherlands and Belgium, its primary target is so-called "senseless violence," involving either an attack on a stranger for trivial reasons – in which the attacker, however, often acts according to the revived traditional honor that he feels at stake – or a killing in a street robbery, when the public feels that, in view of the minor spoils, the victim should not have died. The reactions include silent vigils, as well as the laying of flowers and placing of a memorial at the spot. Germany and England witness frequent commotion and protest at racist murders in particular. The commemoration of victims is current in French *banlieues*, especially when they have been killed by the police. Public anxiety in Switzerland concentrates on sexual violence against children. Thus, the rise in sensitivity is European-wide, but its manifestations and main emphases, influenced by media reporting, differ by country. Everywhere, commemorative groups tend to adopt each other's methods. They recite the names of victims, for example – a practice that originated with Holocaust commemorations and extended to

Figure 7.2: Plaque for a victim of "senseless violence," The Hague. Photo: Pieter Spierenburg

forms of natural death such as aids. The emotions involved have different nuances depending on the offense. In cases of sexual assault, vindictiveness is the main reaction, whereas "senseless" murder leads to a diffuse feeling of not wanting to resign without a particular hatred for the perpetrator. Vindictiveness is largely absent when it concerns family dramas, usually during or after a divorce and often followed by the perpetrator's suicide. In such cases, sympathy for the victims predominates, especially if they are children. The commemoration of racist murders, finally, always has political implications.

These political implications have been magnified since September 2001, when events in New York shifted the target of anxiety. Fear of the terrorist threat was real, as the bombings in Madrid in 2004 and London in 2005 demonstrated. The randomness of the attacks made everyone conscious of being a potential victim, unlike with individual murder. Public attitudes toward crime-related murders, on the other hand, are often characterized by a measure of indifference. Many people do not care much if criminals kill each other, as long as they refrain from hitting innocent bystanders. Even the police sometimes delight in the fact that they can close their dossiers on a murdered suspect. Officers and magistrates, however, tend to consider such killings as an intolerable breach of their monopoly on violence. In January 2007, Amsterdam's chief of police Bernard Welten proudly announced that the 2006 fall in the city's murder rate was due to the force's successes in combating organized crime. The public reaction is typical of a society in which the large majority has no direct experience of violence. This is manifested in the relative helplessness that is felt when someone is, after all, attacked. An exploratory study of assault victims in 1998 found that three-quarters offered no resistance whatsoever, even though this failed to persuade the perpetrator to moderate his aggression.[35]

The 1990s spurt in sensitivity concerning violence can be situated within a wider context of cultural change. In 1979, the French philosopher Jean-François Lyotard announced "the end of grand narratives," providing a program for the postmodern movement that became visible in the 1980s. The sociologist Nico Wilterdink (2000), while critical of the scholarship that calls itself postmodern, accepts postmodernism as a label characterizing the culture of the late twentieth and early twenty-first centuries. The markers of this culture include a fluidity of boundaries in literature and the visual arts, which often merge with advertising; quick changes in fashions and popular views; a decline of faith in political ideologies; and the appearance of social movements – of women, gays, and ethnic minorities – that emphasize personal identity. Above all, postmodern culture is characterized by eclecticism and relativism concerning general rules, hierarchical principles, and solid forms. As explanatory factors, Wilterdink points at the commercialization of leisure, the appearance of new media, individualization, and the declining influence of organizations such as churches and trade unions. It is my hypothesis that the inherent mentality of "anything goes" requires an unacknowledged substratum of absolute certainty. This assumes the form of the widespread expectation of personal security and an absence of risk. Any challenge of that expectation causes great anxiety. Within the postmodern climate of relativism, safety from violence is one of the few collectively agreed-on demands.

Today's concern about domestic and sexual violence, murder, and terrorism indicates that the majority of Europe's population is not enmeshed in a great wave of de-civilization. The book's conclusion examines this issue against the background of the preceding seven centuries.

Conclusion

Over the past seven centuries the image of murder has changed considerably. At the beginning of the period examined, contemporaries often viewed homicide as an act of honorable defense or vengeance. Nowadays, murders regularly give rise to anxiety among the general public. Whereas all social classes, the elites even more than others, were involved in personal violence during the Middle Ages and after, physical force gradually became the exclusive domain of underprivileged groups. During an intermediate phase, respectable citizens regularly had to defend themselves, but they refused to become enmeshed in a knife fight. In the wake of these social and cultural changes, homicide rates declined enormously – a long-term development offset by just a slight rise in recent times. These quantitative trends, outlined from the start, are well known. The systematic examination of qualitative changes in murder has placed the bare numbers within a comprehensive framework.

It is less clear from the evidence whether the nature of murder has moved along the axes of violence described in the Introduction. A significant minority of recent homicides is related to criminal dealings, but many of these incidents entail confused reactions rather than calculated eliminations. Hence, they do not necessarily point at an increasing prominence of planned violence. It can be argued, on the other hand, that the degree of impulsiveness of overall aggression has diminished over time. At the most general level, the great decline in murder rates, whatever else it meant, points at an average increase of controls over aggressive impulses among Europe's population. The qualitative evidence, moreover, indicates that the remainder of murders in later times involved a somewhat lesser degree of impulsiveness than the homicides earlier on in the period examined. In particular, male fighting among core Europe's working classes in the nineteenth century involved greater restraint than in preceding periods, as evidenced by the shared understanding to refrain from using knives. Indications are again scarce for a shift over time in the balance between ritual and instrumental violence. The steep rise in robbery rates of recent decades may point at a greater share of the instrumental element in overall non-fatal aggression. However, many modern murders still have a decidedly ritual element.

These conclusions pertain especially to male-on-male fighting. As its incidence began to dwindle, the other three possibilities acquired greater visibility. Simultaneously, the proportion of murders in an intimate relationship was on the rise. Their total incidence, however, declined, just like that of altercations among strangers or acquaintances, though much more modestly. Trends in wife murder, in particular, reflected a diminution of power differentials between men and women. From the eighteenth century onward, as a husband's right of chastisement was increasingly questioned, fewer wife murders were punishment-related. The second half of the nineteenth century and the last decades of the twentieth witnessed further accelerations in concern over violence against women, in the second period also against children. The story is different again for murders that lack an element of overt aggression. Poisoning, always a minority method, shows no definite pattern over time. Infanticide is characterized by an n-curve. The qualitative evidence unequivocally confirms that this crime was closely linked to moral preoccupation with extramarital sex and the economic consequences of bastardy.

All the evidence combined provides powerful support for the theory of civilization. For one thing, this theory encompasses the diminution of power differences between various social groups, including the genders. To the extent that murder trends reflected a shift in the power balance between women and men, these trends are in line with the explanatory framework adopted here. In particular, the character of domestic murder changed from a dominance of hierarchy-related punishments that got out of hand to the dominance of an egalitarian type of emotional conflicts in the intimate sphere. In their respective periods, moreover, the former were more frequent – in incidence, if not in proportion of all homicides. On the other hand, the absolute frequency of tension-related intimate homicides alone has probably increased since the eighteenth century. It is unclear yet how this increase links up with the trajectory of civilizing processes over the last 100 years. The frequency was high, for example, on the eve of as well as during the modern rise in divorce rates. The evidence about women and murder also confirms another important tenet of civilization theory: even in societies with relatively low standards of emotional control, human behavior depends for a large part on learning. Medieval women had some room for aggressive conduct – inciting men to take vengeance, for example – but learned gender roles prevented nearly all women from becoming murderers.

The fit between the evidence about male fighting and the theory of civilization is so obvious that it hardly needs stating. The quantitative long-term trend of decline coincided with the expansion of the European state system, urbanization, and a differentiated economy. During the first phase of these societal transformations, the feud, lacking a code of fairness of numbers, gave way to the stylized duel. At about the same time, the criminalization of homicide entered a decisive phase. Within the monarchies and republics of early modern Europe, internal pacification progressed. As a concomitant, the homicide level had fallen considerably by 1800 and the spiritualization of honor was well under way then. Consistently, regions in which feuding or knife fighting remained prevalent for a longer time, and murder rates continued to be relatively high, were also economically less-developed areas in which state institutions penetrated to a lesser extent. In Europe's core area, but less so in England, dueling, which continued until World War One, formed the principal exception to both the pacification of the elites and the spiritualization of honor. Nevertheless, later-day duels were less lethal than their predecessors. By the 1950s and '60s the trough of homicide coincided with economic prosperity and internal pacification and cohesion on one side of the Iron Curtain.

The recent rise in murder rates challenges the theory of civilization, but on closer examination the evidence allows a refinement of that theory. In recent times, national states and their internal monopolies of violence have come under pressure from the forces of globalization, on the one hand, and renewed localism, on the other. Migration as well as organized crime link metropolitan centers in different parts of the world, largely bypassing the national level. In some ways, this state of affairs is comparable to the uncertain situation in the later sixteenth and early seventeenth centuries, preceding the consolidation of nation-states. In that transitional period, territorial principalities had already ceded a large measure of power and influence, but overarching national states had not yet fully replaced them. The consequences included, not a rise in individual murders, but increased chances for private armies and a number of civil wars. Today, the relative weakness of national states leaves social niches for violent activities. On the one hand, criminal organizations occupy these niches and, on the other hand, the niches encompass a series of relatively depacified neighborhoods. The consequences include an increased homicide rate. In the future, perhaps, the European Union may step in, but there is nothing inevitable about this development. In any case, European society is going through a transitional phase, rather than witnessing a complete trend reversal. The idea of a coming age of de-civilization appears unwarranted.

More than anything else, modern-day anxiety about violence contradicts that idea. This anxiety implies the breakdown of another age-old pattern, that of a negative correlation between the extent of fear of homicide and its incidence. In the Middle Ages, when the homicide level was high, people were not afraid of it. Fears increased as homicides decreased well into the nineteenth century. In the course of the twentieth century, however, the negative correlation subsided. Other social concerns predominated during the trough of violence in the 1950s and '60s, whereas the increase in homicide after 1970 was accompanied by a rising sensitivity toward violence. The new spurt in this process during the 1990s implies that, to a large extent, civilizing tendencies are continuing. They do so not with state-formation processes as their main motor, but rather with functional democratization. The further decrease of power differences between social groups has brought the informalization of behavior, but also new taboos, in particular on the expression of superiority feelings. While informalization may have contributed to the modest rise in violence, the new taboos appear compatible with the modern anxiety surrounding it. Research beyond the theme of murder is needed to clarify these relationships.

The partial return of traditional male honor, finally, is in line with the observation of depacified islands in modern European cities. It confirms the hypothesis that the concept of honor will lean toward the body-related type, as men are increasingly obliged to rely on their own strength for protection. Traditional male honor is back not simply because non-European immigrants have imported it. That is the belief of many people today, who view honor as belonging to a foreign culture and consider adaptation to the native culture as the only road toward change. Once, however, body-related honor was part of European culture too. It became spiritualized within that culture, as European society changed. In a similar vein, the spiritualization of honor may take root within the culture of communities of immigrant descent. No development is inevitable, however. In the end, we are ignorant about the future of honor, violence, and murder.

Notes

Introduction

1 Maitland, cited in Stern 1956: 29.
2 See my contribution to Body-Gendrot and Spierenburg 2008.
3 The graph in figure 0.1 takes the median year of a century as the measuring point: 1350 stands for the fourteenth century, etc. That is why the initial decline from the Middle Ages to the sixteenth century starts in 1450. The graph ends with 2000 as an extra measuring point.
4 For a more detailed discussion of methodology, see Spierenburg 1996: 67–76.
5 On this process, see also Cooney 1997.
6 Monkkonen 2006; Spierenburg 2006a.
7 Esp. Elias 1969 and 1992. On the theory's application to violence, see Fletcher 1997.
8 Discussed most extensively in Spierenburg 1999: 112–15.
9 Bourdieu 1972 and 1980.
10 Reprinted in revised form in Blok 2001: 173–209.
11 Foyster 1999a: 111 (with incorrect interpretation).
12 Brown (Keith) 1986: 28–30.
13 Jones 1959: 190–2.
14 Discussed in greater detail in Spierenburg 1998a: 4–7.
15 Barton 2001: 281–2.
16 Some of the evidence is supplied by authors who, in spite of it, doubt Elias's theory. Unless necessary, I refrain from refuting their criticisms.

Chapter 1 Romeo's Kindred: The Fragility of Life in Medieval Europe

1 All quotations from *Romeo and Juliet* from the Project Gutenberg: www.gutenberg.net/dirs/etext98/2ws1610.txt (August 26, 2004).
2 When discussing vendetta in Friuli, Muir (1993: xxviii) refers to *Romeo and Juliet* in passing. Of Shakespeare's sources (see below), Muir mentions da Porto, but not the original text by Masuccio.

3 On da Porto and his work, see Clough 1993.

4 "Vieni a veder Montecchi e Cappelletti, / Monaldi e Filippeschi, uom sanza cura: / color già tristi, e questi con sospetti!" – Alighieri 1980: 74 (Purgatorio, canto VI, lines 106–8). The editors explain that all four groups named were factions involved in political struggles. The Montecchi were ghibellines of Verona and the Cappelletti (or Capuleti) were guelphs not even of Verona, but of Cremona.

5 Salernitano 1975: 270–7 (novella XXXIII). The abstract has Ganozza commit suicide at Mariotto's body, whereas the story itself has her parents lock her up in a monastery. The inconsistency is because Masuccio had no opportunity to revise his manuscript, which was published after his death. See the introduction by Salvatore Nigro (p. xi). Individual themes of the story have been traced back even further. Cf. Clough 1993.

6 "La *vendetta* marque vraiment toute la vie médiévale, plus particulièrement dans les villes et ceci jusq'au XVe siècle au moins" – Heers 1974: 116. In this and later chapters, the words "feud" and "vendetta" are used interchangeably.

7 Bowsky 1967: 4 (quote), 14.

8 Given 1977: 5–6, 10–11, 36, 69–79. Given's erratum concerning Warwick's population figures has been considered.

9 Hanawalt 1976: 300–2. This figure is based on the mean (42,500) of the estimated range of the population which Hanawalt provides. She also mentions a number of 575 homicides in Northamptonshire in 70 years between 1300 and 1420 (hence 8.2 per year), but she provides no population figures.

10 Hanawalt 1979: 272.

11 Hammer 1978: 11, 16. The figure of 110 is the average of the rates of 120/130 and 90/100 that Hammer calculates for the years 1342–8 and 1342–6, respectively. For a critical note about Hammer's calculations, see Dean 2001: 113–14.

12 Becker 1976: 287. An average, because he calculates a rate of 152 for the years 1352–5 and 68 for 1380–3.

13 Spierenburg 1996: 66 (Freiburg), 79–80 (Utrecht, Amsterdam).

14 Schüssler 1994: 166–70. Where Schüssler gives separate figures per subperiod, I have averaged them. Kracow in Schüssler 1998: 216.

15 Österberg in Johnson and Monkkonen 1996: 44. I have averaged the figures for all sub-periods.

16 For the Regensburg data, see Kolmer 1997: 276 (Kolmer lists 602 *Wundungen* (woundings), 73 *Lähmungen* (paralyzings), 37 *Hausfriedensbrüche* (domestic disturbances). I took the first two together as physical injuries; I took the population figure to be 11,000 as mentioned by Bairoch et al. 1988 for 1300; the exact period of the wound book is specified in Schüssler 1994, note 68). For the Kracow data, see Schüssler 1998: 225.

17 Wernicke 2000: 390.

18 My calculations, based on data in Vrolijk 2001: 132–3. For the first period, Vrolijk provided me with a more precisely calculated total of petitions, which was practically the same as mine. Therefore, I assume that my totals for the two subsequent periods are also valid. Population estimate based on de Vries

and van der Woude 1995: 74, 80. A specification of the calculation is available from the author.

19 The following portrait of (late) medieval cities is based, unless mentioned otherwise, on Nicholas 1997 and Heers 1990.

20 See also Cohn 2002.

21 Given 1977: 69–79.

22 Kolmer 1997: 272–3.

23 Ruggiero 1980: 67. Nuns were among the victims of rape: Chojnacki, in Martines 1972: 199–200.

24 Schuster 2000a: 135–8; 2000b: 365.

25 Brucker, in Martines 1972: 165.

26 Nicholas (1997: 312) calls it a common pattern, but he provides few examples.

27 Wielant, quoted in Vrolijk 2001: 207.

28 Dean 2001: 31.

29 Bellamy 1973: 2; Hanawalt 1979: 273.

30 Dean 2001: 38–9.

31 Ruggiero 1980: 74, 99; Nicholas 1997: 313.

32 Elias 1976 (orig. English edn. 1965).

33 Zorzi 1995: 110–11.

34 Larner 1980: 64–5.

35 Dean 1997: 19–20.

36 Glaudemans 2004: 104.

37 Heers 1974: 190–203 and 1990: 274–97.

38 Covini, in Nubola and Würgler 2002: 139.

39 Ruggiero 1980: 112, 150 (lower-class feuds), 72–3, 175–6 (contract murder; the killer is identified as a carpenter the first time the case is discussed and as a boatman the second time).

40 Brucker 1983: 117.

41 Smail 2003. Cases on pp. 167 and 168. In the first one discussed here, Smail does not mention the outcome.

42 Gauvard 1991: vol. II: 737, 756, 772–9.

43 Glaudemans 2004: 116–18.

44 de Waardt 1996: 20–1.

45 Vrolijk 2001: 424.

46 Dean 2001: 104.

47 Given 1977: 69–70.

48 Given 1977: 50–4, 80, 184.

49 First of two cases discussed in Payling 1998.

50 Bellamy 1973: 55–7.

51 Schüssler 1994: 176–9.

52 Boomgaard 1992: 92–3.

53 Cohen (Esther) 1996: 62.

54 Given 1977: 40–1.

55 Zorzi 1995: 120.

56 Dean 2001: 98.

57 Discussed in detail in Kuehn 1991: 129–42.

58 Algazi 1996.
59 Blockmans, in Marsilje et al. 1990: 15–17.
60 Glaudemans 2004: 38.
61 Muir 1993: 220–1. On the 1511 events, see also Bianco, in Dean and Lowe 1994: 249–73.
62 Bowsky 1981: 288–90; Kempers 1987: 165–72.
63 Nicholas 1970: 1153.
64 Pohl 1999: 241, 251.
65 Zorzi 1995: 115–16.
66 Dean 1997: 8–9.
67 Larner 1980: 123; Zorzi 1995: 117–19.
68 Larner, in Martines 1972: 68–9.
69 Bowsky 1981: 123–7 (quote on 123).
70 Dean 2001: 107.
71 Heers 1974: 119–20.
72 This feud is discussed in great detail in Blockmans 1987.
73 Glaudemans 2004: 138–48.
74 Hoppenbrouwers 1992: 201–5.
75 Heers 1974: 127–9.
76 van Herwaarden 1978: 61–2.
77 Rogge, in Schreiner and Schwerhoff 1995: 110-43; several contributions to Marsilje et al. 1990.
78 All information on Ghent under the Arteveldes is from Nicholas 1988.
79 Glaudemans 2004: 127–9, 106–7.
80 Hanawalt 1979: 172.
81 Burghartz 1990: 127, 147.
82 Gauvard 1991: vol. II: 719–34. For an inventory of insults in Holland, see Glaudemans 2004: 356–8.
83 Schuster 2000a: 102–4. Quote on p. 104: "Das Ehrgefühl sowie die Neigung zum Ehrenhändel nahm mit dem Grad agressiver Enthemmung zu."
84 Given 1977: 135. (135)
85 Hanawalt 1976: 306.
86 Cohn 1996: recalculated from table (pp. 26–7) and specification (pp. 32–3).
87 Gauvard 1991: vol. I: 307–8. The table says 97 percent for the victims and the text both 97 and 79 percent. Gauvard's data set consists of 3,752 pardon letters, more than half of them for homicide, covering the period 1364–1498.
88 Paresys 1998: 17.
89 Häberlein 1998: 148-51.
90 Given 1977: 189; Hanawalt 1976: 310, 319.
91 Burghartz 1990: 146.
92 Schüssler 1998: 310.
93 Cohen (Esther) 1996: 61.
94 Dean in Dean and Lowe 1994: 35.
95 Glaudemans 2004: 113, 341–3.
96 Nicholas 1997: 304–5.
97 McIntosh 1998: 74–8.
98 Langbein 1974: 92.

 99 Gauvard 1991: vol. II: 737; Potter 1997: 288; Cohen (Esther) 1996: 64.
100 Vrolijk 2001: 189.
101 See e.g. Bellamy 1973: 106 (quote); Hammer 1978: 20; Hanawalt 1979: 171.
102 Nicholas 1997: 312–13.
103 The argument is discussed in greater detail in Spierenburg 2001.
104 Smail 2003: 93.
105 Ruggiero 1980: 74. This did not prevent the elite from sometimes humiliat-
     ing their equals with a slap, as in the Borluut/deBrune confrontation dis-
     cussed above. In early sixteenth-century Picardy, nobles did sometimes kill
     commoners, but others refused to fight with such a person: Paresys 1998:
     105-8.
106 Smail 2003: 176.
107 Barker 1986; Given 1977: 80–1; van den Neste 1996; Vale 2000.
108 Guttmann 1986: 35–46.
109 Watanabe-O'Kelly 1990 and 1992.
110 Mehl 1990: 68–75; Muchembled 1989: 297–9.
111 Bowsky 1981: 118–19.
112 Gauvard 1991: vol. II: 737.
113 Spierenburg 1996: 69–70; Jansson 1998: 10.
114 Groebner 2003: 118.
115 Pohl 1999: 239–40.
116 Bellamy 1973: 54–5; Payling 1998 (second of two cases discussed).
117 Schmitt 1976 and, very comprehensive, Murray 1998 and 2000.
118 Murray 1998: 356–62.
119 Given 1977: 106–7.
120 Hanawalt 1976: 313, 320.
121 Hanawalt 1979: 171, 272.
122 Maddern 1992: 20.
123 Bellamy 1973: 86–8.
124 Gyger 1998: 120–31.
125 Geremek 1976: 168–73.
126 Gonthier 1992: 120.
127 Rexroth 1999 (London); Geremek 1976 (Paris).
128 Cohen (Esther) 1996: 49–50.
129 Cohen (Esther) 1996: 73; Gauvard 1991: vol. I: 332–9; Spierenburg 1998b:
     295–300.
130 Nirenberg 1996, esp. chs. 6 and 7.
131 Graus 1987; Gonthier 1992: 58.
132 Brucker 1983: 116.
133 Cohn 2002: 705.
134 Gauvard 1991: vol. II: 785–8.
135 Smail 2003: 16–17.

Chapter 2 Sealed with a Kiss: From Acquiescence to Criminalization

  1 Petkov 2003: 221–4.
  2 Bloch 1965: 228; le Goff 1980: 239–48; Petkov 2003: 12–18.

3 Such etymological shifts are largely accidental (information from Marlies Philippa. See also Philippa 2004: 47–9).
4 Edgerton 1992; Cooney 1998: 49–52.
5 Bloch 1965: 129–30.
6 Petkov 2003: 62 (Galicia), 85–6 (Florence), 96–9 (other Italian towns).
7 Muir 2005: 115–16.
8 Description of the reconciliation ceremony, unless mentioned otherwise, based on van Herwaarden 1978 (chapters 2 and 3), de Waardt 1996 (rich in interpretation) and Glaudemans 2004 (chapter 9).
9 Ylikangas et al. 1998: 31.
10 Nicholas 1970: 1144–8.
11 Petkov 2003: 113.
12 van Herwaarden 1978: 655.
13 Petkov 2003: 120–3.
14 Glaudemans 2004: 365–6 (appendix 8).
15 van Herwaarden 1978: 67.
16 Barraqué 1988: 50; Rousseaux 1993: 73; Dean, in Dean and Lowe 1994: 36–8; Niccoli 1999: 235–6; Nubola and Würgler 2002: 55–6.
17 www.mfa.org/collections. Search accession number 15.1145.
18 Green 1985: 58.
19 See e.g. Burghartz 1990: 152; Smail 2003: 174–5; Glaudemans 2004: 271–3.
20 Dinges and Sack 2000: contributions by Schuster (pp. 67–84) and Schwerhoff (pp. 139–56); Groebner 2003: 36.
21 Gauvard 1999: 6–14, 23–4.
22 Bowsky 1967: 12–13; 1981: 123–7; Pazzaglini 1979: 93–5.
23 Smail 2003: 8–9, 185.
24 Glaudemans 2004: 93–112, 174–5.
25 Green 1985: 30–59, 65–9.
26 Heers 1974: 117.
27 Glaudemans 2004: 79–92 (quote on p. 87).
28 van Herwaarden 1978: 64–86; Glaudemans 2004: 209–24.
29 Schuster 2000a: 149.
30 Pohl 1999.
31 de Waardt 1996: 22–5.
32 Petkov 2003: 33–4.
33 van Herwaarden 1978: 72; Hoppenbrouwers 1992: 208–9; de Waardt 1996: 27, 31–2; Glaudemans 2004: 275–8.
34 Bellamy 1973: 106–15; Dean 2001: 111; Glaudemans 2004: 187–96, 206.
35 Hurnard 1997: 36, 171–93.
36 Green 1985: 69–76.
37 Kesselring 2003: 3 (quote), 95–116 (homicide), passim.
38 Davis (Natalie) 1987: 141–2.
39 Paresys 1998: 15.
40 de Waardt 1996: 22–4.
41 Vrolijk 2001: 27, 35–6, 307–40, 444–61.
42 Muchembled 1989: 20.

43 Langbein 1974: 169–72 (quote on p. 171). Under homicide, Langbein's index has, apart from the passage cited, no references to reconciliation or criminalization; there are no entries at all which relate to private settlements.
44 Vrolijk 2001: 191–5.
45 Boomgaard 1992: 94–5.
46 Hollandts Placcaet-boeck 1645: vol. I: 262–3.
47 Discussed in greater detail in Spierenburg 2006b.
48 Nubola and Würgler 2002: 56 (note 77).
49 Laven in Dean and Lowe 1994: 222–3.
50 Carroll 2003: 106 and passim.
51 Lück, in Rudolph and Schnabel-Schüle 2003: 283–5.
52 Schnabel-Schüle 1997: 247–8; Pohl, in Rudolph and Schnabel-Schüle 2003: 245–8.
53 Wittke 2002: 62–73, 103–10, 119–32, 141–2, 148–51, 197.
54 Stein-Wilkeshuis 1991: 20–3.
55 Ylikangas et al. 1998: 30–58, 151–9.
56 Discussed in greater detail in Spierenburg 1998b: 315–20.

Chapter 3 Swords, Knives and Sticks: The Social Differentiation of Male Fighting

1 R.A. 354, fos. 25vs, 64vs, 67. (Here and in all subsequent such references in chs. 3–5, R.A. refers to *Stadsarchief* [city archive] *Amsterdam*, archive no. 5061 (*oud-rechterlijk archief*). It is followed by the inventory number, and folio numbers.)
2 Carroll 2003.
3 Davis (Natalie) 1987; Muchembled 1989; Paresys 1998; Vrolijk 2001: 66–79.
4 Cellini 1982: 61–2; Rossi, in Dean and Lowe 1994: 181–3.
5 Weinstein 2000; Blastenbrei 1995: 79–83; Cohen and Cohen 1993: first case; Ferraro 1993: 147–8; Stone 1965: 225–6; Greenshields 1994: 73, 87.
6 Raggio 1991; Torre 1994; Graziani 1997: 146–74; Serpentini 2003.
7 Brown (Keith) 1986: 23–4.
8 James 1978 (quote on p. 1).
9 Fehr 1908: 25–6.
10 Mohrmann 1977: 271–7.
11 Cohen (Elizabeth) 1992.
12 Cohen (Thomas) 1992; Cohen and Cohen 1993. See also Strocchia 1998.
13 Spierenburg 2006b: 16–18 (quote on p. 18).
14 Mols 1979: 380.
15 Greenshields 1994: 144–9.
16 Blastenbrei 1995: 71. My calculation from his graphs and tables.
17 Österberg in Johnson and Monkkonen 1996: 44. Jansson (1998: 16) lists a higher figure for the 1610s.
18 Spierenburg 1996: 80–1.
19 Schwerhoff 1991: 282–4.
20 Wittke (2002: 29–32, 77–78) gives a total of 193 homicides in these years. Based on Reekers (1956), I estimated the population at 90,000.

21 According to Greenshields (1994: 68, 120), the annual number of homicides in the years for which there are data during this period averaged about five. Based on Grimmer 1983 and Poitrineau 1965, I estimated the population of Haute Auvergne at 33,000.

22 Cockburn 1991: 76–9.

23 Blastenbrei 1995: 56–68; Blastenbrei, in Dinges and Sack 2000: 127. My calculation (specification available from the author). The "annual rate" mentioned in Spierenburg 2006a: 105 is incorrect; this should have been "monthly rate."

24 Tlusty 2001: 88.

25 Quoted in Peltonen 2003: 3.

26 Fuchs 1999: 220–4; Shepard 2003: 141.

27 Muir 1993: 252–64. Carroll (2003: 75), on the other hand, argues that in late sixteenth–century France, dueling reinvigorated the feud.

28 Brioist et al. 2002: 44–53.

29 Peltonen 2003: 61.

30 Kiernan 1988: 64, 73.

31 Hollandts Placcaet–boeck 1645: vol. II: 320–3; Kelly 1995; Frevert, in Spierenburg 1998a: 39–40; Peltonen 2003: 203.

32 Weinstein, in Dean and Lowe 1994: 213–20; Hughes, in Spierenburg 1998a: 65.

33 Raeymakers 2004: 92–8.

34 Peltonen 2003: 82–5.

35 Raeymakers 2004: 103–8.

36 Billacois 1986: 128, 134; Brioist et al. 2002: 199–200, 221–3. On the code of honor in France, see also Neuschel 1989.

37 Stone 1965: 245; Peltonen 2003: 82.

38 Kelly 1995: 1–50.

39 Frevert, in Spierenburg 1998a: 40–7.

40 Schmidt 1986: 50–1.

41 Andrews 1994: 40–1.

42 R.A. 367, fos. 182, 229vs.

43 Chauchadis 1984.

44 Muir 1993: 260–1.

45 Andrew 1980; Peltonen 2003: 86–92; Brown (Keith) 1986: 184–207.

46 Billacois 1986: 212–18; Peltonen 2003: 109–10; Spierenburg 2006b: 13.

47 Raeymakers 2004: 53–4.

48 Billacois 1986: 148, 247, 295, 302–5, 348–9.

49 Quoted in Billacois 1986: 348.

50 Österberg and Sogner 2000: 83.

51 van Weel 1977; Spierenburg 2006b: 10–13, 24–5.

52 Frevert 1991: 32–4, 65.

53 Häberlein 1998.

54 Hanlon 1985: 247–51, 257.

55 Österberg and Sogner 2000: 76–7.

56 Cooney 1997; Eisner 2003: 115–18.

57 Brennan 1988: 36.

58 Farr 2003; Garnot 2004.

59 Hay, in Hay et al. 1975: 34.
60 Vrolijk 2001: 200.
61 Marci 1618: nr. 35.
62 R.A. 378, fos. 51, 52, 53vs, 100.
63 R.A. 336, fos. 129vs, 132vs, 138, 140vs; R.A. 596, fo. 177vs.
64 R.A. 336, fos. 145, 148, 151vs, 153, 155vs, 192; R.A. 596, fo. 216.
65 R.A. 347, fos. 49, 52, 54vs, 56, 57vs, 59, 66, 81vs, 116vs, 121vs, 122vs, 123, 144, 147.
66 R.A. 640f: March 11, 1721.
67 R.A. 381, fos. 236vs, 238 (year: 1724).
68 R.A. 338, fos. 149, 154vs, 202.
69 R.A. 326, fos. 162, 165, 195, 201, 219, 221vs.
70 R.A. 387, fos. 182vs, 185vs, 196vs (the killer); fos. 116, 125, 137vs, 173, 187, 242vs (his friend).
71 R.A. 374, fos. 203vs, 223vs, 227vs; R.A. 375, fo. 20.
72 R.A. 385, fos. 49vs, 83 (Toon); fos. 74vs, 85vs (the woman) (year: 1726).
73 R.A. 399 (dossier at the end, without systematic foliation); R.A. 400, fo. 24 (year: 1739).
74 R.A. 392, fos. 21, 36, 40vs (year: 1734).
75 R.A. 329, fo. 218 (year: 1685).
76 R.A. 325, fos. 138vs, 140, 141, 143 (year: 1680).
77 R.A. 349, fos. 246, 250, 262vs, 264vs, 265vs, 273, 277vs, 278.
78 A[mpzing] 1633: nr. 10.
79 Petter 1674: illustrations pp. 56–64. With thanks to Joel Rosenthal for first alerting me to the question of how knives were held.
80 R.A. 372, fos. 143vs, 147vs, 171.
81 R.A. 345, fos. 226, 227, 229vs, 257vs, 261vs; R.A. 346, fos. 24vs, 31vs, 36vs, 41vs, 119 (year: 1696)
82 Tlusty 2001: 110.
83 R.A. 321, fos. 209vs, 211vs; R.A. 322, fos. 5vs, 11vs.
84 Spierenburg 1984: 158–60, 231.
85 R.A. 363, fos. 92vs, 98, 131, 139vs, 151, 156, 171; R.A. 640f: April 13, 1717; R.A. 375, fos. 235vs, 239, 248, 248vs.
86 Shoemaker 2001: 199.
87 Faber 1983: 91–8.
88 Roodenburg 1990: 347–61.
89 Spierenburg 1999; Sevilla: Mantecón 2006a; Perry 1980.
90 R.A. 349, fos. 249, 261, 278.
91 R.A. 394, fos. 204vs, 220vs, 244vs, 247; R.A. 395, fo. 1.
92 R.A. 343, fos. 117, 128vs, 131, 145vs (year: 1696).
93 R.A. 356, fos. 100, 102, 129vs (year: 1706).
94 R.A. 640e: November 10, 1705.
95 R.A. 348, fos. 48vs, 57vs, 70vs, 72vs, 209.
96 Petter 1674. About Petter and his book, see *Amstelodamum Maandblad* 57 (1970): 7; 68 (1981): 8.
97 R.A. 327, fos. 56, 59, 76vs, 80, 102, 102vs, 130vs (the son); fos. 74, 82, 85vs, 89vs, 102, 130vs (the father).

98   Brennan 1988: 45–8, 61–3, 74–5; Dinges 1994: 213–15, 341–2.
99   McMahon 2004: 167.
100 Beattie 1986: 92–3; Foyster 1999a: 177–9; Shoemaker 2001: 195–6, 198.
101 Tlusty 2001: 127–33.
102 Jansson 1998: 114–20.
103 Kiernan 1988: 72; Mantecón (Tomás), "Long–term changes of ritualized interpersonal violence. The early modern Spanish *desafíos*." Paper presented at the conference "Crime, Violence and the Modern State," Rethymon, Greece, March 2007.
104 Castan 1980a: 57–8; Hanlon 1985: 258; Farr 1988: 180; Greenshields 1994: 72.
105 Greenshields 1994: 83–5 (year: 1626).
106 Brennan 1988: 34–5; Tlusty 2002.
107 Dean, in Dean and Lowe 1994: 18; Vrolijk 2001: 181.
108 R.A. 640f: Dec. 23, 1718; R.A. 376, fos. 229vs, 235vs, 242vs.
109 Brennan 1988: 55; Dinges 1994: 324–5.
110 Lacour 2001: 650.
111 Shepard 2003: 145.
112 R.A. 354, fos. 39vs, 40, 40vs, 41, 41vs, 42, 49vs, 56, 56vs, 58, 70 (Jan); fos. 42vs, 54, 57vs, 69vs (Lodewijk) (year: 1704).
113 Sabean 1984: 144–73.
114 McMahon 2004: 187–8, 209–10; Greenshields 1994: 77–8; Lacour 2000: 112–64; 2001: 659–60 (total set of categories not exactly the same in both publications); Frank 1995: 247; Ylikangas et al. 1998: 88–94; Koskivirta, in Koskivirta and Forsström 2002: 141.
115 Dupont–Bouchat 1994: 15–17; Jansson 1998: 128–30.
116 Hanlon 1985: 256–7.
117 R.A. 316, fos. 63vs, 66, 67vs, 70vs, 75; R.A. 585, fo. 1.
118 R.A. 403, fos. 105, 113, 123, 124vs, 129, 139vs, 142vs, 146vs, 156vs (the killer); fos. 99, 130, 135vs, 259vs (the contractor) (year: 1742).
119 Gaskill 1998; 2000.
120 From table 2 in Cockburn 1991: 80–1. Periods and a few categories regrouped as in Spierenburg 2000: 184.
121 Watt 2001: 52.
122 Spierenburg 1996: 85.
123 Brioist et al. 2002: 340–9.
124 Cockburn 1991: 86–7.
125 R.A. 310, fos. 121vs, 124vs.
126 R.A. 346, fos. 33, 33vs, 35vs, 36, 38vs, 39, 39vs, 40, 54, 54vs, 55, 98, 98vs, 99, 99vs, 103vs, 104, 119 (leader); fos. 33vs, 34, 34vs, 35, 40, 40vs, 41, 41vs, 100, 100vs, 101, 101vs, 105, 105vs, 106, 119 (accomplice).
127 Brunet 2001: 146–62.
128 Davis (Robert) 1994.
129 Discussed in greater detail in Spierenburg 1999: 140–1.
130 Statt 1995.
131 R.A. 327, fos. 21vs, 22, 25, 25vs, 54.
132 Gemeente-Archief Amsterdam, Keurboek S, fo. 86vs; Handvesten 1748: 1049.

133 R.A. 376, fos. 111, 116vs.
134 R.A. 387, fos. 254vs, 259vs.
135 R.A. 640f, Dec. 15, 1720 and May 29, 1724; Keurboek S, fo. 131vs.
136 Eibach 1998: 374–5.
137 Two were tried but denied: R.A. 313, fos. 201vs, 210 and fos. 202, 206, 210, 210vs.
138 R.A. 510, pp. 120, 169, 410, 430, 435.
139 Hobsbawm 1981 (orig. edn. 1969).
140 Reconsidered, with inclusion of recent studies, in Blok 2001: 14–28.
141 Cobb 1970; Brown (Howard) 1997.
142 Winslow, in Hay et al. 1975: 119–66; Mantecón 2006b; Hufton 1974: 284–305.
143 Ruff 2001: 232.
144 Castan 1980b: 195; Sharpe 2004; Roeck 1993: 135–6.
145 Hufton 1974: 266–83; Sharpe 2004: 106–38; Küther 1976; Danker 1988; Lange 1994; Spicker-Beck 1995; Blok 1991; Egmond 1993 and in Johnson and Monkkonen 1996: 138–52.
146 Cameron 1981: 192; Cockburn 1991: 87.
147 1650–1700: 61 robberies, 62 woundings punished on the scaffold, 780 (estimated) woundings punished non-publicly; 1701–50: 77 (Jaco band excluded), 116, and 220, respectively. No robberies entered my samples of non-public punishments. Calculated from Spierenburg 1984.
148 R.A. 313, fos. 82–5, 89–90.
149 Adapted from Spierenburg 1996: 82–3. I used new population figures for the seven periods (200, 200, 200, 205, 220, 220, 205 x 1,000) based on the most recent estimates in Nusteling 1997: 75–9. As the absolute annual average of homicide in these periods, I took the median between certain and total.
150 Discussed by Lindström in Body-Gendrot and Spierenburg 2008.
151 Based on Watt 2001: 55–6 (from *livres des morts*). Population figures taken from Porret 1992: 473.
152 Calculated from Henry 1994. Pop. of 182,000, based on Bairoch 1988: 39.
153 Mantecón (Tomás), "Homicide and violence in early modern Spain." Paper presented at the CRIMPREV conference on violence, Rotterdam, January 2007.
154 Brioist et al. 2002: 331–7. Pop. from Bairoch 1988: 28. Body inspection reports are available for various jurisdictions in France since the end of the seventeenth century: Garnot 2000: 101–2. The number of 372 murders in Paris in 1643 mentioned by a chronicler (Lebigre 1991: 99) would yield a homicide rate of 93, but this is obviously unreliable.
155 Beattie 1986: 132–9; Shoemaker 1999 and 2001.
156 Farr 1988: 166, 187–91.
157 Mohrmann 1977: 239.
158 Burke 2000: 37.
159 Spierenburg 2006b: 15–16.
160 Shoemaker 2000.
161 Spierenburg 2004: 136–7.

162 "Diese Ehre setze ich keineswegs in das Urtheil anderer über meine
     Handlungen . . . sondern in dasjenige, das ich selbst über sie fallen kann."
     Quoted in Jones (George) 1959: 154.
163 Shovlin 2000; Brioist et al. 2002: 379–413.
164 Österberg and Sogner 2000: 84; Kaspersson, in Godfrey et al. 2003: 78–9.
165 Billacois, in Garnot 1996: 251–6; Peltonen 2003: 135–8, 207–12.
166 Kelly 1995: passim.
167 Brioist et al. 2002: 245–6, 323.
168 Peltonen 2003: 210, 223–62.
169 Porret 1992: 163–77.
170 R.A. 429, pp. 79, 111, 156, 233.
171 See e.g. Fishman 1982.
172 Foyster 1999b.

Chapter 4 Patriarchy and its Discontents: Women and the Domestic Sphere

1 Archives d'Etat de Genève, PC, nr. 10820 (1760). I am very grateful to
  Michel Porret for providing me with a photocopy of the entire dossier. See
  also Porret in Garnot 1996: 182.
2 Quoted in Lebigre 1991: 11
3 van de Pol 1996b: 38 (no date mentioned).
4 Mantecón (Tomás), "Long–term changes of ritualized interpersonal violence. The early modern Spanish desafíos." Paper presented at the conference "Crime, Violence and the Modern State," Rethymon, Greece, March
  2007.
5 Feeley and Little 1991; and forthcoming book by Malcolm Feeley and Hadar
  Aviram.
6 Eisner 2003: 109–12.
7 Groebner in Schreiner and Schwerhoff 1995: 361–80, and Groebner 2003:
  72ff.
8 Cohen (Esther) 1996: 64.
9 Gowing 1994: 32; 1996: 103–4.
10 Foyster 1999a: 182.
11 Dean 2001: 77; Dinges 1994: 346; Hanlon 1985: 259–60; van der Heijden
   1995: 27–30; Lacour 2000: 93. Cheshire appears to be the exception: Walker
   2003: 79–81.
12 Schwerhoff, in Ulbricht 1995: 99–100 (between 1557 and 1620).
13 R.A. 355, fo. 120vs, 124 (year: 1706).
14 Wiltenburg 1992: 188–96.
15 Farge, in Dauphin and Farge 1997: 79.
16 R.A. 409, fo. 187, 190vs, 204vs (year: 1750).
17 van de Pol 1996a: 289–90; Benabou 1987: 480–1.
18 Cohen (Elizabeth) 1992: 609–12.
19 Walker 2003: 52–5.
20 Eisner 2003: 118–19.
21 Watt 2001: 61.

22 Spierenburg 1996: 84–5.
23 Shoemaker 2001: 203.
24 R.A. 346, fo. 33vs, 34, 34vs, 35, 40, 40vs, 41, 41vs, 100, 100vs, 101, 101vs, 105, 105vs, 106, 119.
25 Dinges 1994: 343; Walker 2003: 61–2; McMahon 2004: 157.
26 Greenshields 1994: 83 (year not mentioned).
27 R.A. 371, fo. 208, 212vs, 217, 221vs; R.A. 372, fo. 16.
28 Farr 1991: 408–11. For Amsterdam, see van de Pol 1996a: 80.
29 Mohrmann 1977: 237–8, 278 (note 255).
30 R.A. 353, fo. 234vs, 240 (year: 1704).
31 Overview of the literature in van der Heijden 2000: 624–5.
32 Meyer-Knees 1992: 55–7, 77–103, 161.
33 Vigarello 1998: 13.
34 Vigarello 1998: 21, 57–8 (year in second case: 1667).
35 Greenshields 1994: 107–9.
36 Gowing 1994: 37; Walker 2003: 55–60.
37 Mantecón 2002: 171–2.
38 Cohen (Sherrill) 1992: 64.
39 van der Heijden 2000: 626–7.
40 Emsley 1996: 162; Leclercq, in Ågren et al. s.a.: 177–93.
41 Doggett 1992: 46.
42 Collard 2003: 99–114.
43 Spierenburg 1996: 93–4.
44 Langbein 1974: 41.
45 Lorenz 1999: 265–6.
46 van Hasselt 1772: 24.
47 Gaskill 2000: 276–7; Watson 2004: 16–30, 42–3, 149–73.
48 Turner 2002: 124; Walker 2003: 146; McMahon 2004: 119.
49 Capp 1996: 21–2; McMahon 2004: 223–5.
50 Rublack 1998: 215–18, 318–22; Wegert 1994: 138–9; Göttsch, in Ulbricht 1995: 315–35.
51 Watson 2004: 45–7; Lapalus 2004: 240–3.
52 Septon 1996.
53 www.dodenakkers.nl/artikelen/leidsgif.html (Feb. 23, 2007). For England, see Watson 2004: 89, 97–122.
54 Overview in Spierenburg 1998b: 318–20. More recently: Nolde 2003: 65–211; Pinar 2002: 174–5.
55 Eisner 2003: 120; cf. Cooney 2003.
56 Based on a more complete series of homicides than in Spierenburg 1996: 89–91.
57 Lacour 2000: 180.
58 Jansson 1998: 126; Kaspersson, in Godfrey et al. 2003: 80.
59 R.A. 372, fo. 178, 193 (year: 1715).
60 Spierenburg 2004: second case.
61 Wegert 1994: 150 (year: 1768); Schnabel-Schüle 1997: 248–50.
62 Cohen (Esther) 1996: 63; Schuster 2000a: 159–63.
63 Doggett 1992: 1–32; Walker 2003: 63.

64 For an overview of charivari in Europe, see Spierenburg 1998b: 51–2, 98–103. See also Ingram, in Roodenburg and Spierenburg 2004: 288–308.
65 Schwerhoff, in Roodenburg and Spierenburg 2004: 220–46.
66 Sabean 1990: 133–8. Cited case on p. 135 (year: 1742).
67 Potter 1997: 304.
68 Nolde 2003: 388–92.
69 Mantecón 1997. For England, see McMahon 2004: 83; Bailey 2006.
70 Bailey 2006: 281.
71 Schnabel-Schüle 1997: 252–3 (year: 1737).
72 Gowing 1996: 229.
73 Walker 2003: 138.
74 Nolde 2003: 94–137.
75 Hufton 1990: 83.
76 Nolde 2003: 326.
77 Nolde, in Garnot 1996: 147 (year: 1594).
78 Turner 2002: 130–5; Walker 2003: 143.
79 Rublack 1998: 322–3 (year: 1677).
80 Garnot 1993.
81 R.A. 352, fo 4vs et seq. (both trials); Spierenburg 1984: 59. There was no mention of a poisoning charge in her sentence.

Chapter 5 Marks of Innocence: Babies and the Insane

 1 Walter Scott, *The Heart of Mid-Lothian*. Quotes from vol. I, ch. 21, at the Project Gutenberg: www.gutenberg.org/etext/6944 (March 5, 2007). See also Symonds 1997: 179–93.
 2 See Beattie 1986: 113 (note 84, with criticism of Hoffer and Hull 1981).
 3 Cockburn 1991: 93–6.
 4 See the discussion in Spierenburg 1996: 72–3.
 5 Dean 2001: 79–80.
 6 See, among many publications, van der Heijden and Burghartz, in Roodenburg and Spierenburg 2004.
 7 Hoffer and Hull 1981: 13–17.
 8 Hoffer and Hull 1981: 3; Sharpe 1984: 61.
 9 Hoffer and Hull 1981: 71; Beattie 1986: 117; Spierenburg 1996: 85; Rublack 1998: 244; McMahon 2004: 140 (case of Joan Fountain, 1724).
10 Hufton 1974: 349 and 1990: 77; cited again in Ruff 2001: 153.
11 van Dülmen 1991: 59 (pop. figures), 70–1 (graph).
12 Kaspersson, in Godfrey et al. 2003: 75–6. Fig. 4.2 actually gives a rate of 15 for the sixteenth and eighteenth centuries, but comparison with fig. 4.3 strongly suggests that decimals have been incorrectly omitted from fig 4.2.
13 Spierenburg 1996: 86 (slightly adapted because of new population estimates).
14 Sharpe 1984: 61.
15 Watt 2001: 61.
16 Hufton 1974: 350; van Dülmen 1991: 17, 49–51; Rublack 1998: 237–8; Walker 2003: 150–3.

17 Jackson 1996: 94–5; van Dülmen 1991: 33–5; Faber 1978: 228–9.
18 Hufton 1974: 321–2 (quote) and 1990: 78.
19 Quoted in, among others, Jackson 1996: 32.
20 Österberg and Sogner 2000: 173.
21 Symonds 1997: 2–5.
22 Spierenburg 1984: 120.
23 R.A. 640g: February 1, 1788.
24 Gowing 1997: 89.
25 Faber 1978: 227.
26 Michalik 1997: 56, 69, 112.
27 Hufton 1990: 81.
28 Castan 1980b: 310.
29 Rublack 1998: 247, 260–1.
30 van Dülmen 1991: 77; Ulbricht in Blauert and Schwerhoff 1993: 59; Wegert 1994: 176.
31 Symonds 1997: 70–92.
32 Gowing 1997 (period 1642–80) and Jackson 1996 (period 1720–1800).
33 Gowing 1997: 91, 98 (year 1663).
34 Jackson 1996: 63.
35 Hufton 1990: 82.
36 Porret 1992: 210.
37 Wegert 1994: 164–5 (year: 1747).
38 Dickinson and Sharpe in Jackson 2002: 43–4.
39 van Dülmen 1991: 43–5. For Friesland, see Faber 1978: 234.
40 van Dülmen 1991: 85.
41 Ulbricht, in Blauert and Schwerhoff 1993: 54–85.
42 Gowing 1997: 106.
43 Walker 2003: 152–3 (year: 1681).
44 Spierenburg 1998b: 220–6 (Norwich case on p. 224).
45 Schnabel-Schüle 1997: 259.
46 Mantecón 2004.
47 Schnabel-Schüle 1997: 259–65 (year: 1778).
48 Lorenz 1999: 269–82.
49 R.A. 393, fo. 215vs, 222; 640L: 1736.
50 R.A. 452, pp. 419, 432, 448.
51 R.A. 477, pp. 163, 169, 183, 431; 640g: July 23, 1795; Faber and Krikke 1977.
52 Barras, in Koenraadt 1991: 283–300; Walker (Nigel) 1968; Eigen 1995.
53 Monod 2003 (Breads); Brewer 2004 (Hackman).
54 Spierenburg 1984: 95–6.
55 Jansson 1998: 49–70. Cited case on pp. 56–7 (year: 1686).
56 Lind, in Watt 2004: 78.
57 Göttsch, in Ulbricht 1995: 327; Lorenz 1999: 282–3 (cited case; year: 1778).
58 Lind and Jansson, in Watt 2004.
59 Murray 1998: 368–78 (overviewing figures from earlier studies).
60 Bailey (Victor) 1998: 129; Baumann 2001: 250–1 (averages per decade and five-year period, respectively).

61 Chesnais 1976: 42–3.
62 Jansson 1998: 138–43; Watt 2001: 57.
63 Schär 1985: 68–9; Wegert 1994: 69–70; Lind 1999: 159–67; Watt 2004.
64 Schär 1985: 100–3; Macdonald and Murphy 1990: passim; Spierenburg 1998b: 238–9; Baumann 2001: 106–27; Watt, in Watt 2004: 1–8.
65 Andrew in Watt 2004: 175–90; http://en.wikipedia.org/wiki/Samuel_Romilly (March 20, 2007).
66 Baumann 2001: 145–379.
67 Beattie 1986: 120; Jackson 1996: 98.
68 Rabin, in Jackson 2002: 73–92.
69 Hufton 1990: 79–80; Jackson 1996: 159–76; Symonds 1997: 8–9; Michalik 1997: 19; Österberg and Sogner 2000: 186–7; Tinkova 2005: 50.
70 Symonds 1997: 8–9, 57; McDonagh 2003: 35–96; van Dülmen 1991: 98–108.
71 Marland and Quinn in Jackson 2002 (quote on p. 175).
72 Tillier 2001: 110–27, 153–200.
73 Faber and Donker, in Koenraadt 1991: 67–83.
74 Dupont-Bouchat, in Bard et al. 2002: 75–96.
75 Schulte 1989: 23–6, 126–76.
76 Jackson, in Jackson 2002: 10–11; Watson 2004: 83.
77 Wheelwright, in Jackson 2002: 270–85.
78 Spierenburg 1996: 88.
79 van Ruller, in Koenraadt 1991: 23–33.

Chapter 6 M for Less: The Marginalization of Murder, 1800–1970

1 On the movie, see Tatar 1995: 153–72; Kaes 2000; on Fritz Lang, see http://en.wikipedia.org/wiki/Fritz_Lang (May 16, 2007).
2 De Telegraaf, April 26, 1932; Archive of Marseilles, 1M748 – Presse 1932. I am grateful to Laurence Montel for the Marseilles reference.
3 Taylor 1998. His critics: Morris (Robert) 2001; Wiener 2004: 18; Chassaigne 2005: 92.
4 Eisner 2003: 99.
5 Eisner 2001: 629. Same table, but before 1800 rounded off to figures without decimals, in Eisner 2003: 99.
6 Chesnais 1981: 76.
7 Chesnais 1976: 210, 298.
8 Johnson 1995: 129. He presents rates per million inhabitants, which I adapted to per 100,000.
9 Eisner 1997: 52.
10 Ylikangas 1998: 15–23, 38–45; O'Donnell 2002: 64 and in Body-Gendrot and Spierenburg 2008; Gallant 2000: 362; Boschi in Spierenburg 1998a: 132–3; Serpentini 2003; Wilson 1988: 16.
11 On the problems with these statistics in England, see Emsley 2005: 5–9.
12 Gatrell 1980; Godfrey 2003; Emsley 2005: 19.
13 Johnson 1995: 127; Franke 1991: 23.
14 King 1996; D'Cruze, in D'Cruze 2000: 5; Wiener 2004: 9–39.

15 Emsley, in Emsley et al. 2004: 193–209; Wiener 2004: 17; Chassaigne 2005: 49.
16 Wilson 1988; Gómez Bravo 2005: 66–75.
17 Chauvaud 1995: 176.
18 Beavan 2001; Hett 2004: 172.
19 Malcolmson 1973; Spierenburg 1998b: 256–60.
20 Dunning and Sheard 1979; Emsley 2005: 47–9; Nye 1984: 319–29.
21 Malcolmson 1973: 43–4; Gorn 1986: 19–33; Wiener 2004: 48–50; Wood 2004: 72; Emsley 2005: 45–6.
22 Chassaigne 2005: 111–16; Emsley 2005: 15–18.
23 Davies 1998, 1999, and in D'Cruze 2000: 70–85.
24 Montel 2003: 5–6.
25 Nye 1984: 196–202; Perrot 2001: 351–64; Kalifa 2005: 44–66.
26 Spierenburg 1984: 196–9; Morris 1991: 61–4; Halttunen 1995; Rey 1995; Gilman 1999.
27 Lindenberger, in Lindenberger and Lüdtke 1995: 190–212; Ambroise-Rendu, in Garnot 1996: 447–56.
28 Schwerhoff 1999: 129–30.
29 Wood 2004: 25 and passim.
30 Davies 1999: 77; Wood 2004: 70–94 (cited case on pp. 80–1).
31 Archer, in D'Cruze 2000: 44–6 (quote on 44); Wiener 2004: 55–75.
32 Chauvaud 1991: 44–6, 105–11; 1995: 183–215; and in Garnot 1996: 437–45; Ploux, in Body-Gendrot and Spierenburg 2008.
33 Blasius 1978: 64–8; Schulte 1989: 41–117; Archer 1990.
34 Hanewinckel 1800: 88–94; van den Brink 1991; 1995: 306–21. Rombach (1993: 106–8) claims a continuation of knife fights until the early twentieth century, but refers only to middle-class observers.
35 Sleebe 1994: 264–74; Eggens 2005: 82–94.
36 Haine 1996: 170–7.
37 Chassaigne 2005: 81–107.
38 Johnson, in Johnson and Monkkonen 1996: 238.
39 Eisner 1997: 51; Parrella 1992: 630–1.
40 Dutch figures cited in Spierenburg 2000: 186. For England, see Emsley 2005: 88.
41 Bos 2000.
42 See, among others, Fletcher 1997: 52.
43 Conley 1999a: 33–5, passim and 1999b. On the famine and homicide: conversation with David Miller in 2001. For an analysis of one murder case, see Sweeney 2002.
44 Farrell 2000; Conley 1999a: 165–214.
45 Ylikangas 1998: 98–100 and passim; Spierenburg 1998a: 17.
46 Wilson 1988.
47 Gallant 2000; Avdela, in Bard et al. 2002; Avdela 2006.
48 Boschi, in Spierenburg 1998a: 128–58.
49 Blok 1974; for a discussion of recent literature, see Dunnage 2002: 16–18.
50 Reuber 2002.
51 Simpson 1988; Wiener 2004: 40–6; Emsley 2005: 44–5.
52 Wolf 1984: 38–40 (Breda); van Vree 1994: 201 (minister).

53 Kock 1876 (mildly positive); Beaufort 1881; Anten 1892; Scheuer 1893.
54 Chesnais 1976: 29; Nye, in Spierenburg 1998a: 88; Hughes, in idem: 68.
55 The remainder of this section is based, unless otherwise indicated, on Frevert 1991; Elias 1992; Nye 1993; McAleer 1994; and Frevert, Hughes, and Nye, in Spierenburg 1998a.
56 Chauvaud 1995: 129–30.
57 D'Cruze 1998 and 1999; Jones, in D'Cruze 2000: 104–18.
58 Wiener 2004: 76–122; Chassaigne 2005: 130.
59 Ferron, in Bard et al. 2002: 129–38 (quote on 130); Chauvaud 1995: 72–81.
60 Wiener, in Spierenburg 1998a: 208 (quote); Wiener 1999; 2004: 123–288; Frost 2004.
61 Dupont-Bouchat, in Kurgan-Vanhentenryk 1999: 41–60; Ferket 1999.
62 Emsley 2005: 69.
63 Gagnon, in Bard et al. 2002: 139–47; Parrella 1992: 647–51.
64 Wood 2004: 65; Chassaigne 2005: 125; Töngi 2005: 101; Yvorel, in Chauvaud and Mayaud 2005: 125–36.
65 Wiener 2004: 125; Chassaigne 2005: 126–7.
66 Porret 2003.
67 Lapalus 2004.
68 Guillais 1986: 34–42; Harris (Ruth) 1989: 210–11.
69 Quoted in Shapiro 1996: 79.
70 Hett 2004: 202–19.
71 www.dodenakkers.nl/beroemd/pisuisse.html (May 11, 2007).
72 Guillais 1986: 281; Harris (Ruth) 1989: 312.
73 Chassaigne 2005: 39.
74 Foucault 1973; Lapalus 2004: 377–90.
75 Chassaigne 2005: 61. For classifications and their problems in the present USA, see Fox and Levin 2005: 17–18
76 Varlet, in Chauvaud and Mayaud 2005: 99–112.
77 Chassaigne 2005: 61 (without reference or further information).
78 Gómez Bravo 2005: 189.
79 Guarnieri 1993.
80 Curtis 2001: 19–23; Chassaigne 2005: 58–61.
81 Artières and Kalifa 2001. Most internet references are to a namesake, an actor.
82 http://en.wikipedia.org/wiki/Henri_Desire_Landru (May 24, 2007). The author's father, born in 1911, knew the song about Landru.
83 Tatar 1995; Evans 1996: 526–36, 591–605; Kaes 2000: 30–5.
84 Brückweh 2006a: 288–90, 303–37, and 2006b.
85 Compare Watson 2007: 286–303, who includes poisoners.
86 Compare Elias and Dunning 1986.
87 Vincent 1999.
88 Nemeth, in Bard et al. 2002: 233–41.
89 Chassaigne 2005: 68; Emsley 2005: 84–5. On the spelling, see Curtis 2001: 319 (note 36).
90 Smith 2002 (about the Winter case; Hruza case on pp. 40–1); Hett 2004: 148–55.

91 Chassaigne 2005: 215–24; Emsley 2005: 81–3.
92 Weber 1986: 130–41.
93 Lawrence 2003; Wirsching 2003; Emsley, "A legacy of conflict. The 'brutalized veteran' and violence in Europe after the Great War." Paper presented at the conference "Crime, Violence and the Modern State," Rethymon, Greece, March 2007.
94 Rousseaux et al. in Body-Gendrot and Spierenburg 2008. I excluded the "dubious cases" from the rates cited.
95 Lynch in Chauvaud and Mayaud 2005: 236–41; Chesnais 1976: 22, 210, 298 (statistics missing for 1914–19; rates with two decimals rounded off to one).
96 Chesnais 1981: 67; Dunnage 2002: 131–4; Franke 1991: 28.
97 Dunning et al. 1987 and 1992; Emsley 2005: 124–5.
98 de Regt 1984: 175–239; O'Day, in Emsley et al. 2004: 149–66.
99 Dercksen and Verplanke 1987; Knotter 1999.
100 Hett 2004: 55–103; Chassaigne 2005: 57.
101 Emsley 2005: 34–5, 85–7; Montel 2003.
102 Wagner and Weinhauer, in Dinges and Sack 2000: 265–90; Emsley 2005: 2 (quote), 89–90.
103 Rosenhaft, in Lindenberger and Lüdtke 1995: 238–75; Lessman-Faust, in Dinges and Sack 2000: 241–63; Schumann 2001: 306–7, 320.
104 Emsley 2005: 126–8.
105 Cited in de Haan 1997: 1.
106 Wills 2005; Hood and Joyce 1999.
107 Chesnais 1976: 30–1; Kaiser 1982.
108 Marwick 1998: 479–89; Righart 2003.

Chapter 7 The Tables Turned: 1970 to the Present

1 Lepoutre 1997: 40–2.
2 Eisner, unpublished paper, table 3. For Ireland, see O'Donnell, in Body-Gendrot and Spierenburg 2008.
3 Leistra and Nieuwbeerta 2003: 21–6.
4 Harris et al. 2002.
5 Thome and Birkel 2007: 84–94; Eisner, unpublished paper, fig. 5; Robert, in Body-Gendrot and Spierenburg 2008.
6 de Haan 1997: 4; de Haan et al. 1999: 20–1; several contributions to Albrecht et al. 2001; Egelkamp 2002.
7 Robert, in Body–Gendrot and Spierenburg, 2008; de Haan 2000: 189; van Dijk et al. 2005: 50.
8 Chauvaud and Mayaud 2005: 256–60; Hoogenboezem 1995: 8; Leistra and Nieuwbeerta 2003: 25.
9 Eisner 1997: 157.
10 Thome and Birkel 2007: 81–4; Eisner, unpublished paper; Leistra and Nieuwbeerta 2003: 32–3, 44.
11 Thome 2001; Thome and Birkel 2007.
12 Eisner 1997: 122–4; and unpublished paper.

13 O'Donnell, in Body-Gendrot and Spierenburg 2008.
14 Body-Gendrot 1998: 199–230.
15 Hood and Joyce 1999: 155–6.
16 Hobbs et al. 2005.
17 Bjørgo 2005.
18 van der Ploeg and Mooij 1998: 20, 156.
19 Gemert and Torre 1996.
20 van San 1998: 174.
21 de Haan 2000: 197–8. Cf. Body-Gendrot 2000: 26.
22 Haen 2000: 125.
23 Timmer and Naeyé 2000: 169.
24 van de Port 2001: passim.
25 Mucchielli 2006: 102.
26 van de Port 2001: 38–9.
27 Leistra and Nieuwbeerta 2003: 44.
28 O'Donnell 2002: 83; and in Body-Gendrot and Spierenburg 2008.
29 Zaitch 2002.
30 Emsley 2005: 180–1.
31 <http://en.wikipedia.org/wiki/Marc_Dutroux> (July 12, 2007).
32 Leistra and Nieuwbeerta 2003: 116–21.
33 Cf. Komen 1998.
34 This paragraph is based on a discussion with the editorial board of *Crime, History & Societies*, June 30, 2007.
35 van de Port 2001: 24 (police delighting); Terlouw et al. 2000: 23–4 (no resistance).

References

Ågren, Maria, et al. (eds.) s.a. *Guises of power. Integration of society and legitimisation of power in Sweden and the Southern Low Countries, 1500–1900* (Uppsala: Department of History).

Albrecht, Günter, et al. (eds.) 2001. *Gewaltkriminalität zwischen Mythos und Realität* (Frankfurt a.M.: Suhrkamp).

Algazi, Gadi. 1996. *Herrengewalt und Gewalt der Herren im späten Mittelalter. Herrschaft, Gegenseitigkeit und Sprachgebrauch* (Frankfurt/New York: Campus).

Alighieri, Dante. 1980. *La divina commedia. Purgatorio. A cura di Carlo Salinari, Sergio Romagnoli, Antonio Lanza* (Roma: Riuniti).

A[mpzing], S[amuel]. 1633. *Spigel ofte toneel der ydelheyd ende ongebondenheyd onser eeuwe, voorgestelt in rymen van S.A. tot lere ende beterschap.*

Anderson, Elijah. 1999. *Code of the street. Decency, violence and the moral life of the inner city* (New York/London: Norton).

Andrew, Donna T. 1980. The code of honour and its critics. The opposition to duelling in England, 1700–1850. *Social History* 5: 409–34.

Andrews, Richard Mowery. 1994. *Law, magistracy and crime in Old Regime Paris, 1735–1789*. Vol. I: *The system of criminal justice* (Cambridge: Cambridge University Press).

Anten, W. M. H. 1892. *Het verachtelijke en verderfelijke van het duel* (Amersfoort: Blankenberg).

Archer, John. 1990. *By a flash and a scare. Incendiarism, animal maiming and poaching in East Anglia, 1815–1870* (Oxford: Clarendon Press).

Artières, Philippe and Kalifa, Dominique. 2001. *Vidal, le tueur de femmes. Une biographie sociale* (Paris: Perrin).

Avdela, Efi. 2006. Emotions on trial. Judging crimes of honour in post-civil-war Greece. *Crime, Histoire and Sociétés/Crime, History and Societies* 10,2: 33–52.

Backmann, Sibylle, et al. (eds.) 1998. *Ehrkonzepte in der frühen Neuzeit. Identitäten und Abgrenzungen* (Berlin: Akademie Verlag).

Bailey, Joanne. 2006. "I dye [*sic*] by inches." Locating wife beating in the concept of a privatization of marriage and violence in 18th-century England. *SocHist* 31,3: 273–94.

Bailey, Victor. 1998. *"This Rash Act." Suicide across the life cycle in the Victorian city* (Stanford: Stanford University Press).

Bairoch, Paul, et al. 1988. *La population des villes Européennes. Banque de données et analyse sommaire des résultats, 800–1850* (Genève: Droz).

Bard, Christine, et al. (eds.) 2002. *Femmes et justice pénale, 19e–20e siècle* (Rennes: Presses Universitaires de Rennes).

Barker, Juliet R. V. 1986. *The tournament in England, 1100–1400* (Woodbridge: Boydell Press).

Barraqué, J.-P. 1988. Le contrôle des conflits à Saragosse, 14e – début du 15e siècle. *Revue Historique* 279, 1: 41–50.

Barton, Carlin A. 2001. *Roman honor. The fire in the bones* (Berkeley: University of California Press).

Baumann, Ursula. 2001. *Vom Recht auf den eigenen Tod: Die Geschichte des Suizids vom 18. bis zum 20. Jahrhundert* (Weimar: Verlag Hermann Böhlaus Nachfolger).

Beattie, J. M. 1986. *Crime and the courts in England, 1660–1800* (Oxford: Oxford University Press).

Beaufort, Binnert Philip de. 1881. Beschouwingen over het tweegevecht (Dissertation, University of Utrecht).

Beavan, Colin. 2001. *Fingerprints. The origins of crime detection and the murder case that launched forensic science* (New York: Hyperion).

Becker, Marvin B. 1976. Changing patterns of violence and justice in 14th- and 15th-century Florence. *Comparative Studies in Society and History* 18,3: 281–96.

Bellamy, John. 1973. *Crime and public order in England in the later Middle Ages* (London: Routledge & Kegan Paul).

Benabou, Erica-Marie. 1987. *La prostitution et la police des moeurs au 18e siècle* (Paris: Perrin).

Berghuis, A. C. and Jonge, L. K. de. 1993. Moord en doodslag in 1989 en 1992. Een secundaire analyse. *Tijdschrift voor Criminologie* 35,1: 55–62.

Billacois, François. 1986. *Le duel dans la société française des 16e–17e siècles. Essai de psychosociologie historique* (Paris: Ecole des Hautes Etudes en Sciences Sociales).

Bjørgo, Tore. 2005. Conflict processes between youth groups in a Norwegian city. Polarisation and revenge. *European Journal of Crime, Criminal Law and Criminal Justice* 13,1: 44–74.

Blasius, Dirk. 1978. *Kriminalität und Alltag. Zur Konfliktgeschichte des Alltagslebens im 19. Jahrhundert* (Göttingen: Vandenhoeck & Ruprecht).

Blastenbrei, Peter. 1995. *Kriminalität in Rom, 1560–1585* (Tübingen: Max Niemeyer).

Blauert, Andreas and Schwerhoff, Gerd (eds.) 1993. *Mit den Waffen der Justiz. Zur Kriminalitätsgeschichte des späten Mittelalters und der frühen Neuzeit* (Frankfurt a.M.: Fischer).

Blauert, Andreas and Schwerhoff, Gerd (eds.) 2000. *Kriminalitätsgeschichte. Beiträge zur Sozial- und Kulturgeschichte der Vormoderne* (Konstanz: Universitätsverlag).

Bloch, Marc. 1965. *Feudal society*, trans. L. A. Manyon (London: Routledge & Kegan Paul).

Blockmans, Wim. 1987. *Een middeleeuwse vendetta. Gent 1300* (Houten: De Haan).

Blok, Anton. 1974. *The mafia of a Sicilian village, 1860–1960. A study of violent peasant entrepreneurs* (New York: Harper & Row).

Blok, Anton. 1991. *De Bokkerijders. Roversbenden en geheime genootschappen in de Landen van Overmaas, 1730–1774* (Amsterdam: Prometheus).

Blok, Anton. 2001. *Honour and violence* (Cambridge: Polity).

Body-Gendrot, Sophie. 1998. *Les villes face à l'insécurité. Des ghettos américains aux banlieues françaises* (Paris: Bayard).

Body-Gendrot, Sophie. 2000. *The social control of cities? A comparative perspective* (Oxford: Blackwell).

Body-Gendrot, Sophie and Spierenburg, Pieter (eds.) 2008. *Violence in Europe. Historical and contemporary perspectives* (New York: Springer).

Boomgaard, Jan. 1992. *Misdaad en straf in Amsterdam. Een onderzoek naar de strafrechtspleging van de Amsterdamse schepenbank, 1490–1552* (Zwolle: Waanders).

Bos, Dennis. 2000. Verborgen motieven en uitgesproken persoonlijkheden. Eer en reputatie in de vroege socialistische arbeidersbeweging van Amsterdam. *BMGN* 115: 509–31.

Bourdieu, Pierre. 1972. *Esquisse d'une théorie de la pratique, précédé de trois études d'ethnologie Kabyle* (Genève: Droz).

Bourdieu, Pierre. 1980. *Le sens pratique* (Paris: Editions de Minuit).

Bowsky, William H. 1967. The medieval commune and internal violence. Police power and public safety in Siena, 1287–1355. *AHR* 73: 1–17.

Bowsky, William H. 1981. *A medieval Italian commune. Siena under the Nine, 1287–1355* (Berkeley: University of California Press).

Brennan, Thomas. 1988. *Public drinking and popular culture in 18th-century Paris* (Princeton: Princeton University Press).

Brewer, John. 2004. *Sentimental murder. Love and madness in the eighteenth century* (London: Harper Perennial).

Brink, Gabriël van den. 1991. Van gevecht tot gerecht. Geweldpleging in het Zuidoosten van Brabant, 1811–1875. *AST* 18,3: 96–116.

Brink, Gabriël van den. 1995. De grote overgang. Een lokaal onderzoek naar de modernisering van het bestaan: Woensel, 1670–1920 (Dissertation, Universiteit van Amsterdam).

Brioist, Pascal, et al. 2002. *Croiser le fer. Violence et culture de l'épée dans la France moderne, 16e–18e siècle* (Seyssel, Champ Vallon).

Brown, Howard G. 1997. From organic society to security state. The war on brigandage in France, 1797–1802. *JMH* 69,4: 661–95.

Brown, Keith M. 1986. *Bloodfeud in Scotland, 1573–1625. Violence, justice and politics in an early modern society* (Edinburgh: Donald).

Brucker, Gene A. 1983. *Renaissance Florence*, 2nd edn. (Berkeley: University of California Press).

Brückweh, Kerstin. 2006a. *Mordlust. Serienmorde, Gewalt und Emotionen im 20. Jahrhundert* (Frankfurt/New York: Campus).

Brückweh, Kerstin. 2006b. Fantasies of violence. German citizens expressing their concepts of violence and ideas about democracy in letters referring to the case of the serial killer Jürgen Bartsch, 1966–1971. *Crime, Histoire & Sociétés/Crime, History and Societies* 10,2: 53–81.

Brunet, Michel. 2001. *Contrebandes, mutins et fiers-à-bras. Les stratégies de la violence en pays Catalan au 18e siècle* (Canet, Editions Trabucaire).

Burghartz, Susanna. 1990. *Leib, Ehre und Gut. Delinquenz in Zürich, Ende des 14 Jahrhunderts* (Zürich).

Burke, Peter. 2000. A civil tongue. Language and politeness in early modern Europe. In Burke, et al. (eds.), *Civil histories. Essays presented to Sir Keith Thomas* (Oxford: Oxford University Press): 31–48.

Cameron, Iain A. 1981. *Crime and repression in the Auvergne and the Guyenne, 1720–1790* (Cambridge: Cambridge University Press).

Capp, Bernard. 1996. Serial killers in 17th-century England. *History Today* 46,3: 21–6.

Carroll, Stuart. 2003. The peace in the feud in sixteenth- and seventeenth-century France. *PP* 178: 74–115.

Castan, Nicole. 1980a. *Justice et répression en Languedoc à l'époque des Lumières* (Paris: Flammarion).

Castan, Nicole. 1980b. *Les criminels de Languedoc. Les exigences d'ordre et les voies du ressentiment dans une société pré-révolutionnaire, 1750–1790* (Toulouse: Université de Toulouse-le-Mirail).

Cellini, Benvenuto. 1982. *Het leven van Benvenuto Cellini* (Amsterdam: Querido).

Chassaigne, Philippe. 2005. *Ville et violence. Tensions et conflits dans la Grande-Bretagne victorienne, 1840–1914* (Paris: Presses de l'Université Paris-Sorbonne).

Chauchadis, Claude. 1984. *Honneur morale et société dans l'Espagne de Philippe II* (Paris).

Chauvaud, Fréderic. 1991. *De Pierre Rivière à Landru. La violence apprivoisée au 19e siècle* (Turnhout: Brepols).

Chauvaud, Fréderic. 1995. *Les passions villageoises au 19e siècle. Les émotions rurales dans les pays de Beauce, du Hurepoix et du Mantois* (Paris: Publisud).

Chauvaud, Fréderic and Mayaud, Jean-Luc (eds.) 2005. *Les violences rurales au quotidien* (Paris: Boutique de l'Histoire).

Chesnais, Jean-Claude. 1976. *Les morts violentes en France depuis 1826. Comparaisons internationales* (Paris: Presses Universitaires de France).

Chesnais, Jean-Claude. 1981. *Histoire de la violence en Occident de 1800 à nos jours* (Paris: Robert Laffont).

Clough, Cecil H. 1993. Love and war in the Veneto. Luigi da Porto and the true story of Giulietta e Romeo. In Chambers, David S., et al. (eds.), *War, culture and society in Renaissance Venice. Essays in honour of John Hale* (London: Hambledon Press): 99–127.

Cobb, Richard. 1970. *The police and the people. French popular protest, 1789–1820* (Oxford: Oxford University Press).

Cockburn, J. S. 1991. Patterns of violence in English society. Homicide in Kent, 1560–1985. *PP* 130: 70–106.

Cohen, Elizabeth S. 1992. Honor and gender in the streets of early modern Rome. *JIntH* 22,4: 597–625.

Cohen, Esther. 1996. *Peaceable domain, certain justice* (Hilversum: Verloren).

Cohen, Sherrill. 1992. *The evolution of women's asylums since 1500. From refuges for ex-prostitutes to shelters for battered women* (New York: Oxford: Oxford University Press).

Cohen, Thomas V. 1992. The lay liturgy of affront in 16th-century Italy. *JSH* 25,4: 857–77.

Cohen, Thomas V. and Cohen, Elizabeth S. 1993. *Words and deeds in Renaissance Rome. Trials before the papal magistrates* (Toronto: University of Toronto Press).

Cohn, Samuel K., Jr. 1996. *Women in the streets. Essays on sex and power in Renaissance Italy* (Baltimore/London: Johns Hopkins University Press).

Cohn, Samuel K., Jr. 2002. The Black Death. End of a paradigm. *AHR* 107,3: 703–38.

Collard, Franck. 2003. *Le crime de poison au moyen âge* (Paris: PUF).

Conley, Carolyn A. 1999a. *Melancholy accidents. The meaning of violence in post-famine Ireland* (Lanham, MD: Lexington Books).

Conley, Carolyn. 1999b. The agreeable recreation of fighting. *JSH* 33,1: 57–72.

Cooney, Mark. 1997. The decline of elite homicide. *Criminology* 35,3: 381–407.

Cooney, Mark. 1998. *Warriors and peacemakers. How third parties shape violence* (New York/London: New York University Press).

Cooney, Mark. 2003. The privatization of violence. *Criminology* 41,4: 1377–406.

Curtis, L. Perry, Jr. 2001. *Jack the Ripper and the London press* (New Haven/London: Yale University Press).

Daly, Martin and Wilson, Margo. 1988. *Homicide* (New York: Aldine de Gruyter).

Danker, Uwe. 1988. *Räuberbanden im alten Reich um 1700. Ein Beitrag zur Geschichte von Herrschaft und Kriminalität in der frühen Neuzeit*, 2 vols (Frankfurt a.M.: Suhrkamp).

Dauphin, Cecile and Farge, Arlette (eds.) 1997. *De la violence et des femmes* (Paris: Albin Michel).

Davies, Andrew. 1998. Youth gangs, masculinity and violence in late Victorian Manchester and Salford. *Journal of Social History* 32,2: 349–69.

Davies, Andrew. 1999. "These viragoes are no less cruel than the lads." Young women, gangs and violence in late Victorian Manchester and Salford. *British Journal of Criminology* 39,1: 72–89.

Davis, Natalie Zemon. 1987. *Fiction in the archives. Pardon tales and their tellers in 16th-century France* (Stanford: Stanford University Press).

Davis, Robert C. 1994. *The war of the fists. Popular culture and public violence in late Renaissance Venice* (New York: Oxford University Press).

D'Cruze, Shani. 1998. *Crimes of outrage. Sex, violence and Victorian working women* (London: UCL Press).

D'Cruze, Shani. 1999. Sex, violence and local courts. Working-class respectability in a mid-19th-century Lancashire town. *British Journal of Criminology* 39,1: 39–55.

D'Cruze, Shani (ed.) 2000. *Everyday violence in Britain, 1850–1950. Gender and class* (Harlow, Longman).

Dean, Trevor. 1997. Marriage and mutilation. Vendetta in late medieval Italy. *PP* 157: 3–36.

Dean, Trevor. 2001. *Crime in medieval Europe, 1200–1550* (Harlow, Pearson).

Dean, Trevor and Lowe, Kate J. P. (eds.) 1994. *Crime, society and the law in Renaissance Italy* (Cambridge: Cambridge University Press).

Dercksen, Adrianne and Verplanke, Loes. 1987. *Geschiedenis van de onmaatschappelijkheidsbestrijding in Nederland, 1914–1970* (Meppel, Boom).

Dijk, Jan van, et al. 2005. *EUICS Report: The burden of crime in the EU. A comparative analysis of the European survey of crime and safety* (EUICS).

Dinges, Martin. 1994. *Der Maurermeister und der Finanzrichter. Ehre, Geld und soziale Kontrolle im Paris des 18. Jahrhunderts* (Göttingen: Vandenhoeck & Ruprecht).

Dinges, Martin and Sack, Fritz (eds.) 2000. *Unsichere Grossstädte? Vom Mittelalter bis zur Postmoderne* (Konstanz: Universitätsverlag).

Doggett, Maeve E. 1992. *Marriage, wife-beating and the law in Victorian England* (London: Weidenfeld and Nicolson).

Dülmen, Richard van. 1991. *Frauen vor Gericht. Kindsmord in der frühen Neuzeit* (Frankfurt a.M.: Fischer).

Dunnage, Jonathan. 2002. *Twentieth-century Italy. A social history* (London: Longman).

Dunning, Eric and Sheard, Kenneth. 1979. *Barbarians, gentlemen and players. A sociological study of the development of rugby football* (Oxford: M. Robertson).

Dunning, Eric, et al. 1987. Violent disorders in 20th-century Britain. In Gaskell, George and Benewick, Robert (eds.), *The crowd in contemporary Britain* (London: Sage): 19–75.

Dunning, Eric, et al. 1992. Violence in the British civilising process (Leicester: Leicester University Discussion Papers in Sociology, nr. S92/2).

Dupont-Bouchat, Marie Sylvie. 1994. "L'homicide malgré lui." Les transformations dans la gestion de l'homicide à travers les lettres de rémission, 16e–18e siècle (Paper at IAHCCJ Colloquium, Paris).

Edgerton, Robert B. 1992. *Sick societies. Challenging the myth of primitive harmony* (New York: Free Press).

Egelkamp, Margarethe Maria. 2002. Inflation von Gewalt? Strafrechtliche und kriminologische Analysen von Qualifikationsentscheidungen in den Niederlanden und Deutschland (Dissertation, University of Groningen).

Eggens, Albert. 2005. *Van daad tot vonnis. Door Drenten gepleegde criminaliteit voor en tijdens de Eerste Wereldoorlog* (Assen: Van Gorcum).

Egmond, Florike. 1993. *Underworlds. Organized crime in the Netherlands, 1650–1800* (Cambridge: Polity Press).

Eibach, Joachim. 1998. Städtische Gewaltkriminalität im Ancien Régime: Frankfurt am Main im europäischen Kontext. *Zeitschrift für Historische Forschung* 25: 359–82.

Eigen, Joel Peter. 1995. *Witnessing insanity. Madness and mad-doctors in the English court* (New Haven/London: Yale University Press).

Eisner, Manuel. 1997. *Das Ende der zivilisierten Stadt? Die Auswirkungen von Modernisierung und urbaner Krise auf Gewaltdelinquenz* (Frankfurt/New York: Campus).

Eisner, Manuel. 2001. Modernization, self-control and lethal violence. The long-term dynamics of European homicide rates in theoretical perspective. *British Journal of Criminology* 41: 618–38.

Eisner, Manuel. 2003. Long-term historical trends in violent crime. *Crime and Justice. A Review of Research* 30: 83–142.

Elias, Norbert. 1969 [1939]. *Über den Prozess der Zivilisation. Soziogenetische und psychogenetische Untersuchungen*, 2nd edn. 2 vols. (Bern/München: Francke Verlag). English translation by Edmund Jephcott: *The civilizing process*, 2 vols. (Oxford: Blackwell, 1978–82).

Elias, Norbert. 1992. *Studien über die Deutschen. Machtkämpfe und Habitusentwicklung im 19. und 20. Jahrhundert* (Frankfurt a.M.: Suhrkamp). English translation, with Preface, by Eric Dunning and Stephen Mennell, ed. Eric Dunning: *The Germans: power struggles and the development of habitus in the nineteenth and twentieth centuries* (Cambridge: Polity, 1996).

Elias, Norbert and Dunning, Eric. 1986. *Quest for excitement. Sport and leisure in the civilizing process* (Oxford/New York: Oxford University Press).

Elias, Norbert and Scotson, John L. 1976. *De gevestigden en de buitenstaanders. Een studie van de spanningen en machtsverhoudingen tussen twee arbeiders-buurten* (Utrecht/Antwerpen: Het Spectrum). English translation: *The established and the outsiders: sociological enquiry into community problems* (London: Cass, 1965; 2nd edn. London: Sage, 1994).

Emsley, Clive. 1996. *Crime and society in England, 1750–1900*, 2nd edn. (London: Longman).

Emsley, Clive. 2005. *Hard men. The English and violence since 1750* (London/New York: Hambledon and London).

Emsley, Clive, et al. (eds.) 2004. *Social control in Europe*. Vol. 2: *1800–2000* (Columbus: Ohio State University Press).

Eshof, P. van den and Weimar, E. C. J. 1991. Moord en doodslag in Nederland. Nederlandse gegevens in internationaal perspectief. *Justitiële Verkenningen* 17,1: 8–34.

Evans, Richard J. 1996. *Rituals of retribution. Capital punishment in Germany, 1600–1987* (Oxford: Oxford University Press).

Faber, Sjoerd. 1978. Kindermoord, in het bijzonder in de 18e eeuw te Amsterdam. *Bijdragen en Mededelingen betreffende de Geschiedenis der Nederlanden* 93: 224–40.

Faber, Sjoerd. 1983. *Strafrechtspleging en criminaliteit te Amsterdam: 1680–1811. De nieuwe menslievendheid* (Arnhem: Gouda Quint).

Faber, Sjoerd and Krikke, Bert. 1977. De psychiatrische expertise in de zaak Harmen Alfkens. Een Bataafse primeur? *Tijdschrift voor Gezondheidsrecht* 1: 262–4.

Farr, James R. 1988. *Hands of honor. Artisans and their world in Dijon, 1550–1650* (Ithaca: Cornell University Press).

Farr, James R. 1991. The pure and the disciplined body. Hierarchy, morality and symbolism in France during the Catholic Reformation. *JIntH* 21,3: 391–414.

Farr, James R. 2003. The death of a judge. Performance, honor and legitimacy in seventeenth-century France. *JMH* 75,1: 1–22.

Farrell, Sean. 2000. Rituals and riots. Sectarian violence and political culture in Ulster, 1784–1886 (Lexington: University Press of Kentucky).

Feeley, Malcolm M. and Little, Deborah I. 1991. The vanishing female. The decline of women in the criminal process. *Law & Society Review* 25,4: 719–57.

Fehr, Hans. 1908. *Der Zweikampf* (Berlin: Curtius).

Ferket, Nathalie. 1999. Zwijgen als vermoord. Vrouwenmishandeling en de juridische positie van de gehuwde vrouw in België in de 19e eeuw. *TvSG* 25: 285–304.

Ferraro, Joanne M. 1993. *Family and public life in Brescia, 1580–1650. The foundations of power in the Venetian state* (Cambridge: Cambridge University Press).

Fishman, Jane Susannah. 1982. *Boerenverdriet. Violence between peasants and soldiers in early modern Netherlands art* (Ann Arbor, UMI Research Press).

Fletcher, Jonathan. 1997. *Violence and civilization. An introduction to the work of Norbert Elias* (Cambridge: Polity).

Foucault, Michel. 1973. *Moi Pierre Rivière, ayant égorgé ma mère, ma soeur et mon frère. Un cas de parricide au 19e siècle* (Paris: Gallimard).

Fox, James Alan and Levin, Jack. 2005. *Extreme killing. Understanding serial and mass murder* (London: Sage).

Foyster, Elizabeth A. 1999a. *Manhood in early modern England. Honour, sex and marriage* (London: New York: Longman).

Foyster, Elisabeth. 1999b. Boys will be boys? Manhood and aggression, 1660–1800. In Hitchcock, Tim and Cohen, Michèle (eds.), *English masculinities, 1660–1800* (London: New York: Longman): 151–166.

Frank, Michael. 1995. *Dörfliche Gesellschaft und Kriminalität. Das Fallbeispiel Lippe, 1650–1800* (Paderborn, Ferdinand Schöningh).

Franke, Herman. 1991. Geweldscriminaliteit in Nederland. Een historisch-sociologische analyse *Amsterdams Sociologisch Tijdschrift* 18,3: 13–45.

Frevert, Ute. 1991. *Ehrenmänner. Das Duell in der bürgerlichen Gesellschaft* (München: Beck).

Frost, Ginger. 2004. She is but a woman. Kitty Byron and the English Edwardian criminal justice system. *Gender and History* 16,3: 538–60.

Fuchs, Ralf-Peter. 1999. *Um die Ehre. Westfälische Beleidigungsprozesse vor dem Reichskammergericht, 1525–1805* (Paderborn, Ferdinand Schöningh).

Gallant, Thomas W. 2000. Honor, masculinity and ritual knife fighting in 19th-century Greece. *AHR* 105,2: 359–82.

Garnot, Benoît. 1993. *Un crime conjugal au 18e siècle* (Paris: Imago).

Garnot, Benoît (ed.). 1996. *L'infrajudiciaire du moyen âge à l'époque contemporaine* (Dijon: Editions Universitaires).

Garnot, Benoît. 2000. *Justice et société en France au 16e, 17e et 18e siècles* (Paris: Orphrys).

Garnot, Benoît. 2004. *Intime conviction et erreur judiciaire. Un magistrat assassin au XVIIe siècle?* (Dijon: Editions Universitaires de Dijon).

Gaskill, Malcolm. 1998. Reporting murder. Fiction in the archives in early modern England. *SocHist* 23,1: 1–30.

Gaskill, Malcolm. 2000. *Crime and mentalities in early modern England* (Cambridge: Cambridge University Press).

Gatrell, V.A.C. 1980. The decline of theft and violence in Victorian and Edwardian England. In Gatrell et al. (eds.), *Crime and the law. The social history of crime in Western Europe since 1500* (London: Europa Publishers): 238–370.

Gauvard, Claude. 1991. *"De grace especial." Crime, état et société en France à la fin du moyen âge*, 2 vols. (Paris: Publications de la Sorbonne).

Gauvard, Claude. 1999. Fear of crime in late medieval France. In Hanawalt, Barbara and Wallace, David (eds.), *Medieval crime and social control* (Minneapolis, University of Minnesota Press): 1–48.

Gemert, Frank van and Torre, Edward van der. 1996. Berbers in de dope. Cultuur als verklaring voor vormen van criminaliteit. *Amsterdams Sociologisch Tijdschrift* 23,3: 480–503.

Geremek, Bronislaw. 1976. *Les marginaux Parisiens aux 14e et 15e siècles* (Paris: Flammarion).

Gilman, Sander. 1999. *Making the body beautiful. A cultural history of aesthetic surgery* (Princeton: Princeton University Press).

Given, James Buchanan. 1977. *Society and homicide in thirteenth-century England* (Stanford: Stanford University Press).

Glaudemans, Corien. 2004. *Om die wrake wille. Eigenrichting, veten en verzoening in laat-middeleeuws Holland en Zeeland* (Hilversum, Verloren).

Godfrey, Barry. 2003. Counting and accounting for the decline in non-lethal violence in England, Australia and New Zealand, 1880–1920. *British Journal of Criminology* 43: 340–53.

Godfrey, Barry, et al. (eds.) 2003. *Comparative histories of crime* (Uffculme: Willan Publishing).

Goff, Jacques le. 1980. *Time, work and culture in the Middle Ages*, trans. Arthur Goldhammer (Chicago/London: University of Chicago Press).

Gómez Bravo, Gutmaro. 2005. *Crimen y castigo. Cárceles, justicia y violencia en la España del siglo XIX* (Madrid, Catarata).

Gonthier, Nicole. 1992. *Cris de haine et rites d'unité. La violence dans les villes, 13e–16e siècle* (Turnhout, Brepols).

Gorn, Elliott J. 1986. *The manly art. Bare-knuckle prize fighting in America* (Ithaca, NY: Cornell University Press).

Goudsblom, J. 1998. De paradox van de pacificatie. *Amsterdams Sociologisch Tijdschrift* 25,3: 395–406.

Gowing, Laura. 1994. Language, power and the law. Women's slander litigation in early modern London. In Kermode, Jenny and Walker, Garthine (eds.), *Women, crime and the courts in early modern England* (London: UCL Press): 26–47.

Gowing, Laura. 1996. *Domestic dangers. Women, words and sex in early modern London* (Oxford: Clarendon Press).

Gowing, Laura. 1997. Secret births and infanticide in 17th-century England. *PP* 156: 87–115.

Graus, Frantisek. 1987. *Pest, Geissler, Judenmorde. Das 14. Jahrhundert als Krisenzeit* (Göttingen: Vandenhoeck & Ruprecht).

Graziani, Antoine-Marie. 1997. *La Corse génoise. Economie, société, culture. Période moderne, 1453–1768* (Ajaccio: Alain Piazzola).

Green, Thomas Andrew. 1985. *Verdict according to conscience. Perspectives on the English criminal trial jury, 1200–1800* (Chicago: University of Chicago Press).

Greenshields, Malcolm. 1994. *An economy of violence in early modern France. Crime and justice in the Haute Auvergne, 1587–1664* (University Park, PA: Pennsylvania State University Press).

Grimmer, Claude. 1983. *Vivre à Aurillac au 18e siècle* (Aurillac: PUF).

Groebner, Valentin. 2003. *Ungestalten. Die visuelle Kultur der Gewalt im Mittelalter* (München: Carl Hanser).

Guarnieri, Patrizia. 1993. *A case of child murder. Law and science in 19th-century Tuscany* (Cambridge: Polity).

Guillais, Joëlle. 1986. *La chair de l'autre. Le crime passionnel au 19e siècle* (Paris: Olivier Orban).

Gurr, Ted Robert. 1981. Historical trends in violent crime. A critical review of the evidence. *Crime and Justice. An Annual Review of Research* 3: 295–353.

Guttmann, Allen. 1986. *Sports spectators* (New York: Columbia University Press)

Gyger, Patrick J. 1998. *L'épée et la corde. Criminalité et justice à Fribourg, 1475–1505* (Lausanne: Université de Lausanne).

Haan, W. J. M. de. 1997. *'t Kon minder. Geweldscriminaliteit, leefbaarheid en kwaliteit van veiligheidszorg. Rede uitgesproken bij de aanvaarding van het ambt van gewoon hoogleraar in de criminologie aan de Rijksuniversiteit te Groningen* (Deventer: Gouda Quint).

Haan, W. J. M. de, et al. 1999. *Jeugd en geweld. Een interdisciplinair perspectief* (Assen: Van Gorcum).

Haan, W. J. M. de. 2000. Explaining the absence of violence. A comparative approach. In Karstedt, Susanne and Bussmann, Kai-D. (eds.), *Social dynamics of crime and control. New theories for a world in transition* (Oxford: Hart Publishing): 189–203.

Häberlein, Mark. 1998. Tod auf der Herrenstube. Ehre und Gewalt in der Augsburger Führungsschicht, 1500–1620. In Backmann, Sibylle, et al. (eds.), *Ehrkonzepte in der frühen Neuzeit. Identitäten und Abgrenzungen* (Berlin: Akademie Verlag): 148–69.

Haen, Ineke. 2000. Vuurwapens en geweld in internationaal perspectief. *Tijdschrift voor Criminologie* 42,2: 118–29.

Haine, W. Scott. 1996. *The world of the Paris café. Sociability among the French working class, 1789–1914* (Baltimore/London: Johns Hopkins University Press).

Halttunen, Karen. 1995. Humanitarianism and the pornography of pain in Anglo-American culture. *AHR* 100,2: 303–34.

Hammer, Carl I., Jr. 1978. Patterns of homicide in a medieval university town: 14th-century Oxford. *Past and Present* 78: 3–23.

Hanawalt, Barbara. 1976. Violent death in 14th and early 15th-century England. *Comparative Studies in Society and History* 18: 297–320.

Hanawalt, Barbara. 1979. *Crime and conflict in English communities, 1300–1348* (Cambridge, MA/London: Harvard University Press).

Handvesten ofte privilegien ende octroyen mitsgaders willekeuren, costumen, ordonnantien en handelingen der stad Amstelredam, 3 vols. (Amsterdam 1748).

Hanewinckel, Stephanus. 1800. *Reize door de Majorij van 's Hertogenbosch, in den jaare 1799, in brieven. Met plaaten* (Amsterdam).

Hanlon, Gregory. 1985. Les rituels de l'agression en Aquitaine au 17e siècle. *AESC* 40,2: 244–68.

Hardwick, Julie. 2006. Early modern perspectives on the long history of domestic violence. The case of seventeenth-century France. *JMH* 78,1: 1–36.

Harris, Anthony R., et al. 2002. Murder and medicine. The lethality of criminal assault, 1960–1999. *Homicide Studies* 6: 128–65.

Harris, Ruth. 1989. *Murders and madness. Medicine, law and society in the fin de siècle* (Oxford: Clarendon Press).

Hasselt, Johan Jacob van. 1772. *Rechtsgeleerde verhandeling over de noodzaakelykheid van het schouwen der doode lighaamen* (Amsterdam).

Hay, Douglas, et al. 1975. *Albion's fatal tree. Crime and society in 18th-century England* (New York: Pantheon Books).

Heers, Jacques. 1974. *Le clan familial au moyen âge. Etude sur les structures politiques et sociales des milieux urbains* (Paris: PUF).

Heers, Jacques. 1990. *La ville au moyen âge en Occident. Paysages, pouvoirs et conflits* (Paris: Fayard).

Heijden, Manon van der. 1995. Criminaliteit en sexe in 18e-eeuws Rotterdam. *Tijdschrift voor Sociale Geschiedenis* 21,1: 1–36.

Heijden, Manon van der. 1998. *Huwelijk in Holland. Stedelijke rechtspraak en kerkelijke tucht, 1550–1700* (Amsterdam: Bert Bakker).

Heijden, Manon van der. 2000. Women as victims of sexual and domestic violence in 17th-century Holland. Criminal cases of rape, incest and maltreatment in Rotterdam and Delft. *JSH* 33,3: 623–44.

Henry, Brian. 1994. *Dublin hanged. Crime, law enforcement and punishment in late 18th-century Dublin* (Dublin: Irish Academic Press).

Herwaarden, Jan van. 1978. *Opgelegde bedevaarten. Een studie over de praktijk van het opleggen van bedevaarten in de Nederlanden gedurende de late middeleeuwen* (Assen, Amsterdam: Van Gorcum).

Hett, Benjamin Carter. 2004. *Death in the Tiergarten. Murder and criminal justice in the Kaiser's Berlin* (Cambridge, MA: Harvard University Press).

Hobbs, Dick et al. 2005. Violence and control in the night-time economy. *European Journal of Crime, Criminal Law and Criminal Justice* 13,1: 89–102.

Hobsbawm, Eric. 1981. *Bandits*. Revised edn. (New York: Pantheon Books).

Hoffer, Peter C. and Hull, N. E. H. 1981. *Murdering mothers. Infanticide in England and New England, 1558–1803* (New York: New York University Press).

Hollandts Placcaet-boeck. 1645. *1580 tot 1645* (Amsterdam: Jan Janssen).

Hood, Roger and Joyce, Kate. 1999. Three generations. Oral testimonies on crime and social change in London's East End. *British Journal of Criminology* 39,1: 136–60.

Hoogenboezem, J. Mortaliteit. 1995. Moord en doodslag in Nederland. *Maandbericht Gezondheidsstatistiek* 14,7: 4–10.

Hoppenbrouwers, P. C. M. 1992. *Een middeleeuwse samenleving. Het Land van Heusden, ca.1360–ca.1515*, 2 vols. (Wageningen: A. A. G. Bijdragen 32).

Hufton, Olwen H. 1974. *The poor of eighteenth-century France, 1750–1789* (Oxford: Clarendon Press).

Hufton, Olwen. 1990.Women and violence in early modern Europe. In Dieteren, Fia and Kloek, Els (eds.), *Writing women into history* (Amsterdam: Historisch Seminarium van de Universiteit van Amsterdam): 75–95.

Hurnard, Naomi D. 1997[1969]. *The king's pardon for homicide before AD1307* (Oxford: Clarendon Press).

Jackson, Mark. 1996. *New-born child murder. Women, illegitimacy and the courts in 18th-century England* (Manchester/New York: Manchester University Press).

Jackson, Mark (ed.). 2002. *Infanticide. Historical perspectives on child murder and concealment, 1550–2000* (Aldershot: Ashgate).

James, Mervyn. 1978. *English politics and the concept of honour, 1485–1642* (Oxford: Past & Present Supplement 3).

Jansson, Arne. 1998. *From swords to sorrow. Homicide and suicide in early modern Stockholm* (Stockholm: Almqvist & Wiksell International).

Johnson, Eric A. 1995. *Urbanization and crime: Germany, 1871–1914* (Cambridge: Cambridge University Press).

Johnson, Eric A. and Monkkonen, Eric H. (eds.) 1996. *The civilization of crime. Violence in town and country since the Middle Ages* (Urbana: University of Illinois Press).

Jones, George Fenwick. 1959. *Honor in German literature* (Chapel Hill: University of North Carolina Press).

Jones, Philip. 1997. *The Italian city-state. From commune to signoria* (Oxford: Clarendon Press).

Kaes, Anton. 2000. *M* (London: British Film Institute).

Kaeuper, Richard W. 2000. Chivalry and the "civilizing process." In Kaeuper, Richard W. (ed.), *Violence in medieval society* (Woodbridge: Boydell Press): 21–35.

Kaiser, Hildegunde. 1982. Das Messer als Tatwerkzeug bei Gewaltdelikten. Eine Untersuchung über die Beziehungen zwischen Täter, Opfer, Tatmotiv und Tatwaffe (Dissertation, University of Frankfurt).

Kalifa, Dominique. 2005. *Crime et culture au 19e siècle* (Paris: Perrin).

Kelly, James. 1995. *"That damn'd thing called honour." Duelling in Ireland, 1570–1860* (Cork: Cork University Press).

Kempers, Bram. 1987. *Kunst, macht en mecenaat. Het beroep van schilder in sociale verhoudingen, 1250–1600* (Amsterdam: Arbeiderspers).

Kesselring, K. J. 2003. *Mercy and authority in the Tudor state* (Cambridge: Cambridge University Press).

Kiernan, V. G. 1988. *The duel in European history. Honour and the reign of aristocracy* (Oxford: Oxford University Press).

King, Peter. 1996. Punishing assault. The transformation of attitudes in the English courts. *JIntH* 27,1: 43–74.

Knotter, Ad. 1999. *Rondom de Stokstraat. "Onmaatschappelijkheid" en "onderklasse" in de jaren vijftig* (Maastricht: Sociaal Historisch Centrum voor Limburg).

Kock, Henri François de. 1876. Het duel. Aantekening op boek II, titel VI van het Ontwerp-Wetboek van Strafrecht van 1875 (Dissertation, University of Leiden).

Koenraadt, F., (ed.). 1991. *Ziek of schuldig? Twee eeuwen forensische psychiatrie en psychologie* (Arnhem: Gouda Quint).

Kolmer, Lothar. 1997. Gewalttätige Öffentlichkeit und öffentliche Gewalt. Zur städtischen Kriminalität im späten Mittelalter. *Zeitschrift der Savigny Stiftung für Rechtsgeschichte, Germanistische Abteilung* 114: 261–95.

Komen, Mieke. 1998. Kindermishandeling en sociale verandering. *Tijdschrift voor Criminologie* 40,1: 39–58.

Koskivirta, Anu and Forsström, Sari (eds.) 2002. *Manslaughter, fornication and sectarianism. Norm-breaking in Finland and the Baltic area from mediaeval to modern times* (Helsinki: Finnish Academy of Science and Letters).

Kuehn, Thomas. 1991. *Law, family and women. Toward a legal anthropology of Renaissance Italy* (Chicago/London: University of Chicago Press).

Kurgan-Vanhentenryk, Ginette (ed.). 1999. *Un pays si tranquille. La violence en Belgique au 19e siècle* (Bruxelles: Editions de l'Université).

Küther, Carsten. 1976. *Räuber und Gauner in Deutschland. Das organisierte Bandenwesen im 18. und frühen 19. Jahrhundert* (Göttingen: Vandenhoeck & Ruprecht).

Lacour, Eva. 2000. *Schlägereyen und Unglücksfälle. Zur Historischen Psychologie und Typologie von Gewalt in der frühneuzeitlichen Eifel* (Egelsbach: Hänsel-Hohenhausen).

Lacour, Eva. 2001. Faces of violence revisited. A typology of violence in early modern rural Germany. *JSH* 34,3: 649–67.

Lane, Roger. 1997. *Murder in America. A history* (Columbus: Ohio State University Press).

Langbein, John H. 1974. *Prosecuting crime in the Renaissance. England, Germany, France* (Cambridge, MA: Harvard University Press).

Lange, Katrin. 1994. *Gesellschaft und Kriminalität. Räuberbanden im 18. und frühen 19. Jahrhundert* (Frankfurt a.M.: Lang).

Lapalus, Sylvie. 2004. *La mort du vieux. Une histoire du parricide au 19e siècle* (Paris: Tallandier).

Larner, John. 1980. *Italy in the age of Dante and Petrarch, 1216–1380* (London: Longman).

Lawrence, Jon. 2003. Forging a peaceable kingdom. War, violence and fear of brutalization in post-First World War Britain. *JMH* 75,3: 557–89.

Leany, Jennifer. 1989. Ashes to ashes. Cremation and the celebration of death in 19th-century Britain. In Houlbrooke, Ralph (ed.), *Death, ritual and bereavement* (London: Routledge): 118–35.

Lebigre, Arlette. 1991. *Les dangers de Paris au 17e siècle. L'assassinat de Jacques Tardieu, lieutenant criminel au Châtelet, et de sa femme, 24 août 1665* (Paris: Albin Michel).

Leistra, Gerlof and Nieuwbeerta, Paul. 2003. *Moord en doodslag in Nederland, 1992–2001* (Amsterdam: Prometheus).

Lepoutre, David. 1997. *Coeur de banlieue. Codes, rites et langages* (Paris: Odile Jacob).

Lind, Vera. 1999. *Selbstmord in der frühen Neuzeit. Diskurs, Lebenswelt und kultureller Wandel am Beispiel der Herzogtümer Schleswig und Holstein* (Göttingen: Vandenhoeck & Ruprecht).

Lindenberger, Thomas and Alf Lüdtke (eds.) 1995. *Physische Gewalt. Studien zur Geschichte der Neuzeit* (Frankfurt a.M.: Suhrkamp).

Lorenz, Maren. 1999. *Kriminelle Körper – Gestörte Gemüter. Die Normierung des Individuums in Gerichtsmedizin und Psychiatrie der Aufklärung* (Hamburg, Hamburger Edition).

McAleer, Kevin. Dueling. 1994. *The cult of honor in fin-de-siècle Germany* (Princeton: Princeton University Press).

McDonagh, Josephine. 2003. *Child murder and British culture, 1720–1900* (Cambridge: Cambridge University Press).

Macdonald, Michael and Murphy, Terence R. 1990. *Sleepless souls. Suicide in early modern England* (Oxford, Clarendon Press).

McIntosh, Marjorie Keniston. 1998. *Controlling misbehavior in England, 1370–1600* (Cambridge: Cambridge University Press).

McMahon, Vanessa. 2004. *Murder in Shakespeare's England* (London: Hambledon and London).

Maddern, Philippa C. 1992. *Violence and social order. East Anglia, 1422–1442* (Oxford: Clarendon Press).

Malcolmson, Robert W. 1973. *Popular recreations in English society, 1700–1850* (Cambridge: Cambridge University Press).

Mantecón, Tomás. 1997. *La muerte de Antonia Isabel Sánchez. Tiranía y escándalo en una sociedad rural del Norte español en el Antiguo Régimen* (Alcalá de Henares: Centro de Estudios Cervantinos).

Mantecón, Tomás. 2002. Mujeres forzadas y abusos deshonestos en la Castilla moderna. In *Manuscrits. Revista d'Historia Moderna* 20: 157–85.

Mantecón, Tomás. 2004. Les démons de Martín. Folie et erreur judiciaire dans la Castille du 17e siècle. In Garnot, Benoît (ed.), *L'erreur judiciaire. De Jeanne d'Arc à Roland Agret* (Paris: Imago): 61–84.

Mantecón, Tomás. 2006a. Las culturas criminales portuarias en las ciudades atlánticas. Sevilla y Amsterdam en su edad dorada. In Fortea, José Ignacio and Gelabert, Juan E. (eds.), *La ciudad portuaria atlántica en la historia* (Santander: Autoridad Portuaria de Santander): 161–94.

Mantecón, Tomás. 2006b. Hampas contrabandistas en la España Atlántica de los siglos 17 y 18. In Fernandez de Pinedo, E., et al. (eds.) *El Abra: ¿Mare Nostrum? Portugalete y el mar* (Bilbao: Concejalia de Cultura de Portugalete): 131–72.

Marci, Iacobus. 1618. *Deliciae Batavicae. Variae elegantesque picturae* (Amsterdam).

Marsilje, J. W., et al. 1990. *Bloedwraak, partijstrijd en pacificatie in laat-middeleeuws Holland* (Hilversum: Verloren).

Martines, Lauro (ed.) 1972. *Violence and civil disorder in Italian cities, 1200–1500* (Berkeley: University of California Press).

Marwick, Arthur. 1998. *The sixties. Cultural revolution in Britain, France, Italy and the United States, c.1958–c.1974* (Oxford: Oxford University Press).

Mehl, Jean-Michel. 1990. *Les jeux au royaume de France du 13e au début du 16e siècle* (Paris: Artheme Fayard).

Meyer-Knees, Anke. 1992. *Verführung und sexuelle Gewalt. Untersuchung zum medizinischen und juristischen Diskurs im 18. Jahrhundert* (Tübingen: Stauffenburg Verlag).

Michalik, Kerstin. 1997. *Kindsmord. Sozial- und Rechtsgeschichte der Kindstötung im 18. und beginnenden 19. Jahrhundert am Beispiel Preussen* (Pfaffenweiler: Centaurus Verlag).

Mohrmann, Ruth-Elisabeth. 1977. *Volksleben in Wilster im 16. und 17. Jahrhundert* (Neumünster: Wachholtz).

Mols, R. 1979. De seculiere clerus in de 17de eeuw. In Blok, D. P., et al. (eds.), *Algemene geschiedenis der Nederlanden*, vol. 8 (Haarlem: Fibula-Van Dishoeck).

Monkkonen, Eric. 2001. New standards for historical homicide research. *Crime, Histoire & Sociétés/Crime, History and Societies* 5,2: 5–26.

Monkkonen, Eric. 2006. Homicide. Explaining America's exceptionalism. *American Historical Review* 111,1: 76–94.

Monod, Paul Kléber. 2003. *The murder of Mr. Grebell. Madness and civility in an English town* (New Haven: Yale University Press).

Montel, Laurence. 2003. Genre et criminalité organisée à Marseille du début du 19e siècle à la fin des années 1930. Paper presented at the conference "Gender and Crime in Historical Perspective" (Paris: IAHCCJ).

Morris, David B. 1991. *The culture of pain* (Berkeley: University of California Press).

Morris, Robert M. 2001. "Lies, damned lies and criminal statistics." Reinterpreting the criminal statistics in England and Wales. *Crime, Histoire & Sociétés/Crime, History and Societies* 5,1: 111–27.

Mucchielli, Laurent. 2004. Demographic and social characteristics of murderers and their victims. A survey on a département of the Paris region in the 1990s. *Population-E* 59,2: 1–27.

Mucchielli, Laurent. 2006. L'élucidation des homicides. De l'enchantement technologique à l'analyse du travail des enquêteurs de police judiciaire. *Déviance et Société* 30,1: 91–119.

Muchembled, Robert. 1989. *La violence au village. Sociabilité et comportements populaires en Artois du 15e au 17e siècle* (Turnhout: Brepols).

Muir, Edward. 1993. *Mad blood stirring. Vendetta & factions in Friuli during the Renaissance* (Baltimore/London: Johns Hopkins University Press).

Muir, Edward. 2005. *Ritual in Early Modern Europe*, 2nd edn. (Cambridge: Cambridge University Press).

Murray, Alexander. 1998. *Suicide in the Middle Ages. Vol I: The violent against themselves* (Oxford/New York: Oxford University Press).

Murray, Alexander. 2000. *Suicide in the Middle Ages. Vol II: The curse on self-murder* (Oxford/New York: Oxford University Press).

Neste, Evelyne van den. 1996. *Tournois, joutes, pas d'armes dans les villes de Flandres à la fin du moyen âge, 1300–1486* (Paris: Ecole des Chartes).

Neuschel, Kristen B. 1989. *Word of honor. Interpreting noble culture in 16th-century France* (Ithaca/London: Cornell University Press).

Niccoli, Ottavia. 1999. Rinuncia, pace, perdono. Rituali di pacificazione della prima età moderna. *Studi Storici* 40: 219–61.

Nicholas, David M. 1970. Crime and punishment in fourteenth-century Ghent, Second Part. *Belgisch Tijdschrift voor Filologie en Geschiedenis* 48,4: 1141–76.

Nicholas, David. 1988. *The van Arteveldes of Ghent. The varieties of vendetta and the hero in history* (Leiden, Brill).

Nicholas, David. 1997. *The later medieval city, 1300–1500* (London: Longman).

Nirenberg, David. 1996. *Communities of violence. Persecution of minorities in the Middle Ages* (Princeton, Princeton University Press).

Nolde, Dorothea. 2003. *Gattenmord. Macht und Gewalt in der frühneuzeitlichen Ehe* (Köln: Böhlau).

Nubola, Cecilia and Würgler, Andreas (eds.) 2002. *Suppliche e gravamina. Politica, amministrazione, giustizia in Europa, secoli 14–16* (Bologna: Il Mulino).

Nusteling, Hubert. 1997. The population of Amsterdam in the golden age. In Kessel, Peter van and Schulte, Elisja (eds.), *Amsterdam: Rome. Two growing cities in 17th-century Europe* (Amsterdam: Amsterdam University Press): 71–84.

Nye, Robert A. 1984. *Crime, madness and politics in modern France. The medical concept of national decline* (Princeton: Princeton University Press).

Nye, Robert A. 1993. Masculinity and male codes of honor in modern France (New York/Oxford: Oxford University Press).

O'Donnell, Ian. 2002. Unlawful killing past and present. *The Irish Jurist* 37, New Series: 56–90.

Österberg, Eva and Sogner, Sölvi (eds.) 2000. *People meet the law. Control and conflict-handling in the courts: the Nordic countries in the post-Reformation and preindustrial period* (Oslo: Universitetsforlaget).

Paresys, Isabelle. 1998. *Aux marges du royaume. Violence, justice et société en Picardie sous François Ier* (Paris: Publications de la Sorbonne).

Parrella, Anne. 1992. Industrialization and murder. Northern France, 1815–1904. *Journal of Interdisciplinary History* 22,4: 627–54.

Payling, S. J. 1998. Murder, motive and punishment in 15th-century England. Two gentry case studies. *EHR* 113: 1–17.

Pazzaglini, Peter Raymond. 1979. *The criminal ban of the Sienese commune, 1225–1310* (Milano: A. Giuffrè).

Peltonen, Markku. 2003. *The duel in early modern England. Civility, politeness and honour* (Cambridge: Cambridge University Press).

Perrot, Michelle. 2001. *Les ombres de l'histoire. Crime et châtiment au 19e siècle* (Paris: Flammarion).

Perry, Mary Elizabeth. 1980. *Crime and society in early modern Seville* (Hanover, NH: University Press of New England).

Petkov, Kiril. 2003. *The kiss of peace. Ritual, self and society in the high and late medieval West* (Leiden: Boston, Brill).

Philippa, Marlies. 2004. *Lustwoorden. Over eten en seks in taal* (Den Haag: SDU).

Phillips, Roderick. 1988. *Putting asunder. A history of divorce in Western society* (Cambridge: Cambridge University Press).

Pinar, Francisco J. Lorenzo. 2002. Actitudas violentes en torno a la fornicación y disolución del matrimonio en Castilla durante la edad moderna. In Fortea, José I., et al. (eds.), *Furor et Rabies: Violencia, Conflicto y Marginación en la Edad Moderna* (Santander: Universidad de Cantabria): 159–82.

Ploeg, J. D. van der and Mooij, T. (eds.) 1998. *Geweld op school. Achtergronden, omvang, oorzaak, preventie en aanpak* (Rotterdam: Lemniscaat).

Ploux, François. 2002. *Guerres paysannes en Quercy. Violences, conciliations et répression pénale dans les campagnes du Lot, 1810–1860* (Paris: Boutique de l'Histoire).

Pohl, Susanne. 1999. Ehrlicher Totschlag – Rache – Notwehr. Zwischen männlichem Ehrencode und dem Primat des Stadtfriedens. Zürich 1376–1600. In Jussen, Bernhard and Koslofsky, Craig (eds.), *Kulturelle Reformation. Sinnformationen im Umbruch, 1400–1600* (Göttingen: Vandenhoeck & Ruprecht): 239–83.

Poitrineau, Abel. 1965. *La vie rurale en Basse-Auvergne au 18e siècle, 1726–1789*, 2 vols. (Aurillac: Imprimerie Moderne).

Pol, Lotte van de. 1996a. *Het Amsterdams hoerdom. Prostitutie in de 17e en 18e eeuw* (Amsterdam: Wereldbibliotheek).

Pol, Lotte van de. 1996b. *In en om het spinhuis. In Met Straffe Hand: Tucht en Discipline in het Amsterdamse Rasphuis* (Amsterdam: Universiteitsbibliotheek): 35–42.

Porret, Michel. 1992. *Le crime et ses circonstances. De l'esprit de l'arbitraire au siècle des lumières selon les réquisitoires des procureurs généraux de Genève* (Genève: Droz).

Porret, Michel. 2003. Le drame de la nuit. Enjeux médico-légaux du quadruple égorgement commis en 1885 à Genève par une mère sur ses enfants. *Revue d'Histoire du XIXe Siècle* 26–27: 305–29.

Port, Mattijs van de. 2001. *Geliquideerd. Criminele afrekeningen in Nederland* (Amsterdam: Meulenhoff).

Potter, David. 1997. "Rigueur de justice." Crime, murder and the law in Picardy, 15th to 16th centuries. *French History* 11: 265–309.

Raeymakers, Dries. 2004. *"Pour fuyr le nom de vilayn et meschant." Het duel in de Zuidelijke Nederlanden: aspecten van eer en oneer in de Nieuwe Tijd* (Leuven: Licentiaatsverhandeling Katholieke Universiteit).

Raggio, Osvaldo. 1991. Social relations and control of resources in an area of transit: eastern Liguria, 16th to 17th centuries. In Stuart Woolf (ed.), *Domestic strategies. Work and family in France and Italy, 1600–1800* (Cambridge/New York: Cambridge University Press): 20–42.

Reekers, Stephanie. 1956. *Westfalens Bevölkerung, 1818–1955. Die Bevölkerungsentwicklung der Gemeinden und Kreise im Zahlenbild* (Münster: Aschendorfse Verlagsbuchhandlung).

Regt, Ali de. 1984. *Arbeidersgezinnen en beschavingsarbeid. Ontwikkelingen in Nederland, 1870–1940. Een historisch-sociologische studie* (Meppel, Amsterdam: Boom).

Reuber, Ingrid Sybille. 2002. *Der Kölner Mordfall Fonk von 1816. Das Schwurgericht und das königliche Bestätigungsrecht auf dem Prüfstand* (Köln: Böhlau).

Rexroth, Frank. 1999. *Das Milieu der Nacht. Obrigkeit und Randgruppen im spätmittelalterlichen London* (Göttingen: Vandenhoeck & Ruprecht).

Rey, Roselyne. 1995. *The history of pain* (Cambridge, MA/London: Harvard University Press).

Righart, Hans. 2003. *De wereldwijde jaren zestig: Groot-Brittannië, Nederland, de Verenigde Staten. Bezorgd door Paul Luykx en Niek Pas* (Utrecht: Instituut Geschiedenis van de Universiteit Utrecht).

Roché, Sebastian. 1998. *Sociologie politique de l'insécurité. Violences urbaines, inégalités et globalisation* (Paris: PUF).

Roeck, Bernd. 1993. *Aussenseiter, Randgruppen, Minderheiten. Fremde im Deutschland der frühen Neuzeit* (Göttingen: Vandenhoeck & Ruprecht).

Rombach, Geurt. 1993. Verbalen, vonnissen en volkscultuur. Een nieuwe lezing van bekende bronnen. In Jan van Oudheusden and Gerard Trienekens (eds.), *Een pront wijf, een mager paard en een zoon op het seminarie. Aanzetten tot een integrale geschiedenis van oostelijk Noord-Brabant, 1770–1914* (Den Bosch: Stichting Brabantse Regionale Geschiedbeoefening): 89–124.

Roodenburg, Herman. 1990. *Onder censuur. De kerkelijke tucht in de Gereformeerde gemeente van Amsterdam: 1578–1700* (Hilversum: Verloren).

Roodenburg, Herman and Spierenburg, Pieter (eds.) 2004. *Social control in Europe.* Vol. I: *1500–1800* (Columbus: Ohio State University Press).

Rousseaux, Xavier. 1993. Ordre moral, justices et violence. L'homicide dans les sociétés Européennes, 13e–18e siècle. In Garnot, Benoît (ed.), *Ordre moral et délinquance de l'Antiquité au 20e siècle.* Actes du Colloque de Dijon (Dijon: EUD): 65–82.

Rublack, Ulinka. 1998. *Magd, Metz' oder Mörderin. Frauen vor frühneuzeitlichen Gerichten* (Frankfurt a.M.: Fischer).

Rudolph, Harriet and Schnabel-Schüle, Helga (eds.) 2003. *Justiz = Justice = Justicia: Rahmenbedingungen von Strafjustiz im Frühneuzeitlichen Europa.* Trierer Historische Forschungen, Band 48 (Trier: Kliomedia).

Ruff, Julius. 2001. *Violence in early modern Europe* (Cambridge: Cambridge University Press).

Ruggiero, Guido. 1980. *Violence in early Renaissance Venice* (New Brunswick, NJ: Rutgers University Press).

Sabean, David Warren. 1984. *Power in the blood. Popular culture and village discourse in early modern Germany* (Cambridge: Cambridge University Press).

Sabean, David Warren. 1990. *Property, production and family in Neckarhausen, 1700–1870* (Cambridge: Cambridge University Press).

Salernitano, Masuccio. 1975. *Il Novellino. Reprint a cura di Salvatore Nigro* (Roma: Laterza).

San, Marion van. 1998. *Stelen en steken. Delinquent gedrag van Curaçaose jongens in Nederland* (Amsterdam: Het Spinhuis).

Schär, Markus. 1985. *Seelennöte der Untertanen. Selbstmord, Melancholie und Religion im alten Zürich, 1500–1800* (Zürich: Chronos).

Scheuer, Herman Johannes. 1893. Insubordinatie en militair tweegevecht (Dissertation, University of Utrecht).

Schmidt, Cornelis. 1986. *Om de eer van de familie. Het geslacht Teding van Berkhout, 1500–1950* (Amsterdam: De Bataafsche Leeuw).

Schmitt, Jean-Claude. 1976. Le suicide au moyen age. *Annales ESC* 31,1: 3–28.

Schnabel-Schüle, Helga. 1997. *Überwachen und Strafen im Territorialstaat. Bedingungen und Auswirkungen des Systems strafrechtlicher Sanktionen im frühneuzeitlichen Württemberg* (Köln: Böhlau).

Schreiner, Klaus and Schwerhoff, Gerd (eds.) 1995. *Verletzte Ehre. Ehrkonflikte in Gesellschaften des Mittelalters und der frühen Neuzeit* (Köln: Böhlau).

Schulte, Regina. 1989. *Das Dorf im Verhör. Brandstifter, Kindsmörderinnen und Wilderer vor den Schranken des bürgerlichen Gerichts Oberbayern, 1848–1910* (Reinbek bei Hamburg: Rowohlt).

Schumann, Dirk. 2001. *Politische Gewalt in der Weimarer Republik, 1918–1933. Kampf um die Straße und Furcht vor dem Bürgerkrieg* (Essen: Klartext Verlag).

Schüssler, Martin. 1994. Verbrechen im spätmittelalterlichen Olmütz. Statistische Untersuchung der Kriminalität im Osten des Heiligen Römischen Reiches. *Zeitschrift der Savigny-Stiftung für Rechtsgeschichte, Germanistische Abteilung* 111: 148–271.

Schüssler, Martin. 1998. Verbrechen in Krakau, 1361–1405, und seiner Beistadt Kasimir, 1370–1402. *Zeitschrift der Savigny-Stiftung für Rechtsgeschichte, Germanistische Abteilung* 115: 198–338.

Schuster, Peter. 2000a. *Eine Stadt vor Gericht. Recht und Alltag im spätmittelalterlichen Konstanz* (Paderborn: Ferdinand Schöningh).

Schuster, Peter. 2000b. Richter ihrer selbst? Delinquenz gesellschaftlicher Oberschichten in der Spätmittelalterlichen Stadt. In Blauert, Andreas and Schwerhoff, Gerd (eds.), *Kriminalitätsgeschichte. Beiträge zur Sozial- und Kulturgeschichte der Vormoderne* (Konstanz: Universitätsverlag): 359–78.

Schwerhoff, Gerd. 1991. *Köln im Kreuzverhör. Kriminalität, Herrschaft und Gesellschaft in einer frühneuzeitlichen Stadt* (Bonn/Berlin: Bouvier Verlag).

Schwerhoff, Gerd. 1999. *Aktenkundig und gerichtsnotorisch. Einführung in die historische Kriminalitätsforschung* (Tübingen, diskord).

Septon, Monique. 1996. Les femmes et le poison. L'empoisonnement devant les juridictions criminelles en Belgique au 19e siècle, 1795–1914 (PhD thesis, Milwaukee, Marquette University).

Serpentini, Antoine Laurent. 2003. La criminalité de sang en Corse sous la domination génoise, fin 17e – début 18e siècles. *Crime, Histoire & Sociétés/ Crime, History & Societies* 7,1: 57–78.

Shapiro, Ann-Louise. 1996. *Breaking the codes. Female criminality in fin-de-siècle Paris* (Stanford: Stanford University Press).

Sharpe, J. A. 1984. *Crime in early modern England, 1550–1750* (London: New York: Longman).

Sharpe, James. 2004. *Dick Turpin. The myth of the English highwayman* (London: Profile Books).

Shepard, Alexandra. 2003. *Meanings of manhood in early modern England* (Oxford: Oxford University Press).

Shoemaker, Robert B. 1998. *Gender in English society, 1650–1850. The emergence of separate spheres?* (London/New York: Longman).

Shoemaker, Robert B. 1999. Reforming male manners. Public insult and the decline of violence in London: 1660–1740. In Hitchcock, Tim and Cohen, Michèle (eds.), *English masculinities, 1660–1800* (London: New York: Longman): 133–50.

Shoemaker, Robert B. 2000. The decline of public insult in London: 1600–1800. *PP* 169: 97–131.

Shoemaker, Robert B. 2001. Male honour and the decline of public violence in 18th-century London. *SocHist* 26,2: 190–208.

Shovlin, John. 2000. Toward a reinterpretation of revolutionary antinobilism. The political economy of honor in the Old Regime. *JMH* 72: 35–66.

Simpson, Antony E. 1988. Dandelions and the field of honor. Dueling, the middle classes and the law in 19th-century England. *Criminal Justice History* 9: 99–155.

Sleebe, Vincent. 1994. *In termen van fatsoen. Sociale controle in het Groningse kleigebied, 1770–1914* (Assen: Van Gorcum).

Smail, Daniel Lord. 2003. *The consumption of justice. Emotions, publicity and legal culture in Marseille, 1264–1423* (Ithaca: Cornell University Press).

Smith, Helmut Walser. 2002. *The butcher's tale. Murder and anti-semitism in a German town* (New York: W. W. Norton).

Spicker-Beck, Monika. 1995. *Räuber, Mordbrenner, umschweifendes Gesind. Zur Kriminalität im 16. Jahrhundert* (Freiburg im Breisgau: Rombach).

Spierenburg, Pieter. 1984. *The spectacle of suffering. Executions and the evolution of repression: from a preindustrial metropolis to the European experience* (Cambridge: Cambridge University Press).

Spierenburg, Pieter. 1996. Long-term trends in homicide. Theoretical reflections and Dutch evidence, fifteenth to twentieth centuries. In Johnson, Eric A. and Monkkonen, Eric H. (eds.) *The civilization of crime. Violence in town and country since the Middle Ages* (Urbana: Chicago, University of Illinois Press): 63–105.

Spierenburg, Pieter. 1997. How violent were women? Court cases in Amsterdam: 1650–1810. *Crime, Histoire & Sociétés/Crime, History and Societies* 1,1: 9–28.

Spierenburg, Pieter (ed.). 1998a. *Men and violence. Gender, honor and rituals in modern Europe and America* (Columbus: Ohio State University Press).

Spierenburg, Pieter. 1998b. *De Verbroken Betovering. Mentaliteit en Cultuur in Preïndustrieel Europa*, 3rd. edn. (Hilversum: Verloren).

Spierenburg, Pieter. 1999. Sailors and violence in Amsterdam: 17th–18th centuries. In Lappalainen, Mirkka and Hirvonen, Pekka (eds.), *Crime and control in Europe from the past to the present* (Helsinki: Publications of the History of Criminality Research Project): 112–43.

Spierenburg, Pieter. 2000. Wapens en geweld in historisch perspectief. *Tijdschrift voor Criminologie* 42,2: 183–90.

Spierenburg, Pieter. 2001. Violence and the civilizing process. Does it work? *Crime, Histoire & Sociétés/Crime, History & Societies* 5,2: 87–105.

Spierenburg, Pieter. 2004. *Written in blood. Fatal attraction in Enlightenment Amsterdam* (Columbus: Ohio State University Press).

Spierenburg, Pieter. 2006a. Democracy came too early: a tentative explanation for the problem of American homicide. *American Historical Review* 111,1: 104–14.

Spierenburg, Pieter. 2006b. Protestant attitudes to violence. The early Dutch Republic. *Crime, Histoire & Sociétés/Crime, History & Societies* 10,2: 5–31.

Statt, Daniel. 1995. The case of the Mohocks. Rake violence in Augustan London. *SocHist* 20, 2: 179–99.

Stein-Wilkeshuis, M. W. 1991. Wraak en verzoening in middeleeuwse Friese en Scandinavische rechtsbronnen. In Diederiks, H. A. and Roodenburg, H. W. (eds.), *Misdaad, zoen en straf. Aspekten van de middeleeuwse strafrechtsgeschiedenis in de Nederlanden* (Hilversum: Verloren): 11–25.

Stern, Fritz (ed.). 1956 *The varieties of history. From Voltaire to the present* (Cleveland/New York: Meridian Books).

Stewart, Frank Henderson. 1994. *Honor* (Chicago/London: University of Chicago Press).

Stone, Lawrence. 1965. *The crisis of the aristocracy, 1558–1641* (Oxford: Oxford University Press).

Strocchia, Sharon T. 1998. Gender and the rites of honour in Italian Renaissance cities. In Brown, Judith C. and Davis, Robert C. (eds.), *Gender and society in Renaissance Italy* (London: New York: Longman): 39–60.

Sweeney, Frank. 2002. *The murder of Conell Boyle, County Donegal, 1898* (Dublin: Four Courts Press).

Symonds, Deborah A. 1997. *Weep not for me. Women, ballads and infanticide in early modern Scotland* (University Park, PA: Pennsylvania State University Press).

Tatar, Maria. 1995. *Lustmord. Sexual murder in Weimar Germany* (Princeton: Princeton University Press).

Taylor, Howard. 1998. The politics of the rising crime statistics of England and Wales, 1914–1960. *Crime, Histoire & Sociétés/Crime, History & Societies* 2,1: 5–28.

Terlouw, Gert-Jan, et al. 2000. *Geweld: gemeld en geteld. Een analyse van aard en omvang van geweld op straat tussen onbekenden* (Den Haag: WODC-rapport).

Thome, Helmut. 2001. Explaining long-term trends in violent crime. *Crime, Histoire & Sociétés/Crime, History & Societies* 5,2: 69–86.

Thome, Helmut and Birkel, Cristoph. 2007. *Sozialer Wandel und Gewaltkriminalität. Deutschland, England und Schweden in Vergleich, 1950 bis 2000* (Wiesbasen: VS Verlag für Sozialwissenschaften).

Tillier, Annick. 2001. *Des criminelles au village. Femmes infanticides en Bretagne, 1825–1865* (Rennes: Presses Universitaires de Rennes).

Timmer, Jaap and Neayé, Jan. 2000. Wapens en wapengebruik van de politie. *Tijdschrift voor Criminologie* 42,2: 165–77.

Tinkova, Daniela. 2005. Protéger ou punir? Les voies de la décriminalisation de l'infanticide en France et dans le domaine des Habsbourg, 18e–19e siècles. *Crime, Histoire & Sociétés/Crime, History & Societies* 9,2: 43–72.

Tlusty, B. Ann. 2001. *Bacchus and civic order. The culture of drink in early modern Germany* (Charlottesville/London: University Press of Virginia).

Tlusty, B. Ann. 2002. The public house and military culture in Germany, 1500–1648. In Kümin, Beat and Tlusty, B. Ann (eds.) *The World of the Tavern. Public Houses in Early Modern Europe* (Aldershot: Ashgate): 136–56.

Töngi, Claudia. 2005. Erziehung, Vernachlässigung, Missbrauch. Häusliche Gewalt gegen Kinder und Pflegekinder in Uri im 19. Jahrhundert. *Traverse* 12, 2: 101–17.

Torre, Angelo. 1994. Feuding, factions and parties. The redefinition of politics in the Imperial fiefs of Langhe in the 17th and 18th centuries. In Muir, Edward and Ruggiero, Guido (eds.), *History from crime. Selections from Quaderni Storici* (Baltimore: London): 135–69.

Turner, David M. 2002. *Fashioning adultery. Gender, sex and civility in England, 1660–1740* (Cambridge: Cambridge University Press).

Ulbricht, Otto, (ed.). 1995. *Von Huren und Rabenmüttern. Weibliche Kriminalität in der frühen Neuzeit* (Köln: Böhlau).

Vale, Juliet. 2000. Violence and the tournament. In Kaeuper, Richard W. (ed.), *Violence in medieval society* (Woodbridge: Boydell Press): 143–58.

Venard, Marc, et al. 1992. *Histoire du christianisme des origines à nos jours.* Vol. VIII: *1530–1630* (Paris: Desclée).

Vigarello, Georges. 1998. *Histoire du viol, 16e–20e siècle* (Paris: Seuil).

Vincent, Karelle. 1999. Le régicide en république. Sadi Carnot, 24 juin 1894 – Paul Doumer, 6 mai 1932. In *Crime, Histoire & Sociétés/Crime, History & Societies* 3,2: 73–93.

Vree, Wilbert van. 1994. *Nederland als vergaderland. Opkomst en verbreiding van een vergaderregime* (Groningen, Wolters-Noordhoff).

Vries, Jan de and Woude, Ad van der. 1995. *Nederland, 1500–1850. De eerste ronde van moderne economische groei* (Amsterdam: Balans).

Vrolijk, Marjan. 2001. Recht door gratie. Gratie bij doodslagen en andere delicten in Vlaanderen, Holland en Zeeland, 1531–1567 (Dissertation, Nijmegen).

Waardt, Hans de. 1996. Feud and atonement in Holland and Zeeland. From private vengeance to reconciliation under state supervision. In Schuurman, Anton and Spierenburg, Pieter (eds.), *Private domain, public inquiry. Families and life-styles in the Netherlands and Europe, 1550 to the present* (Hilversum: Verloren): 15–38.

Walker, Garthine. 2003. *Crime, gender and social order in early modern England* (Cambridge: Cambridge University Press).

Walker, Nigel. 1968. *Crime and insanity in England.* Vol. I: *The historical perspective* (Edinburgh: Edinburgh University Press).

Watanabe-O'Kelly, Helen. 1990. Tournaments and their relevance for warfare in the early modern period. *European History Quarterly* 20,4: 451–63.

Watanabe-O'Kelly, Helen. 1992. *Triumphall shews. Tournaments at German-speaking courts in their European context, 1560–1730* (Berlin: Gebr. Mann).

Watson, Katherine. 2004. *Poisoned lives. English poisoners and their victims* (London/New York: Hambledon and London).

Watson, Katherine D. (ed.). 2007. *Assaulting the past. Violence and civilization in historical context* (Newcastle: Cambridge Scholars Publishing).

Watt, Jeffrey R. 2001. *Choosing death. Suicide and Calvinism in early modern Geneva* (Kirksville, MO: Truman State University Press).

Watt, Jeffrey R. (ed.). 2004. *From sin to insanity. Suicide in early modern Europe* (Ithaca: Cornell University Press).

Weber, Eugen. 1976. *Peasants into Frenchmen. The modernization of rural France, 1870–1914* (Stanford: Stanford University Press).

Weber, Eugen. 1986. *France. Fin de Siècle* (Cambridge, MA/London: Harvard University Press).

Weel, A. J. van. 1977. De wetgeving tegen het duelleren in de Republiek der Verenigde Nederlanden. *Nederlands Archievenblad* 81: 282–96.

Wegert, Karl. 1994. *Popular culture, crime and social control in 18th-century Württemberg* (Stuttgart: Steiner).

Weinstein, Donald. 2000. *The captain's concubine. Love, honor and violence in Renaissance Tuscany* (Baltimore/London: Johns Hopkins University Press).

Wernicke, Steffen. 2000. Von Schlagen, Schmähen und Unendlichkeit. Die Regensburger Urfehdebriefe im 15. Jahrhundert. In Blauert, Andreas and Schwerhoff, Gerd (eds.), *Kriminalitätsgeschichte. Beiträge zur Sozial- und Kulturgeschichte der Vormoderne* (Konstanz: Universitätsverlag): 379–404.

Wiener, Martin. 1999. The sad story of George Hall. Adultery, murder and the politics of mercy in mid-Victorian England. *SocHist* 24,2: 174–95.

Wiener, Martin J. 2004. *Men of blood. Violence, manliness and criminal justice in Victorian England* (Cambridge: Cambridge University Press).

Wills, Abigail. 2005. Delinquency, masculinity and citizenship in England, 1950–1970. *PP* 187: 157–85.

Wilson, Stephen. 1988. *Feuding, conflict and banditry in 19th-century Corsica* (Cambridge: Cambridge University Press).

Wiltenburg, Joy. 1992. *Disorderly women and female power in the street literature of early modern England and Germany* (Charlottesville: University Press of Virginia).

Wilterdink, Nico. 2000. *In deze verwarrende tijd. Een terugblik en vooruitblik op de postmoderniteit* (Amsterdam: Vossiuspers).

Wirsching, Andreas. 2003. Political violence in France and Italy after 1918. *Journal of Modern European History* 1,1: 60–78.

Wittke, Margarete. 2002. *Mord und Totschlag? Gewaltdelikte im Fürstbistum Münster, 1580–1620. Täter, Opfer und Justiz* (Münster: Aschendorff).

Wolf, H. J. 1984. *Hoe was het ook weer? Verhalen over Breda, de Koninklijke Militaire Academie en het kasteel van Breda* (Breda: Brabantia Nostra).

Wood, John Carter. 2004. *Violence and crime in 19th-century England. The shadow of our refinement* (London: Routledge).

Ylikangas, Heikki. 1998. *The knife fighters. Violent crime in Southern Ostrobothnia, 1790–1825* (Helsinki: Academia Scientiarium Fennica).

Ylikangas, Heikki, et al. 1998. *Five centuries of violence in Finland and the Baltic area* (Helsinki: Publications of the History of Criminality Research Project).

Zaitch, Damián. 2002. *Trafficking cocaine. Columbian drug entrepreneurs in the Netherlands* (Den Haag: Kluwer).

Zorzi, Andrea. 1995. Politica e giustizia a Firenze al tempo degli ordinamenti anti-magnatizi. In Arrighi, Vanna (ed.), *Ordinamenti di giustizia fiorentini. Studi in occasione del VII centenario* (Florence: Archivio di Stato): 105–47.

Index

Anderson, Elijah, 216
arson, 176–7

banditry, 103–5, 124, 170
Barna da Siena, 49–50
Beattie, John, 107
Bertillon, Alphonse, 170
Blockmans, Wim, 31
Blok, Anton, 8–9, 103–4
Body-Gendrot, Sophie, 214
Bourdieu, Pierre, 8
boxing, 172
Breittmayer, Georges, 184
Brennan, Thomas, 95
Bulger, Jamie, 218, 219
Burke, William and William Hare,
    193

Carroll, Stuart, 59
Chassaigne, Philippe, 177, 193
Chauvaud, Fréderic, 176
Chesnais, Jean-Claude, 168
Churchill, Winston, 197
civilization campaigns, 178, 201
civilizing processes, theory of
    outline, 5–6
    and decline of homicide, 112–13,
        224–5
    and modern homicide, 225–6
clergy, lifestyle of, 70

Cockburn, James, 145
Collard, Franck, 128
Conley, Carolyn, 179
Cooney, Mark, 80
Coubertin, Pierre de, 171
crime passionnel
    cases of, 189–91
    decline of, 192
    definition of, 187–8
    perpetrators of, 188
    with vitriol, 188–9
criminalization
    breakthrough of, 58–61
    and state formation processes,
        61–4

D'Cruze, Shani, 185
dark number, 3–4
Davies, Andrew, 173
Davis, Natalie, 56
dead hand, 53
Dean, Trevor, 22, 26, 29
domestic violence, *see* murder, among
        intimates; violence, among
        intimates
drugs, 216–18
duel, formal
    in the 19th and early 20th centuries
        ideas about, 183–4
        practice of, 182–3

attitudes toward, 73, 77–8
civilization of, 74–5
definition of, 71–2
honor courts for the prevention of, 110–11
incidence of, 75–7, 111
origins of, 72
repression of, 78–80
by women, 114–16, 117
duel, popular
in the 19th century
by boxing, 175–6
with knives, 179–80
attitudes toward, 89–90
characteristics of, 82–5
decline of, 111–12
evidence about, 87
origins of, 81–2
outside the Dutch Republic, 93–6
and social class, 91
techniques of, 88
by women, 117
and youth, 90–1
Dülmen, Richard van, 147
Dunning, Eric, 200
Durkheim, Emile, 6, 160, 212
Dutroux, Marc, 218

Egelkamp, Margarethe, 211
Eisner, Manuel, 3, 80, 106, 117, 122, 168, 212–13
Elias, Norbert, 5, 10, 21, 51, 63, 75, 112, 207
elites, pacification of, 80–1, 223
Emsley, Clive, 186, 218
Esquirol, Jean-Etienne, 163

Farr, James, 124
Ferri, Enrico, 197
feuding
in the 19th century, 179
avoidance of, 26–7
family character of, 22–3, 42, 64
in early modern period, 67–8
in England, 25
in Florence, 21–3
in other Italian towns, 23

in France, 23–4
in Friuli, 27–8
in Ghent, 29–30, 31
in Holland and Zeeland, 24–5, 30–1
in the Holy Roman Empire, 27
prevalence of, 14–15
toleration of, 28–9
and urban revolts, 31–2
fingerprints, 170–1
Foucault, Michel, 193

games, 36–8
gangs, 101–2, 172–3
Gauvard, Claude, 24
Gelli, Iacopo, 182, 183
Given, James, 15, 39
Goebbels, Joseph, 166
Goethe, Johann von, 160
Gowing, Laura, 138
Green, Thomas, 50
Gründgens, Gustaf, 166
Gurr, Ted Robert, 3

Hasselt, Johan Jacob van, 130
hippie movement, 205
Hitler, Adolf, 166
Hobsbawm, Eric, 103–4
Hoffer, Peter and N. E. H. Hull, 145
homicide, see murder
homicide rates
around 1600, 70–1
between 1600 and 1800, 106–7
in the 19th century, 167–9
since 1970, 208–10, 212
definition of, 3
in the Middle Ages, 15–17
after the world wars, 199–200
honor
body-related, 8–9
definition of, 7–8
female, 116
and the formal duel, 72
prevalence among men, 68–9
spiritualization of, 9–10, 108–10, 126
house-scorning, 69–70

Hufton, Olwen, 151
Hume, David, 160

infanticide
  assistance with, 152–3
  attitudes toward, 146, 161–2
  causes of, 154
  definition of, 145
  detection of, 151–2
  incidence of, 145–6, 146–8
  method of, 154
  perpetrators of, 150–1, 153
  prosecution, changes in, 162–3
  punishment of, 148–50
injury rates, 71, 169, 177, 200–1,
  210–11
inquisitorial procedure, 57–8
insanity, 154–5

James, Mervyn, 69
Jansson, Arne, 159
Jews, 40–1
Jones, George Fenwick, 9
jury, origins of, 52–3

kiss, 43–4
Kloppenburg, Joes, 219
Krafft-Ebing, Richard von, 174,
  187

Lamartine, Alphonse de, 184
Lang, Fritz, 166, 167, 195
Larner, John, 21–2
Lassalle, Ferdinand, 183
Lepoutre, David, 206, 213
Lombroso, Cesare, 197
López, Gregorio, 54
Lorre, Peter (László Löwenstein),
  166
Lyotard, Jean-François, 221

mafia, 180–1
Maitland, Frederic William, 1
Mann, Klaus, 166
Michalik, Kerstin, 151
Mohrmann, Ruth, 108
Monkkonen, Eric, 204

monomania, 163–4
Montesquieu, 110, 160
Mucchielli, Laurent, 217–18
Muchembled, Robert, 57
Muir, Edward, 27, 46, 73–4
Murray, Alexander, 159
murder
  of Cönen, Wilhelm, 181
  by contract, 23, 99
  and courtship, 134
  definition of, 1
  by disturbed parents, 156–8, 186–7
  by insane perpetrators, 155–6, 158
  among intimates, proportion of,
    133–4, 141–2, 224
  legally defined, 38–9
  long-term decline of, 3–4, 41–2
  of Mannelli, Lippo, 21–2, 28, 43
  modern trends in, 207–8
  modern anxiety about, 219–22
  and multiple perpetratorship, 25–6
  of parents, 187
  political, 196–8, 202–3
  serial
    cases of, 193–6
    definition of, 193
    explanations for the rise of, 196
    precursors of, 130–1, 165–7
  spousal
    around 1900, 185–6
    commissioned, 139–40
    by husbands, 137–8
    and romanticism, 140–1
    types of, 136
    by wives, 138–9
  of Winter, Ernst, 198
  see also: crime passionnel; homicide
    rates; violence
Muslims, 40–1
Mussolini, Benito, 184, 197
Muzio, Girolamo, 73

Nolde, Dorothea, 137, 138
nose-slitting, 117–19

O'Donnell, Ian, 213, 218
organized crime, 216–18

pardon
    evolution of, 55–6
    petitions for, 56–7
    ratification of, 56–7
Paris *banlieues*, 206, 213–14
Pepe, Gabriele, 184
Pitt-Rivers, Julian, 8
Ploux, François, 176
poisoning, 128–31
police, establishment of, 169–70
Porto, Luigi da, 14
prostitution, 40, 121–2

Rabin, Dana, 161
rape, 125–8, 184–5
reconciliation
    early examples of, 45
    family character of, 49, 64
    geographic limitation to the
        evidence about, 45–6
    opposition to, 58–9
    origins of, 44–5
    outside the Low Countries,
        49–50
    after popular violence, 89
    as precondition for pardon, 58
    and prosecution, 51–4
    and religion, 48–9
    and revenge, 50
    ritual of, 46–8
    sobering of, 54
Ribera, Jusepe de, 117
Ripper, Jack the, 193, 194, 197
Rivière, Pierre, 193
robbery, 39, 105–6, 172
Roché, Sebastian, 212
Romilly, Samuel, 160
Rousseau, Jean-Jacques, 114, 160
Rousseaux, Xavier, 199
Ruggiero, Guido, 36

Sabean, David, 136
Salernitano, Masuccio, 14
sanctuary, 54–5
Schnabel-Schüle, Helga, 155
Schüssler, Martin, 16
Schwerhoff, Gerd, 136

Scott, Walter, 143–4, 150, 162
Shakespeare, William, 13, 42
    Romeo and Juliet, 12–14, 22, 42
Sharpe, James, 153
Shoemaker, Robert, 107, 109
Smail, Daniel, 36, 41
sports, 171
Stewart, Frank Henderson, 9
sticks against knives, 65–6, 91–3
students, 40
suicide
    attitudes toward, 160–1
    incidence of, 159–60
    indirect, 158–9
    in the Middle Ages, 39
Symonds, Deborah, 151
Szabó, István, 166

taverns, 35, 97, 124, 177
Taylor, Howard, 167
Thome, Helmut and Cristoph Birkel,
        210, 212
towns, in Middle Ages, 17–19

uncoiffing, 124–5
underworld, 201–2

vendetta, *see* feuding
victimization surveys, 211
violence
    axes of, 6–7, 105–6, 223–4
    female, 117–21
    and impulse, 36, 88, 121
    and insult, 33–4, 85
    inter-faith, 102–3
    inter-village, 101, 176
    among intimates
        definition of, 132
        marital, 135–6
        origins of, 132–3
    and masculinity, 34–5, 85–7
    by medieval elite, 19–21
    modern urban, 213–16
    monopolization of, 2
    public attitudes toward, 174
    and ritual, 36, 97–8
    in rural areas, 98–9

violence (*cont.*)
  trough of, 203–4
  women as victims of, non-sexual,
    122–4
  and World War I, 199
  see also murder
Voltaire, 160
Vrol k, Marjan, 57

weapons, 35, 99–101, 178, 179, 204,
  216
Weber, Eugen, 176

Welten, Bernard, 221
Wheelwright, Julie, 163
Wielant, Filips, 20
Wiener, Martin, 185
Wiertz, Antoine, 163
Wilterdink, Nico, 221–2
Witsen, Nicolaes, 65
Wood, John Carter, 174
wrestling, 93

zoen, see reconciliation
Zorzi, Andrea, 21